Nonacademic Writing:
Social Theory and Technology

Nonacademic Writing: Social Theory and Technology

Edited by

Ann Hill Duin
University of Minnesota

and

Craig J. Hansen
Metropolitan State University

LAWRENCE ERLBAUM ASSOCIATES, PUBLISHERS
1996   Mahwah, New Jersey

Lawrence Erlbaum Associates, Inc., Publishers
10 Industrial Avenue
Mahwah, New Jersey 07430

cover design by Mairav Salomon-Dekel

Library of Congress Cataloging-in-Publication Data

Nonacademic writing : social theory and technology / edited by Ann
    Hill Duin and Craig J. Hansen.
        p.   cm.
    Includes bibliographical references and index.
    ISBN 0-8058-1627-5 (c : acid-free paper). — ISBN 0-8058-1628-3 (p
: acid-free paper)
    1. Technical writing.   I. Duin, Ann Hill.   II. Hansen, Craig.
T11.N57   1995
808′.0666 — dc20   95-19203
                                                             CIP

Books published by Lawrence Erlbaum Associates are printed
on acid-free paper, and their bindings are chosen for strength
and durability.

Printed in the United States of America
10 9 8 7 6 5 4 3 2 1

Contents

v

Foreword

Clearly, the most exciting area of research and scholarship in writing is the area of nonacademic writing or, as it is alternatively named, workplace writing, technical and business writing, real-world writing, or as Ackerman and Oates suggest in this collection, writing in "settings of consequence." Part of the excitement comes from the relative newness of the area to be explored. Most scholarship on writing (in the disciplines of literature and rhetoric) has focused exclusively on the writing of literary authors (including as "literary" any published writing, regardless of genre, considered to have aesthetic merit). In the mid-20th century, academic writing both of students in classrooms and the scholarly writing of academic disciplines became an object of study for the burgeoning field of composition. And the contemporary study of nonacademic writing began, as this nomenclature belies, when writing teachers, motivated by their concerns about how well they were preparing students for their later writing on the job, employed the new methods and questions developed to study academic writing to look at workplace writing.

Like the refocusing of attention from the writing of literary authors to the writing of students and academics, the shift to studying the everyday writing practices of people on the job marks a shift in the direction of academic research and scholarship, one that is not unique to the interdisciplinary field of writing theory. Across the humanities, scholars have been increasingly concerned with the practices of everyday life, whether it be questions of how people orient themselves in urban spaces, how they construct themselves and their world in watching music videos, or how they are constructed by the institutional practices of mental hospitals or prisons. Like these studies, the study of everyday writing practices on the job strives to understand how social structures affect and are affected by people's purposes in an increasingly technological world. Thus, research on nonacademic writing is also exciting because it demonstrates how the concerns of writing researchers articulate with the concerns of researchers across the humanities.

For me, however, the most exciting thing about research on nonacademic writing is the way it problematizes the traditional assumptions about writers and texts that have been developed in studies of literary and academic writing, assumptions that, indeed, have already become problematic within these fields. Defining nonacademic writing as writing that occurs within settings of consequence reveals its essentially pragmatic function: Nonacademic writing is writing that gets something done, as opposed to writing that serves an aesthetic, cognitive, or affective function. Nonacademic writing excludes literature, personal essays, scholarly writing, writing in popular magazines and newspapers—all that writing that makes us think or feel or believe something; all that writing that can be, and often is, separated from the realm of social, political, and economic interaction; all that writing that finds its essence in the unique individual expression of a unique, individual writer in a unique, individual text. In its focus on getting something done, nonacademic writing subordinates the role of the writer and the status of the text to the job at hand: The writer says what needs to be said in the situation, often borrowing from any other relevant writing and often collaborating; the text is often not stable or permanent or even very consequential in its content. Nonacademic writing is a form of social action in its purest sense, writing whose textual and authorial aspects dissolve (almost) completely into its pragmatic purpose.

Writers working in settings of consequence very often do not sign their writing, and, when they do, it is usually their position that matters rather than their individuality. An enormous amount of nonacademic writing consists of institutional documents—reports, manuals, policy books, product and position descriptions, promotional materials—that are written collaboratively, often in conformity to set outlines and language and make heavy use of boilerplate. Bills introduced in legislatures have sponsors, but the sponsors have not usually written them. Memos and letters very often are not signed by the person who wrote them, but by the person from whom the message is supposed to have come. Memos and letters must always clearly indicate the status of the person from whom they come; letters from constituents to governmental representatives, for example, must claim this relationship to achieve rhetorical effectiveness, for opinions of people who do not live within a representative's assigned district can be disregarded.

Furthermore, nonacademic writing is characteristically incomprehensible outside of its context of construction and use. In most business memos or letters to governmental officials, for example, what is said is not nearly as significant as who is saying it and to whom (and who is getting copies of the correspondence), for such memos and letters are primarily means of restructuring relationships of power and influence in the pursuit of particular goals. Charter documents and contracts, although often regarded as stable texts that regulate institutional structures and relationships, gain their force not from the stability of text, but rather from the consensus established in the process of their writing, and they are continually reinterpreted (or disregarded) within the context of the immediate institution or relationship. Planning documents almost never reach a stable form that is simply implemented, instead undergoing continual revision as part of the process of developing programs, products, or policies. Even such seemingly straightforward texts as job descriptions often serve the purposes of establishing the status of the position or enabling accountants to accurately assess the appropriate salary range of the position rather than informing prospective candidates about the job.

In short, nonacademic writing disrupts our traditional notions about the primacy of the writer and the stability of texts even more radically than have the dominant textual theories of poststructuralism and postmodernism. The increasing reliance in nonacademic writing on nonprint forms of writing technology exponentially also increases this disruption. Producing documents on computers and keeping documents and files in computer rather than paper format encourages the continual updating or revision of texts and makes it easier to boilerplate new documents from old. The use of electronic mail has increased the amount of written communication among people in a particular workplace and broadened the range of people they communicate with outside the workplace. The ephemeral quality of electronic text has also reduced the sense of the printed word as fixed and final and emphasized, again, the pragmatic nature of nonacademic writing. The multiple typographical errors and other mistakes in electronic mail messages testify to the primacy of action over correct form in this style of writing.

At the same time, the composition and circulation of electronic texts in situations of consequence raises important issues about how communication technology interacts with the structures and goals of our society. Such notions as the individual or corporate ownership of information and ideas, the maintenance of hierarchical power structures and the restriction of access to participation in discussions and decision making, the attribution of responsibility for policies and decisions, and the mechanisms by which the communication technology can be controlled, all of which are currently defined in terms of print-based communication, must be redefined in the context of electronic communication and thus are open to change. The current debate over how the information superhighways is to be configured, whether it should be a centralized system or a Jeffersonian-switched network, and how the various cable and telephone technologies and companies are to be articulated, demonstrates the complex manner in which communication technology interacts with and enacts various social purposes and how much is at stake in such seemingly "technical" decisions.

In the study of nonacademic writing we cannot evade these serious questions about the structure and purpose of writing in our postmodern society. This volume is exciting for the breadth of contexts it considers and the variety of perspectives it brings to bear on this study; it invites us all to contribute to and continue the dialogue.

Marylin M. Cooper

Preface

The idea for this edited collection grew out of discussions we had while collaborating on other projects. One of us had just returned to composition after 8 years of middle management in industry. One of us was an active scholar in technical communication. We discussed the differences in perspective between these two fields toward nonacademic writing. We discussed nonacademic writing as an activity located in a dynamic social and political environment, and we discussed the rapid changes in communication technology that are profoundly changing nonacademic writing.

Our discussions led to questions that we posed to nationally recognized scholars from a variety of disciplines:

1. How do we translate research into pedagogy?
   That is, how do we prepare professionals for writing in nonacademic settings?
   What is the relationship between research and pedagogy?
   Are we learning from research what we need to know to enhance pedagogy?
2. What nonacademic settings should we be studying?
   That is, what do we really get from looking at these alternative sites?
   Why do we choose the sites that we do?
   How do we really understand these sites?
3. How are emerging technologies reconfiguring nonacademic writing?
   That is, how do we get researchers and learners to ask significant

questions of the communication technologies they use?
What are the value systems of these technologies?
Whose interests do we really serve with technology?
What is the relationship between social context and technology?

Each chapter in this collection has two purposes: first, to challenge current theory, research, and pedagogy in nonacademic writing; and second, to provoke additional innovative inquiry about nonacademic writing. In the following chapters, methodological, cultural, technological, and political boundaries felt by writers are analyzed, translated, and challenged in a way that will appeal to researchers, theorists, graduate students, instructors, and managerial audiences. Instead of extracting rules from previous research, these contributors have crossed disciplinary boundaries, working to analyze and understand the social and technological contexts surrounding nonacademic writing. What follows are chapters that provide an integral rather than peripheral perspective toward future research on nonacademic writing.

PART I: CHALLENGING THE RESEARCH ON WRITING IN NONACADEMIC SETTINGS

Since the mid-1980s, with germinal works such as *Writing in Nonacademic Settings* (Odell & Goswami, 1985)[1] for composition and *New Essays in Technical and Scientific Communication* (Anderson, Brockmann, & Miller, 1983)[2] for technical communication, writing scholars have relied primarily on qualitative research methodologies to study writing in nonacademic settings: participant/observer data collection (ethnomethodology) and surveys (with statistically processed results). This, we know, is a broad generalization, obscuring many combinations and variations of these methodologies. However, we should be aware of the implications of descriptive research, particularly ethnographic, as we reinterpret theory and design pedagogy based on this research. As Herndl (1991)[3] noted, commenting on a long-standing debate in anthropology, "[I]ts findings [ethnography's] are displaced from their sources in the everyday activities of subjects and become part of a disciplinary discourse whose production of

---

[1]Odell, L., & Goswami, D. (Eds.). (1985). *Writing in nonacademic settings.* New York, Guilford.

[2]Anderson, P. V., Brockmann, R. J., & Miller, C. R. (Eds.). (1983). *New essays in technical and scientific communication: Research, theory, and practice.* Farmingdale, NY: Baywood.

[3]Herndl, C. (1991). Writing ethnograpy: Representation, rhetoric, and institutional practices. *College english, 53(3),* 320–332.

authorized knowledge resists the theoretical self-consciousness of the original research ethos" (p. 320). This section also explores the evolving concept of the social perspective and our relationship to it. Do the cultures that we study affect our concepts of writing? By what culture's value system do we judge relevance? Do we fully integrate the changes technology introduces into our understanding of social contexts for nonacademic writing?

In chapter 1, "Setting a Sociotechnological Agenda in Nonacademic Writing," we briefly describe the social perspective—the lens most often used in examining nonacademic writing—and offer another lens, technology, that we believe is central to any study of the social contexts that surround nonacademic writing. We then combine these lenses and propose an agenda that employs a sociotechnological approach to the study of nonacademic writing.

In chapter 2, "The Transformation of Critical Ethnography into Pedagogy, or the Vicissitudes of Traveling Theory," Carl Herndl extends his previous work and challenges the relationship of research on nonacademic writing and pedagogy. Herndl analyzes the problems involved when technical writing research and pedagogy makes use of ethnography; in particular, he is concerned about the domestication of postmodern theories of ethnography given the devotion of technical writing to an instrumental theory of discourse. He examines several difficult questions: To what extent do the institutional demands of the classroom and the innate authority of textbooks ignore or deny the theoretical critique of ethnographic representation? What happens to the critical ethos of a research community when its findings appear in pedagogical applications? And to what extent does ethnographic research and its translation into pedagogy legitimize dominant discourse practices, occluding oppositional discourse?

In chapter 3, "Nonacademic Writing Into the 21st Century: Achieving and Sustaining Relevance in Research and Curricula," Elizabeth Tebeaux assesses who we are, the rationale for what we do, and the goals that evolve from our identity. Tebeaux's strong traditional stand on nonacademic writing serves as an excellent counterpoint to Herndl. For example, Tebeaux's statement that the relevance of research on nonacademic writing should be measured by "its usefulness in helping prepare students and technical writers for nonacademic writing" articulates the traditional side of the debate that frames research and the teaching of nonacademic writing.

In chapter 4, "The Computer Culture, Gender, and Nonacademic Writing: An Interdisciplinary Critique," Mary M. Lay applies gender and social theory to the development, teaching, and application of computer software. Because a great deal of nonacademic writing research and pedagogy focuses on technology, Lay challenges this computer culture and its accommodation of gender-based learning styles. Although the design and use of technologies present challenges in nonacademic writing, so do the development of the documentation that accompanies these technologies.

PART II: STUDYING WRITING IN SETTINGS OF CONSEQUENCE

Focusing on our second set of questions presented earlier, the essays in part II challenge our preoccupation with traditional corporate settings and examine additional "settings of consequence." Assuming we understand the complications of research on writing in nonacademic settings (as described in the previous four chapters), how do we choose alternate settings and analyze the collected data? Through what theoretical lens? These chapters explore these issues by examining a wide variety of settings in which, for example, people compose texts that rely on symbols other than written language, in which citizens write as a means of civic participation, and in which we examine the social context of texts created 100 years ago.

In chapter 5, "Image, Text, and Power in Architectural Design and Workplace Writing," John Ackerman and Scott Oates consider weaknesses in the academic versus nonacademic writing lens. They analyze the nonacademic writing world of architecture through semiotics, claiming that all discourse practice involves a rich interplay of graphic and verbal signs, and that the design and use of these signs in turn shape and are shaped by cultural space. Their study of architects from the vantage point of multiple signs, the interpretant, semiosis, and cultural ethics, provides an expanded notion of textuality and promotes "space" as a "metaphor for textual play and political displacement."

In chapter 6, " 'Some People Weren't Able to Contribute Anything but Their Technical Knowledge': The Anatomy of a Dysfunctional Team," Rebecca E. Burnett examines a student team within a workplace setting, focusing on the interaction within the team and the broader organizational context that had a dramatic impact on the team's failure. Observing this team offered Burnett a unique opportunity to identify distinctions that characterize and differentiate classroom and workplace collaboration.

In chapter 7, "Writing Well as a Form of Social Knowledge," we return again to pedagogy as Dorothy Winsor explores the student writer's relationship to the culture (or cultures) of the workplace by examining technical communication students' enculturation with workplace writing. She analyzes the acquisition of tacit knowledge about the workplace, discusses its importance for developing writing strategies, and explores its problematic relationship with pedagogy. She also challenges those who portray writing and technological experimentation as a rule-driven activity.

In chapter 8, "Social Theories, Workplace Writing, and Collaboration: Implications and Directions for Research," Jo Allen and Carol Thompson collaborate to explore a range of social theory paradigms that will generate new research questions in nonacademic writing. They explore structural-functionalist theory, conflict theory, interactionist theory, marxist/critical theory, and feminist theory as a means of investigating the relationship between nonacademic writers and their readers. Their discussion includes synopses of these paradigms, research questions stemming from each theory, and implications from each for professional writers.

Catherine F. Smith opens yet another perspective—a historical one—in her development of a heuristic framework with which to study institutional discourse. In chapter 9, "Understanding Institutional Discourse in the U.S. Congress, Present and Past," she reviews the forms and technologies of congressional hearings from the 1790s to the present, identifies models of communication (e.g., using hypertest as a conceptual model to understand the flow of information in modern hearings), and examines the relationship between communication models and technologies.

In chapter 10, "Participatory Writing: Literacy for Civic Purposes," Sandra Stotsky serves the important function of opening a field of inquiry for many readers. She provides a compelling message on the function of writing within a culture as she examines writing that citizens do as part of the process of democratic self-government. Her positive message—that literacy can empower citizens—is an important counterpoint in the debate over the social effects of literacy in our society.

PARTIII: RECONFIGURING NONACADEMIC WRITING THROUGH EMERGING TECHNOLOGIES

One of our basic assumptions in creating this collection was that we could not examine any writing context without considering the rapidly changing technologies that are redefining communication. Thus, the last section examines how emerging technologies—electronic mail over local and wide-area networks, hypertext, multimedia, and even voice mail—are redefining our ideas of authorship and textuality and have become integral to the social contexts of communication.

Thus, in chapter 11, "Issues in Hypertext-Supported Collaborative Writing," Stuart A. Selber, Dan McGavin, William Klein, and Johndan Johnson-Eilola explore hypertext's potential to influence our notions of authorship, group dynamics, and organizational structures as well as the social and structural boundaries resulting from the use of hypertext. They describe how hypertext poses both barriers and opportunities for enacting socially based communication, and how critical analyses such as theirs point to new directions for research.

Chapter 12, "Technology Enhanced Nonacademic Writing: A Social and Cognitive Transformation," by Curtis Jay Bonk, Thomas H. Reynolds, and Padma V. Medury, supports Pea and other neo-Vygotskians who claim that technologies designed to encourage teamwork, networking, joint written communication, and brainstorming will not only alter interaction patterns and organizational structures, but may even transform definitions of writing and reorganize mental functioning. They offer a "reprocessing" framework that considers the value of word processing, self-processing, knowledge/idea processing, and co-processing in nonacademic writing settings. Through this model, they show how technological support for collaboration and information gathering provides opportunities for the reprocessing of thought as opposed to mere transcription.

In chapter 13, "Contextualizing Technology and Communication in a Corporate Setting," Craig J. Hansen presents case studies of employees in a large corporation, drawing connections between their perceptions of corporate cultures and their use of communication technologies. He argues that researchers should move beyond the study of technologies as discrete types (such as voice mail or hypertext) and consider the use of these technologies in context, focusing on the relationship of technology and value systems, both institutional and individual, and the implications for users who must select among a variety of communication technologies.

Finally, in chapter 14, Cynthia L. Selfe and Richard J. Selfe, Jr., in "Writing as Democratic Social Action in a Technological World: Politicizing and Inhabiting Virtual Landscapes," provide an intense critique on the design and use of virtual landscapes as alternative learning spaces. Using a related series of texts by Eagleton, Foucault, Poster, Ferguson, and Deleuze and Guattari, they show how theoretical perspectives can problematize, in productive ways, the current vision of online exchanges and expand the agenda for exploring these spaces within nonacademic settings. This chapter identifies the more subtle and complex social and political aspects of online exchanges, showing how these fully elaborated theoretical visions can enrich and extend the study of electronic forums.

Collectively, these chapters offer a number of challenges to our study of nonacademic writing:

• The centrality of emerging communications technologies in nonacademic writing research and the need for a sociotechnological perspective. New technologies are reshaping the concept of text (Bonk et al., Selber et al., Selfe & Selfe, Tebeaux) and significantly impact the writing process and written products in nonacademic settings (Hansen).
• The relationship between the academy and the workplace. A number

of chapters challenge us—sometimes from opposing perspectives—to scrutinize our role as writing educators in preparing students for the workplace. Should we support the interests of corporate employers, as Tebeaux suggests, or should we resist those interests, as Herndl and Selfe and Selfe suggest? Should we enculturate students in workplace writing practices by placing them in these environments (Burnett), or should we examine the tacit knowledge gained by workplace professionals and deliver this via classroom instruction (Winsor)?

- New theory, new research agendas. Contributors such as Allen and Thompson, Winsor, Stotsky, Smith, and Ackerman and Oates offer new theoretical lenses or use established lenses in innovative ways, expanding the agenda for nonacademic writing research.

REVIEWING AND REVISING

We followed a rigorous review procedure in creating this collection. We provided an initial review when receiving the first drafts of each chapter. This resulted in the first round of revision. Next, two "blind" reviewers reacted to the collection as a whole, providing insightful, detailed feedback to each chapter contributor (and the editors). We asked contributors to revise in response to each of these reviews.

As a third and final review process, we assembled a separate pool of reviewers, made up of individuals likely to be interested in the collection, to react to each chapter (the reviewers are listed on page xxix). This was a somewhat unusual step for a collection such as this, but one that we felt was essential to ensure the quality and usefulness of the text. The pool consisted of individuals from research institutions and from teaching institutions—some established scholars, some just beginning academic careers, and some in graduate school. We also included an industry perspective. Each person in this pool reviewed from one to three chapters, and the responses were quite personal and often surprising. Indeed, this proved to be a highly thought-provoking review cycle, providing contributors with feedback from two or three individuals interested in the area of nonacademic writing, some of whose voices are rarely heard in the current practice of academic scholarship. Again, we asked our ever-patient contributors to revise in response.

Finally, to enhance the overall cohesiveness of the collection, we established a listserv on the Internet so that contributors could share ideas and questions during the revision provess. We used the Internet extensively in the preparation of this text (which is only appropriate given the technological theme) to keep contributors informed about the progress of the text, to answer their questions, and to receive and distribute review comments. We came to know the contributors through their e-mail: those who never used capitalized letters, those who used emotions, those who wrote witty messages about their lives beyond the collection, and those who were strictly business. Indeed, we often pondered about the connections between social and technological contexts in the shaping of the essays in this volume.

ACKNOWLEDGMENT

Let us conclude by thanking some of the people who aided us in the preparation of this collection. First, we must express our sincere gratitude to the contributors who provided us with their invaluable insights and ideas — not to mention their time and commitment. Likewise, we greatly appreciate the thoroughness and conscientiousness of the many reviewers involved with this project: those listed in this volume as well as those who served as blind reviewers. We wish to thank Hollis Heimbouch, Editor, Amy Olener, Editorial Assistant, and Marcy Pruiksma, Production Editor, at Lawrence Erlbaum Associates, for their commitment to this project and their understanding of nonacademic writing. We thank our many colleagues and students who have taught us that to understand and teach nonacademic writing takes flexibility, devotion, and integration. Finally, we thank our families for their incredible patience and support.

Ann Hill Duin
Craig J. Hansen

About the Contributors

John M. Ackerman is an assistant professor in Rhetoric in Educational Studies and the University Writing Program at the University of Utah. He coordinates Professional Writing: Business and teaches courses in cultural literacies, situated meaning, and composing. His current research is on cultural practices in disciplinary and professional sites, and he is now concluding a study of architectural practice, funded by the Spencer Foundation. He has recently taught a course that blends cultural criticism with architectural design and writing to explore some of the boundaries in community practice. How is it that a university curriculum can more accurately address the diversity of people and practices found in the larger culture? He can be reached via Internet at jonacker@cc.utah.edu.

Jo Allen is an associate professor in the Department of English at East Carolina University where she co-directs the Technical and Professional Communication Programs. She has served as the co-founder and coeditor of the *ATTW Bulletin,* the biannual newsletter of the Association of Teachers of Technical Writing, has served in various administrative roles at her university, and has published extensively in technical communication journals and presses. She is particularly interested in pursuing questions about social implications of writing and writing communities—especially from the angle of gender relations. Currently, she is incorporating those interests in her work on a book, tentatively titled *Evolutions in Techical Communication: Changing Perspectives on Significant Issues.*

Curtis Jay Bonk is Program Coordinator of the Learning, Cognition, and Instruction area within the Department of Counseling and Educational

Psychology at Indiana University. Writing this paper has caused Curt to reprocess a few long forgotten thoughts he had over a decade ago when he was a corporate controller and CPA. In reflection, his interests in collaborative learning and intermental processing run counter to the overly competitive nature of his business training and the solitary work life of his "watchdog" buddies spread across "countless" accounting institutions and departments. Currently, Curt is a social constructionist and proud of it. Let's start "assisting" in learning and stop "assessing" it! He can be reached via Internet at cjbonk@ucs.indiana.edu.

Rebecca E. Burnett is an associate professor of Rhetoric and Professional Communication in the Department of English at Iowa State University. She came to ISU from Carnegie Mellon where she completed her Ph.D. in rhetoric. In a former life, she spent 19 years as a secondary school teacher. Her workplace consulting includes Fortune 500, high-tech, and service companies as well as government and educational agencies. Her research focuses on collaborative interaction, both in both the classroom and the workplace. Her primary research agenda has been exploring the relationship between substantive conflict and collaborative decision-making. She is also interested in other issues in professional communication, including the creation and interpretation of visuals for technical documents, metaphor in technical and scientific documents, and international professional communication. She may be reached via Internet at rburnett@iastate.edu.

Marilyn M. Cooper is an associate professor of English in the Department of Humanities at Michigan Technological University in Houghton, America. She is the co-author (with Michael Holzman) of *Writing as Social Action* (Heinemann/Boynton-Cook, 1989). Although her work focuses on the writing of first-year college students, she has also worked in the area of nonacademic writing: it was in 1989, when she studied the development of a memo written to the provost of the university, that she first noticed the "oddity" of workplace writing-in this case, how the various people involved in constructing the memo held very different ideas about the memo's purpose and effectiveness. More recently, she proposed that operators' manuals might benefit from the application of postmodern writing strategies. She may be reached via Internet at mmcooper@mtu.edu.

Ann Hill Duin is an associate professor in the Rhetoric Department at the University of Minnesota where she is director of graduate studies for the M.S., M.A., and Ph.D. degrees in rhetoric and scientific and technical communication. Her interest in pedagogy stems from her teaching experience at the elementary, secondary, college, and corporate levels, and she works to connect learners across these diverse settings via innovative instructional technologies. While she has published in the areas of document design, usability testing, and computers and collaboration, she is particularly interested in exploring a sociotechnological perspective as it applies cross-culturally and internationally. She looks forward to conversations via Internet at ahduin@maroon.tc.umn.edu.

Craig Hansen is an assistant professor in the Writing Department at Metropolitan State University in St. Paul, Minnesota, where he serves as co-chair and coordinator of the professional and technical writing curriculum. His interest in technology derives from eight years in technical and managerial positions in the computer industry, and his interest in social theory derives from eight years of avoiding corporate politics. He has published a number of works on communication technologies and is particularly interested in predicting the social implications of emerging technologies. He may be reached via Internet at chansen@msus1.msus.edu.

Carl Herndl teaches ethnography, discourse theory and cultural studies in the rhetoric program at New Mexico State University. He has published in *College English, College Composition and Communication, Rhetoric Review,* and in edited collections on professional writing and rhetorical theory. He is currently coediting a book on rhetorical analyses of environmental rhetoric. He is interested in the way theories of practice, ideology, and culture help us understand the rhetoric and cultural work of professional or disciplinary formations, especially interdisciplinary sites like the environment. He may be reached via Internet at cherndl@nmsu.edu.

Johndan Johnson-Eilola is an assistant professor in the English Department at Purdue University where he teaches undergraduate and graduate courses in professional writing, computer documentation, and computers and writing. His work has appeared in numerous journals and edited collections. He is currently completing *Nostalgic Angels: Rearticulating Hypertext Writing,* a book for Ablex Press on the production, reception, and reconstruction of communication technologies in different contexts. His research focuses primarily on the social and political dimensions of developing technologies. He can be contacted via Internet at johndan@sage.cc.purdue.edu.

William Klein is a lecturer at the University of Missouri-St. Louis, where he teaches business, technical, and science writing. His interests in electronic communications systems and collaboration in the workplace have been stimulated through his consulting work at various corporations in the St. Louis area. A doctoral candidate at Michigan Technological University, he is currently researching the writing practices and professional development of chemists.

Mary M. Lay is a professor in the Rhetoric Department at the University of Minnesota where she teaches and does research in scientific and technical communication. She is co-editor of the *Technical Communication Quarterly,* the Association of Teachers of Technical Writing journal, and of *Collaborative Writing in Industry: Investigations in Theory and Practice* (Baywood, 1991). She has published a number of articles on gender and professional communication, including two articles written with Elizabeth Tebeaux on the images, styles, and voices of women writing technical texts during the English Renaissance. Her most recent project involves observing the creation of licensing rules for traditional midwives in Minnesota, as the medical, homebirth, and state discourse communities converse and debate issues of gender, power, and technology. She may be reached via Internet at mmlay@maroon.tc.umn.edu.

Dan McGavin has been teaching at Davenport College of Business in the Communication Department for 25 years. He recently returned to school and is completing his Ph.D. at Michigan Technological University. Among his interests are the influences on and between social forces, organizations and technology. He is currently working on a social history of mentoring.

Padma V. Medury is a Multimedia Consultant in the Eberly College of Arts and Sciences at West Virginia University. Her main interest areas are groupware technologies, hypermedia courseware development, multimedia presentation systems, and the design of technology-based constructivistic learning environments. Writing this paper was truly a collaborative experience for Padma. She hopes that this book will help researchers better understand the complex nature of collaboration in the workplace.

Scott Oates, after teaching for fifteen years in Salt Lake's high schools and community colleges, is now a full-time doctoral student in the University of Utah's Educational Studies Department's Rhetoric Composition, and Literacy Program. His interests include a critical, revisionist history of language arts and English education. Recently, his work has taken up the cultural context of discursive, literate practices in the workplace. In his dissertation, a qualitative study of literacy at a two-year college, he will seek to understand student beliefs and interpretations of the social relations of literate practices in the classroom.

Tom Reynolds is Director of the Texas Education Collaborative — a school-university partnership — and faculty member in the Language, Literacy, and Culture Program within the Department of Educational Curriculum and Instruction at Texas A&M University. His interest in written communication stems from early studies in literature and philosophy, forays into creative writing, and his work life as an editor of curriculum materials, workplace writer, and educational scholar. In keeping with his social-interactionist orientation to the world, he is concerned with how learning and performance are mediated in assorted writing environments. He may be reached via Internet at tomr@tamu.edu.

Stuart A. Selber is an Assistant Professor and Internet/Multimedia Specialist in the Department of Technical Communications at Clarkson University. He has published in numerous technical communication journals and edited collections. Selber is currently developing pedagogical frameworks for hypermedia literacy and would like to speak with others who teach about and with computer technologies in technical communication instructional contexts.

Cynthia L. Selfe is a professor of Composition and Communication and Head of the Humanities Department at Michigan Technological University. Selfe is also the current Co-Editor of the *CCCC Bibliography on Composition and Rhetoric* (with Gail Hawisher, University of Illinois, Champaign-Urbana). Selfe has chaired the College Section of the National Council of Teachers of English, and that organization's Assembly of Computers in English and Instructional Technology Committee. Selfe currently serves, along with Gail Hawisher, as editor of *Computers and Composition: An International Journal for Teachers of Writing* (Ablex Publishing Corporation). Selfe and Hawisher are the founders of Computers and Composition Press, which sponsors the publication of books on computers and their uses in composition classrooms. In her work, Selfe examines the uses of computer technology in composition classrooms from the perspectives yielded by social, cultural, economic, political, educational, and gender scholarships. She may be reached via Internet at cyselfe@mtu.edu.

Richard (Dickie) Selfe is a Technical Communication Specialist in the Humanities Department at Michigan Technological University (MTU). He directs, along with 40 student workers, the Center for Computer-Assisted Language Instruction and teaches communication courses in the department. He is also a graduate student in the Rhetoric and Technical Communication program at MTU. In his work, Selfe studies the characteristics, potential, and limitations of electronic communication systems. He is particularly interested in the impact these new technologies will have on social action and community development in and around local sites and on global networks. He may be reached via Internet at rselfe@mtu.edu.

Catherine F. Smith is associate professor of Writing/English and Textual Studies at Syracuse University. In the Syracuse University Writing Program she teaches undergraduate and graduate courses in composition, writing in professional and public communities, discourse analysis, and writing technologies. As a consultant to organizations in government and industry, she trains professionals in preparing and presenting expert testimony in Congressional hearings. Her current research interest is the rhetoric of starting a new country. For a collection she is editing on the rhetoric of nationbuilding, she would be pleased to hear from others interested in rhetorical histories of emerging nations, particularly new democracies, across space and time. She may be reached via Internet at cfsmith@mailbox.syr.edu.

Sandra Stotsky is a research associate at the Harvard Graduate School of Education and director of the summer institute on Writing, Reading, and Civic Education, funded by the Lincoln and Therese Filene Foundation. She also serves as a consultant to the Mershon Center at The Ohio State University for its multi-year collaboration with Polish scholars and educators to develop a civics curriculum for democratic citizenship in the Polish schools, and for a companion project in Lithuania. She has published extensively on the uses of writing for learning and citizenship, and on the relationships between reading and writing. Her most recent book is *Connecting Civic Education and Language Education: The Contemporary Challenge,* published by Teachers College Press in 1991. She is now working on a book that examines the civic content and thrust of the literature and reading programs in American schools. She currently serves as editor of *Research in the Teaching of English,* the research journal sponsored by the National Council of Teachers of English.

Elizabeth Tebeaux is professor of English and Coordinator of Technical Writing at Texas A&M University and current President of the Association of Teachers of Technical Writing. As a member of Texas A&M's Writing Committee, she is responsible for the curriculum for the university's required upper division technical writing course and helps with the maintenance of the first year writing curriculum. She has authored numerous articles on pedagogy of technical writing. This is the sixth article she has written since 1985 on social and technological changes that affect technical writing curriculum. She is currently completing a five-year study of technical writing in the English Renaissance and remains interested in the relevance, solvency, and effectiveness of writing programs as these are examined and reduced by universities seeking to cut costs. She may be reached via Internet at edt9933@zeus.tamu.edu.

Carol Y. Thompson is an assistant professor of sociology at Texas Christian University. Her current research interests include testing feminist theories of crime on women's firearm ownership, explicating the cultural origins of punitive attitudes toward criminals, and the depiction of the violent female in film. Her research on women's victimization and fear of crime, cultural and situational explanations of defensive gun ownership, and the relationship between aging and criminal careers has been published in leading criminological and sociological journals.

Dorothy A. Winsor is a professor of Communication at GMI Engineering & Management Institute in Flint, Michigan. She is interested in the way written representations of technical work interact with the production of technical knowledge, and in the way social context shapes what can be said. Because she lives and works among engineers, she particularly enjoys any opportunity for discussions of her work or similar work with colleagues at a distance. She envies faculty who have graduate students asking them interesting questions and invites them to send some of the questions her way. She may be reached via Internet at dwinsor@nova.gmi.edu.

List of Reviewers

Anne Aronson, Professor, Metropolitan State University, St. Paul, MN

Saul Carliner, President, Carliner & Company, Information Architects, Atlanta, GA

Marilyn M. Cooper, Professor, Michigan Technological University

Stephen Doheny-Farina, Professor, Clarkson University

John David Fleming, PhD candidate, Carnegie Mellon University

Cheryl Giesler, Professor, Rensselaer Polytechnic Institute

Keith Gildersleeve, Director, Information Services, AT&T Corporation, St. Paul, MN

Chet Hedden, PhD candidate, University of Washington

David Kaufer, Professor, Carnegie Mellon University

Robert Krull, Professor, Rensselaer Polytechnic Institute

Lisa D. Mason, PhD candidate, University of Minnesota

Paul Prior, Professor, University of Illinois at Urbana

Janice C. Redish, President, Redish & Associates

Timothy Rosa, President, Rosa & Associates, Newton, MA

Donald Ross, Professor, University of Minnesota

1 Setting a Sociotechnological Agenda in Nonacademic Writing

Ann Hill Duin
University of Minnesota

Craig J. Hansen
Metropolitan State University

We have embraced the term *nonacademic writing* long before we have understood it. We have taught nonacademic writing long before we have studied it. Just as we design and use terms before we fully understand them, knowledge about nonacademic writing has traveled through accomplished practitioners in business, self-government, industry, and education. Depending on the discipline, teaching nonacademic discourse represents participation (Stotsky, chap. 10), liberation (Selfe & Selfe, chap. 14), oppression (Allen & Thompson, chap. 8), or enculturation (Winsor, chap. 7). Depending on the context, nonacademic discourse meets the needs of industry (Tebeaux, chap. 3), students (Winsor, chap. 7), publishers (Herndl, chap. 2), theorists (Bonk, Reynolds, & Medury, chap. 12), employees (Hansen, chap. 13; Selber, McGavin, Klein, & Johnson-Eilola, chap. 11), or educators (Burnett, chap. 6). In any case, nonacademic writing is surrounded by understanding and confusion, recognition and reduction, openness and surveillance, ownership and control, connections and boundaries.

DEFINING NONACADEMIC WRITING

Any attempt to define nonacademic writing results in problems caused either by too broad or too narrow a focus. Indeed, whole fields of inquiry rise up as subsets of nonacademic writing: business communication, organizational communication, technical communication, managerial communication, legal writing, medical writing, scientific writing, and participatory or civic writing. Allen (1990) described the debate surrounding the defining of technical writing, whereas Kogen (1989) noted the multidisciplinarity surrounding business writing. Bazerman and Paradis (1991) defined professional writing as including both technical and business writing, and their contributors examined everything from medieval letter writing to charter documents in psychiatry. Most recently, Freed (1993), a contributor to Blyler and Thralls's collection entitled *Professional Communication: A Social Perspective*, explained his confusion both in defining the term *professional communication* and in envisioning such an audience of practitioners: "Somewhat like gravity, I confess gravely, though *professional communication* was all around me and I could feel it at every step, its meaning wasn't clear . . . More confusing, the related term *nonacademic writing* refers to discourse (e.g., proposals and reports) quite often composed by college administrators as well as professors in the academy" (p. 197). Although these definitions help to clarify the boundaries of our research studies, academic programs, and professional societies, we believe that the term *nonacademic writing* unites us as a common core of practitioners interested in writing that occurs within "settings of consequence" (Ackerman & Oates, chap. 5).

Clearly, a satisfactory definition for nonacademic writing is elusive. As Allen (1990) concluded after her quest for a definition of technical writing, "Perhaps, therefore, we need to get over our embarrassment at not having a perfect definition and abandon the search for it altogether" (p. 76). Rather than abandon this term, we have chosen to use it because it implies a multidisciplinarity that adds strength and adaptability to our collective work as scholars and practitioners. The term *nonacademic writing* is used throughout this volume because the earlier work of these contributors was in part inspired by Odell and Goswami's (1985) groundbreaking *Writing in Nonacademic Settings*. However, although nonacademic writing for Odell and Goswami's contributors was primarily composed of memos and reports, new versions of this concept have emerged along with new technologies.

New technologies will continue to emerge; therefore, nonacademic writing will continue as a dynamic, changing field of study. Technologies must be integral to the consideration of both parts of the term *nonacademic writing*: to process and product. There will be no end to investigating nonacademic writing because there are no limits to the "settings of consequence" (Ackerman & Oates, chap. 5) to be studied and no limits to evolving technologies. There will be no end to defining nonacademic writing because to understand the term one must embrace so many themes.

REFOCUSING ESTABLISHED THEMES IN
NONACADEMIC WRITING

If defining nonacademic writing is difficult, refocusing established themes is more difficult. Who sets an agenda in nonacademic writing research? When research in nonacademic writing is designed, are questions formulated and methodologies determined based on a consensus regarding what constitutes nonacademic writing? Or is dissensus practiced in order to lead to refocused themes? Are ascending agendas surrounded with theoretical and methodological jargon to elevate particular disciplines? Or do we work to bring outside audiences into their realm? Is the agenda isolationist or communal? Is it controlled by disciplinary constraints, corporate giants, political concerns, or taxpaying citizens? Are a multiplicity of audiences, purposes, disciplines, and contexts included in its voice?

The purpose of this chapter and this volume is to set an agenda. Such words may be perilous. Surrounded by corporate grants and political exigencies, we are controlled in part by current or future tenure committees and the general public. An inescapable social landscape demands vision for research and pedagogy in nonacademic writing. Institutions currently question the need for nonacademic writing research and its teaching. Numerous conversations with employers reveal that they question institutional preparation of students for writing tasks required in the next century. Why research in nonacademic writing is conducted and how this research is transferred to pedagogy must be articulated.

The collective agenda set in this text is both reassuring and disquieting. Nonacademic writing is studied through the overlapping lenses of social theory and technology. Social theory and nonacademic writing have been dealt with extensively beginning with Odell and Goswami's (1985) publication and continuing most recently with Spilka's (1993) *Writing in the Workplace* and Blyler and Thralls's (1993) award-winning collection. These volumes, taken together with other studies of nonacademic writing, reveal "a burgeoning field of research, one that fifteen years ago was virtually nonexistent" (Bouldin & Odell, 1993, p. 268).

However, this body of research is not without its critics. Gross (1994), in reviewing a large set of this work, stated that "workplace writing researchers display a . . . defect, a product, perhaps, of their principled drift away from humanities: they ignore the ethical, social, and political implications of their work" (p. 829). The chapters in this collection address these issues in several ways. For example, in studying the contexts and uses for participatory writing, Stotsky explores the ethical purposes built into civic literacy. By applying gender and social theory to the development, teaching, and application of computer software, Lay questions whether computers are used to accommodate gender difference or to imitate ways of thinking that prioritize and exclude difference. When studying the rhetorical and ideological formation of technical disciplines and their textbooks, Herndl disputes the transfer between ethnographic theory and professional writing pedagogy. And Selfe and Selfe identify complex social, cultural, and political forces surrounding the use of computers as wide-area communication devices, exploring their potential as spaces either for collective political action or surveillance and control.

Gross (1994) further criticized the current lack of sophistication in workplace writing research, stating:

> To practice workplace writing research as a human science is valuable only in so far as the enterprise is held to the highest methodological standards these sciences have so far achieved: the standards for experiments and quasi-experiments, enunciated by Campbell and Stanley and their successors, and the standards for case studies currently being developed in comparative political science and in sociology. But current empirical work in workplace writing is too theoretically unsophisticated and too methodologically impoverished to count as a legitimate human science. (p. 829)

However, for those conducting writing research in a variety of nonacademic settings, these kinds of research designs may not be desirable. A focus on scientific methodology is based on positivist assumptions that value truth and taxonomy: These may be inappropriate means to explore constructive meaning making. Ethnomethodological models from anthropology and sociology, employed by many researchers in nonacademic writing, are better suited to gain insight, not truth, about complex social behavior. Further, to adhere to experimental methodological standards entails control of the many variables present in the sites of nonacademic writing research, ignoring the social complexity and dynamism of these sites. The variables are too many, too fluid. Researchers employ experimental and quasi-experimental designs in controlled settings to ensure the reproducibility of results. Consistency in some aspects of nonacademic research design is a valuable goal, but replication, given the pace of change in the many settings of consequence explored, may never be practical or even important.

One of the confounding variables in understanding nonacademic writing and a significant factor in driving change (and one to which we direct particular attention in this volume) is technology. Technology has yet to be paired with social theory in a rigorous way in the study of nonacademic writing. Thought to be a product utilized for rather than a process integral to writing, discussion of technology in nonacademic settings has largely been left to the domain of publications such as the *Journal of Organizational Computing* or *Computers and Composition* or work by organiza-

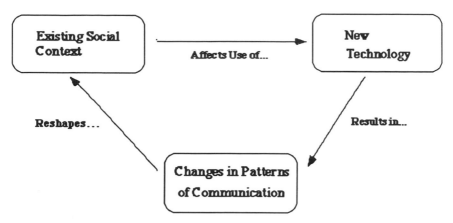

FIG. 1.1.   Interrelatedness of technology and social context.

tional communication scholars such as Galegher, Kraut, and Egido (1991). We must endeavor to explore these links in the field of nonacademic writing as well.

One link illustrating the vitality of the connection between social theory and technology is social context. Social context shapes the use of any new technology, offering new options for connectivity or communication function. Patterns of interaction, formal and informal power hierarchies, and priorities embedded in organizational culture affect the adoption and use of that technology. In turn, characteristics of new technology, access to that technology, and interaction with others via the new technology change the existing social context (see Fig. 1.1). To explore this complex relationship and its impact on nonacademic writing, we need to build an approach that conjoins the social and technological perspectives.

THE SOCIAL PERSPECTIVE

Much of the recent thought on nonacademic writing involves refining the idea of the social perspective. Its well-documented roots are found in an epistemology of social construction where, as described by Clark (1990), "knowledge [is] negotiated by the people who share it, people bound together by common needs and purposes" (p. 3). Within this model, communication is central to a constructive process that is dynamic and nonlinear, that grows from consensus and dissensus, that operates through exchanges of interpretation and meaning. Refinements have taken a variety of forms. For example, Nystrand (1990) distinguished between social construction and social interaction: The former "concerns itself most immediately with communities of writers and readers," and the latter "concerns itself with the individual interactions of writers and readers" (p. 4). Social interaction is the means by which social construction takes place (and is particularly evident in the use of computer networks): Local interactions together make up a larger constructive process (Duin & Hansen, 1994).

Witte (1992) described the relationship of text and largely social perceptions of self. According to Witte, text exists within a perceived context, where context is "something akin to a writer's representation of the externally situated or projected 'self'," and an intertext, an element that relates time and other texts, is "something akin to a writer's representation of the situated 'other,' or the 'social'" (p. 289). We create text in response to our understanding of context and intertext, our intention to communicate shaped by our perception of knowledge we think we share with others. Others have extended the social perspective beyond the constructivist paradigm. Blyler and Thralls (1993) described three theoretical approaches within the social perspective: the social constructivist, the ideologic, and the paralogic hermeneutic. And Allen and Thompson (chap. 8, this volume) offer five models of social theory from sociology that could provide frameworks for research. Clearly, the social perspective, although well established, will continue to change over time, both because scholars will continue to invigorate it with social theory from other disciplines and because it has proven to be a highly flexible framework for nonacademic writing research.

Even a very brief look illustrates the variety of issues, controversies, and approaches social theory has introduced to nonacademic writing research. Faigley (1985) stated that such a perspective "forc[es] researchers to consider such issues as social roles, group purposes, communal organization, ideology, and, finally, theories of culture" (p. 236). Applying a social theory perspective, researchers have considered these issues and others. Some have looked at texts as the result of negotiated meaning (e.g., Cross, 1990; Doheny-Farina, 1991; Flower, 1994); many have defined and explored specific contexts and related these to writing (e.g., Brady, 1993; Segal, 1993); others have explored issues such as collaboration (perhaps most notably, Lay & Karis, 1991), communicative exchanges between pairs of writers (Blakeslee, 1993; Burnett, 1993; Spilka, 1988), and the activities of single writers in organizational contexts (e.g., Winsor, 1989). The variations are endless. But so, too, are the complexities of nonacademic writing and its confounding variables; its multitude of professions, settings, and cultures are essentially alien to many of the academic visitors who study them. Indeed, any one of these elements changes from day to day. Therefore, to comprehend these complexities, research and theoretical models, like the settings themselves, must be dynamic and able to tolerate change, difference, and unpredictability. The goal should be insight, not truth. In this, a social perspective excels.

A social perspective aids the study of contextual influences on writers in nonacademic settings: the ways writers apply their social, political, and cultural experiences to their interpretation and construction of audience; and the ways context inhibits or enables writers to form ideas and transfer them to others. Viewing nonacademic writing through a social lens forces us to identify ourselves, our writing, and our teaching as part of a hetero-glossic social landscape, a complex history in which "writing is potentially responsive to and dependent on everything that is on the social stage" (Bazerman, 1993, p. ix).

A SOCIOTECHNOLOGICAL PERSPECTIVE

Although every player on this complex social stage cannot be identified, certainly one can: technology. Technology merges public and private domains of social theory; technology merges social constructionist and social interactionist perspectives. The assessment of technology's impact on nonacademic writing research and teaching has been far too conservative. Technology can no longer be considered tangential to nonacademic writing. Indeed, nonacademic writing must be viewed through a sociotechnological lens.

Current electronic spaces — virtual classrooms (Selfe & Hilligoss, 1994), virtual corporations (Cronin, 1994), and virtual communities (Rheingold, 1993) — alter our notions of nonacademic writing for students, teachers, employees, employers, and the general public. Instead of assuming that writers meet in the shared space of a conference room, they now meet electronically. Instead of assuming that employers primarily provide employees with experience and practice in the kinds of writing that the corresponding culture most values, technologies allow writers the opportunity to structure interactions and practices that differ from those occurring within traditional workplaces or classroom settings (Barker & Kemp, 1990; Barrett, 1992; Handa, 1990; Selfe & Selfe, chap. 14). Technology provides a feasible means for nonacademic writers to study and practice new forms and forums for learning about writing (Bruce, Peyton, & Batson, 1993; Duin & Mason, in press; Selfe & Hilligoss, 1994). Technology provides a feasible means for national organizations to require members to remain current in their fields (see, e.g., the Office of Rural Health Policy's report on Rural TeleHealth, 1993).

Technological advances offer an opportunity to transform the teaching of nonacademic writing from a passive one-directional transfer of information to a dynamic, interactive, collaborative experience for learners that lies beyond the "traditional" resident-site learner (Handa, 1990; Harasim, 1993). Desktop multimedia in which writers see, hear, and share text with each other from their desktop computers is available for use in education, the community, self-government, and the professions (Duin & Mason, in press). The information highway—at present, the infrastructure known as *Internet*—provides a virtual connection to link academic and nonacademic writers around the world. Interactive multimedia programs such as *Gopher*™ and the *World Wide Web*™ provide college catalogs and entire courses online. Institutions have the capability of recording your classes; learners may then access these courses online at any time and from virtually any country or institution around our tiny globe. Using virtual reality applications, students have the ability to experience laboratory components of courses without being physically present in the laboratory. Students can experience presenting a new product to a corporate board; they can experience persuading a community group to participate in their project; they can experience interviewing people in other cultures; they can experience the look and feel of a design before building it.

These components—desktop multimedia, courses placed on-line, and virtual reality—as well as the myriad of technologies we now use (phone, television/cable, fax, e-mail) will converge into seamless wearable and/or implanted systems. Institutional boundaries will shudder and then shatter as nonacademic writers seek knowledge and know-how from wherever information is located and with whomever they might connect technologically. Nonacademic writing research and teaching must be designed for a transformed world.

Metaphorical Spaces

Although these technologies hold promise for nonacademic writing, there is peril in the potential to create a social system consisting of shared values, vocabulary, status and prestige ordering, and differentiation of members from nonmembers (Hansen, in press; Kiesler, Sproull, & Eccles, 1985; Selfe & Hilligoss, 1994; Selfe & Selfe, chap.14, this volume). We interrogate the nonacademic writing world largely through the computer interface— socially comfortable to some writers but severely uncomfortable to others. The metaphorical structure of this interface guides the processes by which we characterize and then model our understanding of nonacademic writing.

An interface is much more than the screen through which one encounters another. The ancient Greeks spoke of *prosopon,* or "a face facing another face" (Heim, 1993, p. 78). One face reacts to the other face, the other face responds, and so on in a kind of Bahktian dialectic: "The relationship then lives on as a third thing or state of being . . . the ancient word suggests a spiritual interaction between eternity and time" (p. 78). The more we interact through interfaces, the more we face other faces, the more we live in a cyberspace that simultaneously destroys some and erects other demographic, geographical, social, and physical barriers. In 1967, the philosopher Heidegger saw a rising crest of technology that would serve as a resource for a cybernetically organized humankind. Heidegger speculated on an all-enframing *Gestell* (technological system), ominous and threatening as a metaphysical sphinx.

These interfaces are modern-day maps through which writers seek, discover, share, and construct knowledge. According to Wood (1992), maps serve interests, but these interests are often masked. Maps are embedded in a history they help to construct, and maps include signs and myths based on this history. Selfe and Selfe (1993) believe that "the primary interfaces of computer systems which we ask students to use in our classes represent our culture's value on monoculturalism, capitalism, racism, and phallogic thinking. [They provide] a colonial gesture continually extended toward students of color, of non-English speaking backgrounds, and women" (p. 1).

Increasing numbers of nonacademic writing scholars believe that computer interfaces based on the corporate desktop metaphor of layers of files and folders frame reality in the perspective of modern capitalism and thus grant privilege to white middle- and upper class writers. This desktop map does not represent the world in alternative metaphors that would constitute the interface within a different set of social and economic values. But new metaphors for interface design are beginning to change the virtual landscape of writing. Instead of relying on the desktop metaphor, programs now are organized around spatial metaphors such as a stage (*Macromedia Director*™) or geographical locations (*Microsoft Kids*™). Instead of viewing computers as tools, we have shifted to viewing networks of computers as metaphorical places.

Distance and Nonacademic Writing

As these metaphorical places absorb our thought, they also absorb our language and, according to Heim (1993), slide us "from a direct awareness of things to the detached world of logical distance . . . [this] distance . . . offers all the allure of control and power without the pain of having to translate back and forth from our everyday approach to the things we experience" (p. 21). The now common hypertext interface further emulates an almost divine access to information; as nonacademic writers leap through networks of knowledge, intellectual and social distances melt away.

Kaufer and Carley (1993, 1994) theorized about distance and the distancing effect of technology. Whereas Heim spoke of "logical distance" as a writer's detachment from and control over texts, Kaufer and Carley (1994) spoke of distance as "the writer's separation from a reader in space, time, culture or some mix thereof" (p. 8). Although written text introduced the idea of distance between writer and reader, technology has further extended this social distance. By extending a writer's distance, technology also extends a writer's reach, or "the number of people whose mental models can be actually or potentially affected" (p. 32) by the writer. Through the three distancing principles of asynchronicity, durability, and multiplicity, technology breaks the bonds of proximate, or face-to-face, communication. Asynchronous communication allows writers and readers to work at different times; the durability of electronic texts allows communication to extend well beyond the life of the writer; and technology in the form of transcontinental networks allows multiplicity or an increase in the number of communication partners.

Viewing nonacademic writing through Kaufer and Carley's distancing principles shows that when we examine its construction in nonacademic settings, we primarily concentrate on proximate writers rather than on the effects of the resulting texts on their distant audiences. Confining our research efforts to the development and use of texts within their proximate settings limits our understanding of the greater life of a text. Likewise, when we teach nonacademic writing students to develop texts for distant audiences, we primarily teach such courses in the proximate space of the writing classroom. According to Kaufer and Carley (1994), "learning to write within the confines of the classroom entails learning from an ostensibly contradictory premise: that students can get practice in literate communication at a distance with teachers and peers with whom they have, relatively speaking, minimal distance in time and space" (p. 37).

According to Kaufer and Carley (1994), students must "be increasingly confronted with a model of written communication that exposes them to distancing assumptions at a more explicit and theoretical level" (pp. 37–38). One goal in the teaching of nonacademic writing is to teach students how to write for social contexts within a technological world, how to write for a world where an understanding of communicating across distance is imperative, how to write for audiences that inhabit virtual communities and workplaces. Therefore, a crucial goal for research in nonacademic writing is to recognize the importance of sociotechnological issues.

ISSUES WITHIN A SOCIOTECHNOLOGICAL AGENDA

The following are issues surrounding the study and teaching of nonacademic writing in the midst of an overwhelmingly technological age. These issues begin a discussion that continues throughout this volume, and we hope beyond.

Contexts

One of the great challenges of nonacademic writing research is the further study of contexts of writing. This issue transcends the theoretical perspective of scholars such as Witte (1992) and finds focus in the studies by researchers such as Winsor, Ackerman and Oates, and Stotsky in this volume. These authors explore an increasing range of nonacademic sites, sites where texts use different sign systems (such as architecture and other design professions), sites where the common purpose that unites participants is often temporary (such as issue-based organizations) or very focused in purpose (such as neighborhood associations). We could investigate literacy among those who work in the trades, in virtual communities, in the performing arts, or among the homeless. As an aggregate view of nonacademic writing is slowly assembled, diverse vantage points will help us distinguish between the local and the general.

We enter these many settings as strangers and often as guests. We must be aware that our perceptions reflect personal and institutional goals as well as individual value systems. Thus we must define context carefully. A continuing challenge for nonacademic writing research is defining the variables of a sociotechnological context. What social and technological variables should be identified at each research site to tell us how people interact? Without consistency, our ability to comprehend the general will be compromised. As Herndl (chap. 2, this volume) points out, a lack of understanding of the limits of research is particularly dangerous when results are translated to pedagogy. Essentialist views of nonacademic writing that inappropriately freeze dynamic cultures, turning observation into rule, must be resisted.

Power

Analysis of power and politics is essential in understanding nonacademic writing. Power involves control over the distribution of scarce resources. This can take many forms, some very subtle. We must continue to seek out the hidden rules for communication in nonacademic settings, the "tacit knowledge" (as Winsor applies it in chap. 7 of this volume) that is central to organizational enculturation. In sociotechnological theory, the scarce resources are both physical and nonphysical. Power is most often understood in the technology arena as an issue of access. Who receives physical access to machines? Too often this is a function of position in a defined social hierarchy (Hansen, chap. 13, this volume), where it serves to reinforce the status quo. Equally important is the question of who has access to nonphysical resources such as databases and far-reaching networks. Selfe and Selfe (chap. 14, this volume) noted that access is not enough in itself. People must learn to use technologies to meet their needs. They should not have their needs defined by the designers and vendors of the technology (Lay, chap. 4, this volume). In conducting research in nonacademic writing informed by a sociotechnological perspective, we must avoid viewing technology as neutral, as a simple mechanism for information delivery, and actively seek to understand its role in supporting and resisting power structures.

Authorship

Authorship in most large organizations has long differed from notions of academic authorship. Plagiarism of written resources within a single corporation is irrelevant. In many nonacademic sites, intertextuality could be described as a formalized process of appropriation in addition to sometimes subtle influences. Our purview should include not only individual writers or collaborative groups, but the lives of ideas as they evolve through different texts and media. As Selber et al. (chap. 11, this volume) point out, traditional notions of authorship can be irrelevant in some technological settings. Interactive hypertext, multimedia, and virtual reality strain traditional notions of text as well as authorship. We must not ignore evolution in favor of traditional notions of text and authorship.

Connections

Part of provisioning nonacademic writers with the skills for participating in and altering their environments includes connecting them with writers at both academic and nonacademic sites via emerging technologies. Connections constructed and modeled during nonacademic writing courses serve as ongoing connections long after coursework. These connections also serve as a form of apprenticeship learning wherein writers become enculturated into their discourse communities (Winsor, chap. 7, this volume) while at the same time remaining free to resist and question these communities (Selfe & Selfe, chap. 14, this volume). When the physical walls of academia crumble as virtual realities link writers one to one with those people and places that most meet their needs, new forms of nonacademic writing research and teaching ultimately will evolve.

Relevance

Tebeaux (chap. 3, this volume) states that we must achieve relevance in research and curriculum. The control over the study of nonacademic writing has moved from academia (Odell & Goswami, 1985) to the professional site (Blyler & Thralls, 1993) to a call for "mutual constraints"

(Spilka, 1993, p. 210). Nonacademic writers have yet to be empowered with the skills to study themselves from the inside. Only when nonacademic writers gain the skills to transform themselves from the inside out will relevance in research and curriculum be achieved. Teacher-researchers have long known that what matters "is less their learning of a method than their understanding of a point of view about observation that holds regardless of method and that also validates certain methods" (Knoblach & Brannon, 1988, p. 22). Just as teacher-researchers emphasize change from the inside out (i.e., from the classroom to the administration; see Ray, 1992, 1993), so nonacademic writing instructors must equip writers with anthropological, social science, and linguistic skills (e.g., participant observation, journal keeping, interviews, analyses of electronic messages) that will enable them to analyze their sociotechnological writing environments as well as participate in them. Furthermore, such baseline research skills will allow nonacademic writers to enact change rather than depend on either academia or the professional site to alter it.

Although efforts of transfer between traditional theory and research and nonacademic writing pedagogy are questionable (Herndl, chap. 2, this volume), these efforts must be expanded to include a sociotechnological agenda. Integrating social theory and technology in our understanding of nonacademic writing encourages us to face age-old questions through virtual landscapes; it connects scholars and disciplines in a quest to meet the needs of nonacademic writers around the globe.

REFERENCES

Allen, J. (1990). The case against defining technical writing. *Journal of Business and Technical Communication, 4*(2), 68–77.

Barker, T. T., & Kemp, F. O. (1990). Network theory: A postmodern pedagogy for the writing classroom. In C. Handa (Ed.), *Computers and community: Teaching composition in the twenty-first century* (pp. 1–27). Portsmouth, NH: Boynton/Cook Heinemann.

Barrett, E. (Ed.). (1992). *Sociomedia: Multimedia, hypermedia, and the social construction of knowledge.* Cambridge, MA: MIT Press.

Bazerman, C. (1993). Foreword. In N. R. Blyler & C. Thralls (Eds.), *Professional communication: The social perspective* (pp. vii–x). Newbury Park, CA: Sage.

Bazerman, C., & Paradis, J. (Eds.). (1991). *Textual dynamics of the professions: Historical and contemporary studies of writing in professional communities.* Madison: University of Wisconsin Press.

Blakeslee, A. M. (1993). Readers and authors: Fictionalized constructs or dynamic collaborations? *Technical Communication Quarterly, 2*(1), 23–36.

Blyler, N. R., & Thralls, C. (Eds.). (1993). *Professional communication: The social perspective.* Newbury Park, CA: Sage.

Bouldin, T., & Odell, L. (1993). Surveying the field and looking ahead: A systems theory perspective on research on writing in the workplace. In R. Spilka (Ed.), *Writing in the workplace: New research perspectives* (pp. 268–284). Carbondale: Southern Illinois University Press.

Brady, L. (1993). A contextual theory for business writing. *Journal of Business and Technical Communication, 7*(4), 452–471.

Bruce, B., Peyton, J. D., & Batson, T. (Eds.). (1993). *Network-based classrooms: Promises and realities.* Cambridge, England: Cambridge University Press.

Burnett, R. (1993). Conflict in collaborative decision making. In N. R. Blyler & C. Thralls (Eds.), *Professional communication: The social perspective* (pp. 144–162). Newbury Park, CA: Sage.

Clark, G. (1990). *Dialogue, dialectic, and conversation: A social perspective on the function of writing.* Carbondale: Southern Illinois University Press.

Cronin, M. J. (1994). *Doing business on the internet: How the electronic highway is transforming American companies.* New York: Van Nostrand Reinhold.

Cross, G. (1990). A Bahktian exploration of factors affecting the collaborative writing of an executive letter of an annual report. *Research in the Teaching of English, 24*(2), 173–202.

Doheny-Farina, S. (1991), Creating a text/creating a company: The role of a text in the rise and decline of a new organization. In C. Bazerman & J. Paradis (Eds.), *Textual dynamics of the professions: Historical and contemporary studies of writing in professional communities* (pp. 306–335). Madison: University of Wisconsin Press.

Duin, A. H., & Hansen, C. J. (1994). Writing and reading on computer networks as social construction and interaction. In S. J. Hilligoss & C. L. Selfe (Eds.), *Literacy and computers: The complications of teaching and learning with technology* (pp. 89–112). New York: Modern Language Association of America.

Duin, A. H., Lammers, E., Mason, L. D., & Graves, M. F. (1994). Responding to ninth-grade students via telecommunications: College mentor strategies and development over time. *Research in the Teaching of English, 28*(2), 117–153.

Duin, A. H., & Mason, L. D. (in press). Exploring new forms of collaboration: Case studies of computer-mediated mentor activity. In R. E. Burnett & A. H. Duin (Eds.), *Collaboration in technical communication: Research perspectives.* Hillsdale, NJ: Lawrence Erlbaum Associates.

Faigley, L. (1985). Nonacademic writing: The social perspective. In L. Odell & D. Goswami (Eds.), *Writing in nonacademic settings* (pp. 231–248). New York: Guilford.

Flower, L. (1994). *The construction of negotiated meaning: A social cognitive theory of writing.* Carbondale: Southern Illinois University Press.

Freed, R. C. (1993). Postmodern practice: Perspectives and prospects. In N. R. Blyler & C. Thralls (Eds.), *Professional communication: The social perspective* (pp. 196–214). Newbury Park, CA: Sage.

Galegher, J., Kraut, R. E., & Egido, C. (Eds.). (1991). *Intellectual teamwork: Social and technological foundations of cooperative work.* Hillsdale, NJ: Lawrence Erlbaum Associates.

Gross, A. (1994). Theory, method, practice. *College English, 56*(7), 828–840.

Handa, C. (Ed.). (1990). *Computers and community: Teaching composition in the twenty-first century.* Portsmouth, NH: Boynton/Cook Heinemann.

Hansen, C.J. (in press). Networking technology in the classroom: Whose interests are we serving? In J. Dautermann & P. Sullivan (Eds.), *Electronic literacy.* Urbana, IL: National Council of Teachers of English.

Harasim, L. M. (Ed.). (1993). *Global networks: Computers and international communication.* Cambridge, MA: MIT Press.

Heidegger, M. (1967). *Wegmarken.* Frankfurt: Klostermann.

Heim, M. (1993). *The metaphysics of virtual reality.* New York: Oxford University Press.

Kaufer, D. S., & Carley, K. M. (1993). *Communication at a distance: The influence of print on sociocultural organization and change.* Hillsdale, NJ: Lawrence Erlbaum Associates.

Kaufer, D. S., & Carley, K. (1994). Some concepts and axioms about communication: Proximate and at a distance. *Written Communication, 11*(1), 8–42.

Kiesler, S., Sproull, L., & Eccles, J. S. (1985). Pool halls, chips, and war games: Women in the culture of computing. *Psychology of Women Quarterly*, *9*, 451–462.

Knoblach, C. H., & Brannon, L. (1988). Knowing our knowledge: A phenomenological basis for teacher research. In L. Z. Smith (Ed.), *Audits of meaning: A festschrift in honor of Ann E. Berthoff* (pp. 17–28). Portsmouth, NH: Boynton/Cook Heinemann.

Kogen, M. (Ed.). (1989). *Writing in the business professions*. Urbana, IL: National Council of Teachers of English.

Lay, M., & Karis, W. (Eds.). (1991). *Collaborative writing in industry: Investigations in theory and practice*. Amityville, NY: Baywood.

Macromedia director. (1993). Software version 3.1.3. Macromedia, Inc.

Microsoft kids. (1993). Software version 3.1. Microsoft, Inc.

Mosaic. (1994). Network interface: National Center for Supercomputing Applications. Urbana: University of Illinois.

Nystrand, M. (1990). Sharing words: The effects of readers on developing writers. *Written Communication*, *7*(1), 3–24.

Odell, L., & Goswami, D. (Eds.). (1985). *Writing in nonacademic settings*. New York: Guilford.

Office of Rural Health Policy. (1993, September). *Rural teleHealth: Telemedicine, distance education and informatics for rural health care*. Washington, DC: U.S. Department of Health and Human Services.

Ray, R. E. (1992). Composition from the teacher-research point of view. In G. Kirsch & P. A. Sullivan (Eds.), *Methods and methodology in composition research* (pp. 172–189). Carbondale: Southern Illinois University Press.

Ray, R. E. (1993). *The practice of theory: Teacher research in composition*. Urbana: National Council of Teachers of English.

Rheingold, H. (1993). *The virtual community: Homesteading on the electronic frontier*. Reading, MA: Addison-Wesley.

Segal, J. (1993). Writing and medicine: Text and context. In R. Spilka (Ed.), *Writing in the workplace: New research perspectives* (pp. 84–97). Carbondale: Southern Illinois Univeristy Press.

Selfe, C. L., & Hilligoss, S. (Eds.). (1994). *Literacy and computers: The complications of teaching and learning with technology*. New York: Modern Language Association of America.

Selfe, C. L., & Selfe, R. J. (1993, November). *The politics of the interface: Power and its exercise in electronic contact zones*. Paper presented at the Midwest Modern Language Association Conference, Minneapolis, MN.

Spilka, R. (1988). Studying writer-reader interactions in the workplace. *The Technical Writing Teacher*, *15*(3), 208–221.

Spilka, R. (Ed.). (1993). *Writing in the workplace: New research perspectives*. Carbondale: Southern Illinois University Press.

TurboGopher. (1991–92). Network interface. Minneapolis: University of Minnesota.

Winsor, D. A. (1989). An engineer's writing and the corporate construction of knowledge. *Written Communication*, *6*(3), 270–285.

Witte, S. P. (1992). Context, text, intertext: Toward a constructivist semiotic of writing. *Written Communication*, *9*(2), 237–308.

Wood, D. (1992). *The power of maps*. New York: Guilford.

2

The Transformation of Critical Ethnography Into Pedagogy, or the Vicissitudes of Traveling Theory

Carl G. Herndl
New Mexico State University

> Such movement [of theory] into a new environment is never unimpeded. It necessarily involves processes of representation and institutionalization different from those at the point of origin.
>
> —Edward Said (1983, p. 226)

> The theory of practice puts objectivist knowledge back on its feet by posing the question of the (theoretical and social) conditions which make such knowledge possible.
>
> —Pierre Bourdieu (1977, p. 4)

I was talking with a colleague in Anthropology the other day, and he told me a joke that was making the rounds in his department. The joke goes like this: The postmodern anthropologist goes into the field to do ethnographic work; he meets his informant and starts explaining his ideological and disciplinary position. After a couple of hours the informant interrupts, "When do we get to talk about me?"

My friend's joke reflects the frustration many academics feel with postmodernism and its critique of authority, disciplinarity, and representation. The situation here is similar to the one Mailloux describes at the conclusion of *Rhetorical Power* (1989) when he points out the danger that the "rhetorical candor" entailed in postmodern self-consciousness "will be

17

read as narcissistic self-indulgence, that it will not seem a necessary theoretical move required by rhetorical theory but as another case of theory's fashionable rereading of itself — self-critique as self-display" (p. 167). For those of us interested in the interdisciplinary work in cultural studies generally and in ethnographic writing research in particular, the kind of critical self-reflexivity proposed by Mailloux and burlesqued in the joke is indeed a necessity. But the joke indicates not just the objections to the postmodern critical project; it also implies that the rhetorical turn in ethnography is impractical, that it gets in the way of doing anything productive.

For scholars working in nonacademic writing research, the contemporary critique of ethnography opens a number of challenges. The argument that ethnographies construct their findings through discipline-specific rhetorical practices which are legitimized by professional interests has forced us to reexamine both our research methods and our reporting practices (Cintron, 1993; Herndl, 1991; Kleine, 1990), and I turn to these issues shortly. But there is another, more intractable problem confronting contemporary ethnographic theory. Put in its simplest form the problem is this: The critical self-reflexivity of postmodern ethnographic theory does not correspond to the demands of the classroom.

This conflict between self-reflexive postmodern theory and the classroom occurs because the discourse of contemporary ethnographic theory has different institutional and ideological interests than those of professional writing pedagogy. Not surprisingly, what counts as work for theory does not necessarily count as useful work for the classroom. Those of us who read theory and who also teach advanced technical and professional writing experience this difference regularly. And although the conflict between theory and practice is not new, the situation in the case of ethnography is somewhat unusual. The contemporary critique of authority and representation challenges the assumptions and structures of technical and professional writing courses in ways other theories have not.

In this chapter, I examine the uneasy relationship between the contemporary critique of ethnography and cultural representation, and the institutional practice of technical and professional writing with its demands for authority, knowledge, disciplinarity, and practicality. With the emergence of social rhetorics in the 1980s and the growth of research in nonacademic and professional writing, ethnography has become an increasingly popular research strategy for exploring the social and cultural construction of professional discourse. Certainly not all these research reports find their way into textbooks or pedagogical essays, but many do, and many teachers read the research reported in journals and edited collections.

My concern here is twofold: What happens to ethnographic theory when it moves into the discourse of writing research, and what happens to ethnographic interpretation when it moves into the classroom, whether through textbooks, pedagogical articles, or a teacher's class plans? More specifically, I am concerned about a number of questions: What is the conflict between the postmodern critique of ethnography and the institutional discourse of writing pedagogy? How, and how much, does the institutional discourse appropriate and reinscribe the theoretical and the radical in pedagogy? To what extent does the movement into pedagogy domesticate the more radical position of ethnography and its possibilities for critique? What consequences does this conflict have for ethnographic research in rhetoric and composition?

In order to pursue these questions about contemporary ethnographic theory and its relations to writing research and pedagogy, I have borrowed Said's notion of "traveling theory." Said (1983) argued that the environment in which a theory is produced is a first condition which exerts pressure over the theory's formation. He demonstrated the changes a theory undergoes as it travels from one environment to another by describing three moments in the life of Lukâcs's (1919) theory of reification under commodity capital. When he wrote the essay on reification, Lukâcs was a militant activist in the Hungarian revolution, and reification was a radical theory advocating the revolutionary overthrow of the ruling class. In Goldmann's Paris dissertation (1955), Lukâcs's insurrectionary class consciousness gave way to a scholarly exploration of the tragic social vision in Racine and Pascal. Finally, when Williams rewrote the theory of reification in the 1970s, he recognized the trap of Lukâcs's totalizing position. Working in the reflective and textual tradition at Cambridge, Williams recognized that Lukâcs was mistaken when he thought that reification could be totally dominant, and that Lukâcs's theory had become reductive in its repeated applications.

The strategy Said developed for evaluating the way a theory travels involves four operations. He suggested that we examine the origins of a theory, estimate the "distance" it travels, consider the conditions that will lead to the theory's being accepted or resisted, and gauge the degree to which the theory is transformed as it is reinscribed in a new environment. Although the contemporary critique of ethnography does not have as long a history as Lukâcs's theory of reification, Said's strategy for describing the movement and development of theory provides a useful guide for our analysis of ethnographic theory and its relation to the research and teaching of professional writing.

DEPARTURES: SLICK DESCRIPTION, MÉNAGE A TROIS, AND THE JANUS-FACED WRITER

The contemporary critique of ethnography and cultural representation is a result of the Marxist and poststructuralist critique of discourse, disciplinarity, and cultural representation. There are certainly fractures and differences within the work covered by such global terms, but the work of Foucault, Said, Williams, and White constitute a strong position for studying the rhetorical and ideological formation of disciplines and their texts. These theorists have argued that disciplines themselves construct the objects about which they make knowledge claims, and that the authority of disciplinary discourse is maintained and legitimized not by truth or an appeal to facts, but by historically developed and ideologically interested discourse structures. Thus one might argue, as Hacking (1982) has, that "although whichever propositions are true may depend on the data, the fact that they are candidates for being true is a consequence of an historical event" (p. 56). And the historical event in this case is the emergence of a discipline with what Hacking called a peculiar "style of thinking."

From this position, ethnography is the telling of stories about a constructed reality where there is an interpretation already in place at each location, the ethnographer's and the ethnographic subject's. That is, if interpretive ethnography in the tradition of Geertz assumes that the culture under study constructs reality through a socially maintained set of interpretive strategies, then the anthropologist's own culture of study (i.e., the discipline of cultural anthropology) has its own interpretive strategy, ethnography, already in place as well. This disciplinary formation determines what counts as significant data and objects of study; what kinds of claims are possible objects of knowledge; and how these claims can be made and adjudicated.

In anthropological ethnography, this critique emphasizes the rhetorical nature of all cultural accounts, rejects positivist epistemology and the notion of an independent subject, and demands a thoroughgoing reflexivity on the part of the writer and the discipline. Taking Geertz's essays in *The Interpretation of Culture* (1973) as a representative text, Boon (1990) summarized this position when he argued that:

> What has come to be called Balinese culture is a multiply authored invention, an historical formation, an enactment, a political construction, a shifting paradox, an ongoing translation, an emblem, a nonconsensual negotiation of contrastive identity, and more. (p. ix)

The position Boon articulated emerged from the work of the Rice circle — James Clifford, George Marcus, Michael Fischer, and Stephen Tyler — supplemented by Geertz's own analyses of ethnographic writing in *Works and Lives: The Anthropologist as Author* (1988). This critique argues that ethnography is primarily a textual practice and a rhetorical activity whose authority depends on the narrative structures, textual tropes, and argumentative topoi of anthropology. This rhetorical turn in anthropology has led critics to examine ethnography as a disciplinary practice and to regard these textual strategies not as modes of representing the anthropological subject, but as disciplinary strategies for constituting the ethnographer's authority and knowledge (e.g., Crapanzano, 1986; Marcus & Cushman, 1982; Pratt, 1986; Tyler, 1985).

For these critics, textual strategies such as "thick description" popularized by Geertz or the idea of triangulation prominent in sociological ethnography have become disciplinary tropes that warrant ethnographic claims. These strategies present the ethnographic text not as storytelling embedded in a network of disciplinary texts and conventions, but as a valid representation of another culture. As Tyler (1985) put it, these textual practices ostensibly "present a factual description of 'the way things are,' as if they had not been written and as if an ethnography really were a 'picture' of another way of life" (p. 84). The disciplinary fiction inherent in this operation turns thick description into a slick description and makes the validity claims generated by triangulation a suspicious affair.

Perhaps the most ubiquitous and powerful rhetorical strategy in ethnography is that of the participant observer, the Janus-like figure who looks both ways and provides knowledge of an alien culture. For Tyler, the fable of the participant-observer is the central motif in the disciplinary myth of objective representation. But as Fabian has argued, this rhetorical trope reflects a fundamental contradiction created by the historical development of anthropology. The emergence of ethnographic fieldwork and the notion of the participant observer consolidated anthropology as a science and an academic discipline, but it also introduced a contradictory praxis. Fabian (1983) concluded:

> As soon as it is realized that fieldwork is a form of communicative interaction with an Other, one that must be carried out coevally, on the basis of shared intersubjective Time and intersocial contemporaneity, a contradiction had to appear between research and writing because anthropological writing had become suffused with the strategies and devices [e.g. participant observation] of allochronic discourse. (p. 148)

In other words, the temporal and spatial distance inherent in the idea of observation transforms the intersubjective ethnographic experience on which anthropology was based — participation — into a representation of the other in terms of the objectified accounts of informants (Ulin, 1991, p. 69). One consequence of this is that, as Bourdieu (1977) argued, the ethnographer "in his preoccupation with *interpreting* practices, is inclined to introduce into the object [of his study] the principles of his relation to the object" (p. 2).

These contemporary critics have come to regard anthropological ethnography in much the way Said described the discourse of Orientalism, "a system of opportunities for making statements about" the subject culture. And, like Said, the critique of ethnography holds that ethnography operates "as representations usually do, for a purpose, according to a tendency, in a specific historical, intellectual and even economic setting" (1978, p. 273). One result of this critique is that the authority of ethnographic description is now seen to lie not in representational realism, in some objective relationship to a cultural reality, but in the rhetorical tradition of arguments and figures developed by the professional and institutional history of anthropology. Another consequence of the critique is that ethnographic representations are recognized as partial, not simply incomplete, but also partial in the colloquial sense, as driven by desire. Ethnographies and their writers cannot be separated from their conditions of production, the institutional, professional and material interests which these cultural representations both serve and form. This position does not assert an epistemological relativism so much as eschew the question of epistemology, objective or relativist, altogether. To return to Hacking for a moment, studying these rhetorical strategies and their discursive consequences has become a way of describing the discipline's "style of thinking," its method of defining both its object of study and itself as a field of study.

TRAVELS: INSTRUMENTAL DISCOURSE VERSUS *PRAXIS*

In *Writing Culture: The Poetics and Politics of Ethnography*, Clifford and Marcus (1986) described an incident in which a Cree Indian testified in Canadian court about the effects of hydroelectric development on traditional Cree hunting lands. Asked to take the oath, the Cree responded, "I am not sure I can tell the truth. . . . I can only tell what I know." The disparity between the Cree's conception of evidence and truth, and that of the court illustrates the discursive power institutions exert over those who work within them.

Closer to home, Graff (1987) made much the same point when he argued that the work of prominent critics or critical movements does not translate directly into pedagogy and professional practice. Introducing his "institutional history" of English studies, he pointed out that "institutions are not unmediated projections of the values, methods, and ideologies of major individuals and movements." Even dominant critical values and methodologies undergo substantial changes when they "become institutionalized in the form of scholarly fields, curricula, and pedagogy" (p. 5). Graff's point is that we too often think of our discipline in terms of the theories and methodologies that circulate among scholars, and overlook the institutional politics of professional practice. Like the Cree in the anecdote, the ethnographer's self-conscious and partial truth does not always fit the demands of our institutions. It remains to be seen whether the ethnographer's theory of disciplinary reflexivity, and his skepticism of master narratives and objective cultural representation, travels well.

To assess the distance ethnography's critique of cultural representation travels when it is applied in technical and professional writing, we must begin by characterizing the discourse of technical and professional writing. The view of writing that dominates advanced technical and professional writing pedagogy, although changing slowly, is still what Dobrin (1985) called "the Cartesian philosophical tradition which culminates with logical positivism" (p. 237). This "old line" pedagogical position believes (mistakenly) in the objectivity of a technical discourse grounded in an unproblematic relation between experience and writing. This leads to a monologic view of writing that excludes questions of power, value, or interest and considers technical and professional writing as an instrumental discourse designed for stating the facts clearly and efficiently.

That this should be the dominant view of technical discourse is not surprising if we consider how technical writing courses developed. In his history of technical writing instruction, Connors (1982) pointed out that technical writing courses came about as a practical response to the complaints of professional engineers that graduates were illiterate, that they could not write coherent reports or simple business letters (p. 331). The courses that evolved to meet this demand concentrated on "the logical organization and effective presentation requirements of technical articles, reports, and business letters" (p. 337). The instrumental commitment to efficiency and clarity is reflected in Britton's definition of technical writing in 1965 as "the effort by the author to convey one meaning and only one meaning in what he says" (quoted in Connors, 1982, p. 345). This position also derives from a Baconian tradition that combines the authority of an emerging science with a reaction against Ciceronian rhetoric. The textbooks that dominated this curriculum were organized first around the modes of discourse and then around specific formats. This curriculum instantiated Ohmann's (1976) argument that pedagogy and textbooks "can hardly ignore what passes for intellectual currency in that part of the world where vital decisions are made or what kind of composition succeeds in the terms of that part of the world" (p. 206). From this perspective, clarity and instrumentality emerge from what Vitanza (1991) called the discipline's "will to pedagogy," which I take up in the last section of this chapter.

This historical development, with its faith in objectivity and the ideology of service and utility, has led to a pedagogy that too often focuses on writing as a neutral and practical skill aimed at the production of useful texts. Borrowing the distinction between low and high senses of practical from Bernstein, Carolyn Miller (1989) argued that technical writing has traditionally ascribed to the low sense. She associated this low sense of practical with an understanding of *techne* which is concerned only with the production of useful texts in the fashion of how-to manuals and hand-books. The high sense of practical she argued for is a form of *phronesis*: prudent conduct concerned with social action. Where the first sense aims at the immediate benefit to the individual or the private interest, the second, prudent conduct, aims at the benefit to the larger public community. Miller associated this second sense of practical, and the form of technical writing she advocates, with the notion of *praxis* as "a measure of responsibility for political and economic conduct" (p. 24).

In arguments very similar to this, Thomas Miller (1991) and Sullivan (1990) have recently urged us to redefine technical writing as social *praxis*, to consider technical and professional writing as the work which shapes our values and allows for political and ideological action. Miller (1991), for example, argued that technical and business communication "have often been taught as a set of formulaic genres, more recently as a formulaic process, rather than a social practice that involves important political issues" (p. 64). He attributed this, as I have, to the old line belief in scientific objectivity which reinforces the idea that technical writing can be a value neutral *techne*. Miller closed his essay by saying:

> While it may sound like a terribly idealistic and theoretical way to think about technical and business writing, the point is that we cannot be both technicians of the word and humanists because there is a basic contradiction between teaching writing as a technique for information processing [in this the "information age"], and teaching writing as a negotiation of shared values and knowledge. (p. 70)

There are two ways in which Carolyn Miller's and Thomas Miller's arguments are relevant to the question of critical ethnography in technical and professional writing. First, both of these discussions argued for a laudable change in the definition of technical writing, but in doing so they defined the current professional practice as dominated by the low sense of practical, by Dobrin's old-line position, by a philosophically bankrupt positivism. This helps us assess the very considerable distance a critical theory of ethnographic representation has to travel before it enters the discourse of technical and professional writing. When Thomas Miller said that his position seems a "terribly idealistic and theoretical way to think," the "terribly" indicates his sense of how foreign to the discipline is the notion of technical writing as social *praxis*.

The second way these discussions apply to our current task is as evidence that the discourse on technical and professional writing is not monolithic and uncontested. If the essays by Miller, Miller, and Sullivan suggest the degree of resistance critical ethnography will face, they also establish grounds for accepting critical ethnography within technical and professional writing. The move away from the immediate utility and objectivity of *techné* and toward a theory of technical writing as social *praxis* is compatible with ethnography's critique of authority and representation. The current attempt to redefine technical writing opens up a wider discussion of the nature of community, of ethical issues, of the self-construction inherent in *praxis*, which allows us to consider the questions of power and politics on which ethnography's critique depends. Furthermore, scholars working in technical and professional writing have increasingly used sophisticated rhetorical analyses to explore the way power and knowledge interact in writing that circulates in professional and technological institutions (e.g., Katz, 1993; Richardson & Liggett, 1993; Sauer, 1993). Rhetorical analyses of knowledge claims and authority have become common in professional writing research. Whether scholars and researchers in professional writing will apply this critique to their own ethnographic work, and what consequences that would have for both their research reports and their pedagogy, is uncertain. As Graff has argued, this critical movement will be mediated by institutional practice and the material conditions of the university.

DESTINATIONS: TEXTBOOKS, PRACTICE, AND THE WILL TO PEDAGOGY

Despite the attempts to redefine writing by scholars like Miller, Miller, and Sullivan, the practice of technical and professional writing remains dominated by the textbook tradition. Many, if not most, technical and professional writing courses are staffed with lecturers and part-time instructors who have less exposure to and participation in the scholarly and critical debates and, often, little time or incentive to make radical changes. And for many teachers of whatever rank, the textbook largely determines the structure and ethos of their course. Thus, if we are to measure the possible reception and transformation of critical ethnography in the practice of technical and professional writing, we must consider the existing textbooks. Certainly, these textbooks are changing and the scholarship in specialized journals has had an effect. Nevertheless, textbooks remain circumscribed by a discursive formation dominated by the instrumental view and responsive to the perceived demands of potential employers for practical skills in Miller's low sense of the term. This disciplinary formation operates, like those Foucault has described, to delimit the field of objects and legitimate perspectives, and to produce institutional procedures and pedagogical forms which designate both choices and exclusions.

Evaluating the degree to which this disciplinary formation will transform or, more strongly, domesticate, critical ethnography—the last of Said's strategies for understanding traveling theory—is difficult for two reasons. First, with only rare exceptions (e.g., Barnum & Carliner, 1993), very few technical writing textbooks list their sources, and this makes it difficult to trace precise connections between research and theory, and their representation in pedagogy. A second difficulty is the fact that critical ethnography has only recently entered the discourse of nonacademic writing research. Researchers are still developing strategies for accommodating this theoretical position and few if any reflexive and critical ethnographies have emerged—yet. Thus the last section of this chapter is speculative, a cautionary tale about this discipline and its possibilities.

Despite these difficulties, there are textbooks which offer suggestive examples of the relation between the ethnographic study of writing and its translation into pedagogy. *Technical Writing and Professional Communication*, a prominent textbook written by Olsen and Huckin (1991), is somewhat unusual not only because it cites its sources, but also because it makes explicit use of current research in professional and technical writing. But the institutional conditions that shape the production of textbooks— classroom application, publisher's concerns for marketability, the demand for "teacher-proof" texts—legitimize perspectives and pedagogical approaches that domesticate the radical and reduce the critical to the instrumental.

In order to gauge the nature and degree of this transformation, I examine two passages from *Technical Writing and Professional Communication*. The first passage describes an early ethnographic study of professional writing. This study was conducted without the benefit of the contemporary critique, but its representation in the textbook suggests the kind of transformation ethnography experiences as it becomes pedagogy. The second passage I examine involves references to a number of important early essays on the social study of scientific and technical writing.

The passage that describes the ethnography reads as follows:

> Bear in mind, though, that [stylistic] guidelines are merely suggestions, not rules; they should not be considered infallible. Stylistic choices involve not only readability but also sociocultural acceptability, that is, conformity to the ways in which groups of people prefer to express themselves—and sometimes these two goals are in conflict. For example, in a study of two *Fortune 500* companies, Robert L. Brown, Jr. and Carl Herndl found that the most respected writers in these companies sometimes used wordy expressions like *undertake an examination* instead of more concise alternatives like *examine*. Apparently it was common, accepted practice in that particular corporate culture for employees to express themselves that way. The more concise *examine* might be more readable, but *undertake an examination* would help

identify the writer as a member of the group. In general, when making stylistic choices, do not follow guidelines blindly. Expressing an idea in a certain way may have not only some benefits but also some undesirable side effects. Expressing the same idea in a different way may have fewer (or more) benefits but also fewer (or more) undesirable side effects. Keep this trade-off in mind and strive for optimization, not perfection. (p. 470)

This reference to an ethnographic study of professional and corporate writing appears as a cautionary note in a chapter entitled "Editing for Emphasis." The text offers common advice about emphasis, concise wording, sentence combining, the use of "signal words," and highlighting. The ethnography to which the text refers argued for writing as a cultural action of self-definition, the construction of a social self through discourse. The discussion of stylistic features appeared as evidence for the more central claims about the social construction of discourse and the writing subject. Reinscribed in the discourse of pedagogy, this argument for the social construction of self appears as a hedge against the ubiquity of rules and the relative importance of readability and local custom. The controlling metaphors in this passage are those of instrumentality; students are advised to weigh "benefits" against "undesirable side effects" in the attempt to achieve "optimization." My point is not that the textbook offers bad advice—the discussion of "guidelines" instead of rules is good advice. Rather, my point is that the more radical implications of the ethnographic report seem irrelevant to the pedagogical task and disappear from the scene. In Foucault's terms, they have been excluded by the disciplinary formation.

The tendency of textbooks to domesticate ethnographic work is not unique. As a second passage suggests, it is part of a more general leveling effected by the constraints of textbook production. In a chapter entitled "Generating Ideas," the authors cited a number of articles on the social construction of writing and written knowledge:

There have been a series of impressive considerations and studies of "real world" communication in organizational or professional settings. Taken as a group, *these studies outline the importance for a communicator of involving others in the planning and design of communication.* Lester Faigley, Lee Odell, Charles Bazerman, Karen LeFevre, and Steve Doheny-Farina have argued that to be effective in the workplace, technical and professional communicators must understand the social contexts in which they are working. *They need to understand what kinds of questions their readers are likely to ask about their topic, what concerns these readers will want to see addressed.* (Olsen & Huckin, 1991, pp. 36–37; emphasis added)

The passage cites these studies of nonacademic writing to warrant its advice that students involve others in their writing process so that they will have a better sense of their audience. This representation is generally accurate for some of the works cited; Odell's (1985) essay, for example, advocates that we ask students "to engage in discussion and work collaboratively with their classmates" (p. 276). But for others of these citations this representation is partial and excludes the more radical implications of the social constructionist position they share. The essay by Charles Bazerman which this passage cites, for example, is an exhaustive review of the sociological study of science and scientific writing. Although this review covers a daunting amount of material, it spends considerable time detailing the economic and political analysis of both science, for example, Kuhn, Toulmin, Ziman, and of scientific texts, for example, Latour and Woolgar, Mulkay, Bloor. In discussing these historical and sociological analyses, Bazerman outlined the social critique of authority and knowledge that lies at the heart of recent social constructionist thought. To represent his essay as concerned with "social context" interpreted as audience analysis is a powerful pedagogical reduction which excludes the disciplinary and epistemological critique of these sociological analyses. Faigley's (1985) essay was similarly truncated. Faigley argued for a "social perspective" that considers the way "individual acts of communication define, organize, and maintain social groups," concluding that "the social perspective, then, moves beyond the traditional rhetorical concern for audience, forcing researchers to consider issues such as social roles, group purposes, communal organization, *ideology*, and finally *theories of culture*" (pp. 235–236; emphasis added). Faigley's demand that we move "beyond the traditional rhetorical concern for audience" toward questions of ideology and theories of culture disappeared when his essay was inscribed in the pedagogy.

To see this process of exclusion and domestication as the fault of the author or of the individual textbook misses the point. Rather, we should consider the material and political conditions within which both textbook authors and teachers work. As Bourdieu (1988) has argued, the more an academic field is seen as socially necessary and having direct application, the less autonomy it will have (pp. 62–74). Bourdieu compared practical, applied disciplines to speculative, critical, or research disciplines and found that the disciplinary formation for the first class is much more closely tied to the field of power outside the university which in turn exercises more influence in defining and restricting disciplinary procedures and pedagogy. This is, I think, the case with technical and professional writing as it currently exists.

Although it is sometimes tempting to argue that this disciplinary formation is a monolithic position determined by the Althusserian ideological state apparatus, that is an inaccurate and unhelpful reduction. Rather, I suggest that we adopt the language Said used to describe how theories develop, and think of institutional and material constraints as first conditions which exert pressure on disciplinary formations as the theory travels into the textbooks. This allows us to see the discourse of writing as a practice that emerges from what Bourdieu calls the *habitus* within and through which writing researchers and teachers work. The concept of *habitus* and the model of practice Bourdieu provided allow us to understand how and why textbooks and pedagogy domesticate theory without forcing us to accept this as an absolute or permanent arrangement.

Like many other critics of structuralism in the social sciences, Bourdieu argues that the notion of a structure which determines our action contains at least two crucial errors.[1] First, theories that invoke the idea of structure to explain social activity describe structure as static and unchanging. Bourdieu (1977, pp. 1–71) demonstrates that social activity is better thought of in terms of processes that occur in the flux of real time in which agents can act and react. This allows Bourdieu to avoid the second error of structuralist explanations — their inability to explain change. As we will see, practices are open to what Bourdieu calls "regulated revolutions" and "regulated improvisation." Thus the practice of technical and professional writing exerts powerful pressure on theory, but it also allows for counter-argument such as that offered by Miller, Miller, and Sullivan.

For Bourdieu *habitus* is "history turned to nature"; it is the way of thinking we inherit from past experience which then makes sense of our current experience and allows us to act. Furthermore, this *habitus* is itself continuously produced by our ongoing activity. Bourdieu (1977) defined *habitus* as "systems of durable, transposable *dispositions,* structured structures predisposed to function as structuring structures, that is, as principles of the generation and structuring of practices" (p. 72). He referred to "dispositions" to suggest that these are not rules that perforce must be obeyed, but the collective wisdom, sayings, commonplaces, ethical precepts, and *ethos* of a community (p. 77). These durable dispositions that constitute the *habitus* are "structured" because they are the organized result of past experience; they are "structuring" because they provide the "commonsense world endowed with the *objectivity* secured by consensus on meaning" (p. 80).

Because Bourdieu rejects the idea of a static structure that works with divine power and detachment, he uses the concept of *habitus* to explain practice as a dialectical relationship between "objective structures [conditions] and the cognitive and motivating structures which they produce" in

---

[1]Bourdieu's critique of structuralism and his rejection of the opposition between voluntarist and objectivist explanations is very similar to Giddens's argument for the theory of structuration in *Central Problems in Social Theory* (1979). Both Bourdieu and Giddens are trying to construct a theory of agents and social action that departs from the determinism of structure and the dualism of the individual versus the subject. For a brief explanation of Giddens's theory and its relevance to writing see Herndl (1993).

agents (p. 83). That is, the disciplinary formation or practice develops out of an exchange between the current situation and agents' *habitus*, the way of thinking they have developed through past practice. Thus, the *habitus* produces practices, like technical and professional writing pedagogy, through a dialectical relationship with the contemporary conditions within which it operates. The durable dispositions of the *habitus* mediate between the agent and the conditions within which she works. Because the practices thus produced exist in the junction between the past and present, they are both conservative and revolutionary. That is, they tend to maintain the historic common sense of things, yet they are capable of change.

In the case of technical and professional writing, the most commonly taught kind of nonacademic writing, the *habitus* of the community translates research and theory into practice through the textbook. Because the dispositions which constitute the *habitus* have a conservative influence "the most improbable practices are excluded, either totally without examination, as *unthinkable*, or at the cost of a *double negation* which inclines agents to make a virtue of necessity, that is, to refuse what is anyway refused and to love the inevitable" (Bourdieu, 1977, p. 77). Bourdieu's description here echoes Thomas Miller's sense that his theory of writing as *praxis* is terribly idealistic and theoretical, unthinkable.

The conservative function of the *habitus* produces what Vitanza (1991) described as our disciplinary "will to pedagogy." Vitanza argues that contemporary theory threatens to throw the field of composition into a crisis, placing in doubt cherished notions such as: authorship, the self, representation, the distinction between fiction and truth, "especially the revealed wisdom of even teaching students to write" (p. 140). In the face of such threats, the field exerts its will to pedagogy, which Vitanza described as "(1) the will to systematize (the) language (of composing), (2) the will to be its author(ity), and (3) the will to teach it to students" (p. 140).

For technical and professional writing, this will to control and regulate the language of pedagogy reduces the critical to the instrumental in the name of practicality. As Bourdieu's theory suggests, the will to pedagogy comes not from individual scholars, but from the field, from the *habitus* shared by teachers of writing and the discipline's "love of the inevitable." It is a response to the institutional and social demand that writing courses teach practical skills; to the disciplinary need for authority and credibility; to the *habitus*'s common sense of the world; to teachers' desire, finally, to meet students' expectations.

Fortunately, the conditions within which we work include not only the institutional and social demands I have just described, but also the arguments by critics and theorists. Because our *habitus* includes an openness to argument, to theory, to critique, it is possible for the work in critical ethnography to alter our practice. The experience that confronts us and that our *habitus* must make sense of includes these disruptive voices. As interdisciplinary work in ethnography enters our theoretical debates, the practice produced by our *habitus* is liable to change. Because Bourdieu described *habitus* as a process, an ongoing, regulated revolution, it suggests that there might be a lag between theoretical innovation and institutional practice. This explanation of the theory-practice split does not deny the institutional and ideological conflict I have described, but it does suggest another, partial, but encouraging, explanation. As researchers and teachers become more reflexive about their own disciplinary discourse and its representational strategies, they may begin to recognize that the rhetorical candor Mailloux described is a necessary part of our practice. The arguments for redefining writing as social *praxis* may become part of our *habitus*, making it possible that the critique of contemporary ethnography will change our practice, that ethnographic theory will not take the form of the joke with which I opened. Indeed, recent work on theory and pedagogy (e.g., Thralls & Blyler, 1993) has begun to suggest alterations in pedagogy in response to recent theoretical developments.

CONCLUSION

The conservative urge of the *habitus* is powerful, and the shape of a future practice is uncertain, but composition and rhetoric must engage the challenge presented by critical ethnography. The evidence of textbooks and disciplinary history suggests that critical ethnography may be radically reduced by our disciplinary formation, that pedagogy may use some ethnographic findings, but ignore the cultural theory with its built in critique. But this need not be the case. If ethnography has experienced a rhetorical turn, technical and professional writing has begun a return to rhetoric. The rhetorical analysis of authority, ethos, and knowledge, which is now common in our research, exerts its own pressure on the pedagogical discourse.

My analysis of ethnographic theory and my partisan plea that we alter our practice comes with one important caution. One liability in interdisciplinary work is that a theory generated at one disciplinary or cultural site may be codified and mechanically repeated when it travels to another discipline. Thus, important as it is that we engage the critique generated by interdisciplinary work in anthropology, we need to recognize the dangers of uncritically adopting their position. The contemporary critique of anthropological ethnography was partially motivated by anthropologists' awareness that their practice was connected with colonial domination of the third world. Ethnographers came from world powers like France, Britain, and America to study relatively powerless cultures, and their ethnographic writing too often reproduced that cultural and political colonialism. The situation in the case of professional and technical writing is radically different in this respect. In studying powerful nonacademic discourse, writing research "studies up" rather than down a cultural hierarchy of power. As Wells (1986) observed, technical and professional writing has readily accepted its subordination to industry (p. 247). In many ways, it is the discourse of writing research and pedagogy that is colonized by nonacademic power rather than the reverse. It is in the context of this political configuration that we must rethink both our practice and the ethnographic critique.

REFERENCES

Barnum, C., & Carliner, S. (1993). *Techniques for technical communicators*. New York: Macmillan.

Bazerman, C. (1983). Scientific writing as a social act: A review of the literature of the sociology of science. In P. V. Anderson, R. J. Brockman, & C. R. Miller (Eds.), *New essays in technical and scientific communication: Research, theory, practice* (pp. 140–156). Farmingdale, NY: Baywood.

Boon, J. (1990). *Affinities and extremities*. Chicago: University of Chicago Press.

Bourdieu, P. (1977). *Outline of a theory of practice* (R. Nice, Trans.). Cambridge, UK: Cambridge University Press.

Bourdieu, P. (1988). *Homo academicus* (P. Collier, Trans.). Stanford: Stanford University Press.

Cintron, R. (1993). Wearing a pith helmet at a sly angle: Or can writing researchers do ethnography in a postmodern era? *Written Communication, 10*(3), 371–412.

Clifford, J., & Marcus, G. (Eds.). (1986). *Writing culture: The poetics and politics of ethnography*. Berkeley: University of California Press.

Connors, R. (1982). The rise of technical writing instruction in America. *Journal of Technical Writing and Communication, 12*(4), 329–351.

Crapanzano, V. (1986). Hermes dilemma: The masking of subversion in ethnographic description. In J. Clifford & G. Marcus (Eds.), *Writing culture: The poetics and politics of ethnography* (pp. 51–76). Berkeley: University of California Press.

Dobrin, D. (1985). Is technical writing particularly objective? *College English, 47*(3), 237–51.

Fabian, J. (1983). *Time and the other*. New York: Columbia University Press.

Faigley, L. (1985). Nonacademic writing: The social perspective. In L. Odell & D. Goswami (Eds.), *Writing in nonacademic settings* (pp. 231–248). New York: Guilford.

Geertz, C. (1973). *The interpretation of cultures*. New York: Basic.

Geertz, C. (1988). *Works and lives: The anthropologist as author*. Stanford: Stanford University Press.

Giddens, A. (1979). *Central problems in social theory: Action, structure, and contradiction in social analysis*. Berkeley: University of California Press.

Goldmann, L. (1964). *The hidden god: A study of tragic vision in the "pensees" of Pascal and the tragedies of Racine* (P. Thody, Trans.). London: Routledge and Kegan Paul.

Graff, G. (1987). *Professing literature: An institutional history*. Chicago: University of Chicago Press.

Hacking, I. (1982). Language, truth, and reason. In R. Hollis & S. Lukes (Eds.), *Rationality and relativism* (pp. 48–66). Cambridge, MA: MIT Press.

Herndl, C. G. (1991). Writing ethnography: Representation, rhetoric and institutional practices. *College English, 53*(3), 320–332.

Herndl, C. G. (1993). Teaching discourse and reproducing culture: A critique of professional and nonacademic writing. *College Composition and Communication, 44*(3), 349–363.

Katz, S. B. (1993). Aristotle's *Rhetoric*, Hitler's program, and the ideological problem of *praxis*, power, and professional discourse. *Journal of Business and Technical Communication, 7*(1), 37–62.

Kleine, W. M. (1990). Beyond triangulation: Ethnography, writing, and rhetoric. *Journal of Advanced Composition, 10*(1), 117–125.

Lukaĉs, G. (1971) *History and class consciousness: Studies in Marxist dialectics* (R. Livingstone, Trans.). Cambridge, MA: MIT Press.

Mailloux, S. (1989). *Rhetorical power*. Ithaca: Cornell University Press.

Marcus, G., & Cushman D. (1982). Ethnographies as texts. *Annual Review of Anthropology, 11*, 25–69.

Miller, C. R. (1989). What's practical about technical writing. In B. E. Fearing & W. K. Sparrow (Eds.), *Technical writing: Theory and practice* (pp. 14–24). New York: Modern Language Association.

Miller T. (1991). Treating professional writing as social *praxis*. *Journal of Advanced Composition, 11*(1), 57–72.

Odell, L. (1985). Beyond the text: Relations between writing and social context. In L. Odell & D. Goswami (Eds.), *Writing in nonacademic settings* (pp. 249–280). New York: Guilford.

Ohmann, R. (1976). *English in America: A radical view of the profession*. New York: Oxford University Press.

Olsen, L., & Huckin, T. (1991). *Technical writing and professional communication* (2nd ed.). New York: McGraw-Hill.

Pratt, M. L. (1986). Fieldwork in common places. In J. Clifford & G. Marcus (Eds.), *Writing culture: The poetics and politics of ethnography* (pp. 27–50). Berkeley: University of California Press.

Richardson, M., & Ligget, S. (1993). Power relations, technical writing theory, and workplace writing. *Journal of Business and Technical Communication, 7*(1), 112–137.

Said, E. (1978). *Orientalism*. New York: Random House.

Said, E. (1983). *The world, the text, the critic*. Cambridge, MA: Harvard University Press.

Sauer, B. (1993). Sense and sensibility in technical documentation: How feminist interpretation strategies can save lives in the nation's mines. *Journal of Business and Technical Communication, 7*(1), 63–84.

Sullivan, D. (1990). Political-ethical implications of defining technical communication as a practice. *Journal of Advanced Composition, 10*(2), 375–386.

Tyler, S. (1985). Ethnography, intertextuality and the end of description. *American Journal of Semiotics, 3*(4), 83–98.

Thralls, C., & Blyler, N. R. (1993). The social perspective and pedagogy in technical communication. *Technical Communication Quarterly, 2*(3), 249–270.

Ulin, R. C. (1991). Critical anthropology twenty years later: Modernism and postmodernism in anthropology. *Critique of Anthropology, 11*(1), 63–89.

Vitanza, V. (1991). Three countertheses: Or, a critical in(ter)vention into composition theories and pedagogies. In P. Harkin & J. Schilb (Eds.), *Contending with words: Composition and rhetoric in a postmodern age* (pp. 139–172). New York: Modern Language Association.

Wells, S. (1986). Jurgen Habermas, communicative competence, and the teaching of technical discourse. In C. Nelson (Ed.), *Theory in the classroom* (pp. 245–269). Chicago: University of Chicago Press.

Williams, R. (1980). *Problems in materialism and culture*. London: Verso.

3 Nonacademic Writing Into the 21st Century: Achieving and Sustaining Relevance in Research and Curricula

Elizabeth Tebeaux
Texas A&M University

As the chapters in this book suggest, theory in nonacademic discourse is steadily developing connections with allied fields. These chapters help fulfill calls by scholars such as Anderson (1980), Brockmann (1980), Ewing (1983), Gieselman (1980), and Moran (1985) for the development of a theoretical, research-based pedagogy and a resulting, theoretically grounded disciplinary direction for nonacademic discourse. The unstated rationale for these first calls for intellectual depth was clear: Technical and business communication, to be considered a legitimate field of study, needed to move away from its skills image; articulate a theory, a research methodology, and an alliance with well-established respected liberal arts and social science fields; and show that our intellectual goals were commensurate to and as academically worthy as theirs.

As Thralls and Blyler's (1993a, 1993b) recent work in social perspectives has shown, a host of studies has provided a social theory for use in the classroom. But as we enter the closing years of this century, perhaps we need to recall who we are, the rationale for what we do, and goals that evolve from our identity. Herndl correctly described the uneasiness between theory and classroom practice, particularly disparities between ethnographic theory and pedagogy. Although Herndl was correct in recognizing that technical communication pedagogy is driven by nonacademic forces, I would further argue that the current climate of academic accountability, rapid technological change, and decreasing literacy give us major research and teaching challenges. Technical communication is unique in the field of rhetoric: It helps students prepare for the transition from the academy to the world of work.

REAFFIRMING OUR FOUNDATIONS

Although many courses in technical writing and business writing had been taught in colleges since the early years of the century, the initial drop in literacy that began in the late 1960s initiated the rapid growth of writing courses and programs that has continued steadily for 20 years (Gibson, 1978; Rivers, 1985). Corporations complained that employees could not write either clearly or correctly, that college graduates were not able to do the kinds of writing needed in a work environment. Pioneers in the development of technical writing courses such as W. Earl Britton, Herman Estrin, John Harris, Jay Gould, John Mitchell, Tom Pearsall, Jim Souther, followed by Donald Cunningham, J. C. Mathes, and Dwight Stevenson, were among the earliest leaders in our profession to recognize that people at work were doing a very different kind of writing from the kind of writing taught at school. Mathes, Stevenson, and Klaver (1979), following Britton (1975), for example, were perhaps the first to argue that technical writing, not freshman composition, was the best preparation for students in engineering and sciences. Mathes and Stevenson in the Preface to *Designing Technical Reports* (1976) were also perhaps the first to articulate the differences between technical writing (nonacademic discourse) and composition (academic discourse) that still underpin our nonacademic courses and programs. Even though the elements of rhetorical analysis were shared by both academic and nonacademic writing, technical writing by the mid-1970s had its own character: to prepare students for writing on the job rather than for writing in school.

Because industry wanted employees who could write and speak well, technical communication courses were seen as the panacea for beginning to correct the growing problem of employees who could not express themselves clearly. Our most basic goal was this: If technical communication courses could be designed to provide students with the preparation for writing on the job, we could help people be more successful in their careers. Our first published scholarship focused on that goal and attempted to determine the nature of work-based writing and to develop a practical pedagogy to teach this kind of writing.

Numerous departments throughout our universities were delighted that the English department was at last teaching something useful and practical. Enrollment in technical writing courses soared throughout the 1970s and the 1980s. The demand for our services frightened our literature colleagues, who were shocked at the number of credit hours we generated. Because soaring enrollments involved us so heavily in teaching, our first publications reflected our efforts to find ways to prepare students to write on the job. Theory that justified our pedagogy did not begin to emerge until the late 1970s.

With nearly 200 degree and certificate programs in the United States that produce technical writers in addition to the thousands of schools that offer basic courses in technical writing, we can say with pride that we have come a long way in our efforts to become a legitimate academic discipline. A brief survey of our academic journals — *Technical Communication Quarterly, Journal of Technical Writing and Communication,* and *Journal of Business and Technical Communication* — reveal articles having an increasingly formalized, aseptic approach to technical writing. From articles on practical pedagogy, our scholarship has moved toward defining technical communication as a social act. The rhetoric of scientific and technical communication has been explored and affirmed. But with over two decades of development in research, teaching, and professionalism, we need to stop and ask: Has the development of nonacademic discourse as a discipline made itself felt in the world beyond the academy? Do employees who have taken our courses write better?

CURRENT PROBLEMS IN WORKPLACE WRITING

Do employees write better? The answer to this question is no. Recent surveys of employee writing clearly indicate that employee writing problems have not diminished (Laviviere, 1989). If we compare articles about employee writing in current trade journals with articles published a decade or more ago, we see the same communication needs discussed. The lack of reading, writing, and analytical skills of new employees has remained a problem. Studies by consultants report that the employee who can write well is difficult to find and that improving employees' writing is difficult ("On Writing and Relating," 1990). Given the growth in writing programs in general, why are we not making more of an impact on writing in business and industry?

A survey of workplace studies provides an interesting view of current employee writing problems as well as writing needs of the opening years of the next century. For example, Robert Half International, reporting on a pool of 200 executives at the nation's 1,000 largest corporations, reported that the three leading deficiencies in job candidates were interpersonal skills (37%), writing skills (24%), and oral communications (13%). The study also reported that writing still absorbs about 21% of managers' time, or 11 weeks a year. Over 34% of the reports, memos, and letters these executives report receiving are unclear, poorly phrased, or confusing. Forty-one percent of the vice presidents surveyed rated the writing in their organization as "weak" or "poor" ("On Writing and Relating," 1990). Recent essays by Wank in *Advertising Age* (1991) and Breden in *Industry Week* (1991) reported the problems that publications firms are having in finding employees who can produce clear, well-organized prose. Essays by the Wingspread Group on Higher Education (1993), which discuss reform in higher education, emphasize the need for improved writing instruction.

Similarly, the first National Education Goals Report found that reading proficiency of American workers is not improving. Few workers are able to analyze and then synthesize information. Writing skills have not improved since 1975 (Fields, 1991), despite software that helps with invention, organization, and usage (Brody, 1990; Konar, 1986). Still, a comparison of trade journal articles published in 1980 with articles written in 1993 shows a decided difference in guidelines for writing letters, memos, and reports. Our rhetorical perspective in emphasizing the process of designing documents either individually or collaboratively has surfaced. Although organizations still value efficient, concise memoranda and reports, the process of achieving good writing has taken the place of prescriptions for using readability formulas and for squeaky clean prose composed of monosyllabic words. Numerous recent articles emphasize the importance of defining audience and purpose as crucial to the memo's success (Felden, 1989; Gold, 1989; Scott, 1991; Shea, 1992; Straub, 1991). The supervisor's role in establishing the purpose of the document for the employee-writer is also seen as crucial to good writing (Diether, 1992; Gladis, 1991; Zaslow, 1991). In contrast to articles written a decade or more ago, we are seeing top-down organization, based on the document's purpose, not sentence-level clarity, as a crucial issue in the organization of reports and letters (Fahner, 1990). As corporate trainer Petrini (1990) noted, "When the employee knows the purpose of the document, the audience, and the best way to organize the content, style takes care of itself" (p. 31).

In short, the importance of the writer *understanding* the writing process now dominates trade articles on how to write better. The large number of articles on how to write, how to use graphics, and how to give oral presentations suggests that the nonacademic setting is still looking for an *efficient* rhetoric. The abundance of software to assist writers, to enable them to "fill in" content in prescribed report sections that use prearranged formats, the availability of forms, report, letter, and resume-maker software suggests the existence of a major market for technology to circumvent the continuing national decline in writing skills. Ironically, Felden's *Harvard Business Review* (1964) article, "What Do You Mean I Can't Write?" reprinted in a 1990 issue devoted to popular articles published by the journal over three decades ago, remains one of *Harvard Business Review*'s most frequently requested reprints.

ANTICIPATING THE WORKPLACE OF THE FUTURE

A dozen years ago, futurists were hailing information technology as the beginning of a millennium for the workplace. Work would be transformed;

jobs would be streamlined; workers would become more productive. The "electronic cottage" would decrease commuting and allow employees to work at home. The paperless office was imminent. Current futurists, however, look toward 2000 with more caution. Although still hailing the *potential* of leading-edge technology to increase the productivity of the office, futurists recognize that serious problems cloud the workplace, even though communication technology will be essential to keep the United States competitive in a global economy (Brown & Guenther, 1991; Caissey, 1990; Coates, Jarratt, & Mahaffie, 1991; Konar, 1986; Kuehn, 1991; Stewart, 1993).

Technology has become so extensive that organizations have difficulty keeping up with the innovations that technology provides in making work less demanding. Organizations wrestle with decisions about how best to use existing technology, how to evaluate and integrate new technology with existing systems, how to use technology to improve productivity (Ciepiela, 1989; Hammer & Champy, 1993; Karlgard, 1993; Rifkin, 1993). As Wang (1983) once stated, the inevitable problem is that "the human mind is impervious to automation."

Enhanced education strategies designed to improve writing, speaking, and thinking skills have not materialized, despite increased development in writing research and pedagogy. Lack of improvement in writing skills chronicles the larger problem: A workforce that is more skilled, visionary, flexible, and fully able to embrace the changes that technology creates is still illusory (Goddard, 1990). Competitiveness in the global economy requires more than mere reading and writing ability (Erickson, 1991). As the Wingspread Group (1993) has noted repeatedly, competitiveness requires the ability to think critically and solve problems creatively, exercise judgment, and learn new skills and knowledge throughout a lifetime. As Coates, Jarratt, and Mahaffie noted in "Future Work" (1991), almost every job will require knowledge, the ability to think conceptually, to handle complexity, and to extract and communicate information: "Sweeping technological change, the rise of worldwide communications, and competition in the global marketplace require specialized knowledge, but the United States is failing to meet these requirements and struggles to sustain the literacy, math, and other abilities of previous decades" (pp. 15–16).

The challenge created by global competition as it affects survival of U.S. business suggests that education needs to change (Beniger, 1991), but few studies recommend the specific type of education needed in each area. Studies recommend that students learn reading, writing, and mathematics, but few specify what reading, writing, and mathematics (Zuckman, 1991) education will prepare students to live and work in a rapidly changing global society increasingly defined by computer technologies. Although studies of employee writing were numerous in the 1970s and early 1980s, few have been conducted that suggest what we should teach in either nonacademic or academic writing. Toffler, in *Power Shift* (1990), pinpointed what may perhaps be the crucial problem — the increasingly abstract nature of work. And it is this abstraction that must be grasped, transformed into ideas, and then placed into a textual form that will communicate: "Capital has gone from its tangible form, to a paper form that symbolized tangible assets, to paper symbolizing symbols, and finally to electronic blips symbolizing the paper" (p. 62). Literacy is no longer just the ability to read and write, but the ability to grasp intellectually and then link concepts, to turn data into information and information into knowledge that can be communicated in a variety of textual forms. Abstraction requires that communicators be able to help readers visualize concepts (Floren, 1990; Vassalo, 1990). Toffler's (1990) analysis suggests that writing effectively in an organizational framework combines the need for rhetoric with an endless source of information, as keyboard navigation provides access to more and more information networks. Excessive choices in software — which to use, what options to select — adds to the growing information load. The problem is helping writers deal with rhetoric, technology, and economic threat, all at the same time. As Vice President Gore (1991) wrote, "We are now drowning in information. We have automated the process of collecting information, but we have not successfully mastered the task of organizing and distilling the information for our productive use" (p. 21). The issue is that problems emanating from information technology and global competition must underpin any social theory on which technical communication is conceived and taught. Stated in literal terms, technology is currently driving the workplace and nonacademic communication and its rhetoric. Trade literature in marketing, personnel, management, finance, and even education yields the definite sense that neither writing nor productivity will improve.

DISCOURSE AND INFORMATION TECHNOLOGY — CUES FROM THE FUTURISTS

Studies of the changes that information technology is bringing and will bring to workplace writing are beginning to be more informative than they were 5 years ago (LaPlante, 1993). Numerous studies have dealt with the theory of information technology and its impact on society (Browning, 1986; Florida, 1991; Jaikumar, 1991; Krebs, 1988; "The Office of the Future," 1991). The unanswered question, however, is how writing fits into these changes. Computer technology applied to writing has not improved writing (Pearce & Barker, 1991; Wendell & Allerheiligen, 1991).

Despite troubled predictions by consultants and futurists, a number of communication trends have emerged and continue to evolve in their capabilities to generate and deliver communication: Multimedia capability, desktop publishing, fax, video conferencing, and e-mail will continue to be principle modes of written communication. Continuing changes emerging from the use of each provide suggestions for both research and curricular development.

The Integrated Office Communication System

Technology will continue to be the axial concept on which theory and practice hinge (Glaser, 1988). As Bleeker noted in "The Information Age Office" (1991), "Technology establishes the length of our reach. It forms the foundation upon which applications can be constructed. Today, with their new powers, intelligent machines can conform to peoples' needs—not the other way around" (p. 18). Problem-solving teams and networks are making traditional offices outdated because rigid hierarchies hinder flexible networking. Bleeker foresees offices composed of multimedia landing sites equipped with information appliances that combine word processing, e-mail, fax, desktop publishing, and even audiovisual conferencing capabilities.

Desktop Publishing

Computer technology now offers powerful changes in creating communications, but these changes will continue to evolve. For example, improved computer replications of the complete page, rather than VDT textual display, will continue to reduce a reliance on paper (Alesandrene, 1992; Stanton, 1992). Technology for creating and revising text and adding illustrations will provide more extensive options. Workplace writing will require users to understand and be able to manipulate page design—particularly navigational devices such as headings and subheadings. Software will allow individual pages to contain invisible changes that have been made to the page, who made them, who is authorized to read what pages, where the information came from, and what the information is related to. The deep context of the page can be accessed in whatever sequence is needed. To aid deficient writers, more programs will allow writers to design a general format for routine reports, such as sales reports and typical kinds of graphics. Information typed in will be automatically placed in the appropriate section or transformed into the intended graphic (Weinberger, 1991). Using this type of technology effectively has several curricular implications:

1. The employee's knowledge of report design and graphics will dictate the effectiveness of this software in terms of the document generated. Because desktop publishing has merged content generation, document

design, and editing, employees, not just editors, must be able to perform all three functions.

2. The continued emphasis on speed in generating documents suggests that in teaching job-related writing we must emphasize planning rather than revising. Unlike writing as learning, writing at work emphasizes rapid production of documents rather than extensive revising and editing (Haswell, 1988; Selzer, 1983). In writing courses we must emphasize rapid analysis of rhetorical context, getting it right the first time, with editing left to checkers (Krebs, 1988; Straub, 1991).

3. Visual quality of even routine documents has been increased by the mandatory use of word processing equipment and laser printers. Desktop publishing has significantly raised the standards of what is acceptable for business office correspondence and for graphics (Friedman, 1991). Extensive graphics capabilities mandate instruction in how to use computer graphics — choice of graphic, color, labeling, and arrangement of material. Effectiveness of word processing and graphics still depends on the knowledge of design of the person using the system. Theory of page design and then screen design must work and be easily translated into practice.

E-Mail

Although e-mail has been used in writing programs for nearly a decade to familiarize students with the technology and to teach collaborative writing, only since 1983 has the rhetoric of e-mail begun to be understood and transformed into a useful pedagogy. E-mail is notorious for messages that reflect the writer's failure to analyze audiences who will receive the message and the impact of the message.

For example, in a study rich in theoretical and practical implications, Sussman and Golden of the University of Louisville, and Beauclair of Price Waterhouse (1991), in a collaborative study, found that e-mail users "may focus their attention on the process of sending the message while ignoring its impact on the receiver. They may tend to concentrate more on the electronic functions — typing, scanning, and executing commands — than on who will receive the message and how it will be interpreted" (p. 70).

Because e-mail, more than hard copy memos, removes all nonverbal cues, senders have to assume more responsibility for the objective reality of the message. E-mail research is showing that careful rhetorical analysis is even more problematic in e-mail than in standard written memos and letters, in which slower generation forces more careful analysis.

E-mail researchers have discovered that writers are more careful when writing standard memos than when writing on a computer screen. Sims (1991) found that e-mail messages had more of a spoken quality, lacked connections between sentences, exhibited poor spelling and punctuation, and showed little efforts by senders to impress receivers. The use of metadiscourse to control meaning in e-mail needs further study. For example, Sussman, Golden, and Beauclair (1991) recommended that (a) e-mail users need to use more metadiscourse, specifically incorporating parenthetical interpretive cues for the receiver that pointedly tell the receiver the sender's views rather than assuming that the receiver will infer the tone; and (b) that the sender's use of conversational tone without any dramaturgical cues can result in misinterpreted statements.

Fax and Video Conferencing

Decrease in costs of both fax machines and telecommunication channels has suggested to some futurologists that fax will continue as an important source of interoffice communication (Sampson, 1989). Studies of fax have shown that it works particularly well when senders do not need interactive communication to solve a problem, but simply want to send information or directives quickly. Video conferencing has been shown to be more appropriate than fax when interaction between individuals is necessary for problem solving. Although teleconferencing equipment is still more expensive than fax equipment, video conferencing has proven to be worth its cost when it helps businesses avoid costly meetings.

Fax has been found to be particularly useful in communicating information by forms (Alesandrene, 1992; Dzujna, 1991). A new forms development software industry has developed that is attempting to deemphasize prose and hence reading time. Forms are seen by some organizations as a way of compensating for poor employee writing. The increase of forms suggests that forms design could become a new area for technical communication research and pedagogy. Currently, forms design software allows operators to design a form within a rigid framework. Once the form is designed, the software electronically shifts data to the form and eliminates errors from reentering data.

Telecommuting and Collaborative Screen Sharing

Telecommuting and collaborative screen sharing, in work contexts and in distance education, allow participants to respond to each other and view and manipulate the same page layout or graphic. Participants can complete designs, documents, or diagrams by working on the same space. Like video conferencing, collaborative screen sharing and telecommuting work better when those participating already know each other. Major business trade publications illustrate the ways in which telecommuting is allowing business executives to live in one state and manage their corporations several states away (Freedman, 1993). Telecommuting is also allowing more employees as well as college students to do a part of their work at home and avoid costly travel to work every day.

Along with electronic communications and its attempt to create virtual meetings is the need to prepare employees with proper protocols, electronic etiquette, and training in how each works so that the operation of the system demands less of participants' focus. As LaPlante (1993) remarked, "people tend to be much less inhibited—and often less courteous—during such sessions, which can lead to misunderstandings that can fester because there's no immediate confrontation" (p. 117). Another issue for participants is deciding when a virtual meeting will suffice and when the need for group affiliation and personal interaction is a part of the business context. However, virtual meeting technologies produce a record of what was said and by whom. When these conferences are printed, the lack of context in which the discussion was held can create radically different interpretations.

ESTABLISHING RESEARCH AGENDAS IN NONACADEMIC DISCOURSE

Even a cursory survey of nonacademic writing issues reveals several findings: Concerns about the evolving nature of workplace communication are more evident in various business organizations than in published academic research. Academics seem more concerned with describing past and current communication practices and trying to theorize a paradigm for these issues than with predicting future communication environments and determining the best communication solutions for those problems. If technical communication justifies itself as preparing students for the demands of nonacademic writing, and if the form and method of workplace writing are defined by technology, then research in nonacademic writing needs to begin with the workplace—the writing problems of the workplace as articulated by managers, trainers, and communication specialists who deal with workplace writing on a daily basis.

Using the workplace as a point of departure will help ensure the relevance of the research—its usefulness in helping prepare students and technical writers for nonacademic writing and anticipating changes in high- tech workplace communications that should inform university curriculum planning. In their essay, "Theory Building and Relevance," Smeltzer and Suchan (1991) argued:

> The need for academics to provide research relevant to practitioners is particularly compelling given the finding of one study that less than 15 percent of the managers surveyed read academically produced research. . . . [Research] should not be derived from questions unanswered in academic

literature or from the belief that one's research interests are automatically relevant. . . . Rather it is important to look at current trends and predict future ones. (p. 184)

In short, if our research carries no impact beyond the academy (and promotion and salary committees), then the value of nonacademic writing as a separate discipline may be questionable. Most of the interest in anticipating and planning for the future workplace communication emanates from management and marketing consultants and not academics, who seem content to theorize about existing workplace scenarios using academic models developed for academic research in the social sciences. The result is a sometimes ethereal perspective on nonacademic writing as shaped by an alembic of academic theory instead of realities of nonacademic contexts.

Focusing on the workplace can easily begin with surveys, which were abundant in the 1970s and early 1980s but have decreased in the past decade. Surveys of employee writing, like the one conducted by Anderson (1985), provide us with useful insights about the relevance of our curricula as well as our research interests. What is needed are current and continuing studies to further our understanding of writing as it is continually affected by technology. However, the issues and concerns that may emerge may not be what we want to hear.

AN INFORMAL SURVEY

Over the past two years, I conducted personal interviews with upper- level managers who deal with large quantities of writing. These were managers who serve on various university advisory boards. Of the 26 I contacted and who agreed to talk to me, the business profile of the respondents is as follows: three financial services brokers, four corporate training specialists, three senior partners in major accounting firms, four managers in utility companies, three attorneys, five communication specialists in management consulting firms, two managers in major insurance companies, one top-level manager in a major oil company, and one president of a software marketing firm. Each agreed to answer 15 questions and then add additional commentary. Although this survey was purely qualitative and analysis of its findings are clearly beyond the scope of this essay, many of their responses suggest directions for future research in nonacademic writing, several of which surfaced in surveys of trade journal literature.

1. *Do you believe that the writing of employees hired in recent years is better than the writing of employees hired a decade ago? What problems in writing do you believe are the most serious?*
Not one respondent believed that the writing skills of employees who

have joined their organizations in the past 5 to 8 years has improved. The most frequently mentioned problem (12 out of 20 respondents noted this point) was the inability of employees to state their message clearly. Eleven respondents cited the inability of employees to analyze their own writing and understand its ineffectiveness, even when told that their writing was ineffective. Seven respondents noted that convoluted writing that did not address the topic was a typical problem.

2. *What types of writing does your organization do routinely?*

Fourteen respondents stated that their organizations write "relatively short" documents—memoranda, letters, e-mail messages, 2- to 5-page reports. One respondent commented that "the longer the report the worse it is." That perspective was reflected in comments by five other respondents.

3. *Can you explain how you go about composing or writing what you have to write?*

Rapid generation of documents was cited as important by 15 respondents. Twenty of 26 respondents stated that they did all their writing on the computer, from planning to writing to editing. Seven managers stated that they "thought through" reports and letters they had to write while they were traveling or during their commute to work. During travel, 9 reported using a notepad to "get the main ideas." Once at the office, all 20 drafted the reports on a microcomputer, reread the report to check for writing errors, used a spelling checker, printed the document for fax transmission, or sent it by e-mail for intercompany dissemination. Of the 9 respondents who described their individual writing process with some thoughtful reflection, not one cited revision as a major writing activity. As one staff development manager stated, "I revise in my head as I plan, but when I begin to write, I write. I can't spend all day on a memo or report."

4. *How important are communication skills to promotion in your organization?*

Although all respondents stated that good writing and speaking skills were important, only six stated specifically that effective writing skills were used in determining promotions. Fourteen respondents stated that poor writing could block promotional opportunity, whereas good writing was appreciated but (unfortunately) not rewarded. Eighteen noted that oral skills and the ability to conduct meetings were crucial to advancement. Eight respondents noted that technical competence was still the main criteria for promotion. Three respondents stated that prospective employees who submitted writing samples that showed their writing competence had an edge during the recruiting process, but nine respondents stated that grade point average and college attended were the crucial factors.

5. *Do you think that communication skills will improve among future employees, given the increasing stress on writing and speaking skills in university curricula?*

Only two respondents stated that they expected to be able to find employees who could produce the quality writing needed in the organization. Fourteen predicted that writing and thinking will worsen, as the social fabric of the country continues to unravel. Eight said that their firms were using forms whenever possible. Twelve stated that their organizations spent substantial sums for writing software. As two accounting partners commented about the limitations of writing software, "the content will still probably be lousy, but at least the grammar and spelling will be correct."

6. *Do you ever hire writing teachers to conduct workshops for your employees? How do you try to improve employee writing when you see that improvement is necessary?*

Nine respondents reported hiring college faculty to conduct writing short courses, but none felt that the courses had produced long-term significant benefit. Six respondents stated that their organizations had retained outside writing consultants, but within the last three years they had worked carefully with them to ensure the relevance of the topics. This view echoes recent reports on executive education that is being developed within corporations to relate to corporate objectives. The lack of practical application of academic writing values seems to be widespread (Bongiorno, 1993; Richardson & Liggett, 1993). Seven respondents reported that their organizations had purchased computer-aided writing software but that secretarial staff used it more than employees who are responsible for generating their own documents. Eleven respondents reported that employees were encouraged to have a dictionary and a handbook. Five respondents reported that their organizations had used prepackaged, short writing courses developed by executive development companies, but the effectiveness of these short courses was not impressive.

Four respondents stated that their organizations were using forms as much as possible to eliminate the need for writing. All three partners from three major accounting firms stated that their firms routinely developed form letters that could be sent to clients who needed to know about tax law changes so that employees notifying clients did not have to write individual letters. Nine respondents noted that their organizations have standard forms for proposals, status reports, work procedures, and investment plans. The writer just inserts content in the appropriate places. Respondents who reported using forms stated that decreasing writing skills had led to the development of forms. Two respondents reported that their organizations have forms designers who stay busy generating and revising forms that will eliminate the need for original writing.

7. *What would you like college writing faculties to emphasize?*

When queried about suggestions for curricula, seven respondents stated that the legal aspects of documents need to be discussed. All four communication consultants and the marketing firm president, who have studied and taught writing on the college level, believe that communication ethics courses were less important than communication law courses in crowded curricula. Four told me pointedly that rhetoric takes a "back seat" to law, that what a writer may want to say, in terms of effective rhetoric, must be subservient to the legal ramifications of the document. Respondents from law, accounting, and financial services stated that informative or advisory letters to clients had to meet legal specifications; that legality, rather than communication quality, was the most important consideration. Communication consultants stated that they would like to see chapters on communication law in technical and business writing texts with material on conducting meetings eliminated.

Errors in standard usage were the second most important quality mentioned by respondents. Half stated that errors in spelling and usage were unacceptable because they reflected unfavorably on the company.

8. *Do you believe that colleges are preparing students for employment?*

The attitude toward the U.S. educational system in general was pessimistic. Fourteen respondents stated that students needed to do more writing in college classes, but that less writing seems to be the norm. Fifteen respondents thought that at least one course in technical writing and one in public speaking should be required for graduation, whereas three respondents stated that they did not think requiring these courses would make much difference. Five respondents stated that new college graduates seem to know less than graduates they remembered from groups of new hires 5 years ago. Four respondents who said they had been approached to fund technical communication research projects felt that the research proposed had little value for the organization; therefore, they rejected the proposal. None of the respondents believed that college writing courses alone can correct students' writing problems, that writing and speaking skills need to assume a higher priority in elementary and secondary education.

RECOMMENDATIONS FOR RESEARCH IN NONACADEMIC DISCOURSE

To my mind, these responses as well as emerging curricular implications in information systems, desktop publishing, e-mail, and various forms of computer conferencing suggest nine research areas:

1. Current rhetorical principles of nonacademic discourse need to be reexamined. We need to develop a type of WD-40 rhetoric that will work in a variety of contexts: E-mail messages, teleconferencing, collaborative screen sharing, and standard hard-copy documents. The elements of this kind of efficient rhetoric are probably already known but need to be extracted, tested, revised, and then embedded in technical communication

instructional materials. Academics, even in nonacademic discourse, need to understand that what they consider effective "rhetoric" may not work in practice, and that what is intellectually challenging may be of little value to writers in non- academic settings. As Burnett notes in chapter 6 of this volume, collaboration differs in academic and nonacademic settings. However, the extent to which collaboration is used in work contexts suggests that our instruction in collaboration is important and relevant.

2. Because computer conferencing and e-mail seem to operate with short documents, we should find new ways of teaching these technologies, and provide methods for preparing students for computer communication etiquette that discourages flaming, aggressive responses, and tactlessness. Assignments can require development of short documents, e-mail, and paper documents, in a variety of difficult but changing contexts that require the student to analyze rhetorical context quickly but sensitively. Collaborative e-mail assignments can require rapid responses to deep contextual organizational case problems that require the student to determine if he or she wants or needs to communicate and, if so, what and how. Contrary to current writing instruction philosophy, technical communication faculty may want to emphasize product more distinctly than process. Rapid but effective communication product development can occur when students generate more documents rather than working at length on developing one or two.

3. We can then use the connections we establish with professionals in business and industry to continue to study the composing processes of groups and individuals. Can differences in composing processes be attributed to differences among professions or differences among individuals? For example, do financial services workers compose differently from engineers, lawyers, and public relations workers? After extensive study of composing processes, can we determine changes that can be made in the way we tell students to compose? During their working careers, students will likely work in jobs that are outside their disciplinary focus. How can we prepare them for communicating in a variety of disciplines and work contexts?

4. The implementation of total quality improvement (TQI) in higher education with its emphasis on making education responsive to students, the public, and those who employ college graduates suggests the importance of keeping technical communication responsive to the workplace and measuring the effectiveness of technical communication courses. Research needs to be revived that develops performance measures for determining the effectiveness of our technical communication courses.

5. Faculty also need to develop a working knowledge of the legal aspects of written and computer communication, such as privacy rights and legal liability. Texts as well as actual instruction need to emphasize methods of

familiarizing students with the broad legal ramifications of what they produce online and in hard copy. Considering the effect of law on texts raises interesting questions: What constraints on rhetorical strategy are imposed by legal requirements? How can legal constraints be effectively meshed with rhetorical strategies to produce documents that will achieve the writer's purpose and protect the organization?

6. Technical communication faculty should utilize qualitative research to study actual documents. In its adherence to statistical rule, quantitative research often narrows hypotheses to the point that they deal with questions too specific and desiccated to provide any fruitful contextual meaning to nonacademic discourse issues. As Halpern (1988) noted, "What we are short of is not empirical research in general but qualitative research in particular, research that discovers what students and professionals write and how they write it" (p. 25). Halpern, anticipating the emergence of ethnographic research discussed by Herndl, advocates "case studies, informal surveys and interviews, historiography, life histories, observational studies, and textual or content analysis. Each of these methods can help us learn more about business and technical communication" (p. 27). Ethnography should help us understand more about the nonacademic communication context so that we are more able to pursue resesarch that will yield pedagogy that is relevant to students' postacademic needs.

7. Research results must be communicated in language that will be meaningful to nonacademic as well as academic audiences. In the past decade, the development of theory and philosophy of nonacademic discourse has brought with it the development of a jargon that academics have seen as appropriate for discussing theory and research with each other (and for tenure committees). Put another way, technical communication researchers, to give academic credibility to their work, have developed their own exclusionary language. This increasingly allusive, political, ideological, and abstract language gives intellectual stature and a sense of erudition to our work, but also alienates nonacademic users of our research. As Elbow (1991) stated in his objections to academic discourse, this detached medium thus produces writing that is "ungainly or uncomfortable and not infrequently tangled" (p. 141).

Perhaps we should remodel the academic discourse of technical communication research along that suggested by Elbow: "giving reasons and evidence, yes, but doing so as a person speaking with acknowledged interest to others—whose interest and position one acknowledges and tries to understand" (p. 142). In other words, we must write in such a way that our nonacademic readers in business organizations can share our theory and perhaps even collaborate in its development. Without their interest and their help, nonacademic theory will sink into a morass of verbal effluvia that becomes meaningless after it has passed the muster of promotion and salary committees.

8. Because all of our writing instruction will need to respond to accountability requirements and performance measures, those of us who also teach other writing courses should rethink freshman composition courses and make them less directed toward writing as inquiry and writing for academic assignments. In previous articles, I have argued that freshman composition could be adjusted to harmonize with rather than counter the paradigms used in nonacademic writing courses: emphasis on richer contexts (case studies), deemphasis on the essay, introduction to document design, elimination of expressive discourse, and inclusion of writing, such as instructions, that students can identify with and already have encountered in academic and nonacademic settings (Tebeaux, 1988a, 1988b).

9. As Herndl noted, technical communication courses tend to be text-driven, and textual approaches are difficult to change. To improve the relevance of our instructional materials, perhaps we need to study ways of teaching technical communication that is not so rigidly text dictated — reducing single, big texts to separate collections of minitexts, supplementing these with compact disks and online tutorials that can be updated regularly as needed. With distance education becoming increasingly important, building instruction about interactive computing and state-of-the-art software and multimedia can help prepare students for generating communications in the electronic workplace.

CONCLUSION

Since 1988, the Pew Foundation has predicted with startling accuracy the shifts that are occuring in higher education: intense competition for students, decreasing numbers of traditional students, increasing numbers of nontraditional students, growing demands for college education that produces employment opportunities, increasing hostility from the public and legislative bodies who are demanding accountability for higher education's spending (The Pew Higher Education Roundtable, 1993, 1994). The American Association of Higher Education in its annual conferences and its publications (see *Change, AAHE Bulletin*, for example) has argued regularly for a return to accountability in faculty research, teaching loads, and instructional programs. As Hubbard's (1993) collection of case studies of TQI applications in higher education indicate, colleges who are experimenting with various forms of TQI are restructuring their perspectives. They now view students, taxpayers, as well as employers as customers whose needs should be the focus of the university. TQI institutions also recognize that the university is no longer some type of sacrosanct, inviolate entity impervious to the outside world, and that faculty are no longer gatekeepers of knowledge who alone decide what is to be taught. In short, faculty had better care if their subject area is perceived by those outside the department is relevant.

In the face of increasing demands for accountability, technical communication with its focus on the nonacademic world is one of the few liberal arts areas that can show accountability in instruction and research. Ultimately, research in nonacademic discourse, although it must remain palatable to academic review committees, must also remain useful and applicable to the nonacademic settings for which it was initially developed to prepare students. This statement means that the central goal of nonacademic writing researchers should be to study current communication contexts and problems, develop and test solutions to these problems, develop theories to deal with major issues, work with business communities to test these theories as to their value in solving writing problems, attempt to anticipate future nonacademic writing issues, and then translate knowledge gained from these research activities into pedagogy that prepares our students for immediate nonacademic writing demands as well as the probable demands of the future workplace. Futuristic theorizing that moves beyond close analysis of current nonacademic settings is critical. Few organizations are impervious to rapid changes in technology, world events, and legal mandates that antiquate social and rhetorical theories by the time that they are published. Again, technical communication faculty should heed the call for relevant teaching and research.

The value of theory, research, and pedagogy in the teaching of nonacademic discourse still rests on the observations by pioneers such as Britton (1975) and Mathes and Stevenson (1976) that writing at work is very different from writing in school, and that success as an academic writer does not guarantee success as a nonacademic writer. To Britton, Harris, Cunningham, and Mathes and Stevenson we owe the first articulation of these differences that still underpin our current theories. Maintaining our knowledge of that distinction depends on our looking at nonacademic writing from more than an academician's perception, recognizing the legitimacy of the practicing business organization's perceptions and concerns, and understanding that how effectively we aid business in solving communication problems and by sending them students who can also aid in solving these solutions is still our fundamental reason for being.

REFERENCES

Alesandrene, K. (1992). Converting hard copy to "electronic page." *The Office, 115*(5), 51–52.
Anderson, P. V. (1980). The need for better research in technical communication. *Journal of Technical Writing and Communication, 10*(4), 271–282.

Anderson, P. V. (1985). What survey research tells us about writing at work. In L. Odell & D. Goswami (Eds.), *Writing in nonacademic settings* (pp. 3-82) New York: Guilford.

Beniger, J. R. (1991). Far afield—critical connections: Communication for the future. U.S. Congress Office of Technology Assessment. *Communication Research, 18*(3), 428-455.

Bleeker, S. (1991). The information age office. *The Futurist, 25*(1), 18-20.

Bongiorno, L. (1993, October 25). The professor is in: Corporate America's new lesson plan. *Business Week*, pp. 14-16.

Breden, J. (1991). Say it simply. *Industry Week, 240*(14), 19-20.

Britton, W. E. (1975). The trouble with technical writing is freshman composition. In D. H. Cunningham & H. Estrin (Eds.), *The teaching of technical writing* (pp. 70-75). Urbana, IL: National Council of Teachers of English.

Brockmann, R. J. (1980). Taking a second look at technical communication pedagogy. *Journal of Technical Writing and Communication, 10*(4), 283-291.

Brody, H. (1990). Managers turn to grammar, style checkers. *PC World*, No. 8, 72.

Brown, E., & Guenther K. (1991). Desktop publishing: Is it promises, promises? *The Office, 114*(1), 54-55.

Browning, J. (1986). Information technology: Knocking their heads together. *Economist, 300*(745), S13-S16.

Caissey, G. (1990). Skills for the information age. *The Education Digest, 55*, 51-53.

Ciepiela, W. (1989). Putting the great information society in perspective. *Journal of Systems Management, 49*, 15-19.

Coates, J. F., Jarratt, J., & Mahaffie, J. B. (1991). Future work. *The Futurist, 25*(3), 9-19.

Diether, B. V. (1992). Righting rotten writing. *Training, 29*(4), 48-52.

Dzujna, C. C. (1991). Speeding the work flow with electronic forms. *The Office, 113*(6), 56-57.

Elbow, P. (1991). Reflections on academic discourse: How it relates to freshman and colleagues. *College English, 53*(2), 135-155.

Erickson, T. (1991). Competing with technology in the world arena. *Journal of Business Strategy, 12*, 11-16.

Ewing, D. P. (1983). Needed research in business writing. In J. W. Halpern (Ed.), *Teaching business writing: Approaches, plans, pedagogy, research* (pp. 183-199). Urbana, IL: American Business Communicataion Association.

Fahner, H. (1990). The ten commandments of memo writing. *Sales and Marketing Management, 142*, 35-37.

Felden, J. (1989). Clear writing is not enough. *Management Review, 78*, 49-52.

Felden, J. (1990). What do you mean I can't write? *Harvard Business Review, 68*(5), 238.

Fields, H. (1991). Education report finds U.S. reading, writing skills worsen. *Publishers Weekly, 238*(49), 15-26.

Floren, J. (1990). Writing in the age of data drench. *Training, 27*, 57-62.

Florida, R. (1991). The new industrial revolution. *Futures, 23*(6), 539-576.

Freedman, D. (1993, September 13). Culture of urgency. *Forbes ASAP*, pp. 25-28.

Friedman, R. (1991). How desktop publishing adds to communication. *The Office, 114*(3), 23-30.

Gibson, C. (1978). Business as usual: Write, write, write. *CEA Forum*, pp. 3-9.

Gieselman, R. D. (1980). Research in business communication: The state of the art. *The Journal of Business Communication, 17*(4), 3-18.

Gladis, S. (1991). Coaching trainers on winning writing skills. *Training and Development Journal, 45*(6), 31-34.

Glaser, S. (1988). Technology and the future office. *Inc.*, Suppl., 30-34.

Goddard, R. (1990). The rise of the organization. *Management World, 19*(1), 3-5.

Gold, R. (1989). Reader-friendly writing. *Supervisory Management, 34*, 39-43.

Gore, A. (1991). Information superhighways. *The Futurist, 25*(1), 21–23.

Halpern, J. (1988). Getting in deep: Using qualitative research in business and technical communication. *Journal of Business and Technical Communication, 2*(2), 22–43.

Hammer, M., & Champy, J. (1993). *Reengineering the corporation: A manifesto for reengineering business.* New York: Random House.

Haswell, R. H. (1988). Toward competent writing in the workplace. *Journal of Technical Writing and Communication, 18*(2), 161–174.

Hubbard, D. L. (Ed.). (1993). *Continuous quality improvement: Making the transition to education.* Prescott.

Jaikumar, J. (1991). The boundaries of business: The impact of technology. *Harvard Business Review, 69*, 100–101.

Karlgard, K. (1993, September 13). Interview; Mike Hammer. *Forbes ASAP*, pp. 69–75.

Konar, E. (1986). Computer literacy: With ask you shall receive. *Personnel Journal, 65*(7), 83–86.

Krebs, V. (1988). Integrated strategy and information technology. *Personnel Journal, 67*(11), 93–100.

Kuehn, R. H. (1991, June). If technology is the answer, what's the question? *Business Communication Review*, pp. 93–94.

LaPlante, A. (1993, September 13). TeleConfrontationing. *Forbes ASAP*, pp. 110–118.

Laviviere, E. (1989). Writing skills in business: Implications for teachers of technical writing. *The Technical Writing Teacher, 16*(2), 103–114.

Mathes, J. C., & Stevenson, D. (1976). *Designing technical reports.* Indianapolis: Bobbs-Merrill.

Mathes, J.C., Stevenson, D. W., & Klaver, P. (1979). Technical writing: The engineering educator's responsibility. *Engineering Education, 69*(4), 331–334.

Moran, M. G. (1985). Business letters, memoranda, and resumes. In M. G. Moran & D. Journet (Eds.), *Research in technical communication* (pp. 313–349). Westport, CT: Greenwood.

The office of the future. (1991). *Byte, 16*, 204–246.

On writing and relating. (1990). *Training and Development Journal, 44*(12), 10–11.

Pearce, C. G., & Barker, R. T. (1991). A comparison of business communication quality between computer written and handwritten samples. *The Journal of Business Communication, 28*(2), 141–52.

Petrini, C. (1990). Training 101: The write way to write. *Training and Development Journal, 44*(9), 27–33.

Pew Higher Education Roundtable. (1993, November). *Policy Perspectives, 5*(2).

Pew Higher Education Roundtable. (1994, April). *Policy Perspectives, 5*(3).

Richardson, M., & Liggett, S. (1993). Power relations, technical writing theory, and workplace writing. *Journal of Business and Technical Communication, 7*(1), 112–137.

Rifkin, G. (1993, August 19). Reengineering aetna. *Forbes ASAP*, pp. 78–86.

Rivers, W. E. (1985). The current status of business and technical writing courses in English departments. *ADE Bulletin, 82*(1), 50–54.

Sampson, A. (1989). I've seen the future and it's the fax: Bringing back the written word. *World Press Review, 36*(12), 28–30.

Scott, P. (1991). Mail bonding. *Forbes*, Suppl., 156–157.

Selzer, J. (1983). The composing processes of an engineer. *College Composition and Communication, 34*(2), 71–81.

Shea, G. (1992). A case for clear writing. *Training and Development Journal, 46*(1), 63–65.

Sims, B. (1991). Electronic mail and writing in the workplace. In B. R. Sims (Ed.), *Studies in technical communication* (pp. 137–156). Denton: University of North Texas Press.

Smeltzer, L. R., & Suchan, J. E. (1991). Guest editorial: Theory building and relevance. The *Journal of Business Communication, 28*(3), 181–186.

Stanton, M. (1992). Desktop publishing. *Occupational Outlook Quarterly, 35*(2), 2–12.

Stewart, T. A. (1993, August 23). Reengineering: The hot new managing tool. *Fortune*, pp. 40–48.

Straub, J. T. (1991). Memos and reports: Write them right the first time. *Supervisory Management, 36*(7), 1–6.

Sussmann L., Golden, P., & Beauclair, R. (1991). Training for e-mail. *Training and Development Journal, 45*(3), 70–73.

Tebeaux, E. (1988a). The trouble with employees writing may be freshman English. *Teaching English in the Two-Year College, 15*, 9–19.

Tebeaux, E. (1988b). Writing in academe: Writing at work: Using visual rhetoric to bridge the gap. *Journal of Teaching Writing, 7*, 215–236.

Thralls, C., & Blyler, N. R. (Eds.). (1993a). *Professional communication: The social perspective.* Newbury Park, CA: Sage.

Thralls, C., & Blyler N. R. (1993b). The social perspective and pedagogy in technical communication. *Technical Communication Quarterly, 2*(3), 249–270.

Toffler, A. (1990). *Power shift.* New York: Bantam.

Vassalo, M. (1990). Writing for the mind's eye. *Public Relations Journal, 46*(9), 32–34.

Wang, A. (1983, October 3). Office systems for the eighties: Automation and the bottom line. *Fortune*, Suppl., n.p.

Wank, M. (1991). Wanted: Writers who can at least write. *Advertising Age, 62*(8), 21–25.

Wingspread Group on Higher Education. (1993). *An American imperative: Higher expectations for higher education.* The Johnson Foundation.

Weinberger, D. (1991). The active document: Making pages smarter. *The Futurist, 25*(4), 25–28.

Wendell, A. J., & Allerheiligen, R. (1991). Computer assisted writing instruction: Is it effective? *The Journal of Business Communication, 28*(2), 131–140.

Zaslow, R. (1991). Managers as writing coaches. *Training and Development Journal, 45*(7), 61–64.

Zuckman, J. (1991). Labor lists the "competencies" future workers should have. *Congressional Quarterly Weekly, 49*(27), 1835.

The Computer Culture, Gender, and Nonacademic Writing: An Interdisciplinary Critique

4

Mary M. Lay
University of Minnesota — Twin Cities

Within the last two decades, feminist scholars have critiqued social and cultural views of science and technology that assign so-called masculine traits to the subjects or agents of scientific study and feminine traits to objects of that study. In addition, these scholars have questioned objectivity within the scientific method not only by examining the gender stereotypes that link objectivity to masculinity but also by applying the work of social theorists such as Kuhn (1970) who reveal the subjective nature of scientific communities. At the same time, feminist scholars have described the learning and decision-making style that many women assume within their social gender roles, a style that was once dismissed as immature but is now recognized by many as legitimately different.

Now, researchers of the computer culture are beginning to apply these lenses of gender and social theory to the development, teaching, and application of computer software. These studies are valuable not just because they discover or confirm some important cognitive differences that might be determined by gender identity, but also because they recognize difference in general. As researchers of nonacademic writing, we too must acknowledge that differences, some caused by gender identity, exist among computer programmers, designers, and users; our acknowledgment will help ensure that writing about computers will be effective. Also, it is appropriate to turn a critical eye to the computer culture to see how it accommodates difference, as a great deal of nonacademic writing research and pedagogy focuses on that culture. This critical look, to some extent, answers the call of Selfe and Selfe (chap. 14, this volume) to "recognize" not only the "connectedness and extent" of our computer landscape but also the "gaps, partiality, complications, contradictions, and schisms" in that land-scape. Moreover, such a look tests one aspect of Herndl's (chap. 2, this volume) "habitus of the community" within professional and technical writing, a community that "translates research and theory into practice through the textbook," in this case the computer documentation textbook. Finally, this critical look measures the feasibility of Tebeaux's (chap. 3, this volume) appeal for universal computer literacy in the workplace, which includes a need "to learn new software rapidly and to integrate new technology with old."

At this point, it does seem that the computer has created a culture. For example, Kiesler, Sproull, and Eccles (1985) stated, "Based on the infor-mation we have, we believe that computing is more than a set of skills. It is embedded in a social system consisting of shared values and norms, a special vocabulary and humor, status and prestige ordering, and differen-tiation of members from nonmembers. In short, it is a culture" (p. 453). As Keller (1992) stated, "Sharing a language means sharing a conceptual universe" (p. 27). Of course, by this definition the computer has created many cultures. Those who enter an electronic mail conversation, perhaps over an internet bulletin board, soon identify that culture's norms in vocabulary, message length, and topic initiation. Mac users distinguish themselves from IBM users and from UNIX users. Users of specific computer software games seem to speak in code to those unfamiliar with the characters and challenges of *King's Quest IV: The Perils of Rosella*™, *Return to Zork*™, and such. Computer programmers and designers of software may live in similar or different cultures from computer users. And these computer cultures evolved from the antecedent cultures of math, science, and engineering. For the sake of a manageable focus, however, I use the singular in reference to computer cultures often in this chapter, but attempt to acknowledge specific computer cultures—computer software programming/developing cultures, computer user cultures, and computer documentation cultures when finer distinctions are possible and necessary.

With these antecedents and the plurality of cultures in mind, we can identify what motivates a great deal of feminist scholars' scrutiny of the computer—concern over the number of females who refuse to enter or who self-select out of whatever specific computer culture they encounter, not only as users, but also as programmers and developers. Ultimately, the results of these studies must impact computer documentation and lead to different audience analysis and writing strategies in nonacademic writing.

The essential question then is what kind of computer culture have hardware and software developers, programmers, and documenters cre-ated, and what kind of culture do computer documentation textbooks perpetuate? This question leads to a great many others. How does this computer culture contradict, maintain, or derive from our general social or educational culture? How does the culture of the computer software or hardware developer differ and match the culture of the user? When a user becomes literate in this culture, how is literacy defined, and what symbols and values does it include? Is this computer culture pluralistic in prizing diversity and measuring success in terms of each individual's or each group's needs? Does this computer culture strive for assimilation in emphasizing one group's needs and characteristics above subordinate groups who might be termed dysfunctional in maintaining the dominant group? Or, does this computer culture become a melting pot in which a new blend develops, composed of something from each group that strives to enter into it? (I adapted these terms — *pluralistic, assimilation,* and *melting pot* — and their definitions from Ferdman's [1990] essay on general literacy and cultural diversity.)

In this chapter, I first review the scholarship that illuminates the antecedent scientific and technological cultures of the computer culture, in particular the aspects of these cultures that exclude females or characteristics of traditional femininity. Following this review, I identify how scholars define computer literacy, the initial requirement for entrance into any computer culture. Next, I review studies of women's and men's attitudes toward and experiences with the computer application and programming. I then examine the relationship between these studies and one focus in nonacademic writing — computer documentation. Finally, I suggest what instruments might be incorporated into usability testing and research to enable computer documentation to begin to accommodate diversity.

By looking at the computer culture, researchers of nonacademic writing may better see how social theory and technology could intersect to acknowledge and include diversity among writers and users. In this chapter I very much assume that the computer culture should be pluralistic but is instead quite assimilating, and I acknowledge that computer literacy, as with general literacy as defined by Ferdman (1990), "involves facility in manipulating the symbols that codify and represent the values, beliefs, and norms" of the computer culture, symbols that "incorporate the culture's representations of reality" and the "particularistic definitions of the behaviors and skills a person would need to demonstrate" to be considered literate (p. 187). What complicates my examination of the computer culture is juxtaposing it against women's culture(s) at the same time that I attempt to comment on women's values, beliefs, symbols, and learning styles without falling into an uncomfortable and complete dichotomy of women versus men and women versus computers.

GENDER, TECHNOLOGY, AND SCIENCE: THE SOCIAL AND CULTURAL LINKS

Feminist scholars such as Bleier (1986), Harding (1986), and Keller (1985) have explored how stereotypical masculine features have in the past been assigned to science, often through language. Particularly in Baconian science, both science and men were thought to be objective, rational, logical, and therefore distant from the object of science; that object, in turn, is often nature—subjective, irrational, chaotic, and ultimately female. Within this dichotomy a hierarchy emerged, as science overpowered, penetrated, tamed, and conquered nature, according to the language used in science writing. Moreover, the scientific method discouraged connection between scientist and object—only by distance could the scientist remain objective. Keller (1983), however, proposed that connection and closeness, rather than distance, could produce *good* science in her exploration of scientist Barbara McClintock's work, and later Keller (1992) defined *good* science, as "science that effectively facilitates the material realization of particular goals, that does in fact enable us to change the world in particular ways" (p. 5). A *dynamic*, rather than a *static*, objectivity, proposed Keller, "actively draws on the commonality between mind and nature as a resource for understanding" (p. 117). Within technology, such scholars as Hacker (1982, 1983) found that the "pure" or "hard" sciences often emerged at the top of the scientific cultural hierarchy because of their supposed greater objectivity and distance, and that some higher mathematics, often not a subject in which females are taught to be confident, is a cultural rather than technical requirement for some technical subjects.

A great many scientists and technologists have found this view of their fields difficult to accept, even with its focus on the cultural roots of those fields. However, Keller for one is "not about to recant" her findings—nor is she willing to believe that modern science has shed the trappings of that past. In her recent work, Keller (1992) confirmed her "feeling the need for more attention to the logical and empirical constraints that make scientific claims so compelling to scientists, as well as to the technological prowess that makes them so compelling to the world at large" (p. 3).

This debate over masculine distance and feminine connection continues in feminist scholarship on learning and decision styles. Chodorow (1978), within the object relations school of psychology, provided the foundation for the debate. She found that because, in the pre-Oedipal stages of development, girls see nurturing and connection primarily in their gender role model—the mother—they see empathy for others as part of their identity, whereas boys define themselves as separate and distinct, often within competitive hierarchies. Gilligan (1982) explored how this connecting impulse determines females' moral standards and decisions. Moreover, Belenky and her colleagues (1986) defined how these gender roles influence learning styles. Women reach maturation in thinking and knowing, not when they apply objective standards, the sign of maturity as proposed by theorists who focused primarily on men (see, for example, Piaget & Inhelder, 1958), but when they become "connected" knowers, who balance received knowledge from "authority" with personal feeling and experience.

These studies on learning styles too have been subjected to criticism — not exclusively from scientists and technologists or even traditionalists, but also from other feminists. As differences have been used in the past to exclude, isolate, and disadvantage women, and as some studies have demonstrated greater differences among women than between women and men, some feminists warn of associating certain traits to men and other traits to women. Such a caution is warranted. However, we must recognize and respond to those studies that demonstrate the different ways of knowing of *many* men and *many* women within the computer culture, and, even more importantly, the different ways of knowing that have been culturally assigned to masculinity and femininity as they are manifested in the computer culture. Such recognition, even applied cautiously, should enhance our understanding of how users, developers, and programmers may react to this particular technology and how in our writing we might include, rather than exclude, all of our audiences.

COMPUTER LITERACY

To enter the computer culture, whether in the classroom or workplace, one must become computer literate. To understand the entrance (and perhaps survival) requirements of this culture, *literacy* then must be defined not as knowledge of the vocabulary or syntax of any particular language, but as Schuster (1990) defined *literacy*, from the social constructionist view: "the power to be able to make oneself heard and felt, to signify. Literacy is the way in which we make ourselves meaningful not only to others but through others to ourselves" (p. 227). According to Schuster, because of social, economic, and political action by a dominant culture, illiterate people are "denied genuine listeners, denied response on the part of those whom they are purportedly addressing" (p. 229). According to Schuster, excluded from meaning making, illiterate people must either rebel against accepted speech acts or imitate them. But this imitation may be fruitless, as most imitations are obviously only that, or frustrating, as to imitate often means to deny one's own natural language. Using this definition, one seeking entrance into the computer culture also seeks access to a power structure, a structure that makes meaning and takes on not only a particular vocabulary, but also a way of thinking. In the computer culture, membership in other groups such as those determined by gender role can determine who gains easy access to that meaning making and who is naturally literate. In Ferdman's (1990) terms then, the computer culture will assimilate each individual into the culture, based on that individual's success in becoming literate. Although one gender is not deliberately excluded, just as one ethnic or age group would not be consciously excluded, the individual's ties to other groups would not be considered. And the values, needs, and literacy requirements of those other groups would be unrecognized and inconsequential.

Moreover, the computer culture is often what Papert (1987) termed *technocentric*, in that it makes the technical object central, not the culture that defines and applies the technical object (p. 23). This technocentric facade includes "objectivity." Perry and Greber (1990) said that this facade leads to "technological determinism"—the technical tools are considered neutral; therefore, any change their development or application brings about is considered "inevitable" (p. 75). Thus, some individuals find it not only difficult to enter the culture, but also think it impossible to change the culture.

One valued way of thinking within the computer culture is top-down programming. This method is universally understood by all programmers and to many makes programming as simple and efficient as possible. It is presented, particularly within our educational systems, as the culturally prescribed way of thinking, and, upon learning it, the individual assumes socialization into the culture. According to Benston (1983), a skilled top-down thinker and designer works out the model and goals for a program and then can assign to lower level programmers the task of creating modules within the final program; as a result, "debugging is easier and can be done by workers with even fewer skills, since programming styles are no longer individual" (p. 51). Again, this method of thinking is now taught as the culturally accepted way of thinking in the computer community. As Edwards (1990) said, "In contemporary America, computer work—programming, computer engineering, systems analysis—is more than a job. It is a major cultural practice, a large-scale social form that has created and reinforced modes of thinking, systems of interaction, and ideologies of social contact" (p. 102). To become computer literate as a programmer, one is told to learn and use top-down programming, regardless of individual style and the realities of specific jobs.

Structured programming in a way may reinforce hierarchical thinking in that the designer's plan is much more essential than the modules that are eventually written or imported to fit that designer's plan. Moreover, regardless of how creative and intuitive many designers and programmers actually are, regardless of how many have resisted top-down programming or any such standard in general, the image perpetuated to the illiterate is that the computer culture demands linear, formal thinking, a trait often defined in the broader culture as masculine thinking. Thus, said Edwards (1990), "Computers do not simply embody masculinity; they are culturally constructed as masculine mental objects" (p. 125); computers also "literally embody the split between thought and its objects, act as fundamental paradigms of the rationalistic tradition in the modern West" (p. 108). In important ways, then, to be computer literate appears to many to be rational, in control, rule-oriented, abstract, distant, powerful, and ultimately masculine. Ironically, structured programming is relatively new, having developed out of a much less structured way of programming in the past, a past almost exclusively dominated by male programmers. However, it is the presentation of structured programming — the implications of making it the norm — that are most disturbing.

The issue is further complicated when turning from the computer culture of programmers to that of users. At the same time that some scholars identify the masculine ways of thinking that determine computer literacy and therefore alienate individual women from programming, others see the potential for computers in the workplace and the classroom to empower female users. In discussing the pedagogical impact of technology, Selfe (1990) believes that the technology should help "our profession provide wider and more egalitarian access to reading and writing communities via computer networks, ensure our students increasingly active and collaborative engagements with discourse and text, and broaden our traditional notions of unnegotiated, one-way power relationships between writers and readers" (p. 120). Selfe and others see that such pedagogical strategies as computer conferences remove hierarchical cues, such as race, age, and gender, that disadvantage people in the traditional classroom setting or in face-to-face communication. Moreover, text on a computer is so changeable that meaning making can become two-directional, involving both writers and readers.

The computer culture of programming then, technocentric or technologically determined, presented by seemingly exclusive and perhaps masculine ways of thinking, may be uncomfortable or inaccessible to some women. As Selfe proposed, at the same time, using the computer could be advantageous for women. Are the two cultures — programming/developing and using — distinct in their presentation and links to gender roles? Or does each, despite Selfe's optimism, in its own way alienate? We need to identify more precisely why and when certain women select to avoid the computer. That identification will help us reach the means for broadening computer literacy and apply that identification to nonacademic writing.

WOMEN'S ATTITUDES TOWARD COMPUTERS

Researchers who observe women and computers usually ask about women's attitudes toward and experiences with computers. International quantitative and qualitative studies have discovered the following attitudes among many female users: Technology leads to human isolation, intimidating math skills are required for computer education, aggression and competition mark the computer culture, and those who are intrinsically interested in the computer succeed more than those who want to use it as a tool. For example, Gerver and Lewis (1984) used the work of Gilligan (1982) to speculate that women have more difficulty in "establishing a relationship" with a machine that is perceived as "non-intimate" (p. 11). Durndell (1990) confirmed this speculation in a study of 210 first-year Scottish students in higher education. Thus, women may frequently perceive that the computer culture—from both the point of view of programming/developing and of using—is peopled with machines and lonely humans and does not provide the connections that feminist scholars propose are of primary importance to women. These attitudes appear long before students learn about structured programming.

A second attitude that women might share is that higher mathematics skills are required to understand and use computers—here understanding and using includes both programming and application. For example, in early studies Sherman (1983) concluded that it was neither anxiety nor lack of ability that kept women from mathematics, a prerequisite for computer classes at this time, but "a network of sex-role influences which makes mathematics, and the careers mathematics are needed in, appear incongruent with the female role" (p. 342). Australian researchers Kay, Lublin, Poiner, and Prosser (1989) confirmed that women students drop out of computer education because math is overstressed, and communication or problem-solving skills, seeing how the computer could help people, are undervalued. Also working in Australia, Clarke (1990) confirmed that females often have a more difficult time believing that they are good at math and that their successes in the math and other classes are caused by ability rather than luck until they gain more experience with math and computers. But, they often do not stay in computer classes long enough to gain that experience. Perpetuating the idea that higher level math skills are essential prerequisites to computer success, again found by Hacker and others to be a cultural rather than technical requirement particularly for users, discourages some females initially interested in computing. Thus, women who identify strongly with cultural gender roles and value membership in their gender group will see their entrance into the computer culture as incompatible or inappropriate. Of course, individual members of each group—gender and computer—will vary to the extent they "perceive specific attributes as central to their cultural identity and in the value they give these attributes" (as Ferdman [1990, p. 194] would say of ethnic groups). However, both groups send strong messages about gender roles as they are perpetuated within the family, the media, and, to a great extent, the educational system, and about computer thinking as it is almost exclusively taught in classrooms and textbooks.

Researchers also propose that computer classrooms are characterized by aggression and competition. Clarke found that within programming classes, students are "encouraged to compete with each others to complete a program first or to complete it in the fewest number of lines" (p. 60). In lower grades boys often literally push girls aside to occupy the machines. Moreover, researchers Durndell, Siann, and Glissov (1990) working in Scotland discovered that female students take a more "pragmatic, instrumental or practical approach to technology." Females see the computer as "a means to an end," whereas males view computer as more "intrinsically attractive and interesting" (p. 150). Clarke (1990) also found that Australian female students want to treat the computer as a tool and are more interested in what it can do than why (p. 58). In these studies, females appear to find entry into the culture of computer users more acceptable than the culture of computer programmers. However, many computer classes, regardless of the emphasis, make the computer the content of the class, not the application.

Finally, some researchers observing computer anxiety in both the classroom and the workplace determine that lack of computer experience, rather than gender, often leads to negative attitudes toward the computer. For example, Ray and Minch (1990) developed a computer alienation and a computer anxiety scale to assess attitudes of undergraduate and graduate students in marketing and management information systems. In particular, they looked for feelings of powerlessness, "normlessness," meaninglessness, social isolation, self-estrangement, and cultural estrangement. They found that older students and those with less experience feel most alienated and anxious about the computer. In studies of male and female managers, Parasuraman and Igbaria (1990) discovered that computer anxiety seems to be a matter of age, gender, education, and personality. And, in a more recent study, Igbaria and Parasuraman (1991) observed that managers are more comfortable using the computer if they have computer experience, user training, and organizational support. The higher the level of management men and women achieve, the less difference in their computer anxiety. Of course, if females select to avoid the computer in the classroom, they will arrive at the workplace without experience — and so will demonstrate the kind of computer anxiety and alienation that these three studies found in less experienced users.

We must then assess how these attitudes — sense of isolation, lack of confidence in math skills, dislike of competition and aggression, and desire to use the computer as a tool rather than as focus in a course — manifest themselves when many women seek and gain computer literacy. Because the studies cited earlier tend to look at specific classes — some programming classes and some application classes, some peopled with young students and some with college-age students — it is difficult to speculate whether beginning users are more or less alienated than beginning programmers. However, given these studies of attitude, believing that computers can remove hierarchical barriers to communication seems less universally possible. Again, the image and presentation of the computer alienates, not the technology itself. When examining women's actual experiences with the computer, we do see both experiences that reinforce (and perhaps initiate) and experiences that negate women's suspicions about and discomfort with computers.

WOMEN'S EXPERIENCES WITH COMPUTERS

Experience with the computer can start at an early age for both boys and girls—computer games and camps invite them not only to learn elementary programming, but also to associate the computer with entertainment. Yet even at this early age gender makes a difference in computer experience. Boys are three times more likely than girls to participate in computer clubs, attend a computer camp, and use a computer at home (Kramer & Lehman, 1990, p. 158). Moreover, because computer games are primarily designed to interest boys, boys gain more early computer experience. As Hakansson (1990) found, "Because of their more extensive experience with computer games, boys have learned and are more comfortable with traditional computer interfaces. What is daunting to a girl, or to any novice user, has been overcome by boys in pursuit of computer game experiences that are geared to traditionally male themes of conflict, competition, and sports" (p. 126). In their study of computer games, Kiesler et al. (1985) found that the covers of computer games seldom feature women (about 28 men to 4 women), and when the games do, women appear in such ways as the fat queen in *Palace in Thunderland*™ or the princess in a supplicating position in *Wizard and the Princess*™. Lest we think computer games not important, Kiesler et al. remind us, "Playfulness, foolishness, coping with challenge, and exploration are all part of learning to compute, of studying computers, and of working with them" (p. 457). Thus boys seem to receive much more encouragement than do girls to enter the computer culture and will be more experienced when they enter computer classes either as users or programmers.

Moreover, several researchers propose that the programming language that young female and male computer users first encounter may make a difference in positive versus negative experiences. For example, Kiesler et al. (1985), Sanders (1984, p. 33), and others feel that Logo is much more interesting to females than Basic and other languages. Other scholars propose that the arrangement of the computer classroom may make a difference; if chairs are arranged so that students can work in groups, rather than in isolation, females are often much happier (see, for example, Sanders, 1984, p. 33).

However, some studies do find that experiences with computer collaboration, conferencing, and networking activities engage female computer users to the greatest extent. All three of these experiences reinforce what Belenky, Clinchy, Goldberger, and Tarule (1986), Chodorow (1978), and Gilligan (1982) propose is the preferred way of learning for women — connecting with others. Communicating via computer networks seem to be one way that isolated women users can connect (see, for example, Smith & Balka, 1988). Conferencing with classmates allows students to discuss freely ideas that they might hesitate or not be encouraged to bring up in the classroom (see, for example, Jessup, 1991). In conferencing, the computer provides a nonhierarchical tool for exchanging ideas by diminishing authority. Cooper and Selfe (1990) believe:

> that the success of computer conferences as non-traditional academic forums is due to three influences: the synergistic effect of written conversation, dialogue, and exchange; the shift in power and control from a teacher-centered forum to a student-centered one; and the liberating influence of the electronic medium within which the conferences occur. (pp. 857–858)

Collaboration diminishes the feeling of isolation among female computer users (see, for example, Flores, 1990; Hawkins, 1985). In fact, a great deal of research done on computers and composition has centered on the value of using the technology to enhance collaboration. (Even writers of composition textbooks for the computer classroom document their successes using the computer in their own collaboration [see, for example, Duin & Gorak, 1992].)

Thus, to ensure that female computers users enter computer cultures with positive attitudes, it seems more beneficial to offer them early experiences that build on their desire to connect with others in the learning and application process. What is valued in their gender group could then be valued in the computer culture. However, we need to look at one more — and perhaps even more essential — invitation or barrier into the computer culture before turning to nonacademic writing about the computer: learning styles.

GENDER AND COMPUTER LEARNING STYLES

Because Belenkey et al. (1986), Gilligan (1982), and other feminist scholars propose that gender often determines learning style, it is important to test this claim in the computer culture. Attitude and experience with computers would result, to a great extent, from whether a beginning programmer's or user's learning style was accommodated. Some researchers find that even after extensive computer experience and even when females claim the computer strongly as their own, many males still feel more comfortable with the computer (see, for example, Wilder, Mackie, & Cooper, 1985, p. 226) or those who identify with traditionally masculine traits feel more comfortable (see, for example, Ogletree & Williams, 1990, whose use of the Bem Sex Role Inventory is discussed later). These quantitative studies demonstrate that gender and computer learning style affect computer confidence and success in achieving computer literacy in the broadest sense, whether the focus is the student user or student programmer.

A recent study by Davidson, Savenye, and Orr (1992), using Gregorc's measure of learning ability, identified more specifically which learning style might best accommodate computer use. Gregorc's instrument tests which of four styles dominate in an individual: concrete sequential, abstract sequential, abstract random, and concrete random. Davidson et al. hypothesized that students who preferred step-by-step procedures and abstract thinking would enjoy computers more than those who enjoyed "exploring information in their own manner" and tended to be "concrete-based learners" (pp. 350–351). They found that indeed students, whether male or female, with an abstract-sequential style performed best on computer projects and exams and proposed that more students might be successful in computer courses if they were aware of their own particular learning styles.

Perhaps Turkle and Papert (1990) have done the most critical work so far in exploring computer learning style and success, and in linking learning style to gender when studying student programmers. Without accommodating Turkle and Papert's work in nonacademic writing and research, scholars of nonacademic writing will simply reify the computer culture as described by Edwards and others. Turkle and Papert confirmed that "diversity in the practice of computing . . . is denied by its social construction" (p. 128). To reach epistemological pluralism, Turkle and Papert believe that the computer culture must acknowledge and accommodate what they term *bricoleurs*. Turkle and Papert borrowed Levi-Strauss's definition of *bricolage* as the science of the concrete, but depart from Piaget in identifying this concrete knowing as a style, not a stage, in intellectual development. They believe that top-down structured programming style enforces a learning style or way of thinking that makes it difficult for many to become computer literate. However, if the computer culture would recognize epistemological diversity, then Turkle and Papert are as optimistic as such scholars as Selfe. "As a carrier for pluralistic ideas about approaches to knowledge," Turkle and Papert said, "the computer may hold the promise of catalyzing change not only within the computer culture but in the culture at large" (p. 133).

Turkle and Papert's bricoleurs, many but not all of whom are female, tend to anthropomorphize the computer and seek transparency, closeness, and visual manipulation when learning and using the computer. They resist the opacity of the top-down, hierarchical approach, in which black-boxed modules are hidden or created after the programming plan is confirmed. Bricoleurs learn the elements of a program by moving them around "almost as though they were material elements" (p. 136); "While hierarchy and abstraction are valued by the structured programmers' planner's aesthetic, bricoleur programmers prefer negotiation and rearrangement of their materials" (p. 136). In earlier work, Turkle (1984) found that the girls often try to "forge relationships with the computer that bypass objectivity altogether. They tend to see computational objects as sensuous and tactile and relate to the computer's formal system not as a set of unforgiving 'rules,' but as a language for communicating with, negotiating with, a behaving, psychological entity" (pp. 108–109; see also Turkle, 1988). Turkle and Papert (1990) documented a very different learning style, one that seems to be found in more females than males, that fails to be accommodated in the computer culture; in fact, because they resist black-boxing and top-down programming, bricoleurs are often considered computer illiterate and certainly would be as defined by Schuster (1990). And, if indeed the computer culture is based on assimilation, the bricoleurs are seen as dysfunctional until they achieve enough power, and a few do, to be considered eccentric instead.

Thus we have a perplexing mixture of research into gender and computer cultures. Structured, top-down programming is now the norm. It is a norm that individual software developers and programmers may actually resist, but a way of thinking that is presented in many programming classes and work situations as the sanctioned one. This presentation carries what some researchers see as an uncomfortable link to traditional masculinity and fails to accommodate and encourage a bricoleur style. In turn, we see diverse studies that find attitudes and experiences toward computer programming and application differ for some men and for some women. In some cases, negative experiences lead to negative attitudes, and in other cases, negative attitudes are overturned by positive experiences. The majority of the studies propose that women's attitudes and experiences with computer application, particularly with computer programming, may be more negative than men's. Only studies on collaboration, networking, and conferencing suggest strongly that these computer applications can benefit women by overturning a cultural disregard for their voices.

Grouping all these studies for review and speculating about their universal meaning is dangerous, as the research remains at the stage of individual case studies. Leaping from studies about computer programmers and users to computer documentation writers crosses into yet another culture. Yet such a review at least enables us to ask some essential questions about our own field—nonacademic writing—within a new context. For example, if computer documentation perpetuates any tendency to ignore diversity in computer learning styles, then writers do their users quite a disservice. In turn, if textbooks on computer documentation ignore diversity in thinking and writing about the computer, then textbook authors do their student writers a disservice.

A CRITICAL LOOK AT COMPUTER DOCUMENTATION TEXTS AND RESEARCH

Three challenging questions emerge when examining just a few computer documentation texts and research studies. What diversity is possible and beneficial when developing computer documentation? What diversity in that documentation is possible and beneficial to accommodate different types of users? And what images within the documentation invite diverse users into the computer culture? In this chapter, these questions cannot be answered completely, but it can be seen if they are at least being raised.

To examine the first question—what diversity is possible and beneficial when developing computer documentation?—I look at Weiss's (1991) popular *How to Write Usable User Documentation*. Although Weiss recognized different ways of knowing and writing about computers, he prioritized those ways. For example, Weiss distinguished between the *artist,* who puts "little effort" into planning his or her documentation, but whose biggest effort comes with drafting and patching up problems in documentation, and the *engineer*, whose main effort goes into the planning stages of definition, design, and modeling (p. 40). Weiss's artist seems quite similar to the bricoleur (in fact, many of the bricoleurs that Turkle and Papert studied were artists or musicians) in wanting to "play" with the program before committing to a plan. However, Weiss cautioned his readers that "when the projects get complicated and the stakes get high, the artist should yield to the engineer" (p. 41).

Moreover, Weiss stated, "In sum, what documenters must learn from the history of programming is the craft of *top-down design and testing"* (p. 43). His recommendation to imitate the style of "formal, explicit, rule-abiding" top-down programming is based on the same values that Benston (1983) recognized in the computer culture—efficiency and cost over individual style (Weiss, 1991, p. 48). Weiss made absolutely clear the connection between computer programming cultures and computer documentation cultures: "The same structured methods used to make programs and systems most cost effective and maintainable can be applied directly to the job of designing and writing user documentation, and with similar benefits" (p. 49). The documentation writer then "starts with the biggest picture possible, the whole system, with all its interfaces, and adds overlays of detail in successive stages. And at each consecutive level it is tested, using 'stubs' or dummies for the processes below that level" (p. 48).

Again, if there are bricoleur programmers, there are probably bricoleur writers—those who prefer to see and manipulate the elements of a document before creating an outline. That is not to say that these bricoleur writers should not analyze their audience, purpose, and situation, but that they might prefer to write a small portion of the document, an example or sample paragraph, before settling on a plan. Weiss's textbook leaves little room for that kind of writer. Literacy, then, to a computer documentation writer seems to mean a top-down manipulation of symbols and cultural "representation of reality" (Ferdman, 1990, p. 187).

Shneiderman's (1987) *Designing the User Interface: Strategies for Effective Human-Computer Interaction* provides focus for the second question— what diversity in that documentation is possible and beneficial to accommodate different types of users? Shneiderman recognized that writers' styles may not always match users' preferences: "A right-handed male designer with computer training and a desire for rapid interaction using densely packed screens may have a hard time developing a successful workstation for left-handed women artists with a more leisurely and free-form work style" (p. 18). Whether he meant to or not, Shneiderman's example acknowledges possible difference assigned to gender (his male designer and woman artist), although when he later listed measurable human factors "central to evaluation" and "factors affecting perceptual motor performance," he mentioned age but not gender, subjective satisfaction but not what might contribute to that satisfaction (pp. 14, 22). Shneiderman did advise the interface designer that a clear "understanding of personality and cognitive styles can be helpful in designing systems for a specific community of users" and discusses the "fundamental" differences between men's and women's preferences in computer games and women's responses to computer directions such as "kill" and "abort" (p. 23). Moreover, Shneiderman encourages an interactive style in computer interface design—one that encourages direct manipulation in which tasks are visually presented and easy to learn and retain, and in which exploration is encouraged. This style, Shneiderman cautioned, may be hard to program and may require graphics displays and pointing devices, but will lead to "high subjective satisfaction" for many users (p. 58). Finally, and perhaps most importantly, Shneiderman ascribed to Carroll and Rosson's (1985) definition of *design*: "Design is a process. . . . The design process is *nonhierarchical*; it is neither strictly bottom-up nor strictly top-down. . . . The process is radically transformational; it involves the development of particle and interim solutions that may ultimately play no role in the final design. . . . Design intrinsically involves the *discovery of new goals*" (quoted in Shneiderman, 1987, p. 390). Although it is certainly not the primary mission of his book,

Shneiderman does make his reader aware of user differences. Shneiderman introduced a pluralistic computer culture to his student documentation writer, one that would accommodate membership in other groups and the features and symbols of those other groups.

Other documentation texts allow for some diversity among users, but do not acknowledge gender. For example, Horton's (1990) well-respected *Designing and Writing Online Documentation* recommends transparency in "on-line-human dialog" so that a user will get a clear view of information sought or manipulated (p. 32). However, Horton, as do most textbook writers, classified users as novices, occasional users, transfer users (moving from a familiar system to a new one), and experts; he did not recognize ethnicity, age, gender, and familiarity with English in this classification. He did recommend that writers acknowledge the mental model that a user forms of the system; although the interactive program determines that model, Horton did stress the importance of the user knowing the systems "scheme of visual symbology and its pattern of responses" (p. 38). Thus Horton's writers could allow their bricoleur users to "see" the system. However, Horton also advised writers to avoid the "obstacle of animism" or the tendency to "design systems that mimic human characteristics," and recommended chunking and an hierarchical organization, which would inevitably include modular design (p. 44). Horton recommended, "Progressively disclose information, one layer at a time. Start with a small amount of simple information and, as users request, display more complex, detailed information" (p. 125). Again, although Horton did not discuss gender difference (or to a great extent any difference other than experiential), within his recommendations, a writer could find room to design for different learning styles. That writer, however, would have to come to the task and Horton's book with a knowledge of gender difference.

Finally, the writers in one of the latest and most comprehensive research collections on computer documentation, Barker's (1991) *Perspectives on Software Documentation: Inquiries and Innovations*, could have provided an initial focus for the third question — what images within the documentation invite diverse users into the computer culture? But the gaps, rather than information, within this collection demonstrate how in an otherwise excellent collection, gender diversity is generally ignored. For example, whereas in her essay in the Barker collection, Bell (1991) mentioned the problems with metaphors and ambiguity for nonnative English speakers, she did not caution her readers to avoid metaphors that exclude women (p. 85). Perhaps Bell assumes that programmers and writers no longer called for users to "kill" or "abort." Moreover, when Grice and Ridgway (1991) cautioned, "If a product is likely to be used only by men, it is important for men to be evaluators" in the documentation testing stage, they provide no information on how writers design documentation for members of a gender group who identify strongly with the group values, characteristics, and learning styles (p. 220). Finally, in Oram's (1991) essay, "The Hidden Effects of Computer Engineering on User Documentation," in which he deals with the difficulty of writing about important but general modular functions, no mention is made of how modularity might include or exclude diverse learning styles.

The questions of what diversity is possible and beneficial when developing computer documentation and what diversity in that documentation is possible and beneficial to accommodate different types of users are indeed challenging, and at the moment we have made very few attempts to address, let alone answer them, in not only our research, but also our teaching through textbooks. The third question—what images within the documentation invite diverse users into the computer culture?—is much easier to answer and address.

Integrating Gender into Computer Documentation

Applying the results of feminist scholarship to computer documentation writing and research can be done in two ways: We can attempt to make this type of nonacademic writing gender-neutral (e.g., Ferdman's [1990] melting pot literacy); or we can attempt to accommodate gender difference (pluralism). Again, the first effort is much easier; excellent guides exist to help the writer eliminate sex-biased language from documentation (see, for example, Frank & Treichler, 1989). Writers can also select appropriate metaphors for computer functions. For example, Erickson (1990) included in his checklist for selecting an interface metaphor such questions as "How much of the structure does the metaphor provide, how relevant is the metaphor to the problem, how easy is it to present the interface metaphor, is the metaphor *suitable to the audience*?" (p. 65; emphasis added). If the writer remembers that both genders potentially make up that audience, then the documentation could be gender-neutral.

Accommodating gender difference is more difficult but much more important than gender neutrality. For example, if some users, particularly female users, indeed appreciate personification or what Laurel (1990) termed "metaphors with character," then the task calls for the writer to go beyond language. Laurel found the tendency to personify to be a "natural and universal" impulse and the tasks that computers perform for their users require that they "express two distinctly anthropomorphic qualities: *responsiveness* and that capacity to *perform actions*" (p. 358). The "metaphor of agency" then, said Laurel, is fleshed out when the user knows through the metaphor what unique skills, expertise, and predisposition in terms of character traits the particular tool or application possesses. In other words, Laurel acknowledges that impulse to personify through metaphor what the program is designed to do for the user. Building the software and documentation around this metaphor could very well accommodate any female or male users who tend to want this personification. Moreover, Laurel noted that "the agent must be able to distinguish among users, at least on the basis of experience and preferences, in order to be genuinely responsive" (p. 361). If this flexibility is indeed possible, then the documentation could accommodate difference based on gender identity.

The issue of personification in research, however, whether completed by feminist scholars, nonacademic writing scholars, or computing education scholars, is contradictory and incomplete. For example, Hall and Cooper (1990) found that their *male* subjects tended to personify the computer *more* than their female counterparts, but Hall and Cooper speculated that this tendency resulted from males' greater sense of control over the machine and from females' reaction to a "faceless" object that lacked the nonverbal elements to make communication "more complete" for them (p. 58). Researchers Oren, Salomon, Kreitman, and Don (1990) found value in anthropomorphizing the interface agent rather than the machine itself so that users could "engage, project, and suspend disbelief" (p. 376). Ridgway, Grice, and Gould (1992) recommended a transactional analysis approach to computer-human dialogs in which the user perceives an adult-adult collaboration partnership with the computer. However, Burchard and Dragga (1989) found that their student subjects resented attempts to make the computer sound "human" in feedback given during computer-based instruction. It is obvious that much more research on preference of computer personification needs to be done.

Perhaps less contradictory but still somewhat incomplete is the research on icons as well as visual metaphors and manipulation. Turkle and Papert (1990) found that bricoleurs want icons and visual metaphors — so much so that Turkle and Papert speculated that bricoleurs, again many of whom are female, may have "friendlier relationships mediated by the icons, the mouse, and the cozier appearance of a Macintosh" (p. 154). Although many researchers of nonacademic writing believe that standardized icons, especially ones that are close to metaphors, shorten the learning process, they have not merged the research done on bricoleur preference with their own (see, for example, Gurak, 1992).

If computer documentation researchers lag behind in learning how to accommodate gender difference, perhaps the recent research on collaboration may lead the way. Appropriate metaphors, icons, and personification, as Ridgway et al. (1992) mentioned, create collaboration between user and computer. Also, recent studies of the computer and collaboration describe how the technology gives writing teams positive ways to plan, draft, and edit documents (see, for example, Duin, Jorn, & DeBower, 1991; Van Pelt & Gilliam, 1991). Nonacademic writing researchers might use their knowledge about collaboration to accommodate those users who need visualization and connection in computer documentation.

Testing Gender Response to Computer Documentation

Nonacademic writing researchers could begin discovering how to accommodate difference in documentation, how to make computer literacy available broadly regardless of membership in other cultural groups, by testing what individual male and female users find effective in documentation. This effort addresses in specific and concrete terms the second and third questions that emerged earlier in this chapter: What diversity in that documentation is possible and beneficial to accommodate different types of users? What images within the documentation invite diverse users into the computer culture? Building on Grice and Ridgway's (1990) admonition to be aware of gender difference or identity in users, researchers could test and analyze what users with different gender identities or learning styles seem to prefer in documentation. As Haselkorn (1988) suggested, writers should test documentation "not only to adjust documentation, but to feed results back into design and development" (p. 8). Again, very few nonacademic writing researchers have suggested that this testing include a look at difference based on gender identification (for the few who have looked at gender and technical writing, see, for example, Allen, 1991; Bernhardt, 1992; Bosley, 1992; Dell, 1992; Lay, 1991; Raign & Sims, 1993; Sauer, 1993; Tebeaux, 1990). To look at difference based on gender identity, researchers would have to combine existing nonacademic writing testing instruments with gender research instruments.

For example, Shneiderman (1987) has an extensive testing device, "User Evaluation of Interactive Computer Systems," that asks the user to react to such features as frequency of computer terms, instructions for getting help, amount of feedback, display layouts, pace of interaction, helpfulness of error messages, and getting started features (pp. 402–407). Shneiderman's instrument is thorough, yet typical, of such instruments, in that it distinguishes primarily between experts' and novices' reactions to the documentation. On the other hand, McCormick and McCoy (1990) applied a multicultural, nonsexist test to computer software that assesses "elements of invisibility, stereotyping, selectivity and imbalance, unreality, linguistic bias, and fragmentation and isolation" (p. 107). Researchers who look for these features can ensure that documentation is gender-neutral.

Moreover, feminist communication scholars as well as some computer education researchers have found the Bem Sex Role Inventory (BSRI) useful in assessing how closely subjects identify with typical "masculine" or "feminine" features as "independent," "analytical," "sensitive to the needs of others," and "competitive" (Bem, 1977). Ogletree and Williams (1990) used the BSRI to test computer attitudes and aptitude and found, "masculinity significantly related to more positive computer attitudes for females, and to confidence in completing computer science coursework for both females and males" (p. 710). Researchers who use the BSRI must remember that one is measuring how closely the subject identifies with typical masculine traits, not whether one is male or female. However, combining the BSRI and McCormick and McCoy's multicultural nonsexist test with traditional documentation testing instruments could be the first step toward accommodating gender difference.

Again, nonacademic writing researchers who wish to test the effect of gender identity on computer satisfaction should look carefully at Igbaria and Parasuraman's (1991, pp. 558–563) questionnaire. This questionnaire can be applied also to the Myers-Briggs Type Indicator; Davidson's use of Gregorc's identification of concrete sequential, abstract sequential, abstract random, and concrete random style; and Ray and Minch's (1990, p. 483) 14 computer alienation items. All these instruments suggest how difference, based on gender or otherwise, can be accommodated in computer use.

CONCLUSION

In the last 20 years, nonacademic writing research has probably been influenced more by and observed more of the computer culture than any of the other scientific and engineering cultures. Tebeaux is correct in recognizing the need for workers in the 21st century to "learn new software rapidly and to integrate new technology with old"—what she defined as *computer literacy*. But we must also ask if, as technical and professional communication researchers, teachers, and textbook writers, we are perpetuating a computer culture and literacy with all its traditions. These include its suspected failure to accommodate differences in learning style. Or are we challenging that culture, as are feminist scholars and computer education and human factors researchers? Are we finding ways to use the computer to accommodate difference based on membership in other groups, such as gender, or are we imitating ways of thinking that prioritize some values and exclude others? I believe we have not bridged the gap between what feminist scholars—those who look at our broader culture and those who look specifically at the computer culture—say about gender identity and learning style and what we say in nonacademic writing teaching and research.

One immediate way to bridge that gap does exist. In the classroom and workplace, computer collaboration, conferencing, and networking, and in computer documentation, selection of metaphor, icons, visual manipulation, and personification represent specific and concrete ways of accommodating diversity, including possible gender difference. In our testing of documentation effectiveness, we need to research and apply what gender preferences we discover. We need to test each piece of documentation by questioning such characteristics: If those who test high in femininity on the Bem Sex Role Inventory (or perhaps Turkle and Papert's [1990] bricoleurs) find learning a new system satisfying as they first experiment with an example and then learn a method, does our documentation contain such opportunities to experiment? We need to integrate measures used by feminist scholars into our traditional documentation testing instruments.

We must recognize and measure not only males who strongly identify with traditional masculine traits, but also males who identify with traditional feminine traits, with females who score high in femininity on the BSRI, and with females who score low. We must write for not only females and males who strongly prefer the bricoleur style, but males and females who function well with top-down structure. We must write for women who have little confidence with math skills and who have not had experience with computers before they encounter our documentation and for males who have experienced the opposite — or perhaps the same. Accommodating gender difference leads us to accommodating individual difference, whether based on gender, age, experience, race, economic and education background or culture of origin. Fortunately, feminist scholars have already begun the work of recognizing and measuring difference. We need to learn what they have to say and follow their lead if our nonacademic writing research and practice is to be successful. Moreover, this venture into difference grants us insight into how technology and social theory intersect with and illuminate each other.

REFERENCES

Allen, J. (1991). Gender issues in technical communication studies: An overview of the implications for the profession, research, and pedagogy. *Journal of Business and Technical Communication, 5*(4), 371–392.

Barker, T. (Ed.). (1991). *Perspectives on software documentation: Inquiries and innovations.* Amityville, NY: Baywood.

Belenky, M., Clinchy, B. M., Goldberger, N. R., & Tarule, J. M. (1986). *Women's ways of knowing: The development of self, voice, and mind.* New York: Basic Books.

Bell, P. (1991). Cognitive writing: A new approach to organizing technical material. In T. Barker (Ed.), *Perspectives on software documentation: Inquiries and innovations* (pp. 73–89). Amityville, NY: Baywood.

Bem, S. L. (1977). On the utility of alternative procedures for assessing psychological androgyny. *Journal of Consulting and Clinical Psychology, 45,* 196–205.

Benston, M. L. (1983). For women, the chips are down. In J. Zimmerman (Ed.), *The technological woman: Interfacing with tomorrow* (pp. 44–54). New York: Praeger.

Bernhardt, S. A. (1992). The design of sexism: The case of an army maintenance manual.

IEEE Transactions on Professional Communication, 35(4), 217–221.

Bleier, R. (1986). Lab coat: Robe of innocence or Klansman's sheet? In T. de Lauretis (Ed.), *Feminist studies/Critical studies* (pp. 55–66). Bloomington: Indiana University Press.

Bosley, D. S. (1992). Gender and visual communication: Toward a feminist theory of design. *IEEE Transactions on Professional Communication, 35*(4), 222–229.

Burchard, G., & Dragga, S. (1989). Computer-based instruction and the humanizing impulse. *Technical Communication, 36*(1), 13–18.

Carroll, J. M., & Rosson, M. (1985). Usability specifications as a tool in iterative development. In H. R. Hartson (Ed.), *Advances in human-computer interaction* (pp. 1–28). Norwood, NJ: Ablex.

Chodorow, N. (1978). *The reproduction of mothering: Psychoanalysis and the sociology of gender.* Berkeley: University of California Press.

Clarke, V. (1990). Sex differences in computing participation: Concerns, extent, reasons, and strategies. *Australian Journal of Education, 34*(1), 52–66.

Cooper, M., & Selfe, C. (1990). Computer conferences and learning: Authority, resistance, and internally persuasive discourse. *College English, 52*(8), 847–869.

Davidson, G., V., Savenye, W. C., & Orr, K. (1992). How do learning styles relate to performance in a computer applications course? *Journal of Research on Computing in Education, 24*(3), 348–358.

Dell, S. (1992). A communication-based theory of the glass ceiling: Rhetorical sensitivity and upward mobility within the technical organization. *IEEE Transactions on Professional Communication, 35*(4), 230–235.

Duin, A. H., & Gorak, K. (1992). Developing tests for computers and composition: A collaborative process. *Computers and Composition, 9*(2), 15–39.

Duin, A. H., Jorn, L., & DeBower, M. (1991). Collaborative writing: Courseware and telecommunications. In M. Lay & W. Karis (Eds.), *Collaborative writing in industry: Investigations in theory and practice* (pp. 146–169). Amityville, NY: Baywood.

Durndell, A. (1990). Why do female students tend to avoid computer studies? *Research in Science & Technological Education, 8*(2), 163–170.

Durndell, A., Siann, G., & Glissov, P. (1990). Gender differences and computing in course choice at entry into higher education. *British Educational Research Journal, 16*(2), 149–162.

Edwards, P. N. (1990). The army and the microworld: Computers and the politics of gender identity. *Signs, 16*(1), 102–127.

Erickson, T. D. (1990). Working with interface metaphors. In B. Laurel (Ed.), *The art of human-computer interface design* (pp. 65–73). Reading, MA: Addison-Wesley.

Ferdman, B. (1990). Literacy and cultural identity. *Harvard Educational Review, 60*(2), 181–204.

Flores, M. J. (1990). Computer conferencing: Composing a feminist community of writers. In C. Handa (Ed.), *Computers and community: Teaching composition in the 21st century* (pp. 106–117). Portsmouth, NH: Boynton/Cook, Heinemann.

Frank, F. W., & Treichler, P. (Eds.). (1989). *Language, gender, and professional writing: Theoretical approaches and guidelines for nonsexist usage.* New York: Modern Language Association.

Gerver, E., & Lewis, L. (1984). Women, computers and adult education: Liberation or oppression? *Convergence, 17*(4), 5–15.

Gilligan, C. (1982). *In a different voice: Psychological theory and women's development.* Cambridge, MA: Harvard University Press.

Grice, R., & Ridgway, L. S. (1990). Information product testing: An integral part of information development. In T. Barker (Ed.), *Perspectives on software documentation: Inquiries and innovations* (pp. 209–228). Amityville, NY: Baywood.

Gurak, L. J. (1992). Toward consistency in visual information: Standardized icons based on task. *Technical Communication, 39*(1), 33–37.

Hacker, S. L. (1982). The culture of engineering: Woman, workplace, and machine. In J. Rothschild (Ed.), *Women, technology, and innovation* (pp. 341–353). New York: Pergamon.

Hacker, S. L. (1983). Mathematization of engineering: Limits on women and the field. In J. Rothschild (Ed.), *Machina ex dea* (pp. 38–58). New York: Pergamon.

Hakansson, J. (1990). Lessons learned from kids: One developer's point of view. In B. Laurel (Ed.), *The art of human-computer interface design* (pp. 123–131). Reading, MA: Addison-Wesley.

Hall, J., & Cooper J. (1990). Gender, experience and attributions to the computer. *Journal of Educational Computing Research, 7*(1), 51–60.

Harding, S. (1986). *The science question in feminism.* Ithaca, NY: Cornell University Press.

Haselkorn, M. P. (1988). The future of "writing" for the computer industry. In E. Barrett (Ed.), *Text, context, and hypertext* (pp. 3–13). Cambridge, MA: MIT Press.

Hawkins, J. (1985). Computers and girls: Rethinking the issues. *Sex Roles, 13*(3/4), 165–180.

Horton, W. K. (1990). *Designing and writing online documentation: Help files to hypertext.* New York: Wiley.

Igbaria, M., & Parasuraman, S. (1991). Attitudes toward microcomputers: Development and construct validation of a measure. *International Journal of Man-Machine Studies, 35,* 553–573.

Jessup, E. (1991). Feminism and computers in composition instruction. In G. Hawisher & C. Selfe (Eds.), *Evolving perspectives on computers and composition studies: Questions for the 1990s* (pp. 336–355). Urbana, IL: National Council of Teachers of English.

Kay, J., Lublin, J., Poiner, G., & Prosser, M. (1989). Not even well begun: Women in computing courses. *Higher Education, 18*(5), 511–527.

Keller, E. F. (1983). *A feeling for the organism.* San Francisco: Freeman.

Keller, E. F. (1985). *Reflections on gender and science.* New Haven, CT: Yale University Press.

Keller, E. F. (1992). *Secrets of life/Secrets of death: Essays on language, genderr and science.* New York: Routledge & Kegan Paul.

Kiesler, S., Sproull, L., & Eccles, J. (1985). Pool halls, chips, and war games: Women in the culture of computing. *Psychology of Women Quarterly, 9,* 451–462.

Kramer, P. E., & Lehman, S. (1990). Mismeasuring women: A critique of research on computer ability and avoidance. *Signs, 16*(1), 158–172.

Kuhn, T. (1970). *The structure of scientific revolutions.* Chicago: University of Chicago Press.

Laurel, B. (1990). Interface agents: Metaphors with character. In B. Laurel (Ed.), *The art of human-computer interface design* (pp. 355–365). Reading, MA: Addison-Wesley.

Lay, M. M. (1991). Feminist theory and the redefinition of technical communication. *Journal of Business and Technical Communication, 5*(4), 348–370.

McCormick, T. E., & McCoy, S. B. (1990). Computer-assisted instruction and multicultural nonsexist education: A caveat for those who select and design software. *Computers in the Schools, 7*(4), 105–124.

Ogletree, S. M., & Williams, S. (1990). Sex and sex-typing effects on computer attitudes and aptitude. *Sex Roles, 23*(11/12), 703–712.

Oram, A. (1991). The hidden effects of computer engineering on user documentation. In T. Barker (Ed.), *Perspectives on software documentation: Inquiries and innovations* (pp. 103–122). Amityville, NY: Baywood.

Oren, T., Salomon, G., Kreitman, K., & Don, A. (1990). Guides: Characterizing the interface. In B. Laurel (Ed.), *The art of human-computer interface design* (pp. 367–381). Reading, MA: Addison-Wesley.

Papert, S. (1987). Computer criticism vs. technocentric thinking. *Educational Researcher, 16*(1), 22–30.

Parasuraman, S., & Igbaria, M. (1990). An examination of gender differences in the determinants of computer anxiety and attitudes toward microcomputers among managers. *International Journal of Man-Machine Studies, 32*, 327–340.

Perry, R., & Greber, L. (1990). Women and computers: An introduction. *Signs, 16*(1), 74–101.

Piaget, J., & Inhelder, B. (1958). *The growth of logical thinking from childhood to adolescence.* New York: Basic Books.

Raign, K. R., & Sims, B. R. (1993). Gender, persuasion techniques, and collaboration. *Technical Communication Quarterly, 2*(1), 89–104.

Ray, N. M., & Minch, R. P. (1990). Computer anxiety and alienation: Toward a definitive and parsimonious measure. *Human Factors, 32*(4), 477–491.

Ridgway, L. S., Grice, R. A., & Gould, E. (1992). I'm OK; You're only a user: A transactional analysis of computer-human dialogs. *Technical Communication, 39*(1), 38–49.

Sanders, J. S. (1984, April). The computer: Male, female or androgynous? *The Computing Teacher*, pp. 31–33.

Sauer, B. A. (1993). Sense and sensibility in technical documentation: How feminist interpretation strategies can save lives in the nation's mines. *Journal of Business and Technical Communication, 7*(1), 63–83.

Schuster, C. (1990). The ideology of illiteracy: A Bakhtinian perspective. In A. Lunsford, H. Moglen, & J. Slevin (Eds.), *The right to literacy* (pp. 225–232). New York: Modern Language Association.

Selfe, C. L. (1990). Technology in the English classroom: Computers through the lens of feminist theory. In C. Handa (Ed.), *Computers and community: Teaching composition in the 21st century* (pp. 118–139). Portsmouth, NH: Boynton/Cook,Heinemann.

Sherman, J. (1983). Girls talk about mathematics and their future: A partial replication. *Psychology of Women Quarterly, 7*(4), 338–342.

Shneiderman, B. (1987). *Designing the user interface: Strategies for effective human-computer interaction.* Reading, MA: Addison-Wesley.

Smith, J., & Balka, E. (1988). Chatting on a feminist computer network. In C. Kramarae (Ed.), *Technology and women's voices: Keeping in touch* (pp. 82–97). New York: Routledge & Kegan Paul.

Tebeaux, E. (1990). Toward an understanding of gender differences in written business communications: A suggested perspective for future research. *Journal of Business and Technical Communication,4*(1), 25–43.

Turkle, S. (1984). *The second self: Computers and the human spirit.* New York: Simon & Schuster.

Turkle, S. (1988). Computational reticence: Why women fear the intimate machine. In C. Kramarae (Ed.), *Technology and women's voices: Keeping in touch* (pp. 41–61). New York: Routledge & Kegan Paul.

Turkle, S., & Papert, S. (1990). Epistemological pluralism: Styles and voices within the computer culture. *Signs, 16*(1), 128–157.

Van Pelt, W., & Gilliam, A. (1991). Peer collaboration and the computer-assisted classroom: Bridging the gap between academia and the workplace. In M. Lay, & W. Karis (Eds.), *Collaborative writing in industry: Investigations in theory and practice* (pp. 170–205). Amityville, NY: Baywood.

Weiss, E. H. (1991). *How to write usable user documentation* (2nd ed.). Phoenix, AZ: Oryx.

Wilder, G., Mackie, D., & Cooper, J. (1985). Gender and computers: Two surveys of computer-related attitudes. *Sex Roles, 13*(3/4), 215–228.

5 Image, Text, and Power in Architectural Design and Workplace Writing

John Ackerman and Scott Oates
Educational Studies and Writing Program
University of Utah

Writing in Nonacademic Settings (Odell & Goswami, 1985) appeared in the mid-1980s as an example of rhetorical research in untrodden territory, a terrain far different from the composition classroom in its social configurations and discourse practices. Studies of workplace writing illustrated how writers in the marketplace and in technical fields wrote across a wide range of genres and in competitive, hierarchical situations, expanding the world view of those in composition and rhetoric accustomed to classroom scenes and discourses. The term, *nonacademic*, was a convenient shorthand at the time for boundary issues in research and teaching inside and outside of the classroom. For some, nonacademic was the writing *outside* the academy, in the *real world*, and so on. And for others, this positioning resulted in a respect for highly specialized professional discourses, applied to real problems in real situations. But remaining today are contrary attitudes toward workplace writing: As a graduate student remarked recently during a teaching colloquium on business writing, professional discourse pales because of the absence of exemplary texts read for aesthetic or interpretive appreciation.

Such reactions are due partly to a lack of exposure, but also to how studies of workplace writing present textual practice. The *non*academic label further mythologizes the boundaries between literacy in the real world and academic settings. The act of defining what is essential about the "other" is reciprocally an act of self-definition and reification, and often reductive dichotomies (such as professional vs. personal or functional vs. aesthetic) can emerge. And the exercise of separating one world from the other has produced *categories of difference*—in descriptions of composing processes (Selzer, 1983), common textual practice (Anderson, 1985), and contexts for collaboration (Lunsford & Ede, 1990) — that are useful as entry points but that may otherwise obscure and limit participation and inquiry.

As Britton, Burgess, Martin, McLeod, and Rosen (1975, p. 1) mused in the first breath of *The Development of Writing Abilities*, "We classify at our peril," and categories of difference can themselves become the objects of intellectual scrutiny as much as the literate worlds associated with one arena or another. Workplace writing is lodged in a number of sometimes competing systems of belief, depending on whether the project is to prescribe routine practice for the newcomer or to criticize the seemingly conservative nature of workplace writing, when it is tied to the marketplace, science, and the preservation of the status quo. Certainly, the worlds invoked by textbooks are particularly free from political tension, and they remain a stronghold for current/traditional preoccupations with technical, prescriptive, and structural notions of texts. As Gallagher (1989) and Knoblauch (1989) noted, textbooks commonly reproduce clarity and conformity instead of diversity and displacement, and the workplaces that are invoked are not only outside of academia, they appear to be outside of the cultural dynamics of gender, ethnicity, and power (cf. Flower & Ackerman, 1994).

Our analysis of architectural design assumes that a direct relationship exists between the myths and depictions of the worlds in which a given writing practice is situated and the types of analysis and critique that follow. For example, one bias that we brought to the study of architecture was an initial inflexibility toward graphic representations, a logocentricity. However, confronting that bias led to confronting another: An interpretive framework was needed to muddy the boundaries between academic and professional life and between professional or private spheres. In this chapter, architectural design is construed as an activity within a cultural framework, that is, as a specialized professional discourse that has direct consequences on how people live and communicate.

Although in keeping with Faigley's (1985) call for integrating "considerations of individual writers and particular texts into a broader view of the social functions of writing" (p. 241), the social imperative in composition research is only part of what was and is missing in studies of workplace writing. To enter into such inquiry, even more basic questions must be asked of the nature of the "particular texts" associated with a social setting and the cultural spaces for those texts. This chapter is an initial and openly speculative attempt at challenging what researchers traditionally take as the object of their research — the meaningful texts in the workplace and the worlds they invoke. To do this, we have drawn on what Witte (1992) termed a "constructivist semiotic" and on semiotic and critical theory that acknowledges a plurality of "cultural tools" (Wertsch, 1991) inseparable from everyday practice and often at the center of professional and consumer negotiation.

The topic of research and discussion is a comprehensive activity in the field of architecture — how architects conceive and negotiate a program design for a building. As we describe, program design is the first, essential stage in providing an architectural solution for a client's problem, that is, an abstract model of a building or structure that responds to the needs of someone or some group. Through program design, an architect or firm renders a lived or natural space — a meadow, a vacant lot, a bedroom, a neighborhood, a city block — into a *reconfigured* space. The word *reconfigure* is an important one because architects redesign space that has been deeply configured by history, precedent, and patterns of use. Therefore, what is disciplinarily or professionally unique about architectural design is known through its imprint on everyday life.

For the architect, the design problem is both rhetorical and semiotic. The practicing architects that we studied were hired to translate the needs and routines of a client into a plan for a building. But their professional challenge was to read an audience and situation and to produce a design concept that fits their agenda as well as that of their client. This persuasive, rhetorical process involves working with and across a range of graphic and verbal signs. The textual practices of architects are replete with visual acuity, graphic fluency, the laws of physics and the nuances of art, and cultural sites for shelter and communication. Architects begin with a lived or natural site and work back and forth, from image to text, from sketch to verbal description, until they negotiate a reconfiguration of that site. For the writing specialist observing the architectural community, program design appears to be profoundly "nonlinguistic" (Witte, 1992, p. 240).

The nonlinguistic challenge for an architect is one that many people can appreciate. Suppose you decided that a room in your house had outlived its original purposes; let us say a bedroom could be better used as a study. That bedroom probably signifies part of your personal or family history, from gradual changes in life style to perhaps your sense of home and private space. This room materially reinforces that history. Within the room itself, you have observed for years how light plays off the northwest corner, how the willow tree has grown into a bordering element between your house and the neighbor's property, how the the double-hung windows have begun to breathe with age and use, and how the "skins" of the room — walls, ceiling, floors — have faded in style and effect over time. But how will you translate your felt and observed sense of history, need, function and aesthetics into a blueprint for change? Could you compose a statement that captures the intent of your design, your preferences and individuality, the plans to revise one room in concert with the others in your house and life, and the actual devices of light, verticality, and circulation? And how would you design and write in such a way so that other family members could understand you, so that builders know where and when to begin, and so that lenders feel safe with their investments? It is a design problem that you can probably envision more easily than you can articulate, sketch more easily than you can write, a problem riddled with codes and histories of lived spaces and the consequences of whatever you eventually create.

Thus architecture involves the challenge and practice of using a range of verbal and graphic tools to reconfigure a lived space, a semiotics of design and cultural practice. As several have chronicled (Sebeok, 1975; Silverman, 1983), semiotics owes its modern heritage to de Saussure (1966), who proposed the sign as the basic meaning-laden relationship attributed to the referent or object under consideration. A sign in this tradition is formed through a dyadic relationship between the signifier (a word, a gesture, a doorway, a building) and the signified (the concept or meaning attributed). As Eagleton (1983) summarized, de Saussure's semiotics is disinterested in actual practice—what people say and why and with what consequence. His semiotics is an abstract, synchronic, systematic account of linguistic meaning derived through difference. Later treatments of semiotics have infused this theory with discussions of subjectivity (Benveniste, 1971), history (Foucault, 1972), gender (Kristeva, 1980), and ideology (Barthes, 1986). Silverman (1983) offers a useful shorthand for understanding a postmodern treatment of semiotic theory. Drawing from Benveniste's writings, the sign "cannot be detached from discourse, discourse from subject, or the subject from symbolic order" (p. 53). Thus what we take as a sign, discourse, the writer (reader, architect), and culture are interdependent. Our interpretation of one necessitates an interpretation of the other three.

For our research purposes, a semiotic perspective on nonacademic writing offers four vantage points for understanding architectural design and to rethink traditional portrayals of the "particular texts" in workplace settings. First, workplace writing can be approached as a composite of multiple and intersecting verbal, graphic, and spatial tools. Anything can be interpreted as a tool—a word, a quarterly report, a novel, a hallway, an office park—and in daily activity, people communicate, learn, and act by working across graphic and verbal sign systems. De Saussure's semiotic theory, with its linguistic heritage and literary applications, seems to openly promote alphabetic language as the sign system *par excellence* (Silverman, 1983). However, our research supports the views of Geertz and other cultural ethnographers who challenge logocentricity that obscures multisign events and patterns in culture. As Geertz (1973) wrote: "Thinking consists not of 'happenings in the head' but of a traffic in what have been called by G. H. Mead and others—significant symbols—words for the most part but also gestures, drawings, musical sounds, mechanical devices" (p. 45). The cultural tools in architectural design are ones that include a necessary mix of image and print: a vacant lot, a barrio, a brick wall, 80 years of row houses, a steel beam, glass walls, printed instructions, building codes, schematics, and contract law. We do not, with this writing, provide a systematic account of how an architect closely or cognitively works to merge, blend, and revise with multiple signs (for an historical account of such a process, see Gorman & Carlson, 1990). However, we do try to illustrate the complexity of the occasion to do so.

Second, and as Witte (1992) pointed out, Peirce's (1931) theory is helpful in describing writing as one part of a process of iterative representations of meaning. Peirce extended de Saussure's dyadic sign relationship between the signifier and the signified by redefining the latter as the *interpretant*, the mental effect of moving from object to sign to meaning. The interpretant is an equivalent sign in the mind of someone that produces other signs (what a cognitive psychologist might call evolving mental representations). Our research has made clear the primary role of these iterative representations in architecture. Graphic and verbal signs reciprocate and generate through the design work of architects, and representations evolve through an iterative process of internal meaning (mental) and external meaning (sketches, models, written descriptions; cf. Flower & Hayes, 1984). Because architectural design is a cultural practice among architects and between professionals and clients, the interpretant is a cognitive phenomenon mediated through negotiation, conflict, and compromise.

Third, this constructive, multisign process is historically situated. Sebeok and Umiker-Sebeok (1987) called the endless iterations of interpretation a semiotic web and the process of communicating within this web *semiosis*. Interpreting and constructing meaning is bound by the history of one's thinking and the history of those thoughts and actions within a cultural intertext. That is, someone's interpretations and thought processes not only echo within an immediate situation, they echo prior events and traditions. In remodeling a house, an architect might take into account the historial permutations of a given room, but harder to hear would be the traces of social practice that inhabited and surrounded that room—experiences, values, images, knowledges, and the cultural history of the house in a neighborhood, region, and culture. Semiosis, then, is theoretical shorthand for the process of ascertaining meaning in situated experience, with varying levels of historical awareness. The concept of semiosis, for us, embraces individual agency—as a way to make sense of one's world—but binds those meanings to the "traffic" of a material and ideological history.

Finally, our study of architectural practice invokes Foucault's (1972) distinction between disciplinary apparatus and discursive practice, specifically those practices hidden beneath the veneer of institutions. A discursive practice for the architect or a client could be her treatment of the iconographic power of buildings, in the way that buildings can welcome or exclude, or can conserve power. Or a discursive practice might be the ability and choice to render a two-dimensional image into a three-dimensional model. In our research, we found many examples of architectural design that both reproduced institutional power and had the capacity to rewrite cultural space, to break it open for wider participation. For example, should we walk into a school, we might expect to find certain conventions such as the placement of the administration, library, skills center or sports facilities that remind us of school and conserve its traditions. Yet these same configurations compete with less traditional views of schooling that question gender roles, social values, learning, and authority. By construing design as discursive practices, the semiotic process of design is acknowledged as political. As with all discourse (Said, 1983), when a design is wrought, a space is created whereby someone speaks, someone is silenced, and someone is empowered or disenfranchised to act.

To restate, by drawing on semiotic theory, we acknowledge a multiplicity of signs, cognitive and social interpretations of those signs, their historical situation, and their political consequence. But the descriptions that follow, based on empirical data, founder in comparison to the robustness of this theory. We cannot, for example, demonstate how designers and clients translate and negotiate various sign systems or provide a thorough historical account. Instead, we offer a rendering of the design process sympathetic to the theory summarized. Toward the end of this chapter we return to the metaphor of a *space* as a political dynamic in literate practice.

METHODS: RESEARCH QUESTIONS, PARTICIPANTS, AND SETTINGS

This chapter draws from our research of architectural practice and teaching in two venues: graduate students and teachers in a design studio in the Graduate School of Architecture at the University of Utah and the working contexts of practicing architects. The study in its broadest sense has four research agendas:

- To understand architecture as a collage of discursive practices, consisting of formal and subterranean knowledges, beliefs, conventions, rituals, and identitites;
- To study how practicing and student architects represent and solve complex design problems;
- To study, over a 3-year period, the socialization process of a profession;

- To explore whether collaboration, planning, and the habits of mind from architectural design can enhance writing instruction.

To pursue these questions, we combined participatory, observational, process tracing, and interview methods within the guiding framework of ethnomethodology, and we tried to correspond our data gathering with meaningful events in our academic and professional sites. Brandt (1992) broached the difficulties writing researchers face when they simultaneously take on discourse communities, culture, and human agency. For her, ethnomethodology offers at least a partial and worthwhile compromise by advocating research on "contingent" meaning: "[E]thnomethodology, a radical form of analysis that studies the methods that people use for 'doing everyday life' . . . is intensely empirical—grounded as it is in scrupulous observation of people engaged in real-life activity, including discourse . . . its aim is to understand the hermeneutics of real life" (p. 4). For this chapter, we present specific examples and descriptions taken from interviews with seven area architects; our interpretations, however, were drawn from the totality of our experience in architecture, reflecting our research activities with students as much as with professionals.

The seven architects interviewed were chosen to represent both independent and corporate design environments. Three of the architects are principal partners in two of Salt Lake's larger firms that specialize in commercial projects, housing developments, and an occasional single-family dwelling. The fourth principal is a partner in a smaller firm that specializes in historic restorations. For example, this architect recently prepared a report and proposal concerning a controversial shopping center development on the site of a pioneer fort. This report included an inventory of historic buildings and relics on the site, a feasibility study of moving the structures, and a proposal that attempts to mediate between the interests of the developer and the interests of preservationists. All four principal architects are immersed in program design, but as managers they delegate specific design problems to junior partners and most of the technical work of preparing detailed construction documents and models to staff and technical assistants. And as managers, they decide how these various design processes maintain their firm's interests: how best to effectively market a product and streamline design and production.

Of the other three architects we interviewed, one is a woman who, as a staff architect, commonly works with a principal, for example, to develop an atrium centered in the lobby of one wing of an office building. Our final two interviewees are independent architects: One is on staff at a local community college and the other specializes in custom homes and remodeling. The differences in design for a principal or staff architect in a large firm and a freelance designer are considerable: Besides the obvious differences in scope and the option of delegation, they vary in how much they rely on technical support, such as computer-assisted design (CAD) and the pace and style of design. The self-employed architects that we interviewed oversee all facets of the production of a building, including design development, drawing construction documents, and observing the construction. In a large firm, one architect's artistic stamp is subsumed by the collective sense of a corporate design.

Our interview questions ranged from requests to describe design processes and to provide (for data-based interviews) examples, such as notes, sketches, drawings, or contract documents. We visited architects on site, asking them to teach us about the design problems they face. Using an open format, we urged them to talk about the collaborative nature of their work, that is, how clients, other architects, builders, city officials, and financiers influenced their design and administrative processes. We especially sought accounts of the challenge of explaining and demonstrating their designs with people unversed in the graphic codes of architecture. As one informant commented, "They don't speak our lingo. . . . I wish they would trust us more." Another informant spoke of designing in three dimensions for clients who visualize only two. Finally, we tried to elicit comments on the political consequences of design: how an entrance way served as both an invitation to private home space and a territorial boundary in an exclusive neighborhood, or, as one architect explained, how a reconfigured high school design might challenge some of the patterns and assumptions in schooling, such as the engendered social and spatial boundaries separating *fine* and *industrial* arts.

In the offices we visited, architects referred to four distinct phases in the overall process of designing and constructing a building:

- *Program Design*—the personal and collaborative process of generating a concept that solves a design problem and often leads to a financial commitment;
- *Design Development*—the refining and revising of the design concept after the contract is drawn;
- *Construction Documents*—producing the blueprints and instructions that guide builders and contractors and further elaboration of the design;
- *Construction Observation*—advice and guidance for the owner, builders, and inspectors during the construction process with further interpretation of the construction documents and troubleshooting.

Although we collected data on all of these stages of architectural design, the phase of program design, to us, best exemplifies the rhetorical and semiotic power in architectural practice.

OUR RESEARCH: A CAMEO OF ARCHITECTURAL PROGRAMMING DESIGN

Architectural programming is a constructive process and a social and rhetorical negotiation that temporarily "closes" with a text. Programming often results in a written document for the client that is as conventionally specialized as what we might find in engineering or the sciences. A program report is comparable to a feasibility study; it analyzes and reports the client's needs and includes a site analysis and *schematics*, the rough drafts of the spatial concepts of the floor plan and elevation drawings, and proposed arrangements of the building on the site. One key result of programming is the basic design concept, which may be represented with CAD as a virtual reality video or with a three-dimensional, physical model. All of these graphic representations are the groundwork for what most people take as the most common architectural genre: the blueprint or working drawing. All of the arhitects we interviewed spoke of programming as a service to the client, to help them identify their needs and develop a three-dimensional grasp of the design concept, but also a service by proposing construction timelines, a budget, and an outline of the next phases of development. Programming for large commercial projects, such as a health clinic or a high school, can take from two months to a year to agree on and proceduralize a design concept. For smaller firms or self-employed designers, programming appeared to be a general and often idiosyncratic process of moving from the client's needs and constraints (such as site and funding) to a concept design.

We collected several examples of architectural programming—a health clinic, a custom house, a high school, a high-rise office tower, and a corporate office for a regional airline. We chose the last example for our specific illustration. Generally, program design can be broken down into three activities:

- An *assessment* or drawing out of information on clients' needs, their world view, as well as site analyses, functional requirements, and financial constraints;
- The *transposing* of design concepts and verbal data to schematics with floor plans, site plans, elevation drawings, and often with scaled models;
- A momentary *closure* with the intellectual, ideological, and fiscal commitment to a design, often codified in a program report that summarizes and concludes the negotiations between the architect and client.

As we illustrate these three activities, we comment on their consequences, addressing four aspects of semiotic theory: a multiplicity of signs, a process of interpretation, an historical semiosis, and discursive practices in a political landscape.

Assessment

Assessment, for practicing architects, is an exercise in problem identification as a first step in problem solving. Assessment might begin with an idea presented by a client: a company's need to modify its existing structure to accommodate expansion; a developer's inquiry into a firm's previous designs; a state's request for a public service building such as a school, a hospital, or an office tower; or a request for a prototype design as in a fast-food or supermarket chain. The concepts that clients bring to architects are relatively ill defined, for the most part, and the architect's first step is to gather as much specific information as possible about the client, the functions and routines that will occur in the building, and the site. One informant, speaking of designing custom homes, told us that he began by:

> familiarizing myself with the facts. . . .What is the site like; what are the needs of the owner? Try to get as much information about that as you can. I like to let the data suggest a direction. Usually the most influential aspect that suggests a direction is the site. Where is this thing going to be built? If you go and stand at the site, certain things become evident. The sun does certain things, the winds, there are views in certain directions. You just try and get as much information rolling around in your head as you can.

The architect specializing in historic restorations spoke of getting to know the client's world view as a way to assess how sensitive he might be to the expenses and challenges of historic reconstruction. He showed us sketches, photographs, and notes from city-county archives of an old granary that he was working on, and he told us that he uses these methods to gain as much of an understanding about the building as possible: its history, including the original builder, owners, previous renovations, architectural period, and original building material and technology. "I try to understand everything I can about the building. Then I try to understand everything I can about the client. And then how the client and building relate." The female informant also spoke of designing homes and reported that she tries to pick up psychological insights from conversations with the client. One informant gave us a checklist of "concept and special appointments," that he uses with clients. As shown in Fig. 5.1, this checklist asks clients to identify the features that they find desirable in a home, a disclosure of a kind that we found to be common across programming practices. Architects interpreted and tallied this data to help them assess their clients' world views and as a way to locate and commence negotiations.

CONCEPTS

1. High ceilings and spatial feelings
2. Formal and informal rooms
3. Beamed ceilings
4. Exposed trusses
5. Special effect mirrors
6. Stairs (special?)
7. Entry doors (large, hand carved, glass)
8. List items "disliked" in houses
9. Use of plants
10. Basement apartment
11. Basement kitchen
12. Second entry--apartment
13. Kids' entry
14. Kitchen family room nucleus
15. Separation of master bedroom from others
16. Traditional or contemporary
17. Proximity (one room to another)
18. Acceptable combined spaces
19. Solar (passive, active)
20. Earth sheltered
21. Patios & decks (formal, informal, both)
22. "Gotta have" list
23. Second kitchen/pantry concept
24. Pantry, utility, hobby concept
25. Views (panorama, focused)
26. Morning sun (kitchen-breakfast, master bedroom)
27. Building materials (liked--interior and exterior)
28. Building materials (disliked--interior and exterior)
29. Favorite colors (warm, earth, cool, pastel)
30. Furniture styles (traditional, contemporary, mixed)
31. Where buy furniture?

SPECIAL APPOINTMENTS

1. Island kitchen
2. Large range hood
3. JennAir range
4. Commercial range
5. Dishwasher
6. Trash compactor
7. Countertop appliance center
8. Roll top appliance center
9. Microwave
10. Double oven
11. Special sink (stainless, enamel)
12. Interior sprinkler shutoff
13. Cutting board (wood, corning)
14. Marble block
15. Refrigerator (size and accessories)
16. Countertops (tile, stainless, granite, wood)
17. Bar (eating, work surface)
18. Bar stools (moveable, fixed)
19. Pass through (shelf, outdoor, dining room)
20. Garbage disposal
21. Garbage can space (outdoor)
22. Number cars (garage, other)
23. Motorcycles, bicycles
24. Garage door openers (outside key)
25. Outdoor sports storage
26. Yard equipment storage
27. Indoor storage (non-freeze)
28. Chair and table storage
29. Gun storage (hidden, built-in)
30. Fireproof files
31. Safe (built-in, master bedroom)
32. Secret storage (hidden room, vault, etc.)
33. Silver storage (tarnish resistant)
34. Laundry sink
35. Clothes chute
36. Ironing board (built-in, master bedroom)
37. Drip dry hanging rod
38. Folding table
39. Broom and vacuum closet (cleaning supplies)
40. Buffet service
41. Number persons dining (maximum, average)
42. Master bedroom number of beds
43. Dressing mirrors (full, angled)
44. Oversized sprinkler lines
45. Cedar closet (first)
46. Dressing and make-up table
47. Separate toilet closet
48. Bidet
49. Steam shower
50. Sauna
51. Hot tub
52. Jacuzzi whirlpool
53. Separate wash areas
54. Linen storage
55. Separate closets
56. Separate dressing areas
57. Shoe shelves (boxes, displayed)
58. Jewelry drawers (locked)
59. Clothing lights
60. Countertops (marble, corian, tile, carpet)
61. Pedestal sink handpainted

FIG. 5.1. Concept and specific appointments for clients.

Thus, in the earliest moments of assessment, architects and clients struggle with systems of graphic and verbal signs, working from image to text, from text to site, and from bias to category — all to figure out a starting point for the client and the designer. A catalog of concepts and special appointments can serve as a catalyst for assessment, and it points to the architect's expertise in reconfiguring lived space. The ensuing exchange of ideas in graphic and verbal signs will depend on the client's fluency with designing and building, the "ability to think and talk in three dimensions." For example, a builder and developer, in their first meeting with the principals in one firm, presented a land survey of a lot for 12 exclusive homes, designating that they envisioned a home design similar to an exclusive development designed by the firm that they had seen in Phoenix. However, the developer stipulated in the very first meeting with the principal architects that he wanted these homes to place the garage and kitchen adjacent, in order to accommodate and facilitate the flow of the family returning from shopping and entering into the house from the garage to the kitchen. More typical is what our informants called the challenge of negotiating and collaborating with clients who "don't see . . . don't think visually." This comment may seem contradictory when we have already noted that clients often come to architects with photos, sketches, or references to buildings that are familiar. But when we pressed our informants about this contradiction, they said that clients visualize in only two dimensions, such as floor plans, elevation drawings, or a vague idea about how their building should look.

Architects, of course, are hired to think in three dimensions, but what impressed us about these moments of early assessments and trading back and forth of graphic and verbal images is the powerful advantage of thinking and visualizing in full relief. As business people, architects may withhold an initial design concept and strategically delay graphic design until they have learned enough about client, problem, and site. Like all professionals, their expertise allows them to control the discourse, and their graphic fluencies mean that they bring a different kind of intertext to the business table for concept and contract negotiation. Architects have skill in recognizing the generic, social functions of many buildings and the way space is configured in them to actualize daily routines and social traditions. They recognize, but may or may not articulate, messages of invitation or exclusion in the entrances and lobbies of office towers, or the gridded separation of upper level administration from the flow of customers or other employees, or the proximity of child care facilities to the waiting room in a health clinic. Such design *precedents* are coded graphically and verbally, and whether or not they are presented as such, are coded economically and politically as well.

In the case of the corporate airline office, programming began with a business problem: The airline company was outgrowing its current corporate office, and they wanted to use programming to determine whether or not it would be profitable to build a corporate office on a new site. The architect and client first made the decision to enter into a contract to do the programming. Such meetings were high-level business meetings, our informant told us, between the principal architects brokering their services to a consumer who is looking for the right firm to develop and execute their goals and ideas. Once the principal architect and the client had decided to enter into a contract for programming, a series of meetings were planned and held for the purpose of drawing out enough information to begin to articulate the design problem. Although this process was overseen by the principal architect, he did not engage directly in the collecting and analysis of information. For this firm, staff architects, called the "interiors department" were trained to make the initial assessments of a client, a process the principal characterized as:

> Close people work . . . it's us directing at them . . . asking questions "These are typical [operations] in a corporate office; do you have these?" (answered) "Oh yes, and we have a personnel department . . . a marketing department . . . so we'll need people for that too" . . . they come up with not so much diagrams but lists of people . . . we deal with people.

Our informant told us that his firm was particularly successful because they had programming down "to a science." We interpreted this to mean that this firm had developed a reputation for finding swift and efficient design solutions to problems, with procedures to turn designs into a plan for building. In other words, the science of programming was central to the economic gain of both architectural firm and client, by efficiently closing the gap between a designer's ideas and a client's needs. This swift and efficient "directing" allowed the client to occupy the building as soon as possible, and their science was a process of using a coding of lived space. Like the gathering of facts about the preferred features of a personal home noted earlier, this informant's firm used forms and worksheets to represent their precedents for design and buildings and to elicit information and preferences from the client: "We tell them what we are doing. We don't just give it to them. We hand it out in a meeting and go over it, item by item . . . and give them about a week to go through it . . . and ask more questions . . . go through things, explain them, and fill it out with them." The interiors department distributed documents to the airline staff (see Figs. 5.2, 5.3, 5.4, and 5.5) that had the same purpose as the concepts and appointments tally we saw earlier.

We noticed that these forms were directed to managers or directors of departments who were asked to describe the job functions of personnel they

FORM A

This form should be complete for each space required by this department which has <u>special functional, environmental or equipment criteria</u>. Duplicate this form for each space type.

DEPARTMENT: _____

SPACE TYPE: _____

COMPLETED BY: _____

LOCATION: _____

Are there any factors that should be considered which may possibly impact personnel and space requirements in the future?

A. FUNCTION

Describe briefly, the primary function of this area.

_____

_____

Based on your knowledge, outline any organizational or technological change which will affect the size or performance of your space.

_____

_____

_____

Number of personnel who occupy space: _____

What are their job functions?

_____

_____

Based on your own experience and observations, suggest any changes to the efficiency, size and operation of your space (you may also sketch or diagram your desired space on form A cont.)

_____

_____

Do they have assigned work stations within this area? _____

_____

FIG. 5.2. Departmental functions, environments, and equipment.

B. SPECIAL REQUIREMENTS:

FORM B

List any special requirement that should be considered in planning the space on form A.

Approximate net area of current space: _____

Acoustical: _____

Approximate net area desired in a future space: _____

Lighting: _____

Wall Finishes: _____

Special shapes and/or dimensions: _____

Ceiling Requirements: _____

Entry/Access: _____

Special height requirements: _____

Electrical: _____

HVAC: _____

Plumbing: _____

NOTES: _____

Communications: _____

Security: _____

Other Requirements: _____

FIG. 5.3. Space requirements for departments.

OFFICE PERSONNEL PROGRAMMING

SPACE NUMBER	CHAIRS/SEATING					EQUIPMENT						SPECIAL SERVICE							LIGHTING				ENVIRONMENT				
	Executive	Secretary	Conference	Stool	Guest	Typewriter	PC/CRT	Printer	Phone	Plug-in Calc.		No. of Outlets	Phone Lines	Data Lines	Ded. Circuit	Copy Machine			General	Task	Special		Temperature	Humidity	Acoustic		

EXISTING CONDITIONS

FORM C

FIG. 5.4. Existing conditions for office personnel.

OFFICE PERSONNEL PROGRAMMING

FINANCE

SPACE NUMBER	Open Area	Open W/Low Divider 40	Semi Priv W/High Div 60	Semi Priv W/High Div 80	Private W/Door	Secure Area	DEPARTMENT	CURRENT NEEDS					EXPANSION				
								Total Personnel	No. of Stations	Net Area	Gross Area	Total Area	Total Personnel	No. of Stations	Net Area	Gross Area	Total Area
							GENERAL ADMINISTRATION										
					X		Vice President / CFO	1		225	293	293	1				293
					X		Vice President / Treasurer	1		225	293	293	1				293
					X		Controller	1		144	187	187	1				187
			X				Internal Auditor	1		144	187	187	1				187
	X						Secretary	1		64	96	96	1				96
			X				Financial Analyst								144	187	187
							Conference Room	1		144	187	187	1				187
							Conference	1		216	280	280	1				280
							Copy / Woork Room	1		48	72	72					72
			X				File / Storage Room	1		120	156	156					156
							Extra Office						1				187
							Total					1751					1956

FIG. 5.5. Programming space for finance office personnel.

supervise (Figs. 5.2 and 5.3), as well as to catalog numbers of personnel, equipment, furniture, electrical services and such (Fig. 5.4). True enough, with the inclusion of the corporate staff's recommendations for changes in the lived work space, we find evidence of the social, negotiative nature of designing a building. But because we see in these forms no evidence that supervised employees are asked to participate in describing job functions or making recommendations, this exchange of information is doubly hierarchical: Architects proceed from their precedents for generic structures and operations in workplaces, and management (as we would expect) decides, given the architect's questions and categories, how prescribed space can be allocated. This observation does not mean that architects do not care about the occupants of buildings. When we visited a high school that was scheduled to open its doors in a few weeks, we asked a custodian how he felt about the new building. He enthusiastically reported that he, along with other custodians, were asked by the architectural firm to participate in programming, offering their suggestions for design features, given their job functions, that might make the building more comfortable and efficient. Discursive practice in architecture is full of such potential for access, and fluency with sign systems and with a democratic declaration of precedents.

For the airline project, the client information is represented in Fig. 5.5, which is a completed tally of the allocation of space in the finance department. Data collected from these tallies are later combined with the data concerned with an organization's growth, thus allowing the architect to show the clients exactly what they have, and exactly what they need. Further renderings of this programming data include the Functional Relationship Matrix (Fig. 5.6), where the "proximity requirements between the departments" are plotted by computer onto a matrix.

This programming form seemed to be a clear example of how programming data can be proceduralized in such a manner as to demarcate spatial/business relationships between the areas and departments within a building. This form is also an example of linguistic and graphic signs that carry the potential to translate social functions and political arrangements among the departments. This matrix powerfully guides and constrains the design solutions that we eventually see in the schematic drawings of floor plans (in Fig. 5.12).

Even within the earliest moments of programming, as architects assess a client, the design process raises political questions. It appears to us that the scientific precision of these forms belies the interpretive and political processes at work. The forms used to draw out information are part of and signify the professional intertext of the architects. This we may expect to see in any profession. This is why, for example, architectural firms may choose to specialize in designing schools or hospitals. One architect told us of firms that specialize exclusively in programming for hospital remodeling, because

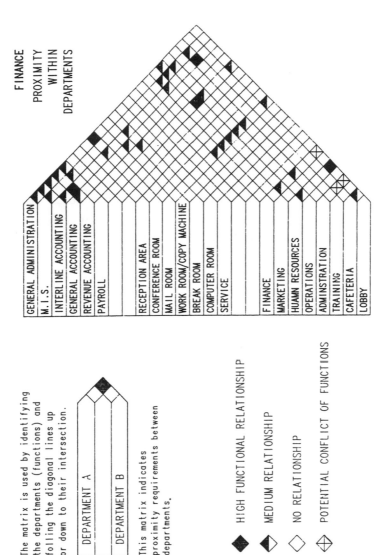

FIG. 5.6. Functional relationship matrix for finance.

99

the ongoing development of medical technology forces departments such as radiology to regularly rethink their operations. This professional knowledge allows them to efficiently direct programming at the client, thus eliciting the data that will guide a design solution that is not merely generic, but customized to meet the needs of the client.

But architects have a choice in how they initiate their assessments as they choose what texts and precedents are offered as essential. Whereas the precedents of a building genre can be viewed as enabling, allowing a group or organization to judge itself, we also view such precedents as evidence of how access to and control over a discourse can shape the space for negotiation. For example, we observed in the data collected from the airline's corporate staff the attention given to *existing* departmental relationships, job functions, and space allocations. In Fig. 5.11, for example, we noted the social and cultural precedents in the allocation of 293 square feet for a vice president when juxtaposed with the 96 feet allocated to a secretary, or the 16 square feet allocated to data entry personnel. And in the principal's comments, we noted who gets to say what is "typical" in any organization's configuration and activities. The genre of a building will conserve and control daily practice, but it may also provide an opportunity for critique if the people who occupy that building have access to it.

Transposition

The empirical, interpretive, and negotiative processes of assessment continue throughout programming, but we observed that assessment gradually gives way to the architect's personal and in-house challenge of transposing verbal data, images, and impressions into a detailed graphic design. The data assessed are both transposed, as they move back and forth from graphic to verbal representations, and transformed, as diverse data are gathered and shaped into concepts. There are rhetorical and strategic choices for the architect as businessperson such as when these transpositions and transformations are shared with a client. Graphic representations, such as a sketch of a building front, are often strategically delayed until the necessary data about the structure, functions, and routines of the corporation have been amassed and analyzed. As one informant reminded us several times, "a lot of people cannot see it [a design concept] until you draw it." Another informant showed us the programming book prepared for a health clinic that was under construction. Pointing to a schematic of a floor plan for the health facility (similar to Fig. 5.12), he told us:

> They'll think it through, and they'll have the answer for where the nurse goes, every step of the day. They'll know that, but they won't be able to visualize what it means till it's down here [points to the floor plan schematic]. And then

you find out that you have the nurse station in the wrong place. They'll say, "It's not right, it won't work. The nurse won't be able to see down the hall."

In the case of the airline's corporate office, the data from these early assessments were transformed into visual, conceptual representations (Fig. 5.7).

Our informant called these representations *bubble diagrams*, which are computer-generated sketches aimed at visualizing a building or structure. These bubble diagrams are conceptually coherent and reflect basic functional relationships and roughly indicate space requirements. Although the design solution at this point does not portray literal rooms, the design concept is starting to make sense as a building. Architects may use representations such as these to direct the client to further assess issues such as "Where's your parking going to be? Where's your main entry?"

At this point, the transposing process for the airline was one of refining and detailing the functional relationships among departments and areas, organizing them along hallways, into wings, (in this case) around a cafeteria, lobby, and atrium. This work is collaborative, with the architect showing the client schematics that indicate the circulation among these areas and a rough floor plan (Fig. 5.8).

The arrows in these schematics indicate the flow of people, but also

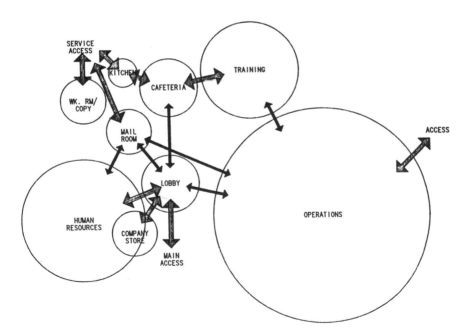

FIG. 5.7.   Bubble diagrams of space and working relationships.

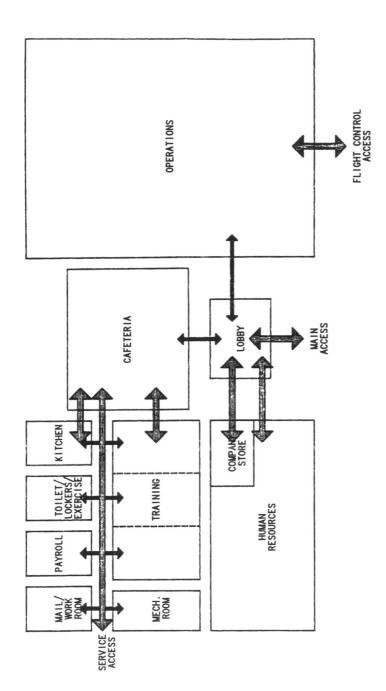

MAIN FLOOR SPACE DIAGRAM

FIG. 5.8.   Main floor diagram.

indicate the larger operations of the business or client at hand. These general schematics are then detailed, area by area (and often as delegated subprojects within the firm), to learn, for example, how much space is optimally required for each employee. The sketches and hierarchy of office space in Fig. 5.8 was used to sharpen the design of one functional area and as the basis for an eventual detailed elaboration of areas within larger schematic drawings of the building layout, as in Fig. 5.12. The presentation of these schematics to the client, which in the case of larger commercial projects are often isolated into blow-up and detailed studies of departments and areas, leads to more collaboration on problem identification and problem solving. We noted the interplay of client and architect precedents during the development of schematics, as they begin to imagine how well a floor-plan schematic matches routines. Architects rely on and challenge the client's knowledge of the daily, lived routines that occur in their spaces and how they portray this knowledge. As our informant told us:

"Routine," that's a good word. Because they're there everyday, and they have to walk 20 times back and forth across a long hallway of a corridor to reach something, back and forth, you know. And a lot of that we can get [in earlier programming treatments]. But sometimes, it's even after going through this process, we'll end up with a full set of schematics and they'll say, "You know, you're right, that's where it belongs according to this [the functional relationship matrix] but if we put it right here, you know, that's better. Can you make that work?" And we go back to the diagram, and figure things out.

Other examples that suggest the exercises of transposing and transforming include hand drawn sketches (Fig. 5.9) that are often the earliest representations of the shape of spaces and functions.

Architects vary in the tools they use for this conceptual work. Some prefer two and three dimensional drawings, while others prefer to work with computer-aided design (CAD) or physical models such as cardboard or foamboard cutouts.

The precision suggested by the CAD bubble drawings belies the conceptual and semiotic struggle in sketching out a basic design concept. Figure 5.9 is an example of an architect's quick sketches of concept possibilities, and we might discover a number of such sketches, especially if the design problem is open-ended. From our observations of student design processes, these sketches are moments of transposition, where precedent appears in unrefined form and is transposed through the architect's idiosyncratic graphic and verbal processes. Figure 5.10 is an example of a student working with the problem of a shelter for a homeless community that tends to congregate beneath an overpass in downtown Salt Lake City.

We see traces of what we are calling the active transposing of graphic and

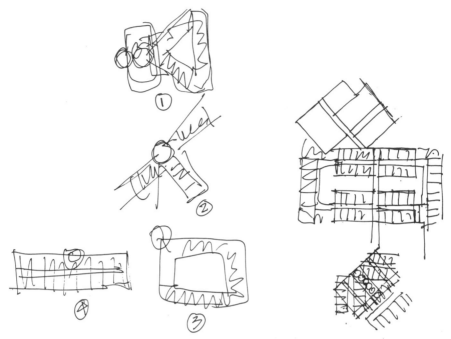

FIG. 5.9.   Hand sketching of space relationships.

verbal representations. Here on one page, we see attempts to transpose verbal and graphic texts with the architect's reflections on what constrains and motivates design. These sketches and notes were borrowed from a student's "visual journal" and are 2 of around 50 pages of sketches for this problem that gave rise to the design concept. The specialized and proceduralized design processes at an architectural firm appear to severely limit this process, yet both student and practicing architects face the "muck" of transposing the ill-defined images and the conceptual leap of transforming fragments into a coherent image and text.

It is in these early drawings and renderings that design motifs appear. For the airline office, a building structure is arranged around one or two levels with jutting corners and a gridded overlay of rectangles. We asked all of our informants about conceptual motifs or preferences, noticing patterns of design in each firm or office. Many denied set patterns, but acknowledged similarities—such as a preference for one material over another, or one shape over another. Informants also spoke of the influence that region played on design motifs. For example, regional climate can function as a determinant: Custom homes in exclusive mountain development sites tend to have steeply raked roofs to meet the demands (and building codes) for heavy snow. The principal of the airline project said the jagged design (seen in Figs. 5.12 and 5.13) gave the building more surface, allowing a play of light and the incorporation of corner offices, with glass on two walls. The location of this office building in southern Utah led to the use of earth-tone stucco and painted tiles and the incorporation of reflective glass walls to take advantage of natural lighting and spacious views of the horizon.

The informants gave us accounts of the transposition phase that further suggest social and rhetorical dynamics. Sometimes the firm takes a persuasive stance, trying to convince the client to trust the design solution that they have developed. One informant told us about the negotiation that ensued with clients over the design of an office tower:

> We knew what we wanted to see, and so, we drew it up in models, drawings, everything. Finally, we talk them into it. And even after that . . . well, we put up a mock-up of the skin panel over in a warehouse, a full size model, which means the actual stone, the actual glass, but just a sample. And everybody came unglued, they said, "No, we can't have it, there's too much mottling. It's too different between the light and dark [stone]." We said, "Take it easy, no, don't worry about it. It will all melt together, it's a big building." But they went on for a month or so, "No, it's too much, it's too busy." And finally, they just settled in and said, okay. . . . You know, we're not talking to somebody who understands our lingo [who has with them] somebody who understands it and can then whisper into the director's ear and say, "Trust them, they're doing the right thing." It's more like trying to convince bankers, attorneys, you know, very conservative, a bunch of black suited guys and they were concerned that it not be too . . . well, they wanted it ostentatious, but they didn't want it gaudy or something.

This comment unravels the scientific facade of a linear programming process that smoothly moves the architect and client from the ill-defined to a well-defined concept model. As we noted earlier, powerful precedents are enacted by the genre of the building. Other sources for architectural precedents include professional magazines, which may research treatments of a building genre, as in a public school. One informant told us that he had an idea for an atrium/lobby and that he was waiting for a client with the appropriate building needs to come along so he could develop his idea into a design concept. We also observed architectural precedents that evidence the stable image (for a certain class) of the upper middle-class family in the 1990s, with a garage adjacent to a kitchen to accommodate the return of shoppers, which promotes consumerism. In the specific case of the airline's corporate office, we see how particular design genres conserve the edifices of position and status. The upper level administration is separated from the flow of activity around the cafeteria, the lobby entrance, and general operations, creating the phenomenon of a two-way mirror: Administration can choose to view itself and those outside itself, whereas the public and common domains of the corporation are architecturally circumscribed.

Hot a sign to indicate I-15 but the journey to the next
polestar - suicide rock ... the next fragment of society—

WHERE ARE THEY GOING TO?
WHERE ARE THEY COMING FROM?
WHO IS TRAVELLING?

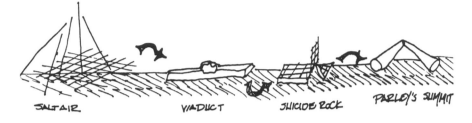

SALTAIR   VIADUCT   SUICIDE ROCK   PARLEY'S SUMMIT

The past leads into the future...

THE W/BILYE GIVES DIRECTION

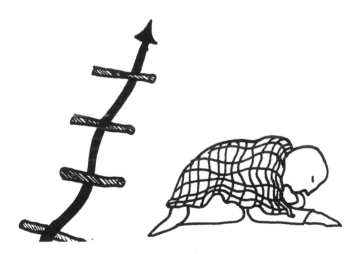

FIG. 5.10.   Transposition in a student design process.

Programming, then, is as much about conserving traditional routines, spaces, and power relationships as it is about designing something new. The facade of a building and the newness of its interiors can mask otherwise hegemonic practices of cultural reproduction. In the Office Layout tem-

As far as program goes- there seems to be two distinct groups of people WHO WILL BE AFFECTED by this polestar. The Traveller- It seems logical to create something to make the traveller's journey easier, faster, more efficient. I could switch this program to one that makes the journey less pleasant - a detour... It could drive them down into the area of these people who are users of the area under the freeway. Or - the road could turn to gravel, force them to slow down & take a look at the area. However, the term "Polestar" implies height, a very obvious marker. Where are you coming from? Where are you going? Where are you? ORIENTATION.

HERE   THERE

THERE

remember - this traveller is in a car.

For the people who use this space (homeless, gangs, etc) they are "Here" and understand here. They are the ones who have the "sense of place" of 'here'- already. How will a polestar in their place affect them? To them, this place under the freeway is complete- or they don't worry about what lacks... until it gets hot in the summer/lack of shade) or cold in the winter (lack of a heater/walls/roof). The logical solution is to make the environment more pleasant - Add trees, roofs, solar panel

FIG. 5.10.   (*Continued*)

plate (Fig. 5.11) the graphic presentation of space allotments signifies and reifies social practice.

Technically, this template is an aid for visualizing and configuring blocks of space within a department; an exercise in transposing and transforming

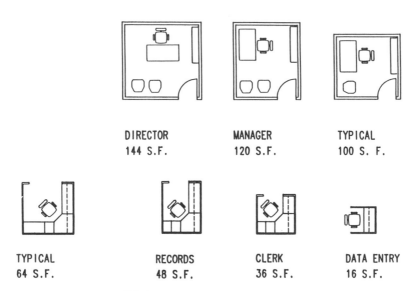

FIG. 5.11.   Office layout of workstations.

data about personnel and job functions into rooms along hallways within a department. However, if the visual exercise became a built environment, it would conserve culturally coded notions of space, circulation, and status. Therefore, in architectural program design, we can find examples of semiosis as a seemingly neutral system of transposing and transforming, rendering the inchoate into the conceptually sound. But these same moments of semiosis may reveal historical and cultural patterns, whereby space is linked to power and authority.

We find it interesting to imagine either client or architect designing *against* such cultural determinants and templates. We were told by the female informant that she was highly conscious of the social and psychological dynamics of space. Speaking of her goals and principles as a designer, she told us: "In office buildings you try to give the emotional feeling to the people working there that they are important . . . that they are in the status of everything, . . . and that they are in an equal working situation . . . and say, in an office setting for a director, how that is set up is basically to put status on where that person is." Later she told us about a project she worked on, where the design problem was to add a new floor to accommodate growth onto an existing office building. The manager of the department she was programming rejected her early schematics because the space that she designed for the supervised personnel was "too luxurious," given their status within the company. In the case of the airline office (see Fig. 5.12), the jagged design and glass walls permitted the allocation of corner offices for directors and chief executive officers that come with a "play of light" that not only rewarded them with an architectural aesthetic, but also approved an actual and ideological view beyond the corridors of corporate conformity.

Closure

Typically, program design reaches an end point when a concept model is developed and detailed by schematic drawings (Fig. 5.12). These designs tend to center and ground whatever business or contractual negotiation is needed to seal the working agreement. The models produced may be a three-dimensional drawing, often aided by computer or a physical model as in Fig. 5.13. We choose the word *closure* to label this end point to allude to the literary notion of premature closure in interpretation. Of course, and as we first explained, the process of design from a business and construction standpoint will continue with the development of floor plans, site plans, and elevation drawings and the ensuing construction and refinement of the actual building. Designing continues through the development of working documents — the specification and contract drawings that include detailed treatments by areas, mechanical systems, roof systems, doorway, and window construction. But the arrival of a design concept, that gives structure to basic human relationships and activity, essentially closes down the negotiative and critical moments of the design process. It is as though once the external and internal images of the building are researched, presented, and accepted, the opportunities for interactive critique of the cultural ethics involved are lessened.

A concept model, then, can achieve the power of a printed document to define a conversation, to limit or promote authority, to displace one voice with another. Looking at Fig. 5.14, which was excerpted from the summary report for the programming on the airline's corporate office, there is literal documentation of design in the presentation of the firm's findings. These findings concern the airline's existing space, "estimated space requirements," and the firm's "development" of space requirements and functional relationships based on "current need and projected future needs." With this "signing off," programming has taken an important semiotic turn, away from graphic representation and toward legal text: A solution has been negotiated. It will serve as the master concept for the development of specific details and features in the next phase of development.

When we observe the design concept as a moment of closure, we note the gathering of intertextual threads: the threads of assessment transposed and

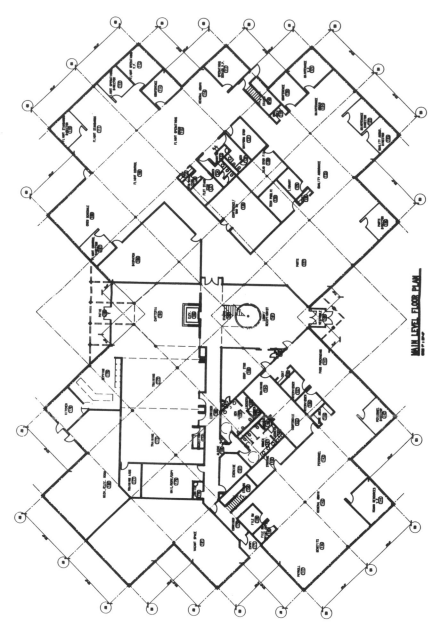

FIG. 5.12.   Completed air terminal floor plan.

110

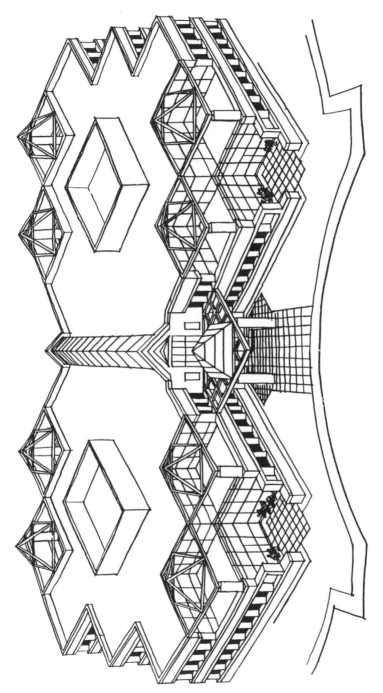

FIG. 5.13. Air terminal model.

111

FINDINGS: Perlmax Architects has prepared the following document to assist in the design of SkyWay Airlines new corporate office building. The purpose of the study was to accomplish the following:

1. To obtain information concerning the present level of personnel, space utilization, functional requirements, equipment use, and functional relationships of the different departments within the existing facility; and

2. To develop space requirements and functional relationships of all departments based on actual current needs and projected future needs.

To gather information on current conditions, Perlmax Architects met with SkyWay and interviewed the various department heads.

The results of this study covers SkyWay's estimated space requirements for the next seven years (see chart in space utilization). This study shows a steady increase in space requirements at both the corporate building in downtown St. Joseph and at the St. Joseph Airport building.

At the corporate office, the finance, marketing, customer service, human resources, and general office spaces were evaluated. Current space requirements account for a total of 21,690 square feet for FY1990. This exceeds the current space available at the building by nearly 4,000 square feet. However, based on space utilization projections for FY1997, this deficiency will amount to approximately to nearly 11,000 square feet.

At the airport facilities in St. Joseph, the operations and maintenance office space was evaluated. Current space needs account for a total of approximately 9,000 square feet which equals the current space available. Projections for FY1995 show a deficit of approximately 4,000 square feet.

At both of SkyWay's operations in St. Joseph there is clearly a growing need for space which will result in major deficiencies within the next five years.

As the first phase of the Space Utilization Program was completed, a major restructuring of the corporate organization was put into effect. The final report that follows incorporates these changes. The following chart shows the corporate administrative structure.

The final phase of the program will be to determine technical requirements for each work area or individual space. Forms used for this analysis are enclosed under Client Data.

EXISTING DEPARTMENTS AT DOWNTOWN BUILDING

	EXISTING 1990
GENERAL OFFICES (INCLUDING HUMAN RESOURCES)	4,203
FINANCE	8,435
MARKETING	3,570
CUSTOMER SERVICE	1,765
TOTAL SPACE NEEDED	17,973
EXISTING SPACE USED	17,973
EXISTING SPACE THIRD FLOOR EAST SIDE	3,595
(NOTE: THE 3,595 SPACE IS UNDER SEPERATE LONG TERM LEASE)	
TOTAL SPACE AVAILABLE	0

EXISTING DEPARTMENTS AT AIRPORT BUILDING

FLYING OPERATIONS	4,500
MAINTENANCE (MANAGEMENT)	1,250
MAINTENANCE (ST. GEORGE FACILITY)	3,750
TOTAL SPACE NEEDED	9,000
EXISTING SPACE USED NORTH SIDE UPPER FLOOR	4,500
EXISTING SPACE USED SOUTH SIDE UPPER FLOOR	4,500
TOTAL SPACE AVAILABLE	0

COST ESTIMATE

Building	49,882 sq. ft.	x	$ 60.00	=	$ 2,992,920.00
Basement		x	L S	=	55,000.00
Site Development	5 Acres	x	L S	=	550,000.00
Interior Furnishings			L S	=	500,000.00

FIG. 5.14. Programming summary report.

transformed graphically and verbally; the threads of precedent, history, and region; and the threads of profit-driven negotiations over concepts, details, and procedures. Closure within the intertext of business is not premature because we would expect nothing less than an architectural firm or self-employed individual to efficiently market their best designs. But closure is premature if an architect or client were to value the possibility of further negotiating the consequences of design. It was apparent that architects are aware of many of the conflicts inherent in design: how the new recreates the old, how functional and aesthetic goals complete, and how the iterative and cumulative refinement of an idea in effect diminishes avenues for inquiry and critique. Our informant on the airline's corporate office reflected on his entrance into the field: "I intended to get in because . . . of my background, studying sculpture. And a lot of people enter architecture because they like to draw and design and create . . . not for the business. But architecture has become that; very strategically planned, carefully manipulated, marketed." All business are such, but architecture uniquely posits art as a counterpart to technical detail and business success. We listened carefully to what our informants had to say about art, culture, and politics. The architect who specialized in historical restoration complained that architecture has forsaken aesthetics and art for attention to structural and engineering concerns. He mentioned specifically that licensing tests have replaced knowledge about the history of architectural periods with structural and engineering codes. We asked him if there was a professional dialogue about a design ethic. He said that there are ethical codes for the practice of architecture as a business, but that there are no ethical principles to guide design. He went on to tell us

> Every bank, every school, every house that is designed is like a direct mirror image of what the people believe in that had that thing built . . . Look at all the bad buildings. That's the disappointing part of the practice to me. So many architects will do bad buildings because there's a way to make money. Ugly churches, houses, shopping complexes. Look at State Street [in Salt Lake City]. Somebody designed and paid money to do those things. It just drives me crazy that we don't have a stronger sense of design. I think this is a cultural thing. Aesthetics are not emphasized as much as all the technical part. It's almost a defensive kind of architecture [because architects have to anticipate all possible structural constraints, such as earthquake footing, flooding, etc. because of growing litigation].

In our interviews, all of these architects were quick to view their field in terms of the art versus function dichotomy, their version perhaps of the political consequences of design closure. Design, they acknowledged, was constrained by conservative clients and financial and structural limits. One informant, after walking us through an example of programming, commented that the role of art and creativity, for his firm, is situated in a competitive, and conservative climate:

> I realized that with a glut of office space and apartment space, that what you needed to do to develop this to bring people to this building [a concept for an office tower] is to make it attractive. A cut above. It's like the ad for Holiday Inns, with a hair dryer in a room. That markets that room so you go there instead of Motel 6. You know, you really want an identification. Something that's going to set it off [the proposed office tower]. What you need to do to bring people [customers, clients, tenants]to this building is to make it attractive. The art, you know . . . it needs to be there, and it is there, and sometimes more than other times. But a lot of what drives architecture is the cheapest envelope for human habitation. And that's business, pure business: There's not much art to it.

If a building's art catches someone's attention and draws them in, that art, as it is integrated into the spatial dynamics of a social structure, has a political consequence for those who own the building and live within it.

THE ARCHITECTONICS OF NONACADEMIC WRITING

Thus far we have characterized program design as an iterative process of negotiation, bound by fluency and access to a wide range of cultural tools. In doing so, we are not scolding practicing architects for not rising to a standard of political sensitivity. We have no evidence that practicing architects are more or less ethical than any other professional group, and all of the informants in our study at least recognized the inherent conflict in designing for people, profit, and aesthetic imprint. Professionalism is always marked by technical and conceptual skill that is encoded into a specialized language, and that is used to exert control and influence in a professional exchange.

We emphasize the cultural antecedents and consequences for architectural design, because this view of workplace writing helps to locate writing processes, texts, and practices closer to the broader cultural situations in which we find them, instead of promoting writing as an acontextual technology (Ackerman, 1993). With regard to architecture, design as semiosis closely links conceptual work with a situational problem or need. When those needs are shelter and a functional environment, we must account for how verbal and graphic fragments and constructs are rooted in the world. With regard to workplace writing, we think the theoretical and critical perspectives of built environment, space, and the politics of displacement can enhance if not challenge some of the traditional representations of technical, professional, and nonacademic writing that appear to treat professional discourse as stable, professionally circumscribed, or insulated from larger cultural practice. In this section, architecture serves as a mirror and metaphor for spatial and political dimensions in workplace writing as we sketch some of the potential in reconsidering print literacy in spatial and graphic contexts.

To begin with, Witte (1992) has argued, similar to reading specialists (e.g., Rowe, 1987; Short, 1987; Siegel, 1984) concerned with the semiotic play of children, that writing practice is intertwined with other tools and representations. To illustrate what this could mean, we offer a reference point: a study of workplace writing that uses linguistic analysis and thus places a linguistic text at the center of inquiry and in the center of the literate world invoked by that inquiry. Rogers and Swales (1990) studied policy statements at the Dana Corporation and used the "standard linguistic technique of *substitution* in order to study the effect of alternative rhetorical choices" (pp. 294–295) for the purpose of uncovering some of the ways a successful corporation encodes and shares its ethics. As Rogers and Swales pointed out, such statements require considerable rhetorical skill, and they inferred (for example) the rhetorical choices evidenced by the frequency of "we" pronouns or sentence-subject references to employee or corporate identities, as in "we believe in study. . . ."

With an eye toward a plurality of tools, the rhetorical effect of this document on an audience can be approached quite differently. First, as an exercise in moving beyond logocentricity, attempts to describe the process or origins of a sample of writing, that is, a text's "document cycle" or intertextual paper trail might note those instances in which a picture, image, or visual aid led to or embellished a printed text. If the origins and intertextual traces of a document were considered to be important clues for writers' rhetorical choices, we would look for contributing sign systems. In the case of the Dana policy statement, a writer's drawings, doodlings, conversations, and visual representations might help to explain why and how the Dana statement builds a particular vision of a corporate community.

In our cameo, we did not detail the rich conceptual process of working back and forth with graphic and verbal signs; neither did we trace the origins of all of the conceptual and rhetorical work of the architects. We could only point to instances and results that suggest this richness. Other studies of architectural (and other) design and writing might pursue some of the choices and circumstances in inventive, creative behavior. As Gorman and Carlson (1990) surmised from their historical sketch of the invention of the telephone, moments of insight and creativity appear to be linked to cycles of internal and external representations, from the conceptual to the physical in graphic and verbal form.

A second question raised from a constructivist semiotic could be how a written text codifies social activity, that is, how a shopping list functions as an orderly aid to memory, and how it signifies the way a shopper envisions the floor plan of a store and predicts movement through it (Witte, 1992). A written text, in this way, has an architectural quality, if a text is assumed to indicate social practice and material circumstances. Rogoff and Lave (1984; Rogoff, 1990) and others interested in "situated cognition" and "everyday practice" have studied writing strategies and cognitive routines as they exist in their circumstances. The Dana statement, then, might provide some insight into the mental and social routines of the policy committee who wrote it and the assumed or actual routines of those who read and participated with the text. A constructivist semiotic suggests that policy statements and other genres in the realm of professional discourse are not read so much as they are integrated into the intertexts of daily conversations and practice (see Devitt, 1991; Hartman, 1991). We would note, then, literally how such a document was found by its readers, how it was designed as a document and distributed, whether its graphic or linguistic qualities echo some physical quality to the Dana environment, and what initial and eventual currency that document held as the intended readers of the document participated with the social and textual spaces in the Dana Corporation.

From this distance, we of course can only pose these questions. But we have learned from our study of architectural design that a powerful relationship exists among a printed document, the built environment in which it is found, and the conversations invited by that environment and document. An architectonic of nonacademic writing would suggest that written texts and writing practices are significantly located in a place, a built environment that itself bears the traces of power, status, and authority. Thus, if we choose to study a sample of workplace writing, we might additionally reference the *places* of workplace writing: collaborative teams, offices, production lines, boardrooms, and professional arenas. The sociolinguistic features of Swales's (1990) discourse communities include "mechanisms of intercommunication" (p. 25) and genres to explain the power gained by participating in socially shared forums. Architecturally, writing practice also bears the stamp of the built environment, whether those environments are viewed as giving form and direction to conversations within a corporate building (e.g., the offices and work spaces in the airline office building) or by shaping the conversations of those who walk in and out of a building. From this angle, we might be curious about the social and physical configuration of the policy committee itself, and consider how these configurations influenced the composing of the statement.

An organizational chart, then, is more than an abstract graphic rendering of lines of authority, responsibility, and communication. It could be read as a road map for some of the spatial dynamics that configure conversation within an organization. Shaver and Shaver (1992) studied the architectural changes in an Indian Health Service Clinic and concluded that modification of physical space directly shaped communication between and among patients and the clinic staff (a social reality you may have experienced at an outpatient clinic, no matter what your gender, race, or economic class). With the Dana statement, we might ask where it is housed, in what physical space was it generated, and how does its presence signify the negative and positive spaces for conversation in the everyday practices and values of Dana employees.

This chapter began by questioning some of the labels and particular texts used to construe various literate worlds inside or outside of academia and the professions. Our study of architectural program design revealed some of the political dimensions, and cultural ethics, within an architect's negotiations with a client to produce a conceptual design for a structure. It is interesting to note that the architects who contributed to our study were uncomfortable with the label and role of social critic, and many complained about their inability to express their thoughts verbally and thus enter into critical debate. But all recognized that the structures they designed (houses, offices, schools, churches, sports arenas, parks, etc.), in some fashion, influenced social and cultural practice.

Architects and critics such as Robert Venturi have recognized and applauded the cultural consequences of architecture, and have helped us to find connections between spatial designs, culture, and literate practice. For Venturi, modernist architecture rejected the immediacies of land, space, and use and adorned them with ornamental buildings, buildings that were announced by and functioned as signs. In *Learning from Las Vegas*, Venturi, Brown, and Izenour (1977) compared the city of Las Vegas to the "pleasure zone" architecture of the mythical Xanadu and the all-too-real Disneyland, with:

> The quality of being an oasis in a perhaps hostile context, heightened symbolism, and the ability to engulf the visitor in a new role: for three days one may imagine oneself a centurion at Caesar's Palace, a ranger at the Frontier, or a jetsetter at the Riviera rather than a salesperson from Des Moines, Iowa. (p. 53)

Las Vegas, then, functions in our culture as an icon for the surreal, an escape route via a carnival in the desert. For Venturi, it fulfills a "literary" role in that architecture, through its explicit signification forces us to reach past modernism. Las Vegas is hardly equal in scale to the seemingly mundane symbolism of a parking garage, but his point is well taken: Architecture always has the potential to distort, reproduce, and transform lived space; to signify larger cultural practices. Houses are built to enhance the illusion of protection and identity, and a high-rise office building suggests authority, coherence, and separateness. Architecture as a discourse about space has its own textual power.

Architecture's spatial politics helps to make clear the power of precedent and lived, cultural spaces and how those spaces seep into daily conversations and activities. It also makes clear how the exposition of these precedents is often stratified to conserve status and power. That is, a room with a view not only signifies success and authority, it signifies to others a boundary for expression and enactment. Texts in the world have a similar architectonic, and the critic Said (1983) wrote to reposition the literary text and critic in the "worldly" domain of everyday activity. For Said, the advanced expertise of the critic falsely removes textuality from worldly practice, isolating texts from the circumstances which and people who generated them. Similar efforts to portray the qualities, features, and rhetoric of specialized discourses and professions are equally faulty, if we assume that texts as systems of signs create and exist in a limited spatial dynamic. For Said, texts do not exist in an unlimited, democratic space (see Banning, 1992); they displace one another. Texts not only record or impressionistically reference their circumstances, they "enact" them. We saw how architectural design creates what superficially or aesthetically is "new," but what politically conserves power relations within an organization.

An architectonic of writing would suggest that all texts, to extend the architectural metaphor, create a sense of space, a place that is neither harmony nor cacophony as theories of heteroglossia seem to suggest. Texts are spatially in opposition to one another. One discourse, one event, one voice displaces another. Just as rooms and space conjoin in the built environment, textual practice involves places in a finite space, with those in power displacing those who have less power. At the Dana Corporation, the committee's policy statement, and all that semiotically went into its generation, displaced other conversations, other documents with similar aims, and other voices that might also comment on values and community operations within the corporation and reach beyond the real and ideological walls of a community.

The maintenance of a text as a built environment for conversation is related to power, to values and authority held by a writer, to community consensus, and to what Said (1983, p. 174) termed "affiliation": a cultural network of associations, institutions, and social forces. For de Certeau (1984), this network is understood as a city with buildings and neighborhoods that maintain the imbalances of class and economic status as competing voices in space. Those who have power have "strategies" for action and agency, whereas those without resort to "tactics" or inventive ploys to work and survive within someone else's system. Here again the Dana policy statement can be read as a strategy by the empowered, written for those who have only tactics with which to translate and make use of its meaning.

We have tried to suggest some of the interpretive potential in bringing semiotic perspectives to bear on workplace writing and in looking to architecture as mirror and metaphor for literate practice. Writing for the architect involves semiotic play and cultural design, and we believe that similar fluencies are part of other specialized discourses in professional settings. The architectural semiotic, for us, exemplifies ownership, the degree to which those in power recognize the worldly expanse of the language practice, the proximities to lived spaces, and the degree to which they enter into a negotiation over the boundaries of language. People do have choices. Our choice is to represent workplace writing as instances of cultural practice where the boundaries of space and text begin to crack, splinter, and shatter.

REFERENCES

Ackerman, J. (1993). The promise of writing to learn. *Written Communication, 10*(3), 334–370.

Anderson, P. (1985). What survey research tells us about writing at work. In L. Odell & D. Goswami (Eds.), *Writing in nonacademic settings* (pp. 3–83). New York: Guilford.

Banning, M. (1992, November). *Expert and formal knowledge in an emergent field: A critical study of snow scientists and field workers.* Paper presented at Speech Communication Association national meeting. Chicago.

Barthes, R. (1986). *The rustle of language.* New York: Hill and Wang.

Benveniste, E. (1971). *Problems in general linguistics* (M. E. Meek, Trans.). Coral Gables, FL: University of Miami Press.

Brandt. D. (1992). Seeing the cognitive as the social: An ethnomethodological approach to writing process research. *Written Communication, 9*, 315–355.

Britton, J., Burgess, T., Martin, N., McLeod, A., & Rosen, H. (1975). *The development of writing abilities 11–18.* London: Macmillan Education.

de Certeau, M. (1984). *The practice of everyday life* (S. Rendall, Trans.). Berkeley: University of California Press.

Devitt, A. (1991). Intertextuality in tax accounting: Generic, referential, and functional. In C. Bazerman & J. Paradis (Eds.), *Textual dynamics of the professions: Historical and contemporary studies of writing in professional communities* (pp. 336–357). Madison: University of Wisconsin Press.

Eagleton, T. (1983). *Literary theory: An introduction.* Minneapolis: University of Minnesota Press.

Faigley, L. (1985). Nonacademic writing: The social perspective. In L. Odell & D. Goswami (Eds.), *Writing in nonacademic settings* (pp. 231–248). New York: Guilford.

Foucault, M. (1972). *The archaeology of knowledge* (A. M. S. Smith, Trans.). New York:

Pantheon.

Flower, L., & Ackerman, J. (1994). *Writers at Work*. Orlando: Harcourt Brace.

Flower, L., & Hayes, J. (1984). Images, plans, and prose: The representation of meaning in writing. *Written Communication, 1*, 120–60.

Gallagher, B. (1989). A critique of the rhetorical and organizational world of business communication texts. In M. Kogen (Ed.), *Writing in the business professions* (pp. 222–245). Urbana, IL: National Council of Teachers of Education.

Geertz, C. (1973). *The interpretation of cultures*. New York: Basic Books.

Gorman, M., & Carlson, W. (1990). Interpreting invention as a cognitive process: The case of Alexander Graham Bell, Thomas Edison, and the telephone. *Science, Technology, and Human Values, 15*(2), 131–164.

Hartman, D. (1991). The intertextual links of readers using multiple passages: A postmodern/semiotic/cognitive view of meaning making. In J. Zutell & S. McCormick (Eds.), *Fortieth yearbook of the National Reading Conference* (pp. 49–66). Chicago: National Reading Conference.

Knoblauch, C. H. (1989). The teaching and practice of 'professional writing'. In M. Kogen (Ed), *Writing in the business professions* (pp. 246–264). Urbana, IL: National Council of Teachers of Education.

Kristeva, J. (1980). *Desire in language: A semiotic approach to literature and art* (T. Gora, A. Jardine, & L. S. Roudiez, Trans. and L. Roudiez, Ed.). New York: Columbia University Press.

Lunsford, A., & Ede, L. (1990). *Singular texts/plural authors: Perspectives on collaborative writing*. Carbondale: Southern Illinois University Press.

Odell, L., & Goswami, D. (Eds.). (1985). *Writing in nonacademic settings*. New York: Guilford.

Peirce, C. S. (1931). What is a sign? Three divisions of logic. *Collected papers* (Vols I-VIII, C. Hartshorne & P. Weiss, Eds.). Cambridge, MA: Harvard University Press.

Rogers, P. S., & Swales, J. M. (1990). We the people? An analysis of the Dana Corporation policies statement. *The Journal of Business Communication, 27*(3), 293–313.

Rogoff, B. (1990). *Apprenticeship in thinking*. New York: Oxford University Press.

Rogoff, B., & Lave, J. (Eds.). (1984). *Everyday cognition: Its development in social context*. Cambridge, MA: Harvard University Press.

Rowe, D. (1987). Literacy learning as an intertextual process. In J. E. Readence & R. S. Baldwin (Eds.), *Research in literacy: Merging perspectives. Thirtysixth yearbook of the National Reading Conference* (pp. 101–112). Rochester, NY: National Reading Conference.

Said, E. (1983). *The world the critic and the text*. Cambridge, MA: Harvard University Press.

de Saussure, F. (1966). *A general course in linguistics* (W. Baskin, Trans.). New York: McGraw-Hill.

Sebeok, T. A. (1975). *The tell-tale sign: A survey of semiotics*. Lisse, Netherlands: Peter de Ridder.

Sebeok, T. A., & Umiker-Sebeok, J. (1987). *The semiotic web*. New York: Mouton de Gruyter.

Selzer, J. (1983). The composing processes of engineers. *College Composition and Communication, 34*(2), 178–187.

Shaver, P. M., & Shaver, L. D. (1992, November). *Signs in the organization: Architectural changes as organizational rhetoric in a public health facility*. Paper presented at Speech Communication Association national meeting. Chicago.

Short, K. (1987). *Literacy as a collaborative experience: The role of critical thinking and intertextuality in learning*. Urbana, IL: National Council of Teachers of Education.

Siegel, M. G. (1984). *Reading as Signification*. Unpublished doctoral dissertation, Indiana University, Bloomington.

Silverman, K. (1983). *The subject of semiotics*. New York: Oxford University Press.

Swales, J. M. (1990). *Genre analysis: English in academic and research settings*. New York: Cambridge University Press.

Venturi, R., Brown, D. S., & Izenour, S. (1977). *Learning from Las Vegas*. Cambridge, MA: MIT Press.

Wertsch, J. (1991). *Voices of the mind: A sociocultural approach to mediated action*. Cambridge, MA: Harvard University Press.

Witte, S. P. (1992). Context, text, intertext: Toward a constructivist semiotic of writing. *Written Communication, 9*(2), 237–308.

6

"Some People Weren't Able to Contribute Anything but Their Technical Knowledge": The Anatomy of a Dysfunctional Team

Rebecca E. Burnett
Iowa State University

> The goal was to put [the students on the team] in a realistic setting so that they learned how to integrate a complex design with many different areas . . . making engineering estimates, working with incomplete information, adhering to a time line when you don't have all the information . . . learning the communications and the writing. (Interview with Ron Paulson, Faculty Facilitator, 1993)[1]

> I think "What have I been doing?" . . . I mean, I was supposed to learn something from this. (Interview with Khuan Chin, Senior in Computer Engineering, 1993)[1]

The potential benefits of cooperative learning and classroom collaboration have been well documented. Benefits include increases in learning (over more teacher-centered methods), support from scaffolding, exploration of substantive conflict, abrogation of solitary authority, and consideration of rhetorical elements that comes from collaborative planning (e.g., Bruffee, 1994; Burnett, 1993; Collins, Brown, & Newman, 1989; Flower, Wallace, Norris, & Burnett, 1994; Sharan, 1990). The widespread use of collaboration in the workplace is equally well documented (Anderson, 1985; Couture

---

[1] Although the names of the organization and the project have not been changed, the names of all but one of the individuals involved — both professionals and students — have been changed for anonymity, although pseudonyms accurately reflect gender. Christianna White is the actual name of the M.A. student in the Business and Technical Communication program at ISU who also had a research assistantship to work on the IDMM team.

& Rymer, 1989; Faigley & Miller, 1982; Lunsford & Ede, 1990). What have not been so well documented are the ways in which classroom and workplace collaboration are similar and the ways in which they are different. Knowing the comparative characteristics of classroom and workplace collaboration could provide insights about similarities and differences that might help educators and practitioners alike strengthen team interaction.

With several notable exceptions (e.g., Cross, 1990, 1994; Doheny-Farina, 1992; Locker, 1992; Paradis, Dobrin, & Miller, 1985), most research about collaboration has examined classroom and workplace teams as independent, discrete units rather than as teams that are analyzed as part of a larger classroom or workplace context. This chapter focuses on the broad organizational context that had a clear and dramatic impact on the successes and failures of a 13-member student team in a workplace setting. This team is a particularly interesting one to study because the distinctions between classroom and workplace are blurred.

In investigating the characteristics of this team, I examined several sources of information, three of which are used for this chapter: notes from observations at selected meetings,[2] transcripts of interviews with team members and professionals,[3] and the final team report. The tapes of interviews as well as observation notes and reports were examined to find instances of purpose, perception, and/or productivity that could characterize the team as it functioned in a workplace environment. In most cases, the student team members and the workplace professionals supervising them had different interpretations of team purpose(s), different perceptions of actions and events as the work progressed, and different criteria about what constituted a productive effort.

This chapter focuses first on my description of the team. After situating the team in the organizational context in which they worked, I concentrate on a series of issues that became problematic for the team. Specifically, I examine six areas: the construction of the team, the organizational impetus for their work, the objectives that guided their actions, the leadership and structure of the team, their management of oral and written communication, and shifting political ground. Once these problematic issues are explored, I move to the second focus: a discussion of a cluster of factors for characterizing and differentiating classroom and workplace collaborations.

---

[2] Observation notes were taken by both Rebecca Burnett and Christianna White at a variety of team meetings from July through December 1993.

[3] All the 90- to 120-minute individual interviews with IDMM team members were conducted by Christianna White. One interview with Ron Paulson was conducted by Christianna White; another interview with Ron was conducted by Helen Rothschild Ewald and Rebecca Burnett, as was the interview with Tim Nelson.

A STUDENT TEAM IN A WORKPLACE CONTEXT

The 13-member student team worked on a conceptual design for a mobile laboratory to screen samples for contamination at Department of Energy (DOE) sites such as Hanford Nuclear Reservation (in Washington) and Rocky Flats (in Colorado). Unlike most student teams, though, this one was not a classroom project; instead, the students worked at Ames Laboratory, operated by Iowa State University (ISU) as one of eight government-owned, contractor-operated DOE national laboratories.[4]

Situating the Team in the Context of Ames Laboratory

Understanding the place of this student team in the organization requires understanding a little about Ames Laboratory. It is a 650-employee organization with 11 scientific programs that act as an umbrella for over 100 research groups working on a variety of projects. One of those programs, Environmental Technology Development, is involved in transferring scientific discoveries from research laboratories to the marketplace, particularly the environmental marketplace. In this technology-transfer effort, Environmental Technology Development established the Technology Integration Program (TIP) in 1992.

One of TIP's responsibilities was to develop a prototype for characterization of contaminated sites. This prototype was named the Mobile Demonstration Laboratory for Environmental Screening Technologies (MDLEST). This demonstration project (self-contained in a 36-foot trailer pulled by a truck cab) uses innovative technologies to conduct on-site analyses of samples. Previously, samples have been analyzed in fixed, off-site labs, a process that is frequently hazardous (because of handling and transportation of contaminated materials), time-consuming, and expensive.

In order for the MDLEST to be manufactured in even limited quantities, the expensive and unwieldy (though mobile) demonstration project had to be modified. One of the first steps in modifying the MDLEST was to develop a conceptual design for downsizing the environmental screening technologies — essentially developing the design for a safe and sensitive but more compact and less expensive mobile laboratory (*The integrated design,* 1993). In deciding how to approach the conceptual design, TIP director,

---

[4]Other DOE national laboratories include Argonne National Laboratory, Brookhaven National Laboratory, Sandia National Laboratory, Los Alamos National Laboratory, Sandia National Laboratory (Livermore), Lawrence Livermore National Laboratory, and Idaho National Engineering Laboratory.

Tim Nelson, consulted with colleagues at TIP and Ames Laboratory; they agreed that although the project was complex, a multidisciplinary student team could do the project: "Our main objective was demonstrating [the downsizing of] this technology. It just turned out that this made a good project for a lot of students."

Thus, Tim approved establishing a student team, called the Integrated Design for Manufacturing and Marketing (IDMM) team, which was formed in the spring semester of 1993, continued through the summer, and ended active work in January 1994.[5] Tim explained that TIP (as well as the rest of Ames Lab) scientists and engineers regularly work with students, although not with large student teams. "We feel like we've been given the opportunity of having these kids here for a while. . . . I think everyone here feels that . . . it's a natural part of what they do." From its beginning, the IDMM team was identified as a part of TIP, as shown in a TIP organizational chart in July 1993 (see Fig. 6.1). Along with other TIP projects, the IDMM team was considered central in TIP's plans. Thus, in many ways, the IDMM team was a workplace team, dealing with an actual technology transfer problem.

Constructing the IDMM Team

Ron Paulson, a faculty member from ISU's Department of Electrical and Computer Engineering (also an Associate Engineer at Ames Lab),[6] was designated by the TIP director, Tim Nelson, as the team facilitator. Ron had several years experience as a coordinator for the senior design course in his department, a course that involved large student teams in solving complex problems for actual workplace clients. As faculty facilitator for the

---

[5]The date the IDMM team started is variously given as January 1993, March 1993, or May 1993, depending on how the individual defined *beginning*, how the individual defined *team*, and when an individual joined the IDMM team. The faculty facilitator said the project started in January 1993; three graduate students who were part of the initial planning said the project started in March 1993 when they started working with the project facilitator; students who joined the team in May 1993 gave that as its date.

The students working on the IDMM for their senior design project completed their course requirements in December 1993. The team ended active work in January 1994, when the financial support for the funded graduate research assistantships ended.

By the end of January 1994, the IDMM team members had individually or collaboratively drafted (and revised and revised) their 14 chapters in the final report. This final report IDMM report was published in May 1994 and distributed to the IDMM team, project advisors, TIP staff, and interested professionals at Ames Lab and DOE.

In October 1994, Christianna White received a Society for Technical Communication Award of Achievement for the IDMM report.

[6]Many ISU faculty do a portion of their work for and receive a percentage of their salary from Ames Laboratory. However, the majority of professionals at Ames Laboratory are full-time scientists and engineers who have no faculty responsibilities (although some of them supervise graduate students who work as research assistants or part-time employees).

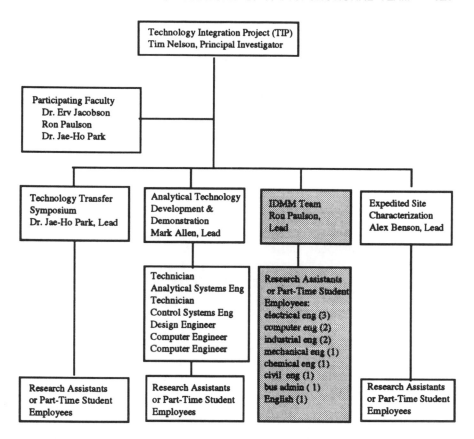

FIG. 6.1.   Technology Integration Program (TIP) Organizational Chart, July 1993.

IDMM team, Ron invited 13 undergraduate and graduate students (4 women and 9 men; 10 native speakers of English, 3 nonnative speakers) to participate as members of the IDMM team (see Table 6.1).

The team members were supported as research assistants (support included research assistant stipends as well as benefits such as insurance and vacation time) or as students taking an independent study research project. Some students worked as research assistants for part of the project and took independent study credit for another part. In some cases, a student's work on the team formed the basis for a senior project or a master's thesis.

The IDMM team was constructed on a "concurrent engineering model" (common in workplace engineering projects as well as upper-level engineering design courses). In this model, all the experts necessary for the completion of a project work together on the same team, mixing, for example, electrical engineers, industrial engineers, computer engineers, mechanical engineers, chemical engineers, civil engineers, and so on. On such an engineering team, everyone gets to explore, argue, and investigate

TABLE 6.1
IDMM Team by Department, Academic Level, Gender, and Native Language

Department	Senior	Masters	Ph.D.
Industrial Engineering	1 (mn)	1 (mn)	1 (mn)
Electrical Engineering	2 (wo[a], mn)	1 (mo[b])	
Computer Engineering	2 (wo[a], mn)		
Civil and Construction Engineering		1 (mn)	
Mechanical Engineering	1 (mn)		
Chemical Engineering	1 (wn)		
Business Administration		1 (mn)	
English		1 (wn)	

Note: w = woman, m = man, n = native speaker of English, o = nonnative speaker of English, wo[a] = Mandarin, mo[b] = Urdu.

ideas and plans concurrently rather than having a project move lockstep through each department and be signed off before moving to the next department. The IDMM team started with 11 engineering students and 1 marketing student; in July (halfway through the project), Ron added a technical communication student to the mix. On the IDMM team, students from electrical and computer engineering comprised more than 38% of the team (5 of 13 members). This overrepresentation had later ramifications as team members assigned each other tasks on the project.

In selecting students for the team, Ron considered three broad characteristics: Some students (particularly the undergraduates who had little workplace experience) were invited because of their enthusiasm; for example, the undergraduates in electrical engineering and computer engineering self-selected after hearing about the project in a presentation for engineering majors about special projects they were qualified to work on. Four other undergraduates were invited because of their academic excellence; for example, 4 of the 7 seniors on the team had been selected as members of Tau Beta Pi, an undergraduate engineering honor society. Other students (particularly graduate students, most of whom brought practical workplace experience) were invited because they were believed to have the added benefit of technical knowledge or field experience that was appropriate to the task.

Because of a number of the students' characteristics — academic excellence, maturity (students' ages ranged from 21 to 42), and field experience — Ron assumed the team members were capable of reading the organizational and project context in order to establish a purpose for the IDMM project and then to construct an agenda that reflected their purpose. During interviews, Ron indicated that he had assumed students would be able to assign each other (or volunteer for) tasks appropriate to their areas of expertise, create a workable schedule, and then complete the necessary tasks. He assumed that they had the experience to function productively on a relatively large nonhierarchical team (which is not a necessary feature of concurrent engineering teams). He assumed their experience would enable them to engage in the problem-solving required for such a complex project. He assumed they would recognize the importance of keeping detailed notes, generating drafts that not only described their work but also presented their recommendations and rationales. He assumed they would see the value of regularly communicating with each other about their decision-making processes.

Recognizing the Organizational Impetus

The organizational or contextual impetus generally establishes part of the basis for a team's sense of purpose and their perception of the task. The impetus for the members of the IDMM team was the belief that their conceptual design could have a major impact on the way in which TIP developed the mobile lab. The TIP scientists' and engineers' need for a modified conceptual design of the MDLEST project gave the IDMM team an important problem with externally established dates for completion and a strong potential market. Not only had officials within DOE shown interest in the prototype of the MDLEST, but the director of TIP had traveled to the former Soviet Union and received inquiries from government officials there who saw the potential for this technology in characterizing the levels of contaminants in the farmlands around, for example, Chernobyl (affected by a 1985 nuclear explosion) and Chelyabinsk (affected by a 1957 chemical plant explosion) ("Spanning the globe," 1994).

The explicit sociopolitical context of the IDMM project meant that the project had a real purpose and a real audience. The purpose was for the IDMM team to produce a conceptual design that would be good enough for the MDLEST project to use in the development of a downsized mobile laboratory. The conceptual design would be presented in a detailed recommendation report that would be reviewed by IDMM project members, by TIP professionals, and by Ames Laboratory and DOE managers, scientists, and engineers. This information about purpose and audience was not presented in a straightforward way to the student team. Rather, before the May start of the team, some of the electrical engineering and computer engineering students had access to documents about the MDLEST project and then met with Ron to talk about the project: "[We spent time] talking . . . through . . . what the objectives were and where to go to find the information and the people. . . . They struggled with it. . . . We did, then, start at the beginning with discussions [of our objectives]. . . . We spent a number of meetings [running 2 ½ to 3 hours] . . . [but] it was not efficient, organized. . . . It was verbal [oral, not written]" (Paulson, 1993). Despite these early spring discussions among some members of the team, there was no apparent consensus about the team's purpose.

Not surprisingly, members of the team developed remarkably different perceptions of their purpose. For example, throughout the summer, some team members believed they would be building something—"soldering cables" (Chin, 1993)—not realizing that the focus of the project was on the conceptual design alone. And the reality that the team's sole product was to be a report that team members would have to write was slow to emerge. The obvious question is "Whose responsibility is it to articulate and clarify the purpose and goals of a student team?" Unfortunately, there are no simple answers—just more complexities of the situation.

The facilities in which the IDMM team worked reinforced the sense that this was a real and important project. The 13 students were not crammed together in a windowless backroom with desks lining the walls, a shared telephone, and no support. Instead, they had professional facilities: Team members had terminals on a networked NeXt system; individual desks, bookshelves, and private workspace; large and small meeting rooms; individual telephones with unlimited long-distance access; photocopying; and fax. They had support systems typical of many workplaces: a small, immediately available professional library (and a university library close by) and secretarial support. They not only had keys to the building so they could come in the evenings or on weekends, but they also had easy access to TIP scientists and engineers—in adjoining offices, on e-mail, in informal meetings—as well as their supportive faculty facilitator and academic advisors (from the ISU program in Rhetoric and Professional Communication as well as from various engineering programs). Treating the IDMM team members like professionals at the beginning of the project created initial commitment. The team members were flattered to have been invited to work on the team and were optimistic about the value of such an experience. They were aware that working on an important DOE project could be a valuable experience (and their involvement on the IDMM project showed up on virtually every resume). And a couple of team members even thought ahead to the potential money to be made if the concept were developed and made commercially available. For example, two of the graduate students on the team (one in marketing and the other in civil and construction engineering) constructed a detailed business plan about developing and marketing the IDMM technology (neglecting to consider that they did not own the technology).

Shaping the IDMM Objectives

The objectives for a team often guide members' overall plans and the tasks and schedules to carry out those plans. Having a clear sense of expectations is critical for any team effort. Of course, individual members always construct their own representations of the task. However, group discussions about common purposes and objectives may bring these individual representations closer together. In the absence of a clear statement of objectives or any discussions to reach consensus about team objectives, there is little chance that individual representations of the team tasks will reflect much common understanding. The discussion in this section deals initially with preliminary planning for the IDMM team, then introduces resulting problems for team members, and finally offers a rationale for Ron's approach in informing the team about their task.

Preliminary Planning.   During what Ron described as the preliminary planning stage of the IDMM team in the beginning of the spring semester 1993, he established a 4-person team (two electrical engineering students and two computer engineering students, one of whom did not stay on the team after the spring semester). During one of his interviews, Ron explained that "[we] spent our time trying to define the problem, set its scope, set its objectives, and get it written down" (Paulson, 1994). By late winter, they added two more graduate students to the team: an M.A. student in marketing and an M.S. student in civil and construction engineering. Commenting on this preliminary planning, Ron identified what was to become a central problem for the team members: "While we worked a lot on definition, objectives, identifying potential markets, the approach to the marketing problem and so forth, I couldn't get them to put black on white. And because of that, when we started in late May [1993] with [most of] the rest of the team, they didn't have what I'd liked them to have had to refine further" (Paulson, 1994).

Ron was not the only one who noticed the lack of clearly articulated definitions and objectives. In fact, it was a recurring theme in virtually all of the interviews with IDMM team members. Chuck Zabrius (1993), a senior industrial engineering major, was specific about the problem: "Our objectives were never spelled out in the beginning. . . . They [the three original graduate students] may have presented the plan on the first day, but the plan was never formalized. Nobody ever really [articulated] the plan: 'This is what we're going to do. These are our objectives.'" Chuck explained that he believed it was critical to get everyone on a team to agree to a common goal and to a commitment to achieving that goal. Making such a commitment, he explained, would have required that everyone begin with the same understanding of the goal and the same level of commitment to the project.

The implication of Chuck's comment is that the teacher should establish the objectives, a theme that is echoed in comments by other team members. His comment also presumed that all the information about the plan for the project was already known, just waiting to be collected, organized, and presented. Whereas an earlier question asked who was responsible for articulating purposes and goals, the obvious question now is, "Whose responsibility is it to articulate and clarify the objectives of a student team?"

Project Development/Problem Development.   Most of the team members expressed the view that the problem of not knowing the objectives was exacerbated as the project developed. "Nobody knew what we were doing. And that's why we went in all different directions" (Zabrius, 1993). Although each person was engaged in a focused inquiry, team members had little sense of whether everything that needed to be explored was in fact being explored, how all the individual pieces might fit together, or how the process of producing a report would proceed.

Realizing that the IDMM team members needed help in planning and producing their report, Ron decided to add a final person to the team. At the beginning of July, Ron invited Christianna White, a master's student in business and technical communication, to join the team as a technical writer/editor. Although Christianna brought a useful background in areas related to the project (professional experience in environmental science as well as in writing and editing), she also had recently completed a graduate course about the theories and practices of collaboration and teamwork. Although Ron and the team knew they needed her, they did not quite know what she should do. Team procedures were well established by the time Christianna joined, so she not only had to create a position on the team, but she had to create her role.

The unorganized approach to the overall project created immediate problems for Christianna. The nature of these problems was spelled out by David Allen (1994), a senior mechanical engineering major on the team:

> I think it'd be safe to say that there . . . wasn't any planning until [Christianna] arrived. . . . When we were first introduced into this project, we were given *minimal* direction. . . . They just basically threw us into the fire. . . . Ron had an idea of where he wanted us to go, but he never stated it. He never guided us in any particular direction. And so, the things that could have been done very early on, the types of questions we could have asked and the type of information we could have obtained very early on was [not guided].

By the time Christianna joined the team, other members realized that a report was going to be written, but they had given little thought to the relationship between their individual work and the team's actual deliverable—a report describing the conceptual design for downsizing the environmental screening technologies for a mobile laboratory.

The Nonhierarchical Approach: Purposeful Nonintervention.   Some of the team members didn't recognize that Ron's nondirective approach was purposeful. He was conscious of their false starts and the frustration. He was aware that he could have eliminated a great deal of the anxiety and complaining by stepping in and identifying the objectives, assigning tasks, laying out a schedule.

Although Ron clearly wanted the IDMM to deliver an outstanding high-level conceptual design to the MDLEST project, he also had clear pedagogical goals. He wanted the students to learn, for example, to make engineering estimates, to work productively in a complex situation when there were no absolute answers, to be willing to make informed recommendations based on estimates. He also wanted them to learn how to work on a team, to define the problems, to establish agendas and schedules, to resolve conflicts, to create arguments (orally and in writing) for their recommendations. Despite the pedagogical purposes for his approach, Ron had reservations: "I wanted them [the whole team] to wrestle with it [the problem definition, etc.] somewhat, but I'd have liked to have given them more finite ammunition to wrestle with to begin; it would have helped" (Paulson, 1994).

Ron explained that he let the flat, nonhierarchical structure "happen" (Paulson, 1993). He said the group discussed team structure, but that the discussion did not lead to any clearcut preferences. "I let them evolve what they felt most comfortable with, and it ended up quite flat. . . . It's not as efficient, but in some respects the results may be better. You may have to work harder to get there, but maybe we can get a better product" (Paulson, 1993). Ron did not object to the IDMM team being nonhierarchical, and he decided to risk the mismatch between the needs of the organization for a conceptual design and the pedagogical needs of the students. Specifically, he hoped that the nonhierarchical structure could be valuable in meeting the pedagogical needs because students would gain experience in setting goals, establishing priorities, organizing schedules, and making decisions. If the nonhierarchical structure did not enable the 13-member inexperienced team to create a conceptual design about manufacturing and marketing a downsized mobile laboratory, he judged that the pedagogical benefits were worth it.

Determining a Team Leadership, Structure, and Approach

In addressing the independence of the IDMM team, Tim talked about Ron's decision to have the students be in charge of their own project. "[Ron's] trying to make this as much their project as possible. . . . We think some additional student-led activities [at Ames Lab] would be beneficial. . . . It's an extremely powerful learning experience" (Nelson, 1994). Although self-discovery is extremely powerful—in fact, at the core of much cooperative learning (Sharan, 1990)—a 13-member team of inexperienced collaborators that has no clear objectives, no leaders, no sense of team structure, no strategies to manage destructive conflict, no strategies to encourage productive conflict, and no consistent approach has been set up for failure. This section begins with a discussion of various aspects of leadership on the IDMM team and then turns to the need for team structure and process skills.

Reluctant Leadership.   When the IDMM team was formed, Ron purposely did not assume a direct, visible leadership role, a decision he frequently examined throughout the project, although he never changed his initial stance of letting the team find its own way. When the majority of the team came together in May (everyone but Christianna), Ron did not explicitly designate anyone as the team leader, nor did the team members make any decisions about selecting a leader or determining how the work of the team would proceed.

In what appeared to be default of rank, Paul Beardshear, the only Ph.D. student on the IDMM team, became the de facto if reluctant leader. Ron said that Paul took the de facto position of leader naturally, "not as a function of educational background." But in an interview, Ron explained the team members' introduction to the project in May: After the initial training (one day of orientation and a second day tour of Ames Laboratory), Ron had arranged for Paul to take "them through the first initial formal training . . . therefore, he was in a position to be seen as the leader" (Paulson, 1993). Paul may have assumed leadership "naturally," but he had been placed in a position that made that leadership look as if it were Ron's choice.

When, at the beginning of July, Paul left the IDMM team to work on another project, the de facto leadership shifted among three of the master's students and one of the undergraduates involved in the original planning, although they were not particularly eager to declare themselves in charge of what they presumed was supposed to be a nonhierarchical team with informal leadership.

The Goal: Developing Leadership.   Although Ron wanted the students to establish their own goals and priorities and determine the most expeditious way to achieve them, he did not sufficiently consider whether they had enough knowledge of and experience with collaboration to accomplish their goals. He brought the group together without giving the students any directive about team structure or organization, believing that having the students decide what to do and how to do it was perhaps one of the most important parts of their learning process.

Ron did mandate two things in the project: weekly meetings and notebooks. Unfortunately, his mandate did not come with instructions or helpful hints. Meetings were frequently lengthy and wandered from subject to subject. Some topics were discussed in excruciating detail; other topics were given cursory attention or ignored all together. Once Paul left in July, one of the occasional leaders took it upon himself to create a regular agenda; even so, meetings frequently ran over the allotted time without covering the items on the agenda. Several team members maintained their bound lab notebooks with some regularity; however, what the notebooks contained was inconsistent and did not follow the rigorous standards for recordkeeping that many research and development engineers and scientists do as a matter of course.

Even though Ron continued to play a background role as facilitator, many of the team members believed that the team would have been more productive if Ron had been more directive. In fact, Kevin Taylor (1993), a master's student from construction engineering and one of the students who joined the project in its planning phase, simply said that "Ron should have been the project manager [from the beginning]." The question here is whether or not it was Ron's responsibility to be more directive.

After the project was over, Ron agreed that progress would have been smoother with clearcut leadership. In retrospect, he said, "We should have had a strong team leader" (Paulson, 1994), but Ron believed that this leader should have emerged from the team. Unfortunately, even team members who probably would have been effective leaders avoided the role because of perceptions about ranks (undergraduates, M.A./M.S., and Ph.D.). For example, Chuck made this comment: "I expected someone to [take a leadership role]. I knew it wouldn't be me [because] I was low man on the totem pole. But I expected someone to [and because no one did] that was *very* frustrating" (Zabrius, 1993).

Leadership and Writing.   Ron's noninterventional approach to facilitation did have a rippling effect on the team's productivity. For example, Ron did not convey to team members — either by directive or example — that writing was essential to their success in this project. Until July, no team members had any concrete sense of the relationship of their work to the team's final report. Eventually, the lack of project planning and the lack of a unified plan for the report had major ramifications. Until a tentative table of contents for the final report was presented by Christianna as a subject for discussion at the weekly team meetings in mid-July, no one (including Ron) knew that a major area of concern had not been investigated:

It was in the process of deciding to put something on paper that . . . these vast differences in concepts started coming out. One group thought, "Oh, we'll just ignore mass spectrometer [MS]," for instance. I think that was one of the big surprises all the way down the line. . . . It was never my intent for them to leave the mass spectrometer out. I saw that as a fairly important subsystem. And the kids were really keyed on AES [atomic emission spectrometer]. And I don't know quite where I lost them. . . . And we still don't have mass spectrometer covered like I thought they would. Again, it's their report, and I didn't want to impose a heavy hand. But frankly I thought [that mass spectrometer should have been included]. (Paulson, 1994)

To her surprise, soon after she joined the team, Christianna was treated as the team leader much of the time. What she considered normal professional behaviors (for example, preparing an agenda for what she wanted to cover at the weekly meetings or maintaining e-mail and memo correspondence with other team members about the developing plans for the final report) were seen by team members as leadership behaviors. Although Ron also recognized Christianna's unexpected leadership, he never anticipated a technical writer to lead a team of engineers: "[She] played as much leadership to the group [as the Ph.D. student, Paul] by forcing them to think about the end product and where they were going in terms of the report as opposed to in terms of the design" (Paulson, 1994). Her impact on the process and progress of the IDMM team influenced Ron's attitude about the importance of having a communication expert on an engineering design team.

Working with a technical communicator gave other team members a sense of unity as they argued and worked toward articulating their overall goal. One result of these team discussions was a short statement in the final project report; the team members explained that their task had been to "complete the conceptual design of the prototype technology . . . [and to] look at the MDLEST elemental analysis technology, modify the design, and determine its viability in the environmental marketplace" (*The integrated design*, 1993, p. x).

The Need for Team Structure.   Although the students were left on their own to develop team structures, they unfortunately did not seem to be aware of any models of collaboration to fall back on. A more experienced team might well have recognized and felt comfortable changing the ground rules — saying, in essence, that a nonhierarchical structure would not work in this situation, that they needed more structure and direction.

The members of the IDMM team did recognize the need to separate their immense task into manageable chunks. For example, they formed subgroups to investigate and prepare recommendations about the various physical components and regulatory restrictions for their conceptual design, including computer and controls, power, prime mover, spectrometer, rastering, laser focus, and so on. Unfortunately, they did not volunteer or assign all of these subsections with each individual's expertise in mind. So, for example, the team member investigating lasers had a background in industrial engineering, whereas the two team members investigating spectrometers had backgrounds in electrical engineering and computer engineering. Team members were working on major areas outside their field of specialization in part because there was an overrepresentation of members in electrical engineering and computer engineering.

More problematic was the lack of interaction between groups, as David Allen (1994) pointed out: "I didn't see as much interaction between some of the groups on some of the design characteristics as I thought I would." The collaborative nature of any productive team (and one of the primary reasons for concurrent engineering teams) includes exchange of new information, feedback about that information, and use of that information as work progresses. But because no vehicle (other than weekly meetings) was encouraged for one subgroup on the IDMM team to share information with the other groups, subgroups seldom built on each other's work.

The Need for Process Skills and Problem-Solving Skills.   The students needed to learn processes of working collaboratively, in part so that they could solve problems together. They had few skills to reach initial agreement about procedural factors, and they had even fewer skills in raising and managing the substantive conflicts typically necessary in negotiating complex decisions. Without a leader, any models of productive team structures, or any training in team interaction, the members did not know how to deal with problems that occurred repeatedly:

> Those of us working on the technological side of this got real frustrated. . . . We had several different, general high-level concepts and were trying to figure out which direction we wanted to [go]. And that was the point—we needed some feedback from marketing. Jay [the marketing member of the team] was of the opinion that he had to have concrete, visual ideas that were worked out way beyond what we could offer him. . . . Instead of asking questions, he was trying to *sell* the ideas. We were no where near prepared to send out a concept that [we] could even back up technologically. We wouldn't even know if it would work. . . . All we wanted to know was [the market response to] the basic configuration: How large can we have the thing? What type of things are they actually looking to get? What things would interest them? . . . But once we gave him [Jay] a few options, he still never went out to the market place and got any feedback until . . . way after we needed that information. (Allen, 1994)

Nothing in the way the project was set up or the way the team functioned gave David Allen or the other IDMM team members the skills or experience to manage problems such as this. Ron was aware of these problems but assumed that working them out was part of the value of working on this project. Such an attitude reflected Ron's unintentional signal that this was a team of students rather than professionals. In his view, having the team members learn to manage conflicts in the process was as important as the report they created. Unfortunately, the majority of the team members did not have theoretical knowledge or the workplace experience to negotiate such problems. The longer they tried to figure the problems out for themselves, the more frustrated they became and the less they maintained their roles as professional experts working on a DOE project. Many of them retreated to a student role of completing their assigned task without regard to the project as a whole; others withdrew from any active participation in the project.

Managing the Oral and Written Communication

Although the IDMM team started as an engineering project, members gradually became aware of the centrality of writing. This section begins by focusing on Ron's view of writing and then explores the process and ramifications of adding a writer to the team.

The Facilitator's View of Writing.   That writing was not stressed at the beginning of the IDMM project, despite the fact that a written report was the only deliverable, was not surprising given Ron's experiences. He came to the project with a model that placed writing at the end of a project — at best as a synthesis of a project, at worst as an afterthought: "Tech writing has been an after the fact in industry for a long time. I've never had the luxury of having the tech writer right on board . . . in the beginning" (Paulson, 1994). Even though Ron explained that discovering information for the conceptual design and for writing were the same thing, extended conversation with him showed that he viewed writing as the transmission of information about the design, an "if you know it, you can write it" view. "It doesn't make any difference in my mind whether you say let's incorporate this in the report or let's incorporate this in the design; they're equal statements" (Paulson, 1994).

From Ron's perspective, not only was writing simply a way of recording what team members already knew, it was a task that occurred near the end of a linear process: "[In my experience,] the design drives everything. You make sure everything's there, then do your darndest to put it together" (Paulson, 1994). Ron's view of the place of writing on a conceptual design project seemed to be shared by some of the engineers with whom members of the IDMM team regularly worked, both at TIP and in their academic departments. Even though the team members kept notebooks, they often waited until the last possible opportunity to turn those notes into prose.

Adding a Writer to the Engineering Team.   As a result of Ron's view of writing, it is not surprising that the original team had no writer/editor, a decision Ron later acknowledged was a mistake. But by mid-June, Ron knew they needed help with writing and decided to add another member to the team; thus, Christianna joined the team at the beginning of July. By this time, everyone on the team had started to realize that they were expected to produce some kind of report. So the arrival of a technical writer/editor was greeted with enthusiasm. People were joyous; finally someone would do the writing. Some team members had fantasies of handing Christianna their notes, which she would turn into polished, professional prose. Their joy was short lived.

Sean Marshall (1993), a senior computer science major, expressed the feeling—and the unsettling realization—that many of the team members felt: "When we finally got a technical writer on the team, we realized that something was going to have to be written." When Christianna joined the team, few members had prose text describing what they had done so far or arguing for a particular decision or position. Some did have lists of equipment features or specifications; others had short, unelaborated chunks of information about their work. Essentially, they had been operating on the model that Ron unintentionally conveyed: "[When] everything's all done, I can put it on paper" (Paulson, 1994). Even though Ron articulated the opposite position at the end of the project—"If you put it on paper before, people've got something to work with. It really facilitates working" (Paulson, 1994)—he did not exert a strong influence in encouraging team members to regularly write memos and interim reports for discussion and circulation among IDMM and MDLEST team members. This lack of interim reports meant that gaps in knowledge and logic were not topics for discussion unless someone on the IDMM team raised an issue during the weekly meetings.

Her third week on the project, Christianna posed a tentative table of contents for the final report; she put it on the table for discussion at the weekly meeting. As the discussions and arguments started about the table of contents, individuals became increasingly aware that many of them had represented the task quite differently. There was no unified sense of the report's purpose, no sense of the report's audience, no report outline, no report schedule, no model of the format—in short, no coherent plan for the design and development of the team's final report.

The Impact of a Writer on the Team.   It did not take long for virtually everyone on the project to recognize the power of writing for developing and shaping consensus. Unfortunately, beyond the weekly meeting, few of the procedures in place for sharing ideas, like e-mail, were heavily used. Christianna, new to the project and idealistic about the role communication would play, reflected about this problem: "[I felt the] frustration of trying [to] get people to even communicate beyond the once-a-week meetings. . . . [Those meetings were] the primary way of communicating, not only among the small groups but between individuals" (White, 1994). This lack of communication was more than interpersonal reticence. It reflected the team's inability to see themselves as a unified group working toward a common goal. Each person had a task, but there was little sense about how that task fit into the project as a whole.

It did not take long for the team members to realize two things. First, they realized that Christianna was not going to turn their rough notes into polished prose (although she made it clear that she would help them plan, draft, and revise their own texts — which she did for many dozens of hours). Managing this situation was challenging for Christianna who did not want to take control of other people's text, nor did she feel comfortable in tacitly approving text that was inaccessible to the audience, inadequately developed, or poorly organized. Most members of the team would have happily given her their text to "fix." She chose, instead, the more difficult role of a technical editor who worked with the experts in marketing and engineering. This meant she not only had to detect and diagnose the problems in their texts, but she had to explain ways to eliminate the problems, frequently modeling alternative solutions, so the individuals would be more likely to do their own detection, diagnosis, and revision when she was not around to help them.

Second, IDMM team members realized that writing was not simply recording what they knew about their areas of the project. And with this realization came an understanding that defining and describing rhetorical elements such as purpose, audience, and organization were important. For example, although the team members had the sense of a general audience of other professionals interested in the IDMM project and the MDLEST project, they had not considered who these people were or what they might need to know: "We never knew specifically what he [Tim, the Director of TIP] wanted. . . . We didn't even have an audience to write to. We were supposed to define the audience as well . . . whether we were writing to just this DOE office, whether we were writing to the Department of Energy in Washington, whether we were writing to potential users of this technology all across the country" (Allen, 1994). David Allen's concern expressed in this quotation raises the question of why he did not realize that part of his responsibility was to identify and define his audiences. Whose responsibility was it to help David Allen know his own professional responsibilities?

The lack of attention to the final report at the beginning of the project began to take its toll. Kevin Taylor (1993) recognized that focusing solely on the technical aspects of the project had been a mistake: "[T]he structure of the report should have been the first thing that we did, even though we didn't have . . . a lot of knowledge about [what] was going to be in it." Although the IDMM team members realized that the transmission model of writing — just recording what they knew about their own investigations — would not work very well for this report, they did not take advantage of methods that Christianna offered to encourage interaction. She wrote memos and sent e-mail to individuals and small groups, she made inquiries that requested a written response, she set up NeXt files to provide convenient opportunities for team members to comment on each other's work. In the end she was frustrated: "There didn't seem to be [a] dialogue. . . . [With] a lot of the things that went on the net[work] . . . there was not a whole lot of interaction. . . . [P]eople didn't access one another's documents and comment or make changes. . . . There was no ownership, and there was very little interaction [about the texts]" (White, 1994).

By October, Christianna had compiled a preliminary draft of the final report and made a number of passes through it to establish consistency in elements such as technical complexity, terminology, tone, organization, and design. Even at this late stage, though, there were still major chunks of the text missing. Initial enthusiasm for being on the IDMM team had waned, and deadlines had become less and less meaningful as the team responded to signals that this was a student project.

Recognizing Shifting Ground

The organizational context in which a team operates shapes its actions and its impact. Sometimes, as happened with the IDMM team members, their inexperience meant that they did not recognize the signs from Tim, the TIP director, that the ground under the IDMM team was shifting. Within a period of weeks, the project went from being treated as if it were central to TIP to being treated as if it were marginal.[7]

The first and most obvious signal was the gradual shift in the reviewing and publication plans. In mid-Fall, plans were underway for a major internal and external review of the final report. The plan that Christianna posed, Ron agreed with, and Tim approved in August 1993, included an internal review (IDMM, MDLEST, faculty advisors) and an external review (Ames Lab and DOE managers, scientists, and engineers). The internal

---

[7]Concurrent with the signals that the IDMM team was being marginalized, Tim spent time in Washington, DC, and returned discouraged about continued and future funding of TIP projects.

review would be completed first, changes would be made based on those reviews, and then the external review would take place. As it became increasingly clear that the document contained a distinctive (but not complete or necessarily functional) conceptual design, Tim kept scaling back the number and range of reviewers. After he had seen some preliminary drafts of the final report, Tim scaled back the external review and then eventually eliminated it. Within weeks he had also scaled back the internal review. Ron commented that the larger peer review did not occur the way it should have "predominantly because of the time and location problem" (Paulson, 1994). He did not acknowledge the possibilities that Tim simply did not want unprofessional work to be widely reviewed or that project funding might be in jeopardy. Surprisingly, no one on the IDMM team seemed to recognize this as a major shift in their organizational position.

Another signal (actually quite a blow) to the IDMM team came during the internal review of their draft for the final report. Some team members were astonished when Dennis Battille, one of the chemists for Ames Lab, responded by saying that the report showed they did not understand critical aspects of the basic technology process. In his judgment, because their recommendations were based on faulty assumptions, their work simply was not acceptable. When these team members asked Dennis why he hadn't mentioned these problems during the previous conversations they had with him, he responded that until he had something to read, a coherent text that laid out the ideas, explanations, and recommendations, he had no way of knowing about the fundamental gaps in their understanding. The draft of the final report was the first text he had been given to read.

IDMM team members had mistakenly presumed that their regular oral communication including corridor conversations, individual and small group meetings, and formal presentations, was sufficient. They had not recognized the value of ongoing writing about their project; memos and interim reports would have established what they knew as they tried out their arguments. A draft document would have given Dennis and others something to respond to early in the project. They also had let slip virtually all the draft deadlines posed by Christianna and agreed to by the rest of the team in August, not realizing the lack of availability of a draft would have later ramifications.

Another signal of the shifting ground was a change in the distribution list for the final report. The August plans for the distribution of the final report provided an extensive list: IDMM; MDLEST; project advisors; interested scientists and engineers at Ames Lab, at DOE, and in related fields; and potential customers. By late Fall, Tim made it clear that the IDMM final report would be a limited-circulation document, distributed only to the IDMM team, TIP scientists and engineers, and selected Ames Lab and DOE professionals.

A final signal was Tim's insistence that a cover letter that identified IDMM as a student project be permanently bound with the final report. This cover letter included caveats about generalizations that could be drawn from the report as well as acknowledgments about the limitations of the investigations. Whereas this letter might be seen simply as an organizational convention — that is, the extension of the disclaimer that DOE requires in all its reports — this particular one drew attention to the limitations based, in part, on the membership of the team.

When the project came to a close in the winter of 1994, everyone on the team recognized the importance of writing, but few saw the problems they had in generating a complete and coherent report as having a connection to the lack of attention that DOE, Ames Lab, or even TIP was giving to their year of work.

FACTORS THAT INFLUENCE PURPOSES AND PERCEPTIONS

Was the IDMM team a workplace team or a student team? Was it a hybrid? Did it start off as a workplace team and revert to a student team due to contextual influences and expectations — a self-fulfilling prophecy? Was it always a student team working in a professional environment? Were team members treated by Ron, Tim, and the MDLEST engineers and scientists as professionals or as students? Did the team members perceive of themselves as professionals or as students?

I believe that the following factors provide a way of teasing out characteristics of workplace and classroom teams, based not on the interactions within a team itself, but on the contextual factors that may influence a team. These factors help us characterize and contribute to the conversation about workplace/classroom distinctions[8]: exigence and expectations, situatedness and context, formation of teams or groups, motivation or buy in, process and strategies, knowledge of details, conventions, impact, and assessment.

Exigence and Expectations

Exigence refers to the impetus for an action. The exigence for a collaborative workplace task is stimulated by some identifiable problem, expectation,

---

[8]Kelvin and Leonard (in press) explored differences between the classroom and the workplace that "significantly influence the kind and quality of collaborative interactions that can occur in each sphere." Their work provides an insightful analysis of five general fields of dissonance that they believe accounts for "collaborative breakdown in the college writing classroom." See also Morgan (1991).

or need (e.g., Cross, 1990, 1994; Locker, 1992; Malone, 1991). The problem, expectation, or need must be addressed even though the priority it is given in someone's work schedule may be flexible. For the IDMM team, the primary exigence was generated by the workplace: The MDLEST project at TIP needed a high-level conceptual design for a safer, faster, and cheaper mobile laboratory.

Although the exigence for a collaborative classroom task is also stimulated by some identifiable problem, expectation, or need, there is an equally important exigence: providing a valuable pedagogical experience for the members of the team. Among other things that the members of the IDMM needed to learn was that every collaboration has an exigence that influences the interaction. As was the case with the IDMM team, the exigence in classrooms is often a double layer: that of the class itself and that specified by the task.

Some of the most basic problems with the IDMM team resulted from the conflict between expectations generated by the workplace exigence and the pedagogical exigence. A number of questions are generated by this conflict: Was letting team members attempt but never quite succeed in defining IDMM project goals and objectives treating them like professionals or like students? Was bypassing the initial training that team members needed treating them like professionals or like students? Was letting team members struggle and attempt to solve their own problems treating them like professionals or like students? Was refusing to intervene when team members could not handle things ranging from the schedule to task completion treating them like professionals or like students?

Although professionals are, of course, hired for their expertise, businesses all over the country have training and development departments to upgrade employee skills. On-the-job training is more the rule than the exception. Even though students usually learn more if they are involved in experiential activities rather than lectures, there comes a point when their level of frustration is counterproductive. Ron had expectations that the IDMM team members could not possibly have achieved without learning some collaborative strategies and changing their view of writing to see it as an ongoing engineering responsibility. The IDMM project might have represented the best of the workplace and the classroom if team members had been provided with initial training in essential areas that they would need for success and with more explicit project management that would defuse their frustration when dealing with complex problems.

Situatedness and Context

Workplace documents are situated—by definition and necessity—in an explicit sociopolitical context. Workplace writers must acknowledge and be responsive to the conventions of this situatedness. The problem, expectation, or need affects individuals, groups, and organizations beyond the people completing the task. Situatedness, as I define it here, refers to the place where the collaborative skills are learned and collaborative interactions occur. These are critical factors in characterizing classroom and workplace collaboration because research in what can be broadly called situated cognition questions whether collaborative skills learned in classrooms are generalizable to workplace situations and, by extension, whether collaborative skills learned in one workplace situation are generalizable to another workplace situation. This view holds that process and content knowledge are inseparable: "The activity in which knowledge is developed and deployed . . . is not separable from or ancillary to learning and cognition. Rather, it is an integral part of what is learned. Situations might be said to coproduce knowledge through activity. . . . Learning and cognition . . . are fundamentally situated" (Brown, Collins, & Duguid, 1989, p. 32). If this view is accurate, then the IDMM team would have benefited from knowing details about how productive concurrent engineering teams functioned so that they could adapt some of those approaches.

Although the interaction of the IDMM team occurred in a workplace setting, as the project progressed, team members were more frequently treated like students than professionals. They also demonstrated an inability to transfer what they might have learned in their undergraduate technical communication courses to their IDMM tasks; either they had no knowledge to transfer, or they simply saw the situations as being too different. Although participation on the IDMM team had the potential to give members the opportunity to acquire new problem-solving strategies, develop collaborative skills, refine individual and collaborative communication skills, and master more advanced content, it did few of these things.

Extending the notion of situatedness suggests that students might be most productive if they learn context-specific skills and knowledge: "Thinking at its most effective depends on specific, context-bound skills and units of knowledge that have little application to other domains. To the extent that transfer does take place, it is highly specific and must be cued, primed, and guided; it seldom occurs spontaneously" (Perkins & Salomon, 1989, p. 19). The complex contexts of writing—whether in the classroom or the workplace—force attention to factors such as audience expectations and organizational constraints, which are affected by social, institutional, and disciplinary factors.[9] These contexts, both in the classroom and the

---

[9]Regardless of the details of a case situation or simulation, a classroom assignment is too often an exercise with only an imagined audience, with a teacher who ultimately holds the final authority, with a product that has no purpose beyond fulfilling the assignment. However,

workplace, are real; however, the natures of these realities are quite different. One of the primary problems of the IDMM team was the fuzzy space they were working in. Were they a workplace team or a classroom team? On the one hand, they were given the resources to conduct one part of a large technology transfer project: a conceptual design for a mobile, on-site lab to test for various contaminants at DOE-designated hazardous waste sites. On the other hand, Ron explicitly made his decision to be a hands-off facilitator in part so that students would learn to be comfortable with the ambiguous contexts that will often face them in their careers.

Formation of Teams/Groups

Another way to characterize classroom and workplace collaboration appears to be the formation or selection of teams or groups. Teachers often determine or influence group membership, sometimes consciously trying to balance a number of factors ranging from gender to ethnicity. Other times, teachers determine group membership based on students' learning styles, grades, or interpersonal relations. Decisions about group membership are usually based on what individual students need to learn as well as on what mix of students will enable the interaction to be most productive.

In contrast, the formation of workplace groups considers the value to the group's successful completion of the task. Bosley (1991) suggested that in the workplace, a "very effective team is a combination of these two considerations: fulfilling the task requirements of the organization and the product, and satisfying the social goals and needs of the team members" (p. 508).

The formation of a team can be confounded by issues of authority. As a case in point, Ron invited IDMM members to join the team based on their disciplinary knowledge, academic excellence, and field experience: 11 engineers, 1 marketing expert, and 1 technical communication expert. In the workplace, this team would have quickly seen that the task was simply too big for the one marketing expert; they needed another one (or a different

---

collaborative assignments, particularly with upper-level students, can be structured so that students have an opportunity to work on real problems for real clients. Instructional texts work particularly well for such assignments. For example, in a graduate course I teach, "Writing Manuals and Instructional Materials," student teams are expected to solicit clients and produce needed manuals/instructions for them (other departments/centers in the university, local businesses and companies, local government). Similarly, in the introductory undergraduate technical writing course that I teach (primarily a service course for students in engineering and agriculture), I also encourage students to write directions for a real purpose and audience (for example, revising the unworkable directions for using the microfilm reader in the library or creating an instruction sheet of the bootup procedure for the new work study student in the computer lab they monitor).

one). But their role as students overshadowed their function as team members. They presumed Ron, the faculty facilitator, would have assigned another marketing expert if they really needed one. As a result of their unwillingness to challenge an initial decision about the formation of the team, the entire project suffered.

Motivation/Buy In

Another characterizing factor involves the rewards, the motivation that students and workplace professionals are offered. Teachers traditionally try to motivate students with grades, which sometimes have incentives for the cooperative achievements of the group or team rather than just the individual (Slavin, 1990). They also try to motivate students with a variety of public acknowledgments (e.g., class publication of well-done papers). We all hope, of course, that the intrinsic value and joy of learning, as well as the pleasure of doing a task effectively, will give both students and workplace professionals some pleasure. Sometimes, however, this internal motivation is simply missing.

Beyond such internal, abstract motivators, though, workplace managers who want to promote collaboration draw on additional means seldom seen in the classroom. They offer a salary, and many try to give employees "a sense of ownership in the company's mission," giving them "a choice in their own projects and tasks" and providing access "into organizational and professional networks" (Bosley, 1991, pp. 508–509). Another intangible motivator is that workplace professionals often see collaborative projects as exciting challenges.

The initial motivation of the IDMM team members dissipated gradually over the course of several months. Their waning motivation became apparent in their lack of adherence to deadlines and their shock when Christianna posed a firm schedule for completing the report. Ron excused their lack of commitment and their casual approach to deadlines as a function of the academic world: "[Because of the way team members contributed to the draft of the report], there should have been the ownership and the signing on, but it didn't materialize like that. . . . There's a distinct difference between the real world and the academic world. In the academic world, the [organization] doesn't live and die on deadlines" (Paulson, 1994). Because by the time of its completion, the project was marginalized, it is not surprising that team members' motivation and enthusiasm for completing their commitments was minimal.

Process and Strategies

Both workplace and classroom collaboration can be characterized by a variety of processes and strategies. Collaborations may commonly involve informal discussions and conversations, meetings, and electronic exchanges of information as well as structured teams and formal paths for the cycle of document development and review (Couture & Rymer, 1989; Kleimann 1991).

Workplace professionals are presumed to have a repertoire of strategies that they can apply in analyzing and negotiating during collaborative interactions. One of the distinctions that marks experts and novices in any number of tasks (ranging from writing to playing chess) is the ability of those with experience to draw on, and if necessary modify, existing strategies. In contrast, students need to learn the processes of working individually and collaboratively so that they can be successful as independent individuals and as members of family, community, and workplace groups. Students also need to develop learning as well as reflective strategies so that they have the ability to assess their own collaborative approaches and progress, to be self-analytical.

Most of the IDMM team members believed that they needed more help than they initially received, as reflected in David Allen's (1994) comment: "[Because most of us were rookies on this project,] there should have been some sort of layout . . . just A-level headings, general topics we need to cover . . . something in order to give us some direction. I think that should have been established before the group came together. . . . There should have been some sort of structure. . . . A lot of arguments could have been avoided." The members of the IDMM team knew that there were gaps in their knowledge; one of their objectives was gaining information they needed to make recommendations. However, when team members realized they did not have technical information they needed to move forward, they were less sure about how to obtain this information. Because there was no one in the role of team leader or project manager, they often fell back on their prior experience as students — looking things up — rather than relying on direct experience or developing computer models or physical prototypes to learn what they needed. From the beginning this had been one of the restrictions imposed on the team members by TIP: The project would be only conceptual, which meant no physical models, no field studies, no data collection, no experiments. The team members did not verify or confirm any of their information by direct observation of any kind.

They took advantage of talking with the TIP scientists and engineers; they brought in people who knew more than they did (for example, a technical sales rep talked to the subgroup about spectrometers); they conducted literature searches of databases (even though some of these searches were inappropriately limited in scope). Simply put, they depended almost completely on what others said in making decisions about what to write about in their final report. Trusting someone else's opinion and/or looking it up were models they were familiar with, even though they were refining the high-level conceptual design for a mobile laboratory that would probably sell for over $900,000 per unit.

The frustration of the team members late in the project encouraged Ron to arrange two seminars to help the team members with process-related skills. One, given by Tim, explained to team members a process for collecting, organizing, analyzing, and making decisions with large amounts of complex data. The second, given by this author, focused on basic technical writing skills such as generating reader-based prose by foregrounding, developing hierarchies of information, selecting appropriate details, and using consistent terminology.

Knowledge of Details

Another area that can be used to characterize classroom and workplace collaboration is the collaborators' knowledge of relevant details. Workplace professionals may not know everything they need to in order to complete a task or to participate productively on a collaborative team. What they have, though, is the ability and access to obtain the needed information and the awareness that such information is essential to the successful completion of their task. They are presumed to have enough knowledge of the content and experience with the process of collaboration to accomplish their goals. They are presumed to know what it is they are supposed to do and then be able to decide how to do it. In practice, of course, workplace professionals often need to seek additional information and gain the experience necessary to accomplish their goals, but they are presumed to be capable of self-assessment and self-direction.

In contrast, students need to learn "content," ranging from philosophy to physics, so that they understand both theory and application, in part to develop as individuals, in part to lead interesting, productive lives, and in part to function productively in the workplace. Part of the problem is that classroom assignments or simulations are often underspecified; however, a greater problem may be that students incorrectly assume that making a task "real" will automatically give them all the relevant details.

Conventions

Another factor that appears to characterize classroom and workplace collaboration is recognition and use of disciplinary conventions. What information should a DOE recommendation report include? What does a DOE report look like? Workplace professionals are presumed to be familiar with the conventions of their discipline as well as their specific organization. Following the conventions (or not) is a choice based on their knowledge of factors such as the context, purpose, and audience. These conventions may include anything from document design to documentation of sources. Students, in contrast, not only need to learn the conventions, they need to learn when to follow the conventions and when to flout them. Students need to learn institutional and disciplinary conventions that will enable them to function in a variety of communication situations and then put these conventions in a broader rhetorical context that helps them recognize the interplay of individual and social factors shaping communication.

The IDMM team members were not sufficiently familiar with the disciplinary conventions of the report they would be producing as a final product to make the process easy or enjoyable. And, unfortunately, they were embarking in new territory so there were not models they could depend on. But the students were also at a disadvantage because they did not have the experience to recognize the interplay of individual and social factors that might affect their investigation.

Impact

Another factor that appears to characterize classroom and workplace collaboration is the impact the collaboration has beyond the group. Most students (and many teachers, too) presume that class collaborations are discrete, self-contained tasks. In fact, what happens in the classroom may have little impact on the class, changing neither the collaborative interactions themselves nor the content and shape of the product. And similarly, little that happens in a class necessarily influences what happens outside that class; completing an assignment — no matter how well or how poorly — often affects no one but the students who worked on it. Students also often naively assume that their product is the task or process itself rather than the report describing that task or process. And, as I describe later, sometimes the thought of actually making an impact is scary when students realize that this impact may be real rather than simply the outcome of a classroom exercise.

In striking contrast, workplace collaborators presume that the completion of a task will have an impact beyond their own reaction. Why would they prepare a report if there were no audience who needed the information? Many workplace tasks are also seen as interrelated rather than discrete and self-contained. These presumptions do not necessarily mark inadequacies of classroom collaborations; they merely highlight the differences between workplace and classroom presumptions that result from different purposes.

Some of the glitches and problems of the IDMM team stemmed from the inconsistent messages they received about the actual impact their final report would have. In the beginning of their work, they were told that they were part of an integral link in the larger research project. The plan was for their report to have a wide audience: IDMM, MDLEST, Ames Lab, DOE, and other interested scientists and engineers. But as the deadline moved closer, the team members seemed reluctant to make recommendations. Instead, they wanted simply to report their findings and let one of the engineers or managers ferret out recommendations based on these findings. The incompleteness of the team's work as well as their reluctance to make recommendations certainly contributed to the minimal impact their report would have.

Assessment

Professionals generally possess the ability to assess their own work, to determine its strengths and weaknesses. Students are typically less willing to assess their own work and often less able. Productive teams in the workplace not only usually have external monitors of a team's progress and success (e.g., supervisors, managers, TQM programs), but they also establish team monitors to provide formative feedback (e.g., progress reports, daily or weekly meetings, updating of milestone charts). Beyond such organizational feedback, successful professionals usually have internal monitors that enable them to assess for themselves whether they are meeting their own individual criteria for success. Student teams, on the other hand, often depend on external monitors (the teacher's feedback) and seldom have team monitors and even less frequently have internal monitors. There was no formal review built into the IDMM team (except for team members whose work on the team was part of independent study or research credit): "Formal reviews? No. I thought about it. I consciously decided against it. I don't want to create that kind of an atmosphere. It's just one more complicating factor. I didn't want to introduce it even though in the real world, yeah, it would be there" (Paulson, 1993).

One of the things that characterized the IDMM team was their ongoing frustration resulting from lack of articulated objectives and plans coupled with their inability to make changes that would improve their situation. If the IDMM team had learned that successful projects often assume a large portion of responsibility for assessing their own progress, and if they had developed the strategies to implement team and internal monitoring of their work, they might have had a more successful project.

In discussing senior design teams (which in many ways Ron sees as similar to the IDMM project), Ron talked about student teams who have difficulty making the transition between the theoretical work they encounter in their classes and the real problems they have to manage on design teams. He recognized the extreme difficulty a faculty facilitator has in deciding whether to intervene: "We have the professional integrity to let them fail rather than go in and—I don't know whether it's professional integrity or whether it's survival. You just flat can't go in and rescue the team. [Interviewer: If they know that's going to happen, they'll wait for you to come.] Exactly!" (Paulson, 1993). Although Ron admitted that he had to restrain himself from actually becoming involved in the technical problems student teams were exploring, he had clear, self-imposed guidelines about the kind of help he would offer. In explaining his responsibility in monitoring student teams, he was very clear about the fact that he should not intervene—even if the team is in trouble: "The faculty monitor's responsibility is to oversee, to coordinate, to cajole, to make sure they consider all the elements, and then let them fail if that's what happens" (Paulson, 1993).

A question that is raised here might be the need to define failure and the need to consider whether failure related to process and product is defined differently for classroom groups than for workplace groups. As a classroom group, would the IDMM team be a failure if the students did not learn something useful that would enable them to be more productive collaborators on their next team? As a workplace group, would the IDMM team be a failure if the students did not produce an excellent conceptual design? As a classroom group, would the IDMM team be a success simply by engaging in an interesting process, even if they did not produce any conceptual design? As a workplace group, would the IDMM team be a success simply by producing an excellent conceptual design, even if their process was haphazard and their interpersonal relations vicious?

Another question might consider the point at which a teacher's responsibility for nonintervention stops. Do students have a right to fail? Of course. Should they fail because they do not know information about processes and procedures that their teachers can provide? Is a teacher responsible for providing background information about collaborative concerns such as group decision making, options for team structure and leadership options, or handling productive and destructive conflict? Educators and workplace managers alike need to make decisions about the point at which self-discovery becomes counterproductive—a point that may vary considerably from one situation to another.

CONCLUSION

What are the key issues raised by examining the IDMM team and by identifying factors to characterize workplace/classroom distinctions? Table 6.2 synthesizes factors that can distinguish classroom and workplace collaboration. Six of these factors have to do with procedure, convention,

TABLE 6.2
Factors that Distinguish Classroom and Workplace Collaboration

Factors that Distinguish Professional and Student Collaboration	Characteristics of Workplace Collaborators	Characteristics of Student Collaborators
exigence and expectations	**Respond to exigence; recognize expectations.** The exigence for a workplace task is stimulated by some identifiable problem, expectation, or need.	**Learn to recognize exigence and expectations.** Students need to learn that every collaboration has an exigence that influences interaction as well as expected outcomes.
situatedness and context	**Recognize power of situatedness and context.** Workplace documents are situated—by definition and necessity—in an explicit sociopolitical context.	**Learn to respond to situatedness and context.** Classroom documents are usually situated in a narrower sociopolitical context.
formation of teams/groups	**Contribute to team formation/ structure.** Workplace professionals sometimes have no say in their placement on a team, but may feel free to change the parameters of that team.	**Participate in teams.** Students sometimes determine group membership, but usually are placed on a team and conform to what they perceive as inviolate parameters of membership or structure.
motivation and buy-in	**Draw on internal and external motivation.** Workplace professionals generally have both internal and external motivation.	**Direct internal and external motivation.** Students usually respond to external motivation but some also develop internal motivation.
processes and strategies	**Use multiple processes and strategies.** Workplace collaboration incorporates a variety of processes and structures. Professionals are presumed to have a repertoire of strategies.	**Learn and practice processes and strategies.** Students need to learn the processes of working individually and collaboratively. They need to develop learning and reflective strategies in order to be self-analytical.
knowledge of details	**Access prior knowledge.** Workplace professionals are presumed to have enough knowledge of content and experience with the process of collaboration to accomplish their goals.	**Acquire content knowledge.** Students need to learn "content."
conventions	**Apply conventions.** Workplace professionals are presumed to know the conventions they need to use in any given situation.	**Learn conventions.** Students need to learn institutional and disciplinary conventions that will enable them to function in a variety of communication situations.
impact	**Recognize impact.** Workplace professionals often use the anticipated impact of their work to make decisions about what processes to use and what product to produce.	**Learn about impact.** Students often naively over- or underestimate the impact of what they're doing. They need to learn that the anticipated importance can guide the processes and products of their work.
assessment	**Assess the process and product.** Workplace professionals are presumed to have criteria and be able to apply these criteria to their work.	**Develop ability to assess process and product.** Students often have no criteria for assessing the processes and products of their work.

affect, and strategy. However, three have to do with sociopolitical concerns: exigence and expectations, situatedness and context, and impact. This clustering of what may broadly be considered social concerns emphasizes their importance in assessing as well as in planning collaborative groups or teams in both the workplace and the classroom.

In designing student teams, we need to ask how students are enculturated into their disciplines, into their professional roles. Placing students in a workplace environment, giving the physical trappings of professionals, and expecting them to complete a complex workplace task may very well fail, as the IDMM team showed. The IDMM project might have had a greater chance of success if team members had been provided early on with information about collaboration, with writing models for the final report, and with a greater understanding of the organizational context. But would it have made enough of a difference? Do we fool ourselves to think that we can expect students to become professionals simply by placing them in a workplace environment?

It is possible that, even with careful training and support, a team made up totally of students will not necessarily succeed. The IDMM team—a student team well supported in a workplace environment—had the potential to combine the best of both worlds. However, pedagogical purposes don't always mesh with workplace purposes; student perceptions are seldom the same as professional perceptions; pedagogical success privileges process, whereas workplace success privileges productivity.

A potentially more successful model might be based on internships or apprenticeship—students working *with* professionals rather than *for* them. Think about how many of us enculturate our graduate students. They work closely with us, follow us, see our work and collaborative processes. Think about how we have really learned about the workplace—through collaboration with workplace professionals, through taking time off from academia and living in the corporation.

To become professionals who can collaborate productively on teams dealing with complex problems, students need to have technical expertise. But technical expertise is just a starting place; alone it is not enough. Although the students were selected to join the IDMM team because of their technical excellence and field experience, in order to work as successful team members, they needed more. David Allen (1994) commented that team members who contributed only their technical expertise simply didn't contribute enough: "[I]t would've worked great if everybody had been able to contribute, but some people weren't able to contribute anything [but their technical knowledge]." David's comment suggests that collaborators who are going to be successful need to understand more than their disciplinary subject matter; they need the skill and sensitivity to communicate in their sociopolitical context.

ACKNOWLEDGMENTS

I thank the following colleagues for insightful observations and stimulating conversation through the drafts of this chapter: Cynthia Myers, Helen Rothschild Ewald, and Charlotte Thralls. I am especially grateful to Christianna White for her contributions to this project.

REFERENCES

Allen, D. [pseudonym]. (1994, February 15). Senior Student in Mechanical Engineering. Unpublished interview with C. White.

Anderson, P. (1985). What survey research tells us about writing at work. In L. Odell & D. Goswami (Eds.), *Writing in nonacademic settings* (pp. 3–83). New York: Guilford.

Bosley, D. (1991). Designing effective technical communication teams. *Technical Communication, 38*(4), 504–512.

Brown, J. S., Collins, A., & Duguid, P. (1989). Situated cognition and the culture of learning. *Educational Researcher, 18*(1), 32–42.

Bruffee, K. (1994). *Collaborative learning: Higher education, interdependence, and the authority of knowledge*. Baltimore, MD: Johns Hopkins University Press.

Burnett, R. E. (1993). Conflict in collaborative decision-making. In N. R. Blyler & C. Thralls (Eds.), *Social perspectives in professional communication* (pp. 144–162). Newbury Park, CA: Sage.

Chin, K. [pseudonym]. (1993, December 13). Senior in Computer Science. Unpublished interview with C. White.

Collins, A., Brown, J. S., & Newman, S. E. (1989). Cognitive apprenticeship: Teaching the crafts of reading, writing, and mathematics. In L. Resnick (Ed.), *Knowing, learning, and instruction: Essays in honor of Robert Glaser* (pp. 453–494). Hillsdale, NJ: Lawrence Erlbaum Associates.

Couture, B., & Rymer, J. (1989). Interactive writing on the job: Definitions and implications of "collaboration." In M. Kogen (Ed.), *Writing in the business professions* (pp. 73–93). Urbana, IL: National Council of Teachers of English.

Cross, G. A. (1990). A Bakhtinian exploration of factors affecting the collaborative writing of an executive letter of an annual report. *Research in the Teaching of English, 24*, 173–203.

Cross, G. A. (1994). *Collaboration and conflict: A contextual exploration of group writing and positive emphasis*. Cresskill, NJ: Hampton Press.

Doheny-Farina, S. (1992). *Rhetoric, innovation, technology: Case studies of technical communication in technology transfers*. Cambridge, MA: MIT Press.

Faigley, L., & Miller, T. P. (1982). What we learn from writing on the job. *College English, 44*(6), 557–569.

Flower, L., Wallace, D. L., Norris, L., & Burnett, R. E. (Eds.). (1994). *Making thinking visible: Writing, collaborative planning, and classroom inquiry*. Urbana, IL: National Council of Teachers of English.

The integrated design for marketing and manufacturing mobile laboratory for elemental analysis [Information Sheet]. (1993, Summer). Ames, IA: Ames Laboratory.

Kelvin, P. R. & Leonard, S. A. (in press). Field dissonance in the collaborative writing classroom. In R. E. Burnett & A. H. Duin (Eds.), *Collaboration in technical communication: Research perspectives*. Hillsdale, NJ: Lawrence Erlbaum Associates.

Kleimann, S. (1991). The complexity of workplace review. *Technical Communication, 38*(4),

520–526.

Locker, K. O. (1992). What makes a collaborative writing team successful? A case study of lawyers and social service workers in a state agency. In J. Forman (Ed.), *New visions of collaborative writing* (pp. 37–62). Portsmouth, NH: Boynton/Cook, Heinemann.

Lunsford, A., & Ede, L. (1990). *Singular texts/plural authors: Perspectives on collaborative writing*. Carbondale, IL: Southern Illinois University Press.

Malone, E. L. (1991). Facilitating groups through selective participation: An example of collaboration from NASA. In M. M. Lay & W. M. Karis (Eds.), *Collaborative writing in industry: Investigations in theory and practice* (pp. 109–119). Amityville, NY: Baywood.

Marshall, S. [pseudonym]. (1993, December 20). Senior in Computer Science. Unpublished interview with C. White.

Morgan, M. (1991). Patterns of composing: Connections between classroom and workplace collaborations. *Technical Communication, 38*(4), 540–545.

Nelson, T. [pseudonym]. (1994). Director of the Technology Integration Program, Ames Laboratory. Unpublished interview with C. White.

Paradis, J., Dobrin, D., & Miller, R. (1985). Writing at Exxon ITD: Notes on the writing environment of an R & D organization. In L. Odell & D. Goswami (Eds.), *Writing in nonacademic settings* (pp. 281–307). New York: Guilford.

Paulson, R. [pseudonym]. (1993, July 23). Integrated Design for Manufacturing and Marketing (IDMM) Faculty Facilitator. Unpublished interview with H. R. Ewald and R. E. Burnett.

Paulson, R. [pseudonym]. (1994, January 16). Integrated Design for Manufacturing and Marketing (IDMM) Faculty Facilitator. Unpublished interview with C. White.

Perkins, D. N., & Salomon, G. (1989). Are cognitive skills context-bound? *Educational Researcher, 18*(1), 16–25.

Sharan, S. (Ed.). (1990). *Cooperative learning: Theory and research*. New York: Praeger.

Slavin, R. E. (1990). *Cooperative learning: Theory, research, and practice*. Englewood Cliffs, NJ: Prentice-Hall.

Spanning the globe: MDLEST technology makes its way to former Soviet Union. (1994, January). *Insider*. Ames, IA: Ames Laboratory.

Taylor, K. [pseudonym]. (1993, December 16). M.S. Student in Civil & Construction Engineering. Unpublished interview with C. White.

White, C. (1994, January 16). M.A. Student in Business and Technical Communication. Unpublished interviews with R. E. Burnett.

White, C. (1994, April 27). M.A. Student in Business and Technical Communication. Unpublished interviews with R. E. Burnett.

Zabrius, C. [pseudonym]. (1993, December 21). Senior Student in Industrial Engineering. Unpublished interview with C. White.

7 Writing Well as a Form of Social Knowledge

Dorothy Winsor
GMI Engineering & Management Institute

The following account was written by an engineering student who was working as part of a cooperative education program:

> When I first reported to the Superintendent of Paint, he told me about a test they were conducting to show the Environmental Protection Agency that the assembly plant was not putting too many contaminants in the air. . . .

> [. . .] Industries conducted the test and gave the results to the Senior Paint Process Engineer. This information was then given to me and I was told to write a short summary of the results showing that the assembly plant was in compliance with its regulations and then give the summary to the Paint Superintendent. I proceeded to write the one page summary.

> After the Paint Superintendent reviewed my work, he decided that he wanted a little more detail explaining how the test was conducted. When he told me this, I was not exactly sure what he wanted and he was too busy to explain it to me so I went to the Senior Paint Process Engineer hoping that he would know what it was that I was to do. Well he was not at all sure himself so he gave me a list of all the things that he and [. . .] Industries had done and he told me to "fluff it up and make it sound impressive." I went back to my desk and looked at this list of approximately 50 things and still did not know what to do. I did not know what half of the things on the list were and it already sounded pretty impressive to me but I tried it anyway. I took my little one page summary and created a five page listing of how the test was conducted.

> I wanted to see if the Senior Paint Process Engineer liked it before I went to the Paint Superintendent because I was scared that if the Paint Superintendent had a question on what I had written I would not be able to answer him. The

Senior Paint Process Engineer made a few changes and then we took the report to the Paint Superintendent. He liked the work "we" had done but then decided that this was going to become the report the assembly plant would send to EPA. He suggested that I add a section explaining the calculations I used to figure out that the plant was in compliance with the regulations.

Well, once more I sat down at my desk and started writing away. This process of showing what I had done to the Paint Superintendent and then him telling me to add more to it lasted for about a week until the day before it was due. It was due on a Monday and I finished it by working on it for thirteen hours on Saturday. My one page summary had become a five chapter report that just barely fit in a three inch binder and it was going to be seen by more people than I could count. After the report had been completed, it was sent to the Production Manager of the assembly plant, the Plant Manager, my company's Central Headquarters, my company's Legal Department, EPA, and New Jersey state environmental officials.

I found out later that it was also seen by every other plant in our division because Central Headquarters had determined that this report was now the standard report for all the plants.

One of the things this story illustrates is that good writing sometimes happens in ways that are mysterious both to us and to the writer. What do we mean when we say that people know how to write? What, for instance, does this student know? How did he come to know it? Presumably, he has some sort of expertise or he could not have written an exemplary report. On the other hand, whatever it is this student knows, he does not seem to be able to articulate it. Nor can he say how he came to know it. In other words, this story suggests that, in Polanyi's (1967) words about tacit knowledge, "we can know more than we can tell" (p. 4). It also suggests that good writing reflects not just our conscious cognitive action, but also our enculturation into what Wittgenstein (1953) calls a "form of life," a way of being that allows us to behave appropriately in our day-to-day existence even without conscious effort.

According to Polanyi (1967), tacit knowledge is the ability to do something without being able to say how. Polanyi's classic example of tacit knowledge is riding a bicycle. A rider cannot tell how he or she balances the bike. Moreover, a physicist's understanding of gravitational forces does not enable the physicist to ride. The ability to ride a bike comes not from propositional knowledge, but from learning to perceive and respond to what happens on a bicycle. This perception is primarily tacit, and, according to Polanyi, the degree to which it can ever become explicit is limited. Many social scientists argue that no matter how much we are able to bring to consciousness, the complexity of daily life and the contingency of events mean that we can never completely say how we know what to do (Collins, 1985; Suchman, 1987, 1990).

In our culture, there is a tendency to downplay tacit, socially contingent knowledge, particularly in discussions of technical expertise. Miller (1978) criticized this tendency, saying that the high-technology characteristic of our culture leads us to see the world as predictable and controllable and to believe that solutions to problems are arrived at through "calculation" and "mechanical procedure" (p. 232). Those who are most deeply involved in technology are thus likely to dismiss knowledge of a form of life as unimportant.

For example, in a study of the creation of an expert system, Collins, Green, and Draper (1985) found that the technicians involved tended to define knowledge as primarily formal and explicable in textbook form. Expert systems are heuristic computer programs that attempt to duplicate and make usable to others the knowledge of an expert in some area. In an assembly plant, for instance, an expert system may be designed to trouble-shoot equipment when it needs repair. Such a system would be created by a "knowledge engineer," who would interview a maintenance person acknowledged to be an expert on the machine in question. The expert might be asked, for instance, what he or she would be likely to check first if the machine went down or what he or she would be most likely to change to achieve a desired condition. The expert's answers to the interview questions would be used to construct a computer program that other maintenance people could consult to service the machine. Creators of expert systems say they are trying to capture experiential as well as formal knowledge. (See Waldrop, 1987, for a discussion of expert systems.) However, even if we assume that experiential knowledge can be fully articulated (and, as I said, there is reason to doubt the possibility of this), creators of expert systems still seem to privilege abstract, rule-based knowledge. In studying one system's creation, for instance, Collins et al. (1985) found that experts did not always draw on their experience-based expertise. The researchers noted that "even where an expert knows that the skills he has are essentially practical he will tend to think of this as a defect rather than an accomplishment" (p. 330). Thus, when experts knew that a textbook version of their knowledge existed, they would sometimes substitute this rule-like version for their own because they saw it as better.

Anthropologist Forsythe (1993) documented this same privileging of textbook knowledge even by the knowledge engineers who theoretically value experiential knowledge. Forsythe contrasted the knowledge engineers' algorithmic idea of knowledge with anthropologists' belief that knowledge is culturally embedded: "Knowledge engineers seem to conceive of reasoning as a matter of following rules. In contrast, social scientists—especially anthropologists—tend to think of it in terms of meaning, and to note that the logic by which people reason may differ according to social and cultural context" (p. 464). Moreover, Forsythe argued that knowledge is not solely a matter of individual cognition. Knowledge, she claimed, is "also encoded in the cultural, social and organizational order. . . . [C]on-textual factors . . . play a role in expertise, and knowledge appears to be a social and cultural phenomenon as well as a cognitive one" (p. 464).

As Forsythe's comments suggest, the rule-driven concept of technology has been challenged by social scientists whose research shows that scientific and technical knowledge are both constituted in social practice and embedded in tacit knowledge (Collins, 1985; Gilbert, 1976; Gilbert & Mulkay, 1984; Hughes, 1987; Latour, 1987; Latour & Woolgar, 1979; Pinch & Bijker, 1987; Suchman, 1987. For a popular view of the social construction of technology, see also Kidder, 1981). In the view of these researchers, learning to do science and technology involves more than learning textbook propositions about the world. It also involves being socialized into the way groups of experts tacitly perceive and respond to part of reality, just as riding a bike involves learning to perceive and respond to what happens on a bike.

Writing scholars have often dealt with our culture's tendency to see technology as rule-bound by distancing writing from it (Dobrin, 1989; Miller, 1979). There is nothing technical about writing, scholars say, meaning that writing is not and cannot be accomplished solely by following rules. Writing, too, is increasingly viewed as a cultural practice, both in and out of the academy. However, once we have dismissed rules, we are left with less than satisfactory explanations for how good writing happens, and a story like that of the student quoted in this chapter's opening seems to leave us without much of an explanation at all. Generally speaking, we know that cultural knowledge is important in writing, but we have not yet explored all of the implications of this fact.

One way to explore these implications is to borrow from some of the findings of the social scientists I have mentioned. That is, if both writing and technology are frequently believed to be rule-governed, but are not, then we may be able to learn about writing, not by distancing it from technology, but by comparing the two. Perhaps we are wrong in saying that writing is unlike technology. Perhaps with a different understanding of technology, we will see that both writing and technology produce and result from a socially encultured way of seeing the world. Technology and writing may both be seen as processes involving knowledge about how to function in a given context, rather than as collections of propositions or products. (See Kostelnick, 1989, for a comparison of the writing process and the design process.)

This chapter presents such a comparison. It applies propositions about how technology is accomplished to statements that student engineers make about how they learned to write at work. The propositions come from the work of sociologist Collins (1985), who studied scientists as they worked with a new kind of laser. The student engineers' statements were written by 190 senior-level engineering co-op students. The students, including the one quoted in this chapter's opening, had worked full time as engineers for 6 months of each year from the time they entered college. As the first assignment for a senior technical writing class, they wrote analytical reports on the writing they had done at work, how they learned to do it, and how well they thought they wrote. The students' remarks about writing offer revealing parallels to what Collins found about technology. Socially ingrained tacit knowledge about how to perceive and respond to the world appears to have an important role in both areas. (These student papers have previously been discussed in Winsor, 1990b. For other remarks from professional writing students, see Anson & Forsberg, 1990; and Winsor, 1990a.)

PARALLELS BETWEEN LASER BUILDING AND WRITING

Collins's work on the experience of scientists learning to build a Transversely Excited Atmospheric Pressure (TEA) laser provides a useful basis for understanding the role of tacit, experiential knowledge in technology and, by extension, in situated writing. In the 1970s, the TEA laser was a relatively new technological artifact that had first been built in government labs in Canada. One might believe that once the achievement had been made public and details of its build had been published, duplicating it would be a relatively straightforward matter. When Collins (1974) studied the seven British facilities trying to construct the laser, however, he found, among other things, that no lab was able to duplicate the laser based on published reports alone. Repeated personal contact with successful builders of the laser was always crucial. A learner might visit a successful lab, then attempt to build the laser, have new questions, talk by phone with the original builders, revisit the original lab and see things he or she had not noticed before, and so on. From his observations, Collins concluded that an aspiring laser builder had to serve a kind of apprenticeship under competent builders because learning to build the laser involved learning to "see" it as did competent builders who couldn't always explain what they knew.

Collins (1985, pp. 51–78) was also a participant-observer when a physicist built TEA lasers in 1974 and again in 1979. The physicist had previous experience in using TEA lasers and had the complete cooperation of another lab that had built one. Despite these advantages, it took the physicist 6 months to build his first laser. Collins said that a large part of this time was spent "debugging" the laser, that is, in correcting what turned out to be mistakes in his various efforts. Collins called this process "developing the relevant tacit skills" (p. 58). That these skills were developed is attested to by the fact that it took the physicist only 2 days to build his second laser, and that in building it he had a much better sense of how to "see" it than he had in his first attempt. He knew what aspects of the device mattered in making it work, what aspects were likely to be trouble spots, and what aspects he could safely vary. (Cf. Amerine and Bilmes's [1990] description of children determining which instructions matter in conducting a scientific experiment.)

From this research, Collins constructed a number of propositions about how people learn to do technical tasks. Five of his propositions seem equally applicable to student engineers' descriptions of how they learned to write at work. They are listed below and should be read to include "writing" where Collins (1985) talked of "experimenting":

. . . Skill-like knowledge travels best (or only) through accomplished practitioners.

. . . Experimental ability has the character of a skill that can be acquired and developed with practice. Like a skill it cannot be fully explicated, or absolutely established.

. . . Experimental ability is invisible in its passage and in those who possess it.

. . . Proper working of the apparatus, parts of the apparatus *and the experimenter* are defined by their ability to take part in producing the proper experimental outcome. Other indicators cannot be found.

. . . Scientists and others tend to believe in the responsiveness of nature to manipulations directed by sets of algorithm-like instructions. This gives the impression that carrying out experiments is, literally, a formality. This belief, though it may occasionally be suspended at times of difficulty, recrystallizes . . . upon successful completion of an experiment. (p. 129)

I take up each of these propositions in turn.

Skill-like knowledge travels best (or only) through accomplished practitioners. (Collins, 1985, p. 129)

As noted earlier, no one succeeded in building a laser without direct contact with a previously successful builder. Similarly, the co-op students overwhelmingly described one pattern in learning professional writing: They examined a previous example of successful writing, attempted to imitate it, and then received feedback from supervisors or coworkers on whether their imitation was successful. (See Winsor, 1990b. See also MacKinnon, 1993, on the importance of feedback to novice writers in a professional setting.) In this recursive process, the model may be compared to the laser that Collins's physicist was trying to duplicate, and the input from experienced writers may be compared to the input the physicist received from experienced laser builders.

Imitating a writing model, like duplicating a laser, is more complicated than it might at first sound. As one student said, "I had to be careful not to follow an old report which had poor format or weak structure. To an uneducated writer, it was easy to follow such a report." Even with a good model, the student had to determine what counted in making the model good and what might be safely ignored or varied. In other words, he or she had to learn how to "see" the model, just as the physicist had to learn how to "see" the laser. The writer's revisions resulted from literal re-vision.

The students' use of models they did not yet completely understand recalls Vygotsky's (1986) description of children successfully using signs to communicate before they understood the signs' full meaning (pp. 93, 101). Vygotsky said that children come to understand the full meaning of language partly by using it, that they learn from a back and forth movement between the generalized concept any word represents and the specific embodiment it refers to (p. 105). The part of reality a word refers to affects the concept children form, but then the concept affects how children see reality. The language they use shapes their perceptions as well as vice versa. "The child begins to perceive the world," said Vygotsky (1978), "not only through his eyes but also through his speech" (p. 32). Given this, we would expect that students would at first use models embodying the local culture's language clumsily, but that clumsy use, coupled with feedback, would eventually help them to build tacit knowledge of the local culture's perceptions of reality. (See Winsor, 1990a, for an example of a student successfully using a model he does not fully understand.)

For the students, the building of this experiential knowledge was facilitated by contact with expert writers who helped them to debug their efforts as Collins' physicist debugged his laser. Some representative comments are as follows: "I consulted a previously published report for the proper format and sentence structure. It didn't take long to catch on to the concise writing style necessary to communicate to fellow employees. After writing my best effort, I showed it to some coworkers, who critiqued it and helped me with the finishing touches before I handed it in to my boss." And, "The engineers I worked with were very helpful and understanding. I would show them what I thought should be written in the report and they would sit down with me, tell me what was good, and what should be added to or deleted from my reports." The learning process described here is, of course, consistent with research on the influence of reading on writing (see Tierney & Shanahan, 1991, for a summary of this research) and on the importance of the interaction between novice and expert in a process variously called *scaf-*

folding (Bruner, 1978; Cazden, 1979) and *guided participation* (Rogoff, 1990).

> Experimental ability has the character of a skill that can be acquired and developed with practice. Like a skill it cannot be fully explicated, or absolutely established. (Collins, 1985, p. 129)

Collins (1985) pointed out that even successful laser builders were not able to explain how they had accomplished their goal. Different labs gave contradictory information about how certain parts had to be shaped, for instance. Each lab believed its own design was essential to success (p. 58; cf. Amerine & Bilmes's [1990] account of third graders who believed one tub of water was more likely to produce a desired experimental outcome than a second, identical tub).

Engineering students frequently commented on the importance of practice versus classroom explanations of how to write. They knew they were improving as writers, but had trouble explaining how the improvement happened. They made comments like the following: "In my college career, nothing has proven more helpful than practice," or "Communication skills cannot be learned solely from a textbook. The style of writing in a workplace can only be learned from experience." Students also downgraded the importance of their freshman technical writing class in their learning to write. Only 14% mentioned it as one of the ways they learned to write for work.

One reason both competent writing and technical expertise are "acquired and developed with practice" (Collins, 1985, p. 129) is their active nature. People who have achieved expert or insider status have learned to see the world as ordered in a certain way. The order they see, however, is not a preexisting form they passively perceive. Rather it is something they learn to accomplish (cf. Vygotsky, 1986, on the active nature of concept formation). Experts have learned to order reality in ways approved by their disciplines or cultures. What's more, because the world does not stand still, this order is something they have to keep on achieving, which is why, as Collins said, their ability is never "absolutely established."

Our descriptions of writing frequently ignore this dynamic aspect of expertise. In our articles and especially in our textbooks, we often seem to describe an order to writing that exists separately from orderers. Such an order is an illusion. As Collins (1985) said, there are no "formal rules which transcend the conventions of the society in which they are embedded . . . .[R]ules are only rules by virtue of social conventions: they *are* social conventions" (p. 145).

A novice in any area must learn to see the world as other group members do.

Experimental ability is invisible in its passage and in those who possess it. (Collins, 1985, p. 129)

Learners did not really know if they knew how to build a laser until they tried to do so. They might think they had learned enough from a visit to a successful lab and then find that they could not make their own device function.

Every teacher has seen students who are surprised by their lack of competence, and the student engineers occasionally fell into this category too: "Once I had all the facts and figures, all I had to do was write the report. I anticipated that this would be an easy task once I had all the data. I was wrong. This turned out to be a nightmare."

Somewhat more unusual is that the students were also often surprised at their competence. The student whose account opened this chapter is a prime example of a writer whose ability is invisible until it is used. Other students too were surprised by their own success: "I was complimented for a job well done and was surprised to learn that what seemed to be a simple job had caused many problems in the past." And, "I really did not expect that I would be required to write the manual. . . .To my surprise, I did a good job documenting the program." Competence, like the lack of it, is invisible even to the possessor.

Proper working of the apparatus, parts of the apparatus *and the experimenter* are defined by their ability to take part in producing the proper experimental outcome. Other indicators cannot be found. (Collins, 1985, p. 129)

A good laser is one that lases. A competent laser builder is one who can build a working laser. There is no other way to test the device or the builder, or perhaps more accurately, any other test can produce only irrelevant results.

Student engineers assessed their success in writing by the perfectly reasonable standard of its effectiveness: "After the first correspondence, I was contacted by the customer to clarify some minor details. I experienced no problems with future letters."

The student assumed that the disappearance of requests for clarification meant his writing was then clear. Whether a writing researcher sees it as possessing the elements making for clarity is irrelevant. Sometimes the emphasis on effectiveness leads to circularity in describing good writing: "Writing these work orders has taught me to write instructions in a logical order, to use explicit detail, and to include sketches to complement my writing. Well-written work orders are essential for getting the job done correctly and for establishing a good working relationship with the technicians doing the work." "Well-written work orders" get the job done; work orders that get the job done are well written.

Applied to writing, this principle accounts for some of the difficulty we have in assessing current practice in writing at work. On the one hand, we conduct research to discover normal practice and then teach it to our students. On the other hand, we feel that much is wrong with normal practice and that we ought to be able to assess it. Against what standards are we to do so? If we and the writer's coworkers agree on a weakness, then we will probably have no problem because our conclusions are supported by the tacit knowledge of the work community. But if a writer is believed competent by others in her environment (if they all believe the passive voice is more appropriate than active voice in a report, for instance), what enables us to say that they are wrong?

In an ethnographic study of writers at work, Brown and Herndl (1986) argued that there is no culturally unbiased way for us to judge a writing practice. They looked at writers who had been trained to avoid overnominalization and narrative form but persisted in using them anyway. Brown and Herndl (1986) concluded that the writers used the forms we think of as less desirable because they felt that those forms marked them as members of the group. The researchers pointed out that there is no culture-free way to decide whether the writers made a good choice (p. 25). We may be able to demonstrate that overnominalization leads to less efficient reading, but efficiency is a culturally determined value just as much as the desire for group membership is. (See Suchan & Dulek, 1990, for similar findings.)

> Scientists and others tend to believe in the responsiveness of nature to manipulations directed by sets of algorithm-like instructions. This gives the impression that carrying out experiments is, literally, a formality. This belief, though it may occasionally be suspended at times of difficulty, recrystallizes . . . upon successful completion of an experiment. (Collins, 1985, p. 129)

The physicist whom Collins worked with believed that he should have been able to build a laser with the directions he was given. He blamed his failure to do so on the unpredictability of his own human behavior, which he took to be a departure from the normal course of technical competence, rather than an expected part of it. While he was still constructing the laser, he saw the procedure as intractable, but once he had succeeded, any difficulty was attributed to the weakness of his own efforts rather than to the nature of the procedure itself. According to Collins, one of the things novices learn as they enter any field is to accept the behavior and perceptions of the field's experts as normal and to blame themselves for any failure to behave and perceive in the same way. This is one of the ways novices make themselves into full-fledged members of a discipline.

The following statement illustrates some of these principles in a student writer: "A journal was used to record facts or important occurrences during projects, so when the time came to write a report there was an account of the happenings to use as a reference. I find that when it comes time to reference my daily journal to write reports or letters it contains data that is not useful. Therefore I feel that more instructions are necessary on what is and what is not important to keep track of." The student saw his inability to know ahead of time what will be important as a flaw in himself rather than as a normal part of work on a project. He asked to be taught something that no teacher is capable of teaching him. Although his ability to guess what will turn out to be worth recording will probably improve, that improvement is likely to come from experience resulting in tacit knowledge of conducting a project.

Students often knew that they themselves had learned to write primarily through experience and, as I have pointed out, they devalued the freshman technical writing class they had all been required to take. Nonetheless, like the student trying to keep his journal, they believed that it should have been possible to give them rules that would have made learning by experience unnecessary. They saw formal training as a possible and desirable replacement for the way they had learned. Thus one finds statements like the following in their reports: "Never having received formal training on how to write a manual, I was completely unprepared for writing one." And, "My 'training' came from the questions I asked the other engineers. I must have learned enough since I did make myself understood. It would be nice to know the best format for all occasions." "For most of the writing I received no formal training, it was just expected that I should have known the proper form to present the information in." "Established classes are rare and it is often up to the individual to 'teach' himself. This, unfortunately, is often by trial and error." Notice that for these students, the only kind of training worthy of the name is formal, class-like training, which could conceivably enable one to know ahead of time "the best format for all occasions." Then writing the report would be, as Collins said, "literally, a formality." On the other hand, if one has not had formal training, one has had no training and is "completely unprepared." Despite overwhelming evidence for the importance of experientially produced tacit knowledge, the students believed in the importance of rules.

In summary, then, tacit knowledge acquired through social interaction seems to be important to both technologists and writers. These activities are part of a communal way of perceiving at least as much as they are part of a communal body of knowledge. Both technologists and writers, however, may believe that their activity is simply rule-driven and perceive their own departures from this ideal as a flaw in their knowledge base.

IMPLICATIONS FOR TEACHING AND RESEARCH

The importance of tacit knowledge to technology and writing has certain consequences for our idea of the nature of expertise and the means by which people achieve it. It implies, for instance, that telling people how writing is done is not the same thing as telling them how to do it. Anthropologist Suchman (1987) provided an extended analysis of the distinction between what she called "plans and situated actions." Plans and instructions can orient an actor, but do not control performance, any more than a map controls a journey. Actions take place in a contingent situation that plans and instructions cannot possibly anticipate fully. In order to write well, a novice has to learn to perceive and react to the world as expert writers do, and we are not able to tell people how to do that.

If we are not able to tell people how to perceive the world as experts, what, if anything, are we able to tell them? If we cannot tell them how to write well, can we still help them to learn how? In other words, what are the implications of this material for teaching? What questions does it raise for further research on how people write well in any context, whether that context be the classroom or the workplace? To some degree, the material discussed here is consistent with a substantial body of research that says that we cannot teach people to do something by telling them the rules. Freedman (1993a) recently summarized the research that questions explicit instruction in genre production. This research has implications for writing in general.

Freedman presented both a strong and a restricted form of the claim that such instruction is of limited value at best. The strong form of the claim draws heavily on Krashen's (1981, 1984, 1992) work on second language acquisition. Krashen argued that the knowledge governing language use in any situation is too complicated to be explicitly taught. As Freedman (1993a) said, Krashen's work implies that people actually learn through "the subconscious inferring of the rules of language use on the basis of comprehensible examples of the target language during the process of authentic language tasks" (p. 230). This position is consistent with the way the student engineers discussed in this chapter described learning to write at work.

However, even in the studies with the most negative findings on explicit instruction, some kinds of explicit teaching seem valuable. For instance, it seems possible to teach explicit rules for format, organization, composing strategies, and some editing (Freedman, 1993a, p. 237). Moreover, many of the studies that Freedman examined take a more moderate position, allowing for effective formal instruction in a wider range of areas if such instruction occurs close to the time when the student needs it (pp. 240–245; see Williams & Colomb, 1993, and Fahnestock, 1993, for counterarguments to Freedman's analysis and Freedman, 1993b, for a response to these counterarguments). One subject for future research, then, would be what is and is not useful to teach by explicit instruction, and what other means of teaching (such as scaffolding) are at our disposal. If writing well depends on some degree of situated knowledge, then how can we best spend our time preparing students for their professional lives?

Another subject for future research is the relationship between school learning (whether by explicit instruction or through such means as scaffolding) and writing in the workplace. In other words, how transferable is knowledge about writing? (See Carter, 1990, for an interesting analysis of this question.) Transferability is difficult to assess. For instance, one possibility is that people learn something at work by socialization and then recognize it as something they have also been taught at school and label it with the school label. Thus even when it looks as if they are applying school learning, they are not doing so in any simple way. The learning came elsewhere, and what they learned may be infinitely more complex than the label suggests. However, it may also be that learning categories at school allows a writer to notice them more at work. This is a possibility that Freedman (1993a, p. 243) suggested. Although such a process is not direct transfer of knowledge, it does imply that knowledge gained in one situation facilitates gaining knowledge in another area. The subject of transferability has not been widely explored in studies of workplace writing, but it deserves to be.

Another subject needing further research is learning from models. (Charney, 1991, presented preliminary work on this topic.) Learning from models has been rather out of favor since Hillocks's (1986) analysis of research on the teaching of writing revealed it to be ineffective. However, the models in the studies Hillocks looked at were generally treated as decontextualized ideals that would be good writing in any circumstances. The use of contextualized models to teach tacit, socially based knowledge is a subject that needs further research.

Research on learning from contextualized models might usefully draw on Miller's (1984) notion of genre as a solution to typical rhetorical problems. Miller argued that the genres used by various discourse communities encouraged their members to perceive certain situations as recurrent, calling for a certain kind of document in response. There is nothing inherent in any situation to force this perception on people. Different knowledge communities sort reality differently. Miller's work suggests why locally endorsed models are so important in the student engineers' accounts of learning to write. They serve not only as objectives the student aims to achieve, but also as embodiments of some of the social knowledge the student lacks. The models provide guidance on what people in a given environment think is worth writing about and on the way they think that writing should be done (cf. Winkler, 1983). A locally endorsed model both constructs and records the order insiders have learned to achieve. It stabilizes the order and makes it easier to see than it is in the normal flow of events. Thus, locally endorsed models, supplemented by expert feedback, provide a bridge between rules a writer might know and the particular circumstances in which the writer must act. This is the area in which, as Suchman (1987) said, "the action is"

(p. 189). It is precisely this area that our studies of situated writing have tended to ignore.

The idea that part of knowledge is tacit and socially based is not easy for writing scholars to accommodate, any more than it is for technologists. It reminds us of our own limitations in knowing and controlling the world. As they are commonly thought of, instructions, whether they be addressed to students or technologists, may be a fiction we use to reinforce our belief in the rational, knowable nature of reality. Seeing instructions as rules that enable us to do something is an example of our belief in and desire for the possibility of rational, rule-driven action. In that sense, they are, to paraphrase Geertz (1973, p. 448), a story we tell ourselves about ourselves. Instructions are chronological narratives of rational action. The ability to write well, however, is not acquired solely by learning rules, although it would be comforting if it were.

REFERENCES

Amerine, R., & Bilmes, J. (1990). Following instructions. In M. Lynch & S. Woolgar (Eds.), *Representation in scientific practice* (pp. 323–335). Cambridge, MA: MIT Press.

Anson, C. M., & Forsberg, L. L. (1990). Moving beyond the academic community: Transitional stages in professional writing. *Written Communication, 7*(2), 200–231.

Brown, R. L., & Herndl, C. G. (1986). An ethnographic study of corporate writing. In B. Couture (Ed.), *Functional approaches to writing: Research perspectives* (pp. 11–28). Norwood, NJ: Ablex.

Bruner, J. (1978). The role of dialogue in language acquisition. In A. Sinclair, R. J. Jarvella, & W. J. M. Levelt (Eds.), *The child's conception of language* (pp. 241–255). New York: Springer-Verlag.

Carter, M. (1990). The idea of expertise: An exploration of cognitive and social dimensions of writing. *College Composition and Communication, 41*(3), 265–286.

Cazden, C. (1979). Peekaboo as an instructional model: Discourse development at home and at school. *Papers and Reports of Child Language Development, 17*(1), 1–29.

Charney, D. (1991, March). *Learning to write science: Rules, models, and practical experience.* Paper presented at the Conference on College Composition and Communication, Boston, MA.

Collins, H. M. (1974). The TEA set: Tacit knowledge and scientific networks. *Science Studies, 4*(1), 165–186.

Collins, H. M. (1985). *Changing order: Replication and induction in scientific practice.* Beverly Hills, CA: Sage.

Collins, H. M., Green, R. H., & Draper, R. C. (1985). Where's the expertise? *Expert systems 85: Proceedings of the fifth technical conference of the British computer society specialist group on expert systems* (pp. 323–334). Cambridge, UK: Cambridge University Press.

Dobrin, D. (1989). *Writing and technique.* Urbana, IL: National Council of Teachers of English.

Fahnestock, J. (1993). Genre and rhetorical craft. *Research in the Teaching of English, 27*(3), 265–271.

Forsythe, D. E. (1993). Engineering knowledge: The construction of knowledge in artificial intelligence. *Social Studies of Science, 23*(3), 445–477.

Freedman, A. (1993a). Show and tell? The role of explicit teaching in the learning of new genres. *Research in the Teaching of English, 27*(3), 222–251.

Freedman, A. (1993b). Situating genre: A rejoinder. *Research in the Teaching of English, 27*(3), 272–281.

Geertz, C. (1973). *The interpretation of culture.* New York: Basic.

Gilbert, G. N. (1976). The transformation of research findings into scientific knowledge. *Social Studies of Science, 6*(2), 281–306.

Gilbert, G. N., & Mulkay, M. (1984). *Opening Pandora's box: A sociological analysis of scientists' discourse.* Cambridge, UK: Cambridge University Press.

Hillocks, G., Jr. (1986). *Research on written composition.* Urbana, IL: National Council of Teachers of English.

Hughes, T. P. (1987). The evolution of large technological systems. In W. E. Bijker, T. P. Hughes, & T. Pinch (Eds.), *The social construction of technological systems* (pp. 51–82). Cambridge, MA: MIT Press.

Kidder, T. (1981). *The soul of a new machine.* Boston: Little, Brown.

Kostelnick, C. (1989). Process paradigms in design and composition: Affinities and directions. *College Composition and Communication, 40*(3), 267–281.

Krashen, S. D. (1981). *Second language acquisition and second language learning.* Elmsford, NY: Pergamon.

Krashen, S. D. (1984). *Writing: Research, theory, and applications.* Elmsford, NY: Pergamon.

Krashen, S. D. (1992). Another educator comments. *TESOL Quarterly, 26*(4), 409–411.

Latour, B. (1987). *Science in action: How to follow scientists and engineers through society.* Cambridge, MA: Harvard University Press.

Latour, B., & Woolgar, S. (1979). *Laboratory life: The social construction of scientific facts.* Beverly Hills, CA: Sage.

MacKinnon, J. (1993). Becoming a rhetor: Developing writing ability in a mature writing-intensive organization. In R. Spilka (Ed.), *Writing in the workplace: New research perspectives* (pp. 41–55). Carbondale: Southern Illinois University Press.

Miller, C. R. (1978). Technology as a form of consciousness: A study of contemporary ethos. *Central States Speech Journal, 29*(2), 228–236.

Miller, C. R. (1979). A humanistic rationale for technical writing. *College English, 40*(6), 610–617.

Miller, C. R. (1984). Genre as social action. *Quarterly Journal of Speech, 70*(2), 151–167.

Pinch, T., & Bijker, W. E. (1987). The social construction of facts and artifacts: Or how the sociology of science and the sociology of technology might benefit each other. In W. E. Bijker, T. P. Hughes, & T. Pinch (Eds.), *The social construction of technological systems* (pp. 17–50). Cambridge, MA: MIT Press.

Polanyi, M. (1967). *The tacit dimension.* London: Routledge and Kegan Paul.

Rogoff, B. (1990). *Apprenticeship in thinking.* New York: Oxford University Press.

Suchan, J., & Dulek, R. (1990). A reassessment of clarity in written managerial communications. *Management Communication Quarterly, 4*(1), 87–99.

Suchman, L. (1987). *Plans and situated actions: The problem of human-machine communication.* Cambridge, UK: Cambridge University Press.

Suchman, L. (1990). Representing practice in cognitive science. In M. Lynch & S. Woolgar (Eds.), *Representation in scientific practice* (pp. 301–321). Cambridge, MA: MIT Press.

Tierney, R. J., & Shanahan, T. (1991). Research on reading-writing relationships. In R. Barr, M. L. Kamil, P. B. Mosenthal, & P. D. Pearson (Eds.), *Handbook of reading research* (Vol. 2, pp. 246–280). New York: Longman.

Vygotsky, L. (1978). *Mind in society* (M. Cole, V. John-Steiner, S. Scribner, & E. Souberman, Eds.). Cambridge, MA: Harvard University Press.

Vygotsky, L. (1986). *Thought and language* (A. Kozulin, Ed.). Cambridge, MA: MIT Press.

Waldrop, M. M. (1987). *Man-made minds: The promise of artificial intelligence.* New York: Walker.

Williams, J. M., & Colomb, G. G. (1993). The case for explicit teaching: Why what you don't know won't help you. *Research in the Teaching of English, 27*(3), 252–264.

Winkler, V. M. (1983). The role of models in technical and scientific writing. In P. V. Anderson, R. J. Brockmann, & C. R. Miller (Eds.), *New essays in technical and scientific communication: Research, theory, and practice* (pp. 111–122). Amityville, NY: Baywood.

Winsor, D. A. (1990a). How companies affect the writing of young engineers: Two case studies. *IEEE Transactions on Professional Communication, 33*(3), 124–129.

Winsor, D. A. (1990b). Joining the engineering community: How do novices learn to write like engineers? *Technical Communication, 37*(2), 171–172.

Wittgenstein, L. (1953). *Philosophical investigations*. Oxford, UK: Blackwell.

8 Social Theories, Workplace Writing, and Collaboration: Implications and Directions for Research

Jo Allen
East Carolina University

Carol Thompson
Texas Christian University

In 1985, Odell and Goswami published a collection of essays on nonacademic writing, including an essay by Lester titled "Nonacademic Writing: The Social Perspective" (pp. 231–248) and Odell's "Beyond the Text: Relations between Writing and Social Context" (pp. 248–280). Both essays acknowledge the social aspects of communication: Communication exists within and between groups of readers and writers and serves to bind those people in some purposeful way for the good of at least one of those groups. Faigley, for instance, noted the textual, individual, and social perspectives of writing, addressing the possibility that "writing . . . is a social act that takes place in a structure of authority, changes constantly as society changes, has consequences in the economic and political realms, and shapes the writer as much as it is shaped by the writer" (p. 226). Because it is not the purpose of his chapter to investigate the means by which these activities and responsibilities control or at least affect the writing endeavor, his work focuses primarily on the kinds of research questions and appropriate methodologies that could be generated by such this assumption.

As a follow-up to Faigley's chapter, Odell cited his research on the particular questions and strategies for communicating from the perspective of one particular group of analysts. He noted the individual writers' justifications for including certain bits of information in the documents they create, as well as whether they are willing to delete various segments of their text. Influencing these writers' decisions are issues of corporate culture—the social attitudes, behaviors, and expectations that pervade a particular corporation's communications. These aspects are informed by the writers' previous experiences in creating documents for a particular reader or group of readers, their experiences in creating successful documents within their corporation (documents that do not require rewrites after they have been passed up the line), and their experiences based on their knowledge of their jobs and roles within the corporation.

In this chapter, we follow up on the broad strokes painted by Faigley on the social aspects of communication and on the company-specific observations noted by Odell. Unlike Thralls and Blyler (1993), who use social pedagogies specifically applied to technical communication classrooms, we take a step back and describe five larger dominant social theories—structural-functionalist theory, conflict theory, interactionist theory, Marxist/critical theory, and feminist theory—as a means of investigating the relationship between workplace writers (as a community) and between these writers and their readers (as interrelated subcultures). We chose these five theories in particular because of their highly influential roles in all aspects of social theory and because of their broad implications for business and technical communication research.

In the first part of the chapter, we briefly explain each theory, some basic criticisms of it, and some examples of how each theory may help clarify the characteristics of the nonacademic writing community and the other communities with which it interacts. Then, we pose some questions about nonacademic writing that the particular theory might address through research. In the next segment of the chapter, we use each theory to acknowledge particular aspects of one writing context—collaboration—one of the more obvious social activities of nonacademic writing. We conclude with some other possible multidisciplinary combinations that might shed new light on the kinds of questions we should be asking about nonacademic writers.

We intend to address these dominant social theories and explore their implications for a particular group of writers—*nonacademic* or *workplace writers*—terms we use to indicate business, scientific, and technical writers. Although these writers may be freelance writers (rather than corporate-salaried writers), they are not writing for popular magazines or newspapers, and they are neither fiction writers nor poets by profession. We should clarify, however, that this group—nonacademic or workplace writers—only excludes professors when they are writing scholarship for publication. It includes them when they are writing to conduct the business of the academy through their memos, letters, proposals, and reports. We assume that workplace writers are sensitive to—although they may disagree over the particular values of—the roles of communication and of ethics within and between various communities and the processes of creating and distributing information.

We should also explain that we use the terms *society* and *community* interchangeably—with the exception that *society* typically denotes a larger group than *community*—to mean a group that is at least loosely bound by the same rules, contexts, understandings, and applications that has set it apart from other groups. Regardless of size, however, the group is not necessarily characterized by consensus, but by a familial ability to tolerate or adjust to each others' general expectations, attitudes, and behaviors. The smaller the community becomes, the more consensus takes over as the characterizing trait of the group. Therefore, as a community within the broader society of writers, technical writers (as a group) tend to value conciseness, design features, and technical accuracy more than the other members of the society of writers. In fact, their appreciation for these and other discipline-specific features brings the group of technical writers together as a community in the first place.

We explore the particular characteristics and understandings that make this group of writers a community, as well as what characterizes or exemplifies deviance in this context. Using various social theories, we address some basic social questions: Who makes the rules? Why do they get to make the rules? What happens if someone breaks the rules? Can the rules change? What kind of social impetus might initiate change? What kinds of consequences result from that change and how, in turn, is this writing community affected? Through our examples and questions for further research, we explore these questions in two ways: in terms of the nonacademic writing community itself (how it creates its own culture) and in terms of this community's relationship with other communities (the technological, business, scientific, political, as well as the general public).

One of the most challenging aspects of integrating the questions of two disciplines — sociology and workplace communication — is finding some way to manage the enormous amount of information generated by the two fields. (Later in this chapter, we devote a section to our own collaborative strategies.) Trying not to overlook important concepts while handling essential tenets means having to make sacrifices: having to opt for one idea, one example, and one set of questions over another. Limiting ourselves to five social theories is one way we have tried to manage the possibilities of this topic. Yet the expansiveness of treating five theories means that only the broadest perspectives can be shaped here. We have chosen to focus these perspectives as suggested avenues for research, avenues that we hope will lead others toward clarifying and exploring the way(s) this particular community of writers works and, then, how it influences other communities and the larger society.

THE NATURE OF SOCIAL THEORIES

Sociologists use the word *theory* in various ways: as loosely organized collections of ideas or as precise statements of ideas that can be clearly spelled out. The latter, of course, is the ideal use of the word, but (like most scholarly terms) *theory* rarely exists in an ideal form. Further complicating the nature of the endeavor, social theorists typically work toward precision of ideas by using working theories. In this case, social theorists are not unlike scientists; for as Kuhn (1970) noted, scientists typically try to clarify or prove particular concepts by assuming the concepts are true. In fact, that stance is the only means by which science can work. For if scientists do not believe a concept is true (at least potentially), the concept is either dismissed or ignored. Similarly, social theorists hypothesize that certain structures and impetuses for societies and communities exist; then, they work to clarify and refine the elements of that structure and impetus.

Unlike scientists, however, sociologists rarely use only one theory to explain or investigate a particular phenomenon. Coser (1981) suggested that social analysis works best when employing not just one theory, but many. He refers to this approach to theory as the "tool kit" model of social investigation (pp. 172–173), meaning that social theorists recognize a feature of the phenomenon and use the appropriate methodology for investigating it or appropriate terminology for explaining it. Thus, he continued, this type of disciplined eclecticism is a productive strategy that allows theorists to apply specific theoretical perspectives to the particular problems they address (p. 173).

What, then, can social theory do? First, it can explain already existing problems or situations. Second, it can facilitate new ideas and ways of understanding or solving problems. Social theory, in other words, can suggest new directions for behavior and policy by sensitizing and/or shaping thoughts or ideas, making theory a guide or map of the social world. Third, social theory can allow us to realistically predict future events. Just as the business/industrial complex becomes increasingly committed to planning and forecasting, its leaders may become increasingly committed to relying on social theories because, clearly, technology and business do not progress by themselves: They require the interaction of human beings. Unfortunately, such applications may become prescriptive, leading business and industry to encourage conformity, rather than creativity, in their writers. The danger, in other words, is the establishment of a monochromatic community of writers, oblivious to the nuances of diversity and its contributions to perspectives, ethics, and other important sociological and communal issues.

What, more specifically, can social theory do for investigations of nonacademic writing? Although in broad terms it can help us describe our present and predict our future conditions, its primary importance may be that it will help us understand the elements peculiar to our community and its interaction with other communities. Recognizing (a) how communication works from a sociological perspective, (b) what our responsibilities are to our own and other communities, and (c) the role of information and its communication in terms of power, enculturation, and social norms may lead us to a clearer sense of our place as professionals, our abilities and responsibilities to interact with other communities or larger societies, and our power to shape policies, thoughts, and behaviors.

Structural-Functionalist Theory

Structural-functionalism has been influenced most by the theory of organicism which asserts that society can be viewed as a living organism or system. The parts of the social system, like an organism, are interrelated, and each part has some specific functions. These roles contribute to the maintenance and equilibrium of the system. If an organism is to survive, it must be able to adapt to environmental changes. When one part of the system is influenced by outside pressures, the equilibrium of the entire system is upset because changes in one part of the system necessitate change in other parts of the system. By gradually adapting or responding to the external pressures, the system evolves. Of course, the evolution of a social system, like a species, is a slow process; thus, change is evolutionary, not revolutionary. If change either inside or outside of the system occurs too quickly or too slowly, the system's survival is threatened.

Structural functionalists argue that a prerequisite for survival is a shared, articulated set of goals. Shared goals assist social cohesion, and a normative system is put in place to help societies regulate individuals. Without normative regulation and consensus, a society would be in chaos. When established norms are violated or compromised, conflict or disequilibrium occurs. This disequilibrium is alleviated once normative consensus is reestablished (Parsons, 1964; Ritzer, 1983; Skidmore, 1979).

The structural-functionalist theory has been widely criticised over the years, primarily because it is impossible to build an empirically testable model based on the theory. It is considered tautological and falsely teleological (Skidmore, 1979). In brief, something is viewed as functional if it exists universally in all social systems and is necessary for those systems to survive. Unfortunately, functionalists go on to assume that if something exists universally and is necessary, it is functional (a circular argument) (Skidmore, 1979, p. 173).

Further, functionalism provides a teleological explanation for the existence of parts of a system with consideration of the parts in the future (Skidmore, 1979, p. 174). For example, a functionalist theory of family would describe the role of, say, the woman as the nurturer because of her biological role as childbearer. Thus, her function within the family is to fulfill the nurturing aspects: nurse, counselor, food preparer. By extension, functionalists say that social structures (norms) emerge and evolve from that division of labor. They predict, further, that those norms will propel her to continue the nurturing role in the future.

Although functionalists see this particular division of labor as providing equilibrium within the family as a social system, critics note that this division of labor is only one way the woman's role could have evolved. In short, functionalism becomes a way of preserving the status quo; without providing any clearer explanation of the causes for the effects they note, functionalists merely argue that because a particular set of behaviors, attitudes, or beliefs exist, they must be functional (useful). Thus, the theory's circular arguments, along with its conservative and limiting stances, are largely responsible for its current unpopularity in sociological circles.

Another problem is that structural-functionalism does not provide reasons for the emergence of certain institutions or forms of societies (capitalist, communist). In other words, the cause is missing from the model, leaving only the effect to constitute the model.

Several concepts utilized within structural-functionalism are helpful for understanding society, but are also problematic because they have been poorly defined. The concept of *system*, for example, suggests relatedness, but when several functioning systems affect each other, they form a larger system that may have its own, even larger structural characteristics (Skidmore, 1979, p. 176). Thus, the notion of system boundaries (which may signal a custom, language, particular rite, or membership) is quite useful at first. When we try to use the term empirically, however, problems arise because these boundaries can be put wherever we want them in order to include or exclude any group, characteristic, or behavior (Skidmore, 1979). (For more on the structural-functionalist theory, see Durkheim, 1895/1964; Giddens, 1972; Parsons, 1954, 1964.)

Given such objections, it may seem inappropriate for us to include this theory in our chapter — much less begin the discussion of social theories and workplace communication with it. Most people outside the field of sociology, however, typically identify most strongly with the ideas espoused by this theory, thinking it best describes what a society is and does. And, for our purposes of discussing rather than building an empirically testable model, it does describe quite accurately the way many workplace writers (and others) see workplace writing; they see it as a set of rules that are not to be violated.

One of the most concrete ways to see this theory working in the nonacademic writing community is to look at several standard textbooks for business or technical writing. They are, for the most part, structured about the same: an introduction discusses the role and importance of communication in business and technological settings, followed by a chapter or two on style and the writing process, a chapter on research methods for finding business/technical information, a series of chapters on particular applications (letters, memos, proposals, reports), a chapter on graphics, a chapter on oral presentations, and a final segment on grammar and mechanics. These texts may be organized in this way either because that is, indeed, the most logical order for students (having them work from a general understanding of what they are doing, through the complex rhetorical and formatting aspects of communication, to the perfunctory last rites of editing and proofreading), or because that is now the way we expect textbooks to be organized. Thus, violations (putting grammar first, for example) imply a disrespect for previous patterns of textbook organization, indicate a reevaluation of what is most important in a text, course, or in workplace communication itself, or may even demonstrate the author's lack of knowledge about this writing genre. Consequently, the matter of expectations—in this case, the expected order of chapters in a text—is critical in terms of whether those expectations are fulfilled or violated and what the fulfillment or violation signals to the community (see also Herndl, chapter 2, and Lay, chapter 4, in this volume).

The fulfillment of normative expectations is, in fact, typically recognized as one of the primary tasks of the workplace communicator (see Thralls and Blyler on social constructivism). Seeking to predict and accommodate readers' expectations, the writer is supposed to know the audience, their background, previous subject knowledge, purpose(s) for reading the document, and educational level. These clues help the writer determine what kinds of information and how many details to include in a document and what kind of style and vocabulary to use. When the writer fails to accommodate the reader, either through content, style, format, or vocabulary, he or she has operated outside the normative boundaries and has produced, supposedly, a noncommunicative/deviant document. Consequently, many teachers of workplace communication courses see students as people trying to belong to a community (competent writers) who must be taught the standards and norms so they can fit in. Thus, if students use fiction or poetic techniques (such as dialogue or rhyme), we say they have created inappropriate documents for either their audience's background or reasons for reading because they have violated the norms of workplace communication. The problem, as Sullivan (1990) wrote, is that this method of teaching requires "teaching the technological mindset, and, thus, enculturating students into the military-industrial complex" (p. 377). Thus, questions arise about the social, political, and ethical responsibilities of writers who are enculturated to produce a particular style, length, voice, format, and content in their workplace documents.

Perhaps the best example of the structural-functionalist theory working in the communication community is the use of standard grammar. Writers are expected by both readers and other writers to adhere to rules of grammatical agreement, appropriate tense and voice, and standard punctuation. When writers violate those norms, other writers and readers react negatively because such a grammatical normative structure serves important purposes (functions) in communication. They set standards by which we evaluate other writers' writings, along with their thinking, backgrounds, intellect, and attention to detail. Violations upset the normative boundaries and create disequilibrium in the writing community and introduce greater possibilities of misunderstandings between the readers and the writers. These violations, at least temporarily, are inconsistent with our purposes for communication and affect our credibility as professionals. Hence, we hear the cry, "Whatever happened to standards?" However, if the external pressure to change certain practices remains, then the community/social system will have to adapt. A temporary period of conflict will end as a new normative framework emerges within the community. Consensus is restored. This portrayal of the need for standard grammar is an example of the conservative leanings of applied structural-functionalism. Although useful, those adopting this theoretical perspective should remain aware of its inherent conservative bias.

What structural-functionalism offers to us as students/teachers of writing, therefore, is a way to understand the writing community as a social system. By applying the concepts of structural-functionalism, we may better understand why certain practices in writing exist and what happens when these practices are threatened. Further, we can ascertain the functional importance of certain practices within writing and writing communities. We can also predict the reactions of the community when changes take place—for example, the change to gender-neutral language in writing. Clearly, pressures on writers to adopt gender-neutral language came from greater social changes taking place (i.e., the women's movement) than a mere revelation within the writing community. This change broke with tradition, threatened the normative order, and expectedly created controversy within the writing community. But the external pressures gave way, and the standard is changing, evidenced by calls for gender-neutral language from our most prestigious journals and professional organizations. If we had utilized this structural-functionalist framework for analyzing how greater environmental/societal change would affect the writing community, we might have predicted this change.

Conflict Theories

Social conflict theories rest on the assumption that society is a complex system marked by inequality and conflict, characteristics that generate social change. This perspective is concerned with power relationships, especially the relationship between those in a position to define normative reality (those with power, prestige, affluence) and those who are not (those who are weak, poor, uneducated, or otherwise disenfranchised).

Dahrendorf (1959) summarized the conflict position, calling it the "coercion" theory of society. He stated that society is subject to the process of change, which is ever present: Thus, social conflict is present at all times, and every element of society contributes to change and disintegration or conflict (p. 159). Consequently, society is based on the coercion of some of its members by others, giving power to those who have the ability to impose their will on others. (For more on conflict theories, see Coser, 1981, and Mills, 1956).

Two models within the conflict perspective offer distinctly different ways of looking at those with power: the power elite model and the pluralist model. The power elite model, best spelled out and championed by Mills (1956), portrays the powerful as a unified elite that controls resources and capital in society. The control of resources and capital ensures that the political, economic, and educational interests and values of this group are protected.

The pluralist model, on the other hand, views power as resting in the hands of many interest groups. These groups utilize the resources available to them to protect their interests. Often interest groups join resources to form powerful alliances that work against other interest groups to protect common spheres of influences. In the pluralists' view of power, it is possible for relatively powerless individuals to band together to ensure that some of their interests are realized. This joining of forces may be recognized among various disenfranchised groups, such as women's rights organizations and gay/lesbian rights organizations. But in technological circles, a good example of this banding together is the software industry, where a small number of companies have much of the power in that industry. Their capital resources are evident from their employment of some of the best programmers, their support by huge conglomerates, and their highly visibile marketing of their wares through expensive advertising campaigns. It is certainly in their capital interest to limit the amount of information given away for free, thus explaining the highly secretive nature and tight security of such companies. Despite these interests, many talented individuals committed to free dissemination of ideas develop "public domain" software, software that is frequently copyrighted, but is free to the user. This sector of the software industry thrives because talented programmers, lawyers, and other professionals believe in the idea of public access to information and band together to create bulletin board systems that successfully compete with develop-for-profit companies (DeMaria & Fontaine, 1987). Of course, those developers committed to public domain software are also seen as deviant from the norm of profit-seeking developers, putting the two groups in conflict. (For more on the pluralist model, see Dahl, 1961, 1982).

One of the problems with conflict theories is that they are often presented as overly conspiratorial in tone. In other words, conflict is seen as pitting good versus evil, terms that become quite abstract when discussing power and problematic when debating writing options. Other criticisms of conflict theory stem from its overemphasis on the powerful political spheres of social life, while ignoring the importance of qualities such as love, respect, dignity, and charisma.

In workplace communication, some of the best examples relating to conflict theory arise from the recent attention to writers' professional ethics (Hall & Nelson, 1987; Jobst, 1987; Little, forthcoming; Shimberg, 1978; Thayer, 1974). Research on ethics, in fact, has led to many questions that can potentially pit writers against each other, their supervisors, and upper-level management. Who owns information, and who can give it away? Under what circumstances? Who has the power to alter information? For what purposes? How should information be communicated? Through what channels? For whose access? How are ethical dilemmas to be resolved in communication cases? Our research may lead to discovering some recognizable patterns of conflict, such as that between profit and accuracy, between various schools of ethics, and between hierarchical layers of corporate societies and their respective responsibilities.

Another example of the role of conflict theory in nonacademic writing is situated in the writer/editor (or student/teacher) relationship. Again, evaluations of quality and matters of choice become fertile ground for conflict, especially factoring in the theory's requirement of power as an essential component of relationships. When editors/teachers have power over writers/students, how are discussions of writing options likely to proceed? Again, issues of good and evil arise: From the writer's perspective, the evil editor/teacher bludgeons the elegant prose that says precisely what the writer intends it to say. From the editor/teacher's perspective, the evil writer has misunderstood, misinterpreted, misused, misinformed, or miscommunicated the message, indicating slovenly thinking (at best) and evil intent (at worst).

Clearly, however, most workplace relationships, even those necessarily based on power, do not fall into such stark and overly dramatic categories of good and evil, and most writers/students do not experience the perpetual angst that necessarily follows from close adherence to conflict theories' tenets. What we may learn from conflict theories, however, is how particular rules, regulations, or hierarchical arrangements are established and maintained. Specifically, we may learn why certain types of writers are given less value than others (from what perspectives and to what ends?). We may also learn why certain forms of writing fail to gain acceptance and others succeed. For example, we might study the fine line between forms of tabloid journalism: the typically unacceptable forms of writing found in the supermarket newsstand tabloids, to the slightly more acceptable forms of television tabloids (syndicated talk shows and current events shows), to the still more acceptable — even award-winning — newsmagazine formats such as *20/20* or *60 Minutes.*

Interactionist Theory

For symbolic interactionsts, interaction is the building block of society, meaning that actors in the social world take account of one another when they act. I act while thinking about you and others, and you interact thinking about me and others. The use of shared symbols, especially language, brings us a way of knowing one another and our selves.

Of most importance to symbolic Interactionists is their emphasis on language and communication. To interactionists language is a vast system of symbols. Words are symbols that stand for things; words make all other symbols possible. Acts, objects, and other words exist and have meaning for us only because they have been and can be described through the use of words. Communicating with shared symbols (such as language) makes it possible for us to take the role of the other, to understand the world from the perspective of another person. Over time and with repeated symbolic interactions, individuals come to have shared meanings and interpretations of the world around them. These repeated and regularized interactions are responsible for the development of society.

We are also capable, through interaction, to modify and alter meanings and symbols for given contexts. For example, requiring one human being to walk behind another symbolizes different things in different contexts. In one context, it may mean the dominance of the leader and the submissiveness of the follower, as in patriarchal societies where women traditionally walk a few steps behind men. In a different context, however, these roles and their corresponding symbolism may be reversed, as in the case of the bodyguard leading the way for a celebrity or dignitary (the follower, in this case). And, of course, the leader/follower distinction may hold absolutely no status significance — as in waiting lines when the participants' positions are based merely on the order of their arrival, not the individual's wealth, intellect, or social standing. The symbolic nature of these and other interactions is the overriding concern and interest of the interactionist.

Thus, the interactionist perspective acknowledges that humans are unique as a species with a mind and a self, qualities that develop through interaction and form the basis of society. There is a fundamental reciprocity between society and the individual. Symbolic interactionists are concerned with the impact of meanings and symbols on human action and interaction, and individuals can create changes in society and others by altering or changing the meanings attributed to acts or symbols. For example, teenagers are notorious for taking a completely innocent term and making it obscene (in American culture, the term usually takes on new sexual connotations). One of the reasons for this appropriation, of course, is to gain ownership of their language, an ownership that will give words a special meaning for those they identify with and also give them the power to exclude unsuspecting adults (especially parents and teachers) who continue to use this term in its original context. Thus, the term now holds symbolic meaning for this group of people, and it may take years before the adult community recognizes the change, adopts the new meaning, or drops the word from its vocabulary altogether. For example, it used to be appropriate to call any eccentric person *queer* and any happy person *gay*. Because of the appropriation of these terms for the homosexual community, adolescents (typically quick to initiate or pick up on such language appropriations) giggled hysterically when their parents said they were *gay* or called the neighborhood misfit *queer*. Clearly, these terms were now beginning to serve in a different context and culture and have, as a consequence of that appropriation, been dropped from contexts unrelated to homosexuality.

Another facet of the interactionist perspective is its view that society emerges from the realities of everyday life (Berger & Luckman, 1967). People relate through the meanings we attach to routine human actions and symbols. Thus, someone who regularly attends religious services and has religious bumper stickers on his or her car is presumed to be a highly religious person—a notion that may or may not be accurate, but nevertheless invokes certain expectations about how this man conducts his life, the kinds of language he does (and does not) use, and his attitudes toward certain issues such as morality, salvation, and the afterlife. Of course, once we get to know this person, we may find our expectations violated (he attends church to support his political aspirations, has bumper stickers on his car because he bought the car secondhand and never removed them, and so on). Nevertheless, the initial symbolism of his actions leads us to expect certain things from him until we see that those expectations were invalid. Thus, when others behave in ways inconsistent with expectations, people react accordingly. They either give off negative cues such as smart comments or nonverbal cues such as avoidance, cues that the original actor likely recognizes as a symbol that he or she has behaved inappropriately, regardless of whether that recognition prompts him or her to alter that behavior. For example, an annoyed bystander frequently reacts to a chronic gum-popper by glaring or turning around to scowl anytime the gum is popped. In the best of cases, the gum-popper recognizes the social *faux pas* and either quits popping the gum or spits it out. This insistence on rule adherence and the subsequent reaction constitute a form of social control over individuals.

Such signals and controls exist with writers as well. Red ink, for instance, on students' papers serves as a very strong symbol of problems, "badness," and so on. To demonstrate the power of symbols, we might wonder (and investigate) how students would interpret *praise* written throughout their papers in red ink. We predict that the element of embarrassment would also likely take its effect in this situation as well, with the student shielding his or her paper from neighbors because he or she does not want them to see (and misinterpret) the red ink—even though the actual comments are praiseworthy.

Because interaction theory further refers to symbols as a matter of culture, a symbol (word, gesture, or behavior) may mean one thing in one culture and something altogether different in another culture. For example, in the American culture, the gesture of nodding (moving the head up and down) signifies agreement or the affirmative. In some other cultures, the same gesture means the opposite: the negative or disagreement. Clearly, failing to recognize the cultural context for certain gestures and other forms of communication can have serious consequences, either in terms of miscommunication or even peril for the communicator.

Interactionist theory also focuses on language as a human creation that emerges within cultures (not separate from them). Language may convey meaning at more than one level, but there is a manifest content or meaning that is explicitly stated and is frequently seen as the only form of content. Drawing on this idea of manifest content, many early definitions of *technical writing* encourage the idea that "good" communication relies on using words, phrases, and sentences, that have "one meaning and only one meaning" (Britton, 1975, p. 11).

What this early definition did not account for, of course, is the role of latent content, ideas that are suggested or implied through language and that create additional assumptions about reality. Sexist language is, per-haps, the most obvious example of latent content. The exclusive use of male pronouns in language communicates the peripheral importance of women and the central importance of men. (For an excellent overview on the effects of sexist pronouns, see Richardson, 1987; for works focusing on sexist language and workplace communication, see Christian, 1986; Corbett, 1986; Hall & Nelson, 1990; Vaughn, 1989; Veiga, 1989; Wilcoxin, 1989.) Less obvious examples arise from ethnic and cultural biases in language, which communicate to the reader meanings that point out social structural arrangements (preferences for, expectations about, or prejudices against certain groups because of their class, race, age, or gender).

The primary criticism of the Interactionist approach to social theory is that many see it as simply an approach, not a full-blown theory. That is, as an approach, interactionism does not have the well-formulated tenets that are testable through positivist methodologies. Further problems arise with its emphasis on the importance of language without a full understanding of language. For example, modern linguists would assert that language is a structured way of communicating. Mead (1934/1974), the leading figure in interactionism, provided an explanation of how words become connected with conduct, but he did not provide insight into whole strings of words that convey thoughts across situations, across time, and between people who use words in infinite ways (pp. 13–15, 74–75). His work, therefore, could not address the aesthetic preference for a particular person's gift of articulation, vocabulary, style, or pitch. Nor would his concept account for purely abstract terms and usages (such as *beauty, handsome, stupid*) that do not link gestures to action. Clearly, a behavioristic account cannot adequately characterize everyday speech, must less the highly abstract thoughts we often have to convey.

Further, interactionism consistently fails to recognize social structure (Skidmore, 1979, pp. 229–231). Saying that there are simple agreements among people who have worked out livable relationships is contrary to the sociological importance of normative rules that direct and constrain individuals from generation to generation — norms that can make individuals feel powerless or alienated. For example, as we become more enlightened about civil rights, the cultures of various groups in our society, and the nature of prejudice, we become more appalled at the social structure and consequences of slavery, racism, and bigotry. As our attitudes change, so does our language — making it unacceptable in intelligent circles to use disparaging terms for African Americans. Similarly, as women have gained more political and economic strength, we learn that terms such as *broad, skirt,* and *babe* are also inappropriate because they misrepresent the entire woman or because they belittle her maturity. Interactionism, however, fails to account for social and political nuances that frame interaction and coerce behaviors and linguistic norms. (For more on interaction theory, see Blumer, 1969; Berger & Luckman, 1967; Mead, 1934.)

In nonacademic communication, however, Interactionist theory may play a useful role in terms of the symbolic uses of our language, particularly as we use writing to motivate certain responses or behaviors. Any form of persuasive writing, therefore, will exemplify this form of manifest and latent content. We might want to investigate the kinds of latent content we draw on in order to motivate certain readers who want power, respect, or money. For as writers more clearly understand the powers of manifest and latent content, they can more easily manipulate their choice of symbols to garner acceptance of their ideas.

A clearer example of the symbolic use of the language, and our understanding of its message, comes from the editorial and proofreading marks used in communicating between writer, editor, and proofreader. For instance, in order for *stet* to generate the kind of response the editor/proofreader wants, both the editor/proofreader and the writer must agree on its meaning. Otherwise, the writer may spend hours wondering what to do with a particular passage marked *stet*, only to find out later that the editor/proofreader does not want him or her to do anything with it. Failing to understand the symbol, in short, means that the two are really not part of the same community at all — at least not at that moment in that situation.

In a larger context, what happens when we readily admit that we are not members of the same community? Anglo-American metaphors, in particular, demonstrate particular attitudes toward time, direction, and relationships that are often unfathomable for those from other cultures and societies. We do not share the same language, symbols, or motivations. Ironically, the meanings of symbols designed to be cross-cultural representations (for example, of airports, nonsmoking areas, restrooms, and no-pets-allowed areas) are specifically designed for those who do not share our communal sense — neither our language, our cultural taboos, nor our sense of propriety (regarding hygiene or decency). Such nuances and rules are designed to inform — but also to immediately enculturate (or punish) — those who are foreign to our ways.

We need to continue our studies by looking at the other symbolic uses of language within the professional communication community. Most technical writers, for instance, rely on a standard pattern of organization for introductions to their work: subject, purpose, audience, scope and limitations, methodology, definitions, and plan of organization. They learn this language of introducing a document from professors, from corporate style manuals, from their editors, or from other on-the-job experience. This strategy, however, is not likely known or practiced among novice writers or among writers in, say, medical or scientific writing. Thus, it serves as a symbolic structure for one subculture of writers, but not another.

We should consider the effects of such symbolic structures on other writers: What, for instance, does the absence of such an introductory structure mean when one technical writer reads the work of another? Does it affect his or her perception of that writer's competence, or at least the writer's organizational skills and knowledge of the genre? What do such symbolic structures mean for readers? Although the workplace writer may intend the introduction to be a map for finding information in the document, how many readers use the introductory material in that way?

What other forms of symbolism do workplace writers use? We should, for instance, investigate more carefully the use of bullets and other graphic elements that signal importance or parallel ideas. Do readers read these signs as intended or do the signs mean something else to different groups of

188 ALLEN AND THOMPSON

readers? Do some readers skip such lists altogether? Although some research has investigated the best techniques for constructing such visual symbols (Arnold, 1963; Lefferts, 1981; Horton, 1993), few researchers have looked at the ways readers interpret and misinterpret these symbols.

Finally, we should consider what various forms of communication symbolize to other nationalities and other cultures. An oil executive from the United States on special assignment to Mexico to enhance coordination shortly after the NAFTA agreement found his Mexican coworkers and subordinates quite offended by the memoranda he sent them — not by their content, tone, or style, but by their very existence. They felt that, given the proximity in which they worked, sending a memorandum was this executive's symbol that he wanted to distance himself from the very gregarious Mexican cohort. Once he understood this interpretation, he began to give his messages orally to his coworkers and send memos later as documents for future references. As this example shows, we need to consider that the very form and distribution of information may be just as symbolic (and, therefore, problematic) as the content, style, and tone of a message. How, for instance, would we interpret the ordering of $500,000 in computer equipment *via* a post-it note? Further investigation from the interactionist perspective, therefore, should help us learn more about the symbolism of information and its distribution.

Marxist/Critical Theory

Marxist theory is probably the most infamous of social theories, the most talked about, but the least understood and used. Marx's theory of class is perhaps the most important component of his work. As explicated in *Capital* (Marx, 1867/1967), class is related to production, and relations of production are viewed as relationships of economic power or property. Differences of power within the production process affect those who benefit from production and those who make decisions about production. Also, those with more power in the production process determine the form of exploitation those with less power will suffer (e.g., wage labor, tenancy, slavery).

Classes emerge from the organization of production, and political forces are based on the relations of property and power. Class is a structural position that can be viewed as separate from individual action, and an individual's actions may or may not be determined by class position. We have all known, for instance, underlings in a corporation who behave as superiors and who act out the will of the superiors. Marx stated that these individuals whose actions are not consistent with their class position have very little effect on the structure of their own class. Instead, the contributions of these individuals, who are typically the more capable of the oppressed class, are usually absorbed into the ruling class to make the ruling class's position stronger and to consolidate power (Marx, 1867/1967). That does not mean that these underlings become powerful or become part of the ruling class; they simply help the ruling class maintain its role as superior.

In workplace communication, we can see the tenets of this theory at work when writers work to fulfill the objectives of the owners of the corporation, with no regard for their own status within the company or even at their own expense. For instance, a writer may work overtime to complete a proposal that will award more business to her company — in spite of the fact that she does not get paid overtime and that the proposal allows for no additional writers to be added to the staff if the contract is awarded. She has, in effect, created a document that will eventually penalize her (in time, stress, and amount of work), while rewarding the company's owners with additional profits. In another case, a writer in a U.S. senator's office may work on a congressional bill that will limit the amount of deductions allowable for certain expenses — even when that new limitation will decrease the amount of his own tax return.

Marx is probably best known for his idea in the "Critique of the Gotha Program" (1848/1972) that people should be allowed to work and live according to the principle "from each according to ability, to each according to need" (p. 338). Although this idea is the heart of his theory, it is also the Achilles' heel. As critics note, it reveals an assumption that reward may be separate from performance — an assumption that may be unrealistic. Criticisms of the Marxist theory rest on its denial of the possibility that to motivate people to perform various social roles requires a system of unequal rewards. The lack of consideration of this possible social truism may account for the generally low productivity of socialist economies around the world.

What may circumvent the popularity of Marxist theories among workplace writers, at least within the American culture, is general admiration for capitalism and the capitalist work ethic: The benefits of having a job far outweigh the benefits of experiencing some kind of equity between the classes. Further fueling a distaste for Marxism is the capitalist belief that anybody can rise to the ruling class, with enough hard work, making it unwise to object to class inequity that may one day provide the lowly worker with great benefits — a concept Marx perceives as wishful thinking and calls "false consciousness." Most notable for our discussion is the idea that workplace writers are often promoted to management positions, a promotion that, in effect, moves a "lowly writer" to a position of more power. Many critics of Marxism, therefore, cite its deterministic elements — the underclass can never rise to become the super class — as oppressive to workers, sapping their initiative. (For more on Marxism, see Adorno, 1950; Habermas, 1984; Marx, 1867/1967, 1848/1972.)

In our research, we can investigate the hierarchical relations between writers and their superiors in the workforce. Primarily, we should look at the ways that writers fulfill the goals of the organization. If it is true that information is power, and we acknowledge that it is the workplace communicator's job to distribute information, then we should investigate how that power is used and for whose benefit(s). Further, we should study various industries in which only certain amounts of information are given to particular groups of writers. For example, in a corporation that handles government contracts, especially defense contracts, very few writers (except those with top security clearances) have more than one or two pieces of the contract puzzle. Whose best interests are served by such security measures? Do the writers (workers) have any rights in determining or negotiating their role or reward as they fulfill the goals of the corporate owners? Again the American work ethic teaches us not to question our superiors at the possible expense of our jobs; furthermore, our patriotic ethics teach us that we are not supposed to know everything about such contracts. But it is certainly illuminating to ponder whose interests are being served by this work ethic and its patriotic complement.

In a renegotiation of Marxist theory, critical theory bridged Marxism for the new socially critical class that emerged in an historical experience foreign to Marxist projections (Wexler, 1991, p. vii). Critical theory reflects the historical/political struggles of the student movement of the 1960s, feminism, and antiracist and ecological social movements (p. viii). It emerged as a result of the failed ideologies that promised a Marxist utopia that would come with the failure of capitalism. This theory sees the entire social world as moving toward commoditization—that everything is becoming a commodity to be produced, packaged, and marketed as some kind of norm in our society. The best examples of this commoditization come from our own contemporary culture: the packaging of crime, law, and order sold weekly to millions of television viewers *via* shows such as *Top Cops* and *American Detective* that give actual film footage of crimes and arrests; self-help books that teach readers to market themselves for jobs, to win friends and influence people, and to become top salespeople (or better lovers); diplomas for any kind of degree in any kind of academic discipline; plastic surgery for any displeasing bodily or facial feature; and even bottled water. Everything is for sale.

This theory emphasizes the extensive development in the means of communication and information, "an intensification of human labor and human domination over labor, both reduced to the status of productive forces and to schemes and ideas of maximum output" (Baudrillard, 1975, p. 33). This commodity culture, according to critical theorists, creates false needs and diverts us from true needs that can be met only by rescripting society and its culture (Agger, 1991, p. 141). Marx's genius, the part that critical theorists hold most dear, is that he visualized a modern system that would create a universal world according to a code of commodity exchange based on industrialized and bureaucratized production (Ashley, 1991, p. 85). Inherent in this theory is the notion (*via* Habermas) that we must all become writers of the public voice (Agger, 1991, p. 140). Such an idea, of course, is inherently democratic; placing it in the industrial complex, however, gives equal power to workers and to owners—a notion many claim may, in fact, come to pass with the ever increasing access to information *via* computers and other forms of contemporary (and developing) technologies. (For more on the changing roles of society *via* communications technology, see Gerbner, Gross, & Melody, 1973.) Others note, however, that prohibitive costs as well as restrictive access are just as likely to sustain the class distinctions, along with (or because of) the access to information as a commodity.

Feminist Theory

Although there are numerous feminist theories, the primary unifying feature is the view that history has generated a distinctly privileged role for men as leaders, intellectuals, and artists. And, correspondingly, women have been appropriated a distinctly marginal role as subordinates, ding-a-lings, and sex objects. Although feminism—as a collective—seeks to balance or equalize those roles and perceptions, various sects of feminism propose different ways of achieving that aim. The feminist theory that arises from Marxist/critical/deconstructionist theories, for instance, contributes to social theory the understanding that gender and gender relations are part of a larger set of social relationships that exist historically in a sociopolitical setting. For example, to understand an African-American woman's experience of gender, one must consider the particulars of the African American's social and historical experiences, as well as the particular experience of being a woman within that context. One must consider her experiences with African-American men, Anglo-American men, and Anglo-American women.

This theoretical approach (seeing gender as rooted in a system of human relations) makes gender a necessary component to consider when looking at all social relations. Gender is inseparable from race, class, history, economics, and politics. Most important, social thinkers can no longer assume fixed notions of gender because gender, unlike *sex*, is socially, not biologically, determined. Thus, men who exemplify certain stereotypically feminine traits (lack of economic, political, or professional power or ambition; "extreme" emotional reactions such as crying—but not violence; or even high-pitched voices) suffer from many of the same gender-based prejudices and inequalities that women face. Eventually, approaching sex and gender as strictly different allows for the possibility of more flexibility in gender role construction. (For more on feminist theory, see Gilligan, 1982; Malson, O'Barr, Westphal-Wihl, & Wyer, 1989; Schur, 1983.)

From a different perspective comes the work of the French feminists Cixous (1986), Irigaray (1985a, 1985b), and Kristeva (1986) who argue for the establishment of a separate, women's language. Claiming that current languages are products and perpetuations of male domination, and thus foreign to and subversive of women's experiences and ways of making meaning, these feminists call for establishing a women's language that would value women and their experiences. Although their aim may be honorable, the problem with such a language, as many critics note, is that it may well lead to more entrenched isolation and discrimination in the systems already characterized by sexism. Thus, the combination of a feminist and interactionist approach to the symbolic nature of language could sabotage the feminist aim of bringing men's and women's relationships into parity—both in the workplace and in other communal establishments. More damaging is that such a language might actually signal the intentional disconnection of men from women: "You don't speak our language; you are not part of our group." Although it may be argued that such is already the case, with women trying unsuccessfully to speak men's language, the appropriation of an entirely new language may well serve prescriptive, negative behaviors that can perpetuate the sexism that feminists have worked so hard to eradicate.

In nonacademic writing research, we have begun to investigate the nature of gender relations from various perspectives particularly from the stances of cognitive developmentalists, social constructionists, and psychoanalysts, all within a variety of applications and contexts. One of the earliest and most influential works is Lay's (1989) work integrating gender theory and collaboration. A 1991 issue of the *Journal of Business and Technical Communication*, moreover, presents a broad range of gender-based issues that merit our attention. In this issue researchers investigated the potential influence of feminist theory on redefining technical communication (Lay, 1991, pp. 348–370), gender issues' contributions for studying the profession, research, and pedagogy of technical communication (Allen, 1991, pp. 371–392), and issues of ownership in writing, focusing particularly on the penalties women writers suffer by personalizing their compositions (Brunner, 1991, pp. 393–411). Baker and Goubil-Gambrell (1991, pp. 412–433) addressed the impact of gender on academic performance and scholarship; Flynn, Savage, Penti, Brown, and Watke (1991, pp. 444–462) investigated gender-based differences in collaboration in engineering courses; and Carrell (1991, pp. 463–468) noted the differences in the ways men and women are presented in workplace communications textbooks. Finally, Halterman, Dutkiewicz, and Halterman (1991, pp. 469–481) presented results of a survey of men's and women's attitudes within their work teams.

More research on gender roles and workplace communication needs to address the current conditions of working as a professional communicator. Recent surveys sponsored by the Society for Technical Communication, for example, show that women, who may make up more of the industry than men, still earn less money than their male counterparts (Cook, 1986). The surveys also show that as this number of women professionals increases, the salaries that all technical communicators earn decreases, corroborating research from other fields that shows that the feminization of a profession typically brings on decreasing salaries (Stoner, 1988). More research needs to address the hierarchical nature of the technical communication industry; the salaries, hiring, and promotion of women technical communicators; the types of assignments given to women technical communicators; and the quality of the professional documents produced by women technical communicators.

Gender theories, of course, have garnered much criticism because of the importance placed on gender as a determining factor in social relations. Too often this perspective ignores individual action and assumes that particular characteristics or stereotypes apply to an entire group or collective. Some critics, moreover, complain that gender theory has a conspiratorial tone, like conflict theory or Marxist theory from which this theory arises, and interpret the feminist mission as one of establishing dominance (and retaliation) rather than equality.

APPLICATIONS OF SOCIAL THEORIES
TO COLLABORATIVE WRITING

As we mentioned earlier in this chapter, most social theorists combine theories in order to understand or explain various behaviors, beliefs, or structures. In this segment, we use the five social theories we have discussed as they may apply to one particular aspect of workplace communication: collaboration. For examples, we frequently refer to our own collaboration in working on this chapter, but also note wider and different phenomena that may arise from the social nature of the collaborative endeavor. (For other ideas about the changing nature and understandings of collaborative partnerships, see Ede & Lunsford, 1990.)

As Toulmin (1958/1964), Foucault (1972), Perelman (1969), and other rhetoricians noted, each discipline has distinct processes and patterns of argument. A relatively new field, rhetoric of inquiry, builds on these rhetoricians' works and investigates such distinctive patterns of academic argument (see Lynne, 1985; Nelson, Megill, & McCloskey, 1987). One of the more interesting aspects of our collaboration on this chapter, therefore, has been our realization of the two separate academic subcultures from which we work. One of us (Allen) is a technical communicator whose primary scholarly interests are the social ramifications of communication, but whose knowledge of these various social theories (until this collaboration at least) was pretty much limited to structural/funtionalism and feminist theories. Thompson, on the other hand, is a sociologist whose primary area of research is deviance. Our working together has meant that we have relied on each other's strengths and filled in any weaknesses with our own experience. While we were making notes, for instance, Allen pressed Thompson for additional explanations of theories, primarily by asking questions about terminology and by posing examples that Thompson would either confirm as valid for the concept being discussed or would replace with a more accurate example. Thompson, on the other hand, was particularly pleased with the introductory segment that clearly spelled out what we would be doing in this chapter—a standard feature of a technical document that Allen includes as a matter of course in anything she writes. As part of the division of labor, Thompson spent much time in the library tracking sources, while Allen worked on various parts of the draft. As the draft progressed, Allen changed some of Thompson's passive voice sentences, while Thompson changed some of Allen's terms that would mean something entirely different to a sociologist than to a technical or business communicator. Clearly, our work required us to learn something about each other's academic subculture—the standard features of content and style, the critical accuracy of sociological terminology, the exploration of examples, the clarification of ideas, and even the means of documenting sources.

A more thorough study of our collaboration (and that of any multiple-authored work) would likely reveal more subtle forms of accommodation and reconciliation. This process means that in some way we have overcome our differences or our conflicts (which seems an awfully harsh term, given the harmony of our collaborative effort). In short, we tried to reach agreement based on the conventions of our subcultures. This agreement acknowledges the structural-functionalist ideas that certain rules do, indeed, apply to what we are trying to create. In fact, structural-functionalists would argue that the agreement about these rules is necessary in order for collaboration to occur. In our own situation, and as far as possible, we have tried to accommodate those rules in order to create a work that will hold significance in both our fields. We have accepted the same rules about grammatical structures, the format for our chapter, the amount of details needed for our audience, and the use of specialized terms and definitions.

Nevertheless, some collaborative efforts are not so harmonious, and conflict is not only a dominant characteristic of the process, but may be either absolutely necessary and desirable (see Burnett, 1991) or, on the other hand, an absolute deal breaker. For many collaborators, of course, the writing must go on: A company's survival may depend on the production of an annual report or a documentation manual. In other situations, however, the writers may simply decide that they cannot work together — whether personality conflicts or cultural conflicts are responsible for the disharmony.

Applying the concepts of conflict theory to this kind of disharmony in the collaborative process would require us to see collaboration as a series of differences, with the power elite model demonstrating that one collaborator has to win an argument about the structure of a sentence, the definition of a term, the arrangement of text, the use of a graphic, and so on. Thus, although conflict may sabotage the collaborative process, conflict theorists would argue that collaboration will necessarily include conflict.

Although some may feel that the two of us worked and wrote on the premise of substantive conflict (Burnett, 1991), we feel that our collaboration is better described altogether in terms of the pluralist model, following the ideas in Lamb's (1991) work presenting collaboration as negotiation and reconciliation, rather than win/lose conflict. This approach, which removes the pejorative qualities of the term *conflict*, adopts the pluralist model on an individual or group basis. This model means that, as Lamb explains, writers look for acceptable means of constructing a text. Most significant within the pluralist models it that the collaborator typically chooses her battle(s) carefully, being willing to give in on the structure of a sentence in one instance, yet holding out for the use of a graphic in a later instance. The pluralist model further requires collaborators to acknowledge strengths — which we have also done in our work. Thompson's strengths are, clearly, the technical explanations of the social theories, whereas Allen's strengths come from applying those ideas to typical communication situations. Whether they are negotiating blocks of time in which to work, the use of particular terms of linguistic structures, or even the format of a text, successful writers work toward agreement rather than domination in the collaborative relationship — a distinction the substantive conflict model does not always uphold.

We would also use the interactionist theory to describe collaborative situations. Most writers who have collaborated on a project know that certain people have particular systems of working. They use particular symbols to acknowledge weak ideas (perhaps a series of question marks or ellipses) to which they want to return in subsequent drafts. Working together means each participant's having to learn this system of symbols.

Further evidence of the symbolic aspects of the collaborative endeavor comes from the roles each individual plays in the process. Certain roles take on particular meanings for the individual; women, for instance, frequently refuse the clerical roles of typing the manuscript because they know that their powers as contributors then get marginalized. Taking the idea of roles and symbolism a step further, the order of authorship on a document or article also projects certain meanings within certain academic cultures, especially when the order is not alphabetical (Brunner, 1991; Ede & Lunsford, 1990). First author typically designates the dominant "idea person" in some disciplines, whereas in other disciplines that designation simply means that this person is the most prominent scholar in the field. Thus, placing his/her name first is expected to garner more attention for the work by virtue of name recognition within the discipline. Even more interesting in workplace communication, of course, is that the actual writers' names may not even appear on the document, being replaced with their superior's or the company's name as a matter of course.

In our case, we appreciated the complexities of assigning first author for this chapter, admiring Ede and Lunsford's (1990) typographic cleverness on the title page of their work *Single Texts/Plural Authors*. Because the proposals for this work were originally sent to Allen, because her name comes first alphabetically, and because of the strong emphasis on nonacademic writing, we agreed that Allen's name would go first.

In other examples of interactionism's influence, we see other roles that take on particular meanings for groups or for members of collaborative groups. One member, for example, will be the schedule maker and keeper, reminding the group of deadlines, time-consuming obstacles, and so on. Another member will be the list maker, copiously charting steps in the research process, the content creation process, and the writing process. Another member may be the devil's advocate (whether for good or bad), noting weaknesses in the process, in the content, or even in the other members' behaviors, attitudes, and contributions. Interactionist theory gives us the opportunity to see the specific roles each member plays in terms of how others in the group expect the person to fulfill that role. Further, the interactionist model allows us to investigate each member's attitudes toward the symbolic structure of writing and collaboration. What does the schedule signify to the members—a flexible good idea for progressing through the project or a rigid timetable that must not be violated? The answer to this question depends largely on the shared understanding of the system of writing and its components. Thus, this approach may explain why someone who works in multiple drafts may have so many problems working with someone who insists that the first draft is the best draft, and why someone who is dogmatic about meeting deadlines resents working with someone who is lackadaisical about such matters. Clearly, these writers do not share the same understanding about the symbols of their profession, whether those symbols involve linguistic variations or elements of process, creativity, and professionalism.

Whereas the interactionist theory requires writers to negotiate a series of symbols, the Marxist/critical theories allow us to sidestep the issue of negotiation altogether. Instead, one begins to recognize hierarchies of power within the collaborative enterprise, and between the writers and the corporate owners. Does one member of the team, for instance, retain the power of veto? Does one member of the team retain the role of assigning specific tasks to individual group members? How are these roles assigned or determined: by group consensus based on personality or competence? Or by strongest allegiance to company ownership?

Marxist/critical theories require us to see the members of the group as tools for the goals of the organization. It may, therefore, even work to the corporation's benefit to have what it perceives as "petty" conflicts within the team — arguments over linguistic structure, format, and terminology — because these conflicts distract the team from larger issues involving conflicts of interest or conflicts of ethics. Many writers, in fact, leave their jobs with certain corporations because of such conflicts. Rather than sell out to the profit motivations of a company whose practices harm the environment, violate the writer's sense of ethics, or promote a political cause with which the writer disagrees, the writer resigns to look for more agreeable work.

Most interesting for our collaboration is that, although we used to work together at the same institution (we have been good friends, have socialized together, have served on committees together, etc.), Thompson moved to Texas after the first draft of this chapter was written. Thus, rather than the immediate accessibility we were used to as we drafted our plans, outline, and even the first draft of this chapter, our collaborative arrangement changed radically when we had to communicate by phone, fax, mail, and e-mail. Fortunately, our editors required few changes in our draft, but we cannot help but wonder what serious revisions might have done — both to the draft and to our now long-distance friendship.

Even more interesting, perhaps, for those in academe is considering (from a Marxist/critical perspective) what differences are implied from the fact that Allen is a tenured, associate professor, whereas Thompson is working toward tenure (at a different institution). How is credit likely to be awarded for Allen? For Thompson? What kinds of differences in personnel and evaluative rules might affect the reward system? Further, what is this publication likely to mean for Allen's reputation? For her institution's reputation? What is it likely to mean for Thompson's reputation? For her institution's reputation? Why, in fact, is publication so important in academe these days? Who benefits?

Finally, we should look at collaboration from a gender perspective, as Lay (1989, 1994) and others have done in recent publications. This perspective may be especially enlightening, given that many collaborative teams are comprised of both men and women. Although their work deals with women *students* in a collaborative setting, Flynn et al. (1991) noted the social implications and manifestations in collaborations:

> We still see evidence of women students being treated as clerical workers, of women being silenced or ignored in group interaction, and of women having difficulty asserting themselves in mixed-group situations. Clearly, the gains that women engineering students have made are fragile and provisional, and there is little evidence that women students are aware of the potentially threatening climate in which they operate daily or of the even greater threat that awaits them once they obtain jobs in industry. These are students who have been socialized to be loyal rather than critical. (p. 460)

Other researchers have addressed the ways women handle conflict in collaborative and management situations, combining gender theory with conflict theory (Borisoff & Merrill, 1987; Henzl & Turner, 1987; Hocker & Wilmot, 1978; Nadler & Nadler, 1987; Rancer & Baukus, 1987; Womack, 1987). In addition to this work, however, we should also consider how often women assume the role of project leader in collaborative encounters. And, if they do, is their work still devalued? Or if it is even somewhat successful, is it perceived as the product of overambition? Bossiness? Ingratiating to management? These suggestions of multiple interpretations recognize the variety of attitudes that, built into the inequitable treatment of women in our society, may carry over into inequitable assessments of their writing in the workplace.

From our own experience in writing this chapter, we may be tempted to dismiss gender theory as an influence on our collaboration. Yet we cannot help but wonder about the harmony of our working relationship as same-gendered writers. Do women work better with other women? If so, why? Do we share the same socialization experiences that let us also share the same language, the same status, and the same voice? Do we fill in the blanks for each other, without having to bring particular issues to the forefront for discussion? Conversely, do men work better with other men? Again, if they do, we should be finding out why. Further, because men and women will inevitably have to work together (won't they?), what can they do to increase the harmony of their relationship? Is androgyny the answer? Is it possible? Clearly, more research needs to go into answering these questions.

COMBINED THEORIES AND COLLABORATION

Finally, combining one of these theories with any other theory or theories gives us an entirely new perspective from which to conduct research. We may study, for example, whether the norms people accept are gender-based. Do women, for instance, accept clerical or token positions in collaborative teams because such positions are the norm? What are the penalties for deviance in this situation?

Combining gender theories with Interactionist theories, we may ask whether men and women have different symbols for communicating in collaborative efforts. In conversation, for instance, women typically nod their heads as men talk to signify that they are paying attention; men, on the other hand, interpret this signal as agreement. Similarly, when a man nods his head at a women, he is, indeed, signaling his agreement with what the woman is saying (and oftentimes his desire to interrupt her). What does this difference in signals mean in the collaborative setting? What other differences exist?

The differences in the ways men and women handle conflict has garnered much attention in sociological studies. We need now to investigate the ways that conflict management (or bias or ignorance) works in collaborative situations. The research of Borisoff and Merrill (1987), Henzl and Turner (1987), Lay (1989), Nadler and Nadler (1987), Rancer and Baukus (1987), and Womack (1987) gives us an excellent starting point for studying conflict management between men and women. In turn, we may apply this research to studies of collaborative communication projects.

Marxist/critical theories, combined with gender theories, would allow us to investigate the dominant roles played by men and women in the corporate structure. We are already well versed in studies of hiring, promotion, and salaries in other fields, but we are only beginning to study these aspects in the professional communication industry. Do men and women see their roles in fulfilling the goals of the organization differently? Do men and women respond differently to the manipulation of workers by management? How and why? In how many ways do men and women recognize their powers as communicators? How do they use or keep that power in check? What do they see as the punishments or rewards for manipulating that power?

This extended discussion of these five social theories and their possible interrelations has allowed us to consider more carefully the role of one social aspect—collaboration—in a nonacademic writing environment. Theories, of course, do not necessarily give us answers; they frequently, and perhaps more usefully, provide different ways to ask questions and help us delve into researching the subtleties of our working relationships. Nevertheless, these theories, and the questions that arise from them, have surely generated plenty of opportunities for additional research into nonacademic writing.

Coupled with the series of questions posed at the end of each segment on social theories that we have addressed, this last section on collaboration may, indeed, prove to be an important starting point for future investigations into the nature of the professional communication environment. For it does seem reasonable to expect the future of this profession to be somewhat dominated by the necessity for collaborative efforts. And if collaboration is, in fact, the dominant feature of communicating within the industrial complex, surely we must invest more time, research, and money into studying the sociological aspects of those working relationships.

Further research should expand sociological theories' usefulness as a perspective for investigating other aspects of nonacademic writing. In relation to business, for example, what issues surround the corporation/client relationship? What happens to corporate communities when the corporation decides to diversity? How do its writers learn about, adjust to, or fit in with the expectations, biases, and needs of new communities of readers? Is there any significance in the order of the document review process through various departments? Whose concerns about a particular document's content, style, or perspective take precedence? The breadth and variety of these questions demonstrate the kind of open territory available for researchers who want to combine two or three disciplines to examine the implications for nonacademic writing.

Further, moving beyond the discipline A + discipline B approach is the unlimited number of combinations represented as A + B + C + D, and so on. With promising avenues arising from linguistics, anthropology, history, adult education, political science, decision sciences, foreign languages, marketing, merchandising, medicine, social work, and women's studies (to name just a few broad fields), these combinations demonstrate both the expansive and narrowed topics and approaches available for our research, along with the particular kinds of questions such combinations might reveal. For example, combining nonacademic writing + marketing + women's studies + social theories, we might easily generate the following questions:

- In what ways are women perceived as a cohesive buying community? What purposes might such a community serve for its members? How does the community relate its communal status to its own members and to those outside that community?
- What kinds of collective initiatives demonstrate the communicative powers of this group?
- What communication strategies work best within this community? How and why would other groups communicate with this community?
- What language features (word choices, structures, tone, metaphors, images, etc.) would be particularly appealing to this community? What would be particularly offensive to this community?

- What kinds of products would appeal to this community? Why? How should their features be described to members of this community?
- How much and what kind(s) of power does this community have? How does it communicate its authority or power to other groups?
- How does this community use its power to perpetuate or disrupt certain (advertising, product, or corporate culture) messages?

Numerous other questions could be asked, of course, but these examples demonstrate the significant multidisciplinary work that can be done in our research of nonacademic writing. Ultimately, however, we must also recognize the potential advantages and disadvantages of such multidisciplinary approaches. First, by being more adaptive, we can recognize entirely new perspectives on writing that will clarify its power in the workplace, perspectives that had previously escaped our attention. But we must also be more critical of our contexts and understandings, along with our methodologies and perspectives when we assimilate the work from various disciplines. Appropriating another discipline's vocabulary, methodology, or paradigm requires a far more thorough understanding of those elements than simple readings allow. Again, the value of collaboration becomes clear: the ability to expand our knowledge, *via* collaborative partnerships — without having to become multidisciplinary experts — creates tremendous opportunities for better understanding our own discipline and how it works throughout the world's communities.

REFERENCES

Adorno, T. W. (1950). *The authoritarian personality*. New York: Harper.

Agger, B. (1991). Theorizing the decline of discourse or the decline of theoretical discourse. In P. Wexler (Ed.), *Critical theory now* (pp. 118–44). New York: Falmer.

Allen, J. (1991). Gender issues in technical communication studies: An overview of the implications for the profession, research, and pedagogy. *Journal of Business and Technical Writing, 5*(4), 371–92.

Arnold, E. C. (1963). *Ink on paper: A handbook of graphic arts*. New York: Harper & Row.

Ashley, D. (1991). Playing with the pieces: The fragmentation of social theory. In P. Wexler (Ed.), *Critical theory now* (pp. 70–97). New York: Falmer.

Baker, M. A., & Goubil-Gambrell, P. (1991). Scholarly writing. The myth of gender and performance. *Journal of Business and Technical Writing, 5*(4), 412–443.

Baudrillard, J. (1975). *The mirror of production* (M. Poster, Trans.). St. Louis: Telos Press.

Berger, P., & Luckman, T. (1967). *The social construction of reality: A treatise in the sociology of knowledge*. New York: Doubleday.

Blumer, H. (1969). *Symbolic interactionism: Perspective and method*. Englewood Cliffs, NJ: Prentice-Hall.

Borisoff, D., & Merrill, L. (1987). Teaching the college course on gender differences as barriers to conflict resolution. In L. B. Nadler, M. K. Nadler, & W. R. Todd-Mancillas (Eds.), *Advances in gender and communication research* (pp. 351–361). Lanham, MD: University Press of America.

Britton, W. E. (1975). What is technical writing? A redefinition. In D. H. Cunningham & H. A. Estrin (Eds.), *The teaching of technical writing* (pp. 9–14). Urbana, IL: National Council of Teachers of English.

Brunner, D. D. (1991). Who owns this work? The question of authorship in professional/ academic writing. *Journal of Business and Technical Writing, 5*(4), 393–411.

Burnett, R. E. (1991). Substantive conflict in a cooperative context: A way to improve the collaborative planning of workplace documents. *Technical Communication, 38*(4), 532–539.

Carrell, D., (1991). Gender scripts in professional writing textbooks. *Journal of Business and Technical Writing, 5*(4), 463–468.

Christian, B. (1986). Doing without the generic he/man in technical communication. *Journal of Technical Writing and Communication, 16*(1), 87–98.

Cixous, H. (1986). *The newly-born woman* (B. Wing, Trans.). Minneapolis: University of Minnesota Press.

Cook, K., Jr. (1986). Profile 85 – Survey of STC membership. *Technical Communication, 33*(1), 27–30.

Corbett, M. Z. (1986). Clearing the air: Some thoughts on gender neutral writing. *IEEE Transactions on Professional Communication, 33*(1), 2–6.

Coser, L. (1981). The uses of classical theory. In B. Rhea (Ed.), *The future of the sociological classics* (pp. 170–182). London: Allyn and Unwin.

Dahl, R. (1961). *Who governs?* New Haven, CT: Yale University Press.

Dahl, R. (1982). *Dilemmas of pluralist democracy: Autonomy vs. control.* New Haven, CT: Yale University Press.

Dahrendorf, R. (1959). *Class and class conflict in industrial society.* Stanford: Stanford University Press.

DeMaria, R., & Fontaine, G. R. (1987). *Public domain software: Untapped resources for the business user.* Redwood City, CA: M & T.

Durkheim, E. (1964). *The division of labor in society.* New York: Free Press. (Original work published 1895).

Ede, L., & Lunsford, A. (1990). *Singular texts/plural authors: Perspectives on collaborative writing.* Carbondale: Southern Illinois University Press.

Faigley, L. (1985). Nonacademic writing: The social perspective. In L. Odell & D. Goswami (Eds.), *Writing in nonacademic settings* (pp. 231–248). New York: Guilford.

Flynn, E. A., Savage, G., Penti, M., Brown, C., & Watke, S. (1991). Gender and modes of collaboration in a chemical engineering design course. *Journal of Business and Technical Writing, 5*(4), 444–462.

Foucault, M. (1972). *The archeology of knowledge* (S. M. Sheridan Smith, Trans.). New York: Tavistock.

Gerbner, G., Gross, L. P., & Melody, W. H. (Eds.). (1973). *Communications technology and social policy: Understanding the new "cultural revolution."* New York: Wiley.

Giddens, A. (Ed.). (1972). *Selected writings.* Cambridge, UK: Cambridge University Press.

Gilligan, C. (1982). *In a different voice: Psychological theory in women's development.* Cambridge, MA: Harvard University Press.

Habermas, J. (1984). *The theory of communicative action* (T. McCarthy, Trans.). Boston: Beacon Press. (Original work published 1981).

Hall, D. G., & Nelson, B. A. (1987). Integrating professional ethics into the technical writing course. *Journal of Technical Writing and Communication, 17*(1), 45–61.

Hall, D. G., & Nelson, B. A. (1990). Sex-biased language and the technical-writing teacher's responsibility. *Journal of Business and Technical Communication, 4*(1), 69–79.

Halterman, C., Dutkiewicz, J., & Halterman, E. (1991). Men and women on the job: Gender bias in work teams. *Journal of Business and Technical Writing, 5*, 469–481.

Henzl, S., & Turner, L. (1987). Rationalizing conflict choices: Do men and women speak the same language?" In L. B. Nadler, M. K. Nadler, & W. R. Todd-Mancillas (Eds.), *Advances in gender and communication research* (pp. 175–188). Lanham, MD: University Press of America.

Horton W. (1993). Pictures please$Presenting information visually. In C. M. Barnum & L. Carliner (Eds.). *Techniques for technical communicators* (pp. 187–218). New York: Macmillan.

Irigaray, L. (1985a). *Speculum of the other woman.* Ithaca, NY: Cornell Univesity Press.

Irigaray, L. (1985b). *This sex is not one.* Ithaca, NY: Cornell University Press.

Jobst, J. (1987). Word processing: Two ethical concerns. *Journal of Technical Writing and Communication, 17,* 1–7.

Kristeva, J. (1986). "Women's time" and "Revolution in poetic language." In T. Moi (Ed.), *The Kristeva reader.* Oxford, UK: Basil Blackwell.

Kuhn, T. S. (1970). *The structure of scientific revolutions* (rev. ed.). Chicago: University of Chicago Press.

Lamb, C. E. (1991). Beyond argument in feminist composition. *College Composition and Communication, 42,* 11–24.

Lay, M. M. (1989). Interpersonal conflict in collaborative writing: What we can learn from gender studies. *Journal of Business and Technical Communication, 3*(2), 5–28.

Lay, M. M. (1991). Feminist theory and the redefinition of technical communication. *Journal of Business and Technical Communication, 5*(4), 348–370.

Lay, M. M. (1994). The value of gender studies to professional communication reearch. *Journal of Business and Technical Communication, 8*(1), 58–90.

Lefferts, R. (1981). *Elements of graphics: How to prepare charts and graphs for effective reports.* New York: Harper & Row.

Little, S. B. (Ed.). (in press). *The rhetoric of ethics in technical communication.* Los Angeles: Roxbury.

Lynne, J. (1985). Rhetorics of inquiry. *Quarterly Journal of Speech, 71*(1), 65–73.

Malson, M., O'Barr, J. F., Westphal-Wihl, S., & Wyer, M. (Eds.). (1989). *Feminist theory in practice and process.* Chicago: University of Chicago Press.

Marx, K. (1967). *Capital* (Vol. 3). New York: International Publishers. (Original work published 1867).

Marx, K. (1972). Critique of the gotha program (T. B. Bottomore, Trans.). In R. C. Tucker (Ed.), *The Marx-Engels reader* (pp. 382–398). New York: W. W. Norton. (Original work published 1848)

Mead, G. H. (1974). *Mind, self, and society.* Chicago: The University of Chicago Press. (Original work published 1934)

Mills, C. W. (1956). *The power elite.* New York: Oxford University Press.

Nadler, M. K., & Nadler, L. B. (1987). The influence of gender on negotiation success in asymmetric power situations. In L. B. Nadler, M. K. Nadler, & W. R. Todd-Mancillas (Eds.), *Advances in gender and communication research* (pp. 189–218). Lanham, MD: University Press of America.

Nelson, J., Megill, A., & McCloskey, D. N. (Eds.). (1987). *The rhetoric of the human sciences: Language and argument in scholarship and public affairs.* Madison: University of Wisconsin Press.

Odell, L. (1985). Beyond the text: Relations between writing and social context. In L. Odell & D. Goswami (Eds.), *Writing in nonacademic settings* (pp. 249–280). New York: Guilford.

Odell, L., & Goswami, D. (Eds.). (1985). *Writing in nonacademic settings.* New York: Guilford.

Parsons, T. (1954). *Essays in sociological theory.* New York: Free Press.

Parsons, T. (1964). *The social system*. New York: Free Press. (Original work published 1951)

Perelman, C. (1969). *The new rhetoric: A treatise on argumentation* (J. Wilkinson & P. Weaver, Trans.). Notre Dame: University of Notre Dame Press.

Rancer, A. S., & Baukus, R. A. (1987). Discriminating males and females on belief structures about arguing. In L. B. Nadler, M. K. Nadler, & W. R. Todd-Mancillas (Eds.), *Advances in gender and communication research* (pp. 155–173). Lanham, MD: University Press of America.

Richardson, L. (1987). *The dynamics of sex and gender: A sociological perspective*. New York: Harper & Row.

Ritzer, G. (1983). *Sociological theory*. New York: Knopf.

Schur, E. M. (1983). *Labeling women deviant: Gender, stigma, and social control*. Philadelphia: Temple University Press.

Shimberg, H. L. (1978). Ethics and rhetoric in technical writing. *Technical Communication, 25*(4), 16–18.

Skidmore, W. (1979). *Theoretical thinking in sociology* (2nd ed.). London: Cambridge University Press.

Stoner, R. B. (1988). Economic consequences of feminizing technical communication. *Proceedings of the 35th International Technical Communication Conference* (pp. MPD-108–110). Washington, DC: Society for Technical Communication.

Sullivan, D. L. (1990). Political-ethical implications of defining technical communication as a practice. *Journal of Advanced Composition, 10*(2), 375–386.

Thayer, L. (1974). *Communication: The ethical and moral issues*. New York: Gordon and Breach.

Thralls, C., & Blyler, N. (1993). The social perspective and pedagogy in technical communication. *Technical Communication Quarterly, 2*, 249–269.

Toulmin, S. (1964). *The uses of argument*. Cambridge, UK: Cambridge University Press. (Original work published 1958).

Vaughn, J. (1989). Sexist language—Still flourishing. *The Technical Writing Teacher, 16*(1), 33–40.

Veiga, N. E. (1989). Commentary: Sexism, sex stereotyping, and the technical writer. *Journal of Technical Writing and Communication, 19*(3), 277–283.

Wexler, P. (1991). *Critical theory now*. New York: Falmer.

Wilcoxin, S. A. (1989). He/she/they/it? Implied sexism in speech and print. *Journal of Counseling and Development, 68*(1), 114–116.

Womack, D. F. (1987). Cooperative behavior by female negotiators: Experts or masochists? In L. B. Nadler, M. K. Nadler, & W. R. Todd-Mancillas (Eds.), *Advances in gender and communication research* (pp. 219–241). Lanham, MD: University Press of America.

9 Understanding Institutional Discourse in the U.S. Congress, Present and Past

Catherine F. Smith

Descriptive research proceeds by observation and interpretation. These are historical acts. A researcher is always grounded in intellectual traditions and presuppositions, social and cultural organization, time, and place. In the study of discourse, this assumption doubly applies—the embedded researcher is always paralleled by the situated subject. The people whose discourses we study are, like ourselves, sense makers in context. A fundamental task of discourse analysis, therefore, is to understand how our subjects' interactions relate to their settings and situations. The other side of that purpose, like the other side of the moon, is to recognize how we are approaching the analysis. Thus, for the intellectual activity of describing in our own terms the discourse of others, we need analytic methods that preserve both the complexity that we find in our subjects and that we bring as researchers.

The book in which this chapter appears has the goal of reconsidering what we do as a research community of specialists in the study of nonacademic writing. That goal encouraged me to consider a 200-year-old case, for the challenge and pleasure of exploring what is found when we shift our analytic gaze from present to past, from individuals to groups, and from workplaces to other kinds of social institutions. My purpose in this chapter is to offer a method—conceptual framing—for descriptive study of discourse that aims to preserve complexity while interpreting it. Use of conceptual framing is illustrated by analysis of an example of historical discourse taken from institutional government.

Institutions manage public life. Governments, for example, are more than temporary, provisional arrangements. They are social macrostructures for stabilizing and legitimating relationships within and between groups as those relationships evolve. Institutions do this through microstructures of spoken and written exchanges that occur in, for example, legislative committees and subcommittees; executive and administrative offices; banks; hospitals; police and military organizations. Scholars of language practices in organizational life are justifiably interested in studying organizations that make and implement public policy for a society as a whole.

The subjects in the following example are elected political representatives instituting a national government in a new democracy. Many such examples might be found in the present late 20th century, as new nations continue to emerge and to attempt democracy. Near the end of 1993, Russia, for example, for the first time democratically elected a parliament and voted on a new constitution. South Africa has done the same. Eighty percent of the present world's national constitutions have been written since 1965, I recall reading somewhere. Here, however, I focus on an example from the late 18th century during the establishment of the United States as a republic, for two reasons. First, a wealth of sources from working sessions in the world's first large-scale attempt at governing by representative democracy awaits description as rhetorical history, rather than political history. I want to draw attention to those sources. Second, revisiting the past makes the present strange, freshens interpretation in our own time. Late 18th century American discourses to institutionalize democratic governance can inform our understanding of the rhetoric of present-day nation-building in Russia, Poland, Latvia, South Africa, and Central and South America.

AN INTERPRETIVE TASK:
MAKING SENSE OF GOVERNMENTAL DISCOURSE

Any discourse event is inherently complex, with multiple layers of activity and influence, some not immediately apparent. Institutional events are especially so. Any given moment of a Congressional hearing, for example, engages multiple and conflicting political viewpoints. Moreover, from governmental hearings (like other institutional meetings) flows a mingled stream of official and unofficial records—all relevant source material for the discourse analyst—of what was said, what was not said, and what any of it meant.

This is business as usual for historians or journalists who interpret the public discourses of government. An extended quotation from a *New York Times* report on Congressional plans for national health care reform suggests the usual richness of the context:

> They all say their health care plans are the most sensible approach to a pressing national problem. They have to.

But the major plans put forward to rival President Clinton's have other important purposes, too, chief among them being to establish the authors and supporters as players who will have a voice when a final bill is put together. Some want to push a certain provision into the law or keep out an offensive item.

And there are even simpler political motives in play. The bills establish lawmakers as concerned about a crucial national issue. Representative Jim McDermott, the Washington Democrat who has been pressing for a Government-run program like Canada's for some time, explained the spate of recent imitators: "This is no time to walk out and say, 'I got no idea what to do.'"

In fact, the authors of the five plans with widespread Congressional support do think they have better approaches than Mr. Clinton's. . . . But it seems unlikely that Mr. McDermott and the four other authors, Senators John H. Chafee and Phil Gramm or Representatives Robert H. Michel and Jim Cooper, really believe that if the 103d Congress passes a health care bill, it will not resemble Mr. Clinton's more closely than it resembles any of theirs.

But they cannot say that, so any analysis of their realistic hopes and true motives has to be assembled indirectly, by inference, from gossipy Congressional aides, and from a lawmaker's occasional 'don't quote me, but' statements. (Clymer, 1993)

My experience in a project of observing committee and subcommittee hearings during the 102d Congress in 1991 and 1992 went much like this reporter's. I came to understand that the work of Congress is to publicly process opposed interpretations of reality in order to construct a course of action. The hearing is a principal site for doing that work. A basic task of understanding the process I was observing, therefore, was to identify what all was underway in a given hearing. Basic construction would always include the announced purpose of the hearing—either legislation, authorization, appropriation, oversight, or confirmation of a nomination in progress. Beyond that, what else? Was the hearing a stage for elaborating positions on issues wider than the hearing's specific objective? If so, what positions were at issue? Major political party relations? Committee or subcommittee jurisdictions? The chair's agenda? Staff agendas? The constituency-based agendas of members?

We would also have to consider the two institutional mandates for holding a hearing: communication and information gathering. The Congress is now obliged to hold hearings to tell the public (communicate) what the Congress is doing, and to enable the Congress to learn (gather information) from experts, advocates, and spokespersons about issues in public life. Official outcomes of a hearing thus are a public record and public policy. The force of policy is bidirectional. Policy refers in as it affects institutional relations (majority/minority party "gridlock," for example) or the constitutional separation of powers between the branches of government. Policy refers out as it establishes or changes conditions of life in a society.

Given the layered, bidirectional, open-ended character of the situation, my strong inference was that multiplicity and dynamism characterize the discourse processes of a hearing.

One theory potentially useful for developing that inference is the proposal that institutions constitute collective thought styles, or social schemata underlying individual cognition (Douglas, 1986). In the terms of cultural anthropology, institutions are organizations for action based on a normative, shared idea of how the world is — or how it should be. Traceable in an individual's processes of categorizing, classifying, and making decisions are influences of that individual's affiliations with social institutions such as family, trade or profession, religious association, school, or political party.

This theory affirms *what* happens in governmental hearings. However, it cannot account for *how* it happens. Schema theory is too monolithic and too static to account for the transactional nature of communal interchange. A synthesis of theory concerned with social interaction and the human processing of information, strongly focused on pragmatics, is more useful. Although it is outside the scope of the present discussion to describe its development, the synthesis from which I derived the conceptual framework discussed here has its roots in theory of symbolic interaction as social organization (Goffman, 1974; Vygotsky, 1978) and draws on hermeneutics, or the study of interpretation (Gadamer, 1975); social constructionism (Gergen, 1985); pragmatic linguistics, particularly conversation theory (Grice, 1975); cognitive anthropology, particularly thought style theory (Douglas, 1986); cognitive psychology, particularly knowledge representation (Kintsch, 1988); and information processing theory, particularly cooperation and collaboration theory (J. B. Smith, 1994).

A MEANS OF INTERPRETATION:
A CONCEPTUAL FRAMEWORK

In observational research, deciding what is interesting or significant in the booming, buzzing confusion (or maybe the droning monotony) of a real situation can be difficult. A framework helps to prompt and ground conceptualization. As a research device, a conceptual framework points (more loosely than a formal model) to meaningful data in a situation. A framework does this, initially, by identifying broadly applicable concepts or features that characterize similarity or that reveal difference across situations.

To broadly identify Congressional hearings, I first reviewed open-ended notes made over approximately six years of varying experience, including the 1991–92 project, in observing hearings and interviewing participants. From these notes, I compiled a general list of symbolizing practices, for example, writing a statement, writing questions, rehearsing answers, testifying, audiotaping or videotaping, transcribing oral speech by shorthand writing, or editing print transcripts. Out of context, the resulting list made little sense. It did make sense, however, when I associated the practices with the constructions likely to be underway in a hearing. These associations yielded four categories of discourse development in hearings, or four large clusterings of many small context-sensitive symbolizing acts that constitute the hearing situation.

The categories, each comprising a cluster of attributes, include:

- *Collectivity*, or the intentional coming together of individuals around a bonding commitment, a shared idea, or a common interest. Attributes of belonging and membership; of assembling for a purpose. Examples affecting hearings would be belonging to a political party or forming a coalition or caucus for political action.
- *Performance,* or role playing. Attributes of behaving as a representative; of enacting and personifying collective agency; of accommodating one's actions to others' actions; of dramatic inter-action. An example in hearings would be an expert testifying to represent one organization's position on an interactive panel of experts representing other organizations' opposing positions.
- *Historicity,* or action in relative time. Attributes of being embedded in a flow of time, of influences of institutional history on present situations. Examples in hearings would be the constant referrals to precedent and the strategic uses of scheduling and timing.
- *Mediation,* or influences and interventions in a situation by communication modes (spoken language, written language); representations (handwriting, print, sound, pictures); enabling technologies (printing press, copier, microphone, camera). Examples in a hearing would be the multiple media of written statements orally presented, manually transcribed for printing, televised, and digitized for re-presentation in varied forms.

Any one, or any combination, of these categories—collectivity, performance, historicity, or mediation—creates perspective on a hearing. Like Deep Throat guiding investigative journalists ("follow the money") in the film *All the President's Men,* this framework directs analysts of discourse in hearings to "follow mediation" or "look at mediation historically."

Unlike Deep Throat, however, the framework does not specialize in exposing conspiracy. Hearings, like any other public forum, can be misused. However, that is not what this chapter is about. My topic is more mundane. I am concerned with ordinary complexity in a particular institutional form. Governmental hearings are naturally messy. They are superficially messy, as in people talking and no one listening; apparent questions or answers that are actually political speeches; arcane rules for who sits where and who speaks when, and so on. They are fundamentally messy, as in multiple issues interconnecting; amounts of information too large for one mind to hold; and authority overlapping among antagonistic organizations.

A conceptual framework helps us to understand these kinds of situations. The conceptual framework presented here is in some ways arbitrary. It reflects my interests in discourse analysis. Its categories are drawn from public political discourse, and its examples are from institutional government. Any framework is inevitably specialized and selective; framing necessarily highlights some aspects and suppresses others. Nevertheless, the use of an acknowledged framework carries the same rational benefits for any subjective process of interpretation. The benefits include making perspectives and analysis explicit, consistent, and capable of comparisons. Frameworks are a generalizable heuristic for studies of discourse. In a given study, a framework provides magnets for relevant data, principles for sorting observations, dimensions along which to see relationships among the data, and constraints on unsupportable interpretation.

APPLYING THE FRAMEWORK: UNDERSTANDING GOVERNMENTAL DISCOURSE HISTORICALLY

The framework used here was developed through attending hearings, watching televised broadcasts or listening to radio broadcasts of hearings, and interviewing participants. Working out the categories of the framework helped me to interpret contemporary hearings. Trying to make sense of what was happening in a particular 1991 hearing, for example, I relied mainly on cues provided by participants who said that I might usefully conceive of the event as performance. I have reported the resulting analysis elsewhere (C. F. Smith, 1993).

Some events were not present-day and could not be directly observed, as in the case of archival records from the earlier history of the Congress. That raised the problem of historical interpretation. I assume that events in the past were equally as complex as events in the present. However, discerning the past's complexity from a printed record is different from figuring out what is happening right now. In archival research, observation becomes reenactment. Situations must be reconstructed. In projective reconstruction of this sort, an explicitly acknowledged conceptual framework is perhaps even more necessary to the researcher than in live observation. What follows, then, illustrates use of the conceptual framework presented earlier to analyze an archival record from the first session of the First Congress, held in 1789–1801.

The Text to be Interpreted

The following is the record I chose to interpret, a verbatim entry from the diary of Senator William Maclay of Pennsylvania recording transactions in the Senate on August 22, 1789.

Senate met and went on the Coasting bill, The Door Keeper soon told Us of the Arrival of the President. The President was introduced and took our President's chair – he rose and told us bluntly that he had called on Us for our advice and consent to some propositions respecting the Treaties to be held with the Southern Indians – said he had brought Genl. Knox with him who was well acquainted with the business. He then turned to Genl. Knox Who was seated at his on the left of the Chair. Genl. Knox handed him a paper which he handed to the President of the Senate, who was seated on a Chair on the floor to his right. our President hurried over the Paper. Carriages were driving past and such a Noise I could tell it was something about Indians, but was not master of one Sentence of it. Signs were made to the door Keeper to shut down the Sashes. Seven heads (as we since learn) were stated at the End of the Paper which the Senate were to give their advice and consent to. they were so framed that this could be done by Aye or No. Our Presid. The President told Us a paper from an Agent of the Cherokees was given to him just as he was coming to the Hall. he motioned to General Knox for it, and handed it to the President of the Senate. it was read, it complained hard of the unjust Treatment of the People of North Carolina & ca. their Violation of Treaties & ca. Our President now read off, the first article to which our advice and consent was requested. it referred back principally to some statements in the body of the Writing which had been read. Mr. Morris rose and said the Noise of carriages had been so great that he really could not say that he had heard the body of the paper which was read and prayed it might be read again. it was so. It was no sooner read than our President. immediately read the first head over and put the Question do you advise and consent & ca. There was a dead pause. Mr. Morris wispered me, we will see who will venture to break silence first. Our Presi – Our President was proceeding *As many As* – I rose reluctantly indeed, and from the length of the pause, the hint given by Mr. Morris, and the proceeding of our President, it appeared to me, that if I did not, no other one would. and we could have these advices and consents ravish'd in a degree from us. Mr. President. The paper which you have now read to Us appears to have for it's basis Sundry Treaties and public Transactions, between the southern Indians and the United States & and the

States of Georgia North and south Carolina. The business is new to the Senate, it is of importance, it is our duty to inform ourselves as well as possible on the Subject. I therefore call for the reading of the Treaties and other documents alluded to in the paper now before Us. I cast an Eye at the President of the United States, I saw he wore an aspect of Stern displeasure. General Knox turned up some of the Acts of Congress, and the protests of One Blount Agent for North Carolina — Mr. Lee rose and named a particular Treaty which he wished to read. the Business laboured with the Senate, there appeared an evident reluctance to proceed. The first Article was about the Cherokees, it was hinted that the Person just come from then, might have more information. The President of U.S. rose said he had no objection to that article being postponed and in the mean time he could see the Messenger. the 2d Article which was about the Chickasaws and Choctaws was likewise postponed. The 3d Article more immediately concerned Georgia and the Creeks. Mr. Gun from Georgia moved this to be postponed to Monday he was seconded by Few Genl. Knox was asked, when Genl. Lincoln would be here on his way to Georgia. he answered, *not untill Saturday next* the Whole House seemed against Gun and Few. I rose & said When I considered the Newness and the importance of the subject, that One Article had already been postponed, That Genl. Lincoln the first named of the ~~Trustees had~~ Commissioners would not be here for a week. The deep interest Georgia had in this affair, I could not think it improper that the Senators from that State should be indulged in a postponement untill monday. more especially as I had not heard any inconvenience pointed out that could possibly flow from it. the Question was put and actually carried. But Elsworth immediately began a long discourse on the Merits of the Business. he was answered by Mr. Lee Who appeald to the Consti < tu > tion with regard to the powers of making War. Butler & Izard answered & ca. Mr. Morris at last informed the disputants that they were debating on a Subject that was actually postponed. Mr. Adams denyed in the face of the House that it had been postponed. this very trick has been played by him and his New England Men more than Once. the Question was however put a 2d time and carried. I had at an early stage wispered Mr. Morris that I thought the best way to conduct the business was to have all the papers committed — my reasons were that I saw no chance of a fair investigation of subjects while the President of the U.S. sat there with his Secretary at War, to support his Opinions and over awe the timid and neutral part of the Senate — Mr. Morris hastily rose and moved that the papers communicated to the Senate by the P. of the U.S. should be referred to a committee of 5, to report ~~immediately~~ as soon as might be, on them. he was seconded by Mr. Gun. several Members Grumbled some Objections. Mr. Butler rose made a lengthy speech against committment. said we were acting as a Council no Councils ever committed anything, Committees were an improper mode of doing business, it threw business out of the hands of the Many into the hands of the few. &ca. &ca. I rose and supported the mode of doing business by Committees, asserted that Executive Councils did make use of ~~Council~~somittees, that Committees were used in all public deliberative bodies &c. &ca. I thought I did the Subject Justice, but concluded, the Commitment cannot be attended with any possible inconvenience, some articles are already postponed untill Monday, Whoever the Committee are (if committed) they must make their report on Monday morning. I spoke thro' the Whole in a low tone of Voice. Peevishness itself I think could not have taken offence at anything I said. as I sat down the President of the U.S. started up in a Violent fret. *This defeats every purpose of my coming here,* were the first words that he said, he then went on that he had brought his Secretary at War with him to give every necessary information, that the Secretary knew all about the Business — and yet he was delayed and could not go on with the Matter — he cooled however by Degrees said he had no objection to putting off the Matter untill Monday, but declared he did not understand the Matter of Committment, he might be delayed he could not tell how long, he rose a 2d time and said he had no Objection to postponement untill Monday at 10 O'clock . by the looks of the Senate this seemed agreed to. a pause for some time ensued. We waited for him to withdraw, he did so with a discontented Air. had it been any other, than the Man who I wish to regard as the first Character in the World, I would have said with sullen dignity I cannot now be mistaken the President wishes to tread on the Necks of the Senate. Committment will bring this matter to discussion, at least in the Committee when he is not present. he wishes Us to see with the Eyes and hear with the ears of his Secretary only, the Secretary to advance the Premisses the President to draw Conclusions. and to bear down our deliberations with his personal Authority & Presence, form only will be left for Us — This will not do with Americans. but let the Matter Work it will soon cure itself. (Bowling & Veit, 1988, pp. 128-131)[1]

Analysis

The framework is useful in this case for illuminating the context and the internal dynamics of this event. Maclay's diary entry is used as source material only. It is not my intention here to examine features of his diary or ways that the genre of the diary constructs history. Rather, I want to understand how discourses emerge in the situation he writes about.

Collectivity

The initial cue to this event is *collectivity*. Collectivity — belonging or not belonging — functioned on several levels. We are shown the first national

---

[1]Referred to here are: George Washington, President of the United States; John Adams, Vice President of the United States and President of the Senate; General Andrew Knox, Secretary of War; General Benjamin Lincoln, Commissioner to the southern Indians; William Blount, North Carolina agent; and Senators Robert Morris (Pennsylvania), Richard Henry Lee (Virginia), James Gunn and William Few (Georgia), Oliver Ellsworth (Connecticut), and Pierce Butler and Ralph Izard (South Carolina).

assembly of elected representatives to the federal government of the new United States. We are seeing particularly the Senate, or upper body of a bicameral legislature. The Senate met, literally, in the upstairs room of the refurbished old city hall in New York City. Downstairs in the same building, the House of Representatives, or lower body, met. As intended by the Constitution, the two bodies also represented higher and lower social strata and different political constituencies. So knowing that Maclay was describing the Senate, not the House, is significant.

Only the senators, the Senate secretary, the vice president, and (as a special circumstance) the president and his War Department secretary would have been present. No others would have been permitted, as will be discussed later. Outside the Senate door was a Cherokee delegation accompanied by Bennet Ballew, a trader of Scottish origin acting as their agent, interpreter, and negotiator. The Senate was convened on that day as a Committee of the Whole.

Performance

If collectivity is fundamental structure, then *performance* is the action to watch in this event. Maclay shows us people performing roles scripted by (in his view) their responsibilities and commitments as political representatives, their character, and their purposes on that particular day. However, he does not provide certain information essential to our historical reconstruction of the event. To situate Maclay's details, I will interject here, like overlays on his diary pages, (my) retrospective explanations of historic conditions, political context, and broad institutional struggles embedding the specific treaty discussion in the Senate on that day.

The Congress members and the president were conscious that they were historically the first political actors to interpret the minimal script for an American government, the blueprint 1788 Constitution. That document called for a federal government of three branches—legislative, executive, and judicial—but did not elaborate the structure, operation, or coordination of the branches. The legislative Congress had been elected first, with responsibility for instituting the other branches. Worldwide, there was no comparable example of representative democracy for the Congress to follow. The new republic, with a population of approximately 4 million on a land area larger than any European nation, was the first to attempt to govern by representation based on the consent of the governed. Moreover, there was little in contemporary political theory to support the feasibility of such a plan.

The historic obligation of the first Congress, shared after the first electoral college vote with the first president, was thus to invent a government that had been conceived. It did so, while operating daily under conditions of crisis. Still politically unstable six years after formally gaining independence from the British empire in 1783, the United States in 1789 faced secession from its intended union of former colonies (by North Carolina and Rhode Island), states' rights and constitutional amendment conflicts in several of the new states, absence of a national currency, lack of revenue (without established taxation or trade), and large war debts. Scattered local wars could not be controlled and threats of foreign attack continued. To understand how the first Senate performed, we need to know what political representation meant in its context.

Constitutionally, the senators represented separate states in a federated union. Two senators for each state were elected by the state legislatures, not by direct popular vote as were members of the House of Representatives. Eleven former colonies (all but North Carolina and Rhode Island) had accepted the new constitution and joined the federal union as states. With full attendance, 22 senators would have been present on August 22, representing both pluralism — 11 very different states — and singularity — the voting public of adult White males in each state.

Demographically, the senators represented elites. In wealth, property, education, professions, and prior experience in government (in the English parliament, in colonial and state assemblies, or in the American confederation congresses and constitutional conventions), the first senators conformed to the constitutional framers' intentions that the upper house of government should represent social stability and authority (Swift, 1989, pp. 52–57).

Politically, the Senators held a spectrum of positions on how to govern a democratic republic. Few would have agreed, for example, on what democracy meant or on how much democracy was good for the new country.

In light of these historic conditions and this political context, two broad institutional struggles can be discerned in the deliberations specific to a treaty with the Cherokees on that August Saturday. They are struggles to institute the republic, itself, as well as its government.

Instituting a Republic.   The United States was not alone on its continent in 1789. Two political cultures and two governmental systems competed there. One was European political culture and its derivative, the new republican government of the United States. The other was indigenous political culture and diverse governmental systems based on it. Again, I will summarize conditions before proceeding.

Geographically, the United States in 1789 was a slender strip between the Atlantic Ocean and the Appalachian mountains. Limits on further western occupation were the physical barriers of the mountains and the political barrier of the so-called Indian Boundary line.[2] This boundary had been determined earlier by the British government in negotiations with tribes to define land under tribal control and not available to colonists. Each state in the narrow American corridor was ill defined. As colonies, their boundaries had been ideals, only. (Some, for example, were shown on maps as extending from the Atlantic to the Pacific ocean.) Borders had been only partially surveyed and were commonly disputed between and among states, native groups, and European powers. (The British colony of Canada, for example, bordered several states.)

Diarist William Maclay's Pennsylvania was an example. Implementation of the Penn family's proprietary land grant from the English king Charles II had required land purchases from the Iroquois, negotiations with the state of New York to resolve conflicting claims to western parts of the grant, and adjudicated resolution of armed conflicts between Pennsylvania militia and settlers who claimed eastern parts for Connecticut.

The states' populations were ill-defined, too. The first census was not conducted until 1790. The colonies' inhabitants had included varying proportions of British and European migrants of differing origins and ethnic loyalties; slaves and freed former slaves from Africa and the Caribbean; and indigenous tribal groups. (Massachusetts, for example, was a mixed population of English and non-English Whites, whereas South Carolina's population was predominantly Black and Georgia's predominantly indigenous.) Moreover, loyalties divided between sympathy for England, for the new republic, and, anarchistically, for no government at all. Continuing British military alliances with tribes added to the complexity (*Atlas of Early American History*, 1976, pp. 86–90).

Instituting a republic comprising these heterogeneous populations and contested borders depended on defining criteria for citizenship and on

---

[2]Terminology for describing people is historical. Names for population groups on the North American continent were shifting in 1789. Prior to the colonial revolt in the late 1770s, Europeans and the British used American to refer generally to indigenous peoples on this continent, who were also called Indian. Americans were thus the Indians who lived here. However, with the establishment of the United States as a nation in the 1780s, a new national identity emerged and usage changed. Former European and British colonists living in the new United States became consciously American. Thomas Jefferson, after growing up in the Virginia colony as a British subject, was led by his political commitments and activities to assert that he, born in Virginia to English parents, was a first-generation American. William Maclay, born in Pennsylvania to Scottish parents, asserted the same consciousness, which he extended institutionally to the elected representatives in the Senate when he criticized behavior by saying, "This will not do with Americans." For Maclay, Americans were inside the Senate doors on August 22. The Cherokees outside the door were a delegation from a foreign nation. I have used late 20th-century terminology here, except in quoting verbatim from historical documents.

defining territorial boundaries. Territorial boundaries were the issue in the Senate session on August 22. Where was the western border of Georgia, South Carolina, and, if it joined the union as hoped, North Carolina? And, what were the relative jurisdictions of the federal and state governments in that territory?

However, the deeper conflict was between Euro-American and indigenous definitions of territory. Legal jurisdiction over land areas was a European-derived concept of nationhood defined as territory. In contrast, settled (nonnomadic) indigenous peoples understood territory very differently. Some groups did not acknowledge ownership of land. Access to land was commonly defined by inherited occupation and use. Under this definition, a group's land area was defined by living on it and using it over generations. Legal jurisdiction had nothing to do with it. To draw lines around land and to claim control over what was inside the lines, regardless of the land's occupation and use, violated a hereditary system. Moreover, experience taught the Cherokee and others that legal governmental jurisdiction did not work, anyway. European and British colonial boundaries, and then state boundaries, had meant nothing to immigrants determined to settle wherever they wanted. Little prevented them, with the absence in 1789 of established procedures for land titles and ownership. "The whole white race is a monster who is always hungry and what he eats is land," a western territory Shawnee leader, Chiksika, said, after years of encroachments on Indian lands by the British, French, and Americans (Eckert, 1992, unpaginated epigraph).

Neither the Euro-American nor the indigenous governmental systems prevailed in 1789. The political reality was that they were separate and had to negotiate relationships. Among the first U.S. president's principal duties, therefore, was codifying U.S. boundaries in treaties with numerous tribal groups. Washington recognized the southwestern border question as entailing all facets of the new republic's foreign relations. Thus, the treaty he read aloud began:

> To conciliate the powerful tribes of Indians in the southern district, amounting probably to fourteen thousand fighting men, and to attach them firmly to the United States, may be regarded as highly worthy of the serious attention of Government.

> The measure includes not only peace and security to the whole southern frontier, but is calculated to form a barrier against the colonies of a European Power, which in the mutations of policy, may one day become the enemy of the United States. The fate of the Southern States, therefore, or the neighboring colonies, may principally depend on the present measures of the Union towards the Southern Indians. (Gales, *Annals of Congress,* Vol. 1, p. 66)

For their part, the Cherokees acknowledged the republic's potential for protecting tribal rights against the depredations of states such as North Carolina. As their appointed agent Bennet Ballew wrote in a Cherokee statement included among the treaty's supporting documents:

> We now make known to the great Congress of america, that Our Desire and intention is to live in the most perfect & Strict Friendship and Alliance with our Elder brothers the americans: That we shall for ever listen to and abide by their instructions Advice and determination, placing the Strongest Confidence that the Great Council is composed of such who have eyes of pitty and hearts of humanity and Compassion, that they will not devest us of our rights and possessions, which our ancient Fathers have enjoyed time out of mind.
>
> We still remember and abide by the treaty held with your Commissioners in south Carolina in the year 1785. And tho our hunting grounds and towns north of tenesee and holeson rivers is sold unto white people for the Settle upon without our Consent, we still hope Congress will have mercy Upon us: For if our country is all taken from us we shall not be able to raise our children, neither there any place left for us to remove too.
>
> We rejoice much to hear that the Great Congress have got new powers And have become Strong. we now Hope that whatever is done hereafter by the Great Council will no more be destroyed and made small by any State. (DePauw, Bickford, & Siegel, 1972, p. 186)

The basis for this plea is made clear in a proclamation of the earlier Continental Congress in 1788:

> And Whereas it has been represented to Congress, that several disorderly Persons settled on the Frontiers of North-Carolina . . . have, in open violation of said treaty (Hopewell 1785), made intrusions upon the said Indian Hunting Grounds, and committed many unprovoked outrages upon the said Cherokees, who by the said Treaty have put themselves under the Protection of the United States, which proceedings are highly injurious and disrespectful to the authority of the Union. . . . The United States in Congress assembled. . . . Do hereby issue this Proclamation, strictly forbidding all such unwarrantable intrusions and hostile proceedings against the said Cherokees; and enjoining all those who have settled upon the said Hunting Grounds . . . to depart with their Families and Effects. (DePauw et al., 1972, pp. 184–185)

The Continental Congress had no statutory power of enforcement, however. Cherokee agent Ballew described the continuing conflict more directly in the letter handed to Washington outside the Senate door as "war carried on with all its horrors, between a party of the North Carolinians and Cherokees" (DePauw et al., 1972, pp. 200–201).

August 22, 1789 illustrates the interaction between political cultures surrounding the new federal Congress. Obvious, of course, is the lopsided representation. Cherokee viewpoints were presented only in documents written for communication with the Senate by agent Ballew. Evidently, Ballew was accepted as spokesperson by the Cherokees as, in his own description, "a neutral person, & one who was formerly acquainted with that nation (having lived among them as a prisoner of war during part of our war with the British)" (DePauw et al., 1972, p. 200). Similarly, the viewpoints of North Carolinians (still outside the American union) were summarized in statements by William Blount, a state legislator and Continental Congress member.

The senators were able to read these documents in light of their own experience and interests. Several (including Maclay and Washington) had fought in British military operations against tribal groups, purchased land for the states, surveyed state boundary lines, and at the time of this debate were land speculators holding private claim to untitled lands used by tribes and occupied by settlers.

Instituting a government.   The second broad institutional struggle that day concerned interbranch cooperation in the government. Animating the struggle were sharp differences of political philosophy among the elected representatives. As noted, the senators represented the states in a federated union. The president represented the union. The senators and the president shared a strong commitment to the union. However, beneath that shared commitment, ideology was considerably more diverse.

Participants on August 22 were committed to opposing philosophies of government: federalist and republican. Generally, federalists distrusted democracy and favored a strong national government to prevail over weaker state governments. Republicans trusted democracy and favored a weak national government checked by internal balances and by state governments. The majority of the first senators were federalists. These differences shaped the exchanges reported between the diarist Senator Maclay, a republican, and President Washington, a federalist.

Mediation

Inseparable from the ideological conflict was concurrent maneuvering, related to institution-building, over procedures for communicating between the branches of government. Performance of representation, it turns out, was melded to *mediation*.

The session on August 22 was a test of the constitution's "advise and consent" provision that the president and the Senate would share executive power to appoint government officers and to negotiate treaties with other nations. To facilitate these shared executive functions as well as general needs for coordination, a committee of senators had been delegated to work out procedures for communication between the two branches. Earlier in August, a procedure had been established. Nominations for appointment to government office would be communicated by the president in writing, and the Senate's only action would be to consent or reject, in writing. Treaties, in contrast, would be orally communicated because the president had said he wished to seek the Senate's advice directly and continually throughout a treaty process.

President Washington tested the procedure for treaties by coming in person to the Senate on August 22. Because this was an executive session, the legislative record of the day was silent about his visit. That record read:

Saturday, August 22, 1789

The Senate assembled,

Present as yesterday.

The memorial of John Cox and others, citizens of the State of New-Jersey and of the State of Pennsylvania, praying that the future Seat of Government might be established on the Banks of the Delaware, and proposing a cession of a tract of land of ten miles square, was read, and together with a draught of the said tract, was laid on the table for consideration.

Proceeded on the THIRD reading of the bill, entitled, "An Act for registering and clearing of Vessels, regulating the Coasting Trade, and for other Purposes" — And after progress,

Adjourned until 10 o'clock on Monday morning. (DePauw et al., 1972, p. 127)

Unofficially, in Maclay's personal diary we have a record of the contest that developed that day over what oral communication by the president with the Senate would actually mean. The president exercised one option: reading aloud a near-final treaty before calling for immediate Senate reaction by voice vote. The Senate insisted on a different option: a review and discussion of all relevant documents by committee, followed by deliberation in the whole body with the president invited to participate. Deliberation would conclude in a written summary of advice sent later to the president.

Republican fear of a strong presidency likely shaped this conflict, but probably more directly influential was the Senate's institution-building wish to define itself as a deliberative, rather than a reactive, partner to the president. The Senate wanted to advise and to consent and to deliberate. The president on this occasion seemed to want only consent, with or without deliberation. The Senate's preference prevailed. The test of procedure ended with this first, and last, visit by Washington to the Senate. After a follow-up session on August 24 to hear the Senate deliberate, he did not return for more face-to-face discussion. Subsequent treaties were developed by written communication.

Cued to follow mediations in this event, I have thus far considered how communication practices configured institutional relations. But there is more to be seen. How, for example, did the choice of media and the state of communication technology condition participants' working knowledge of the issues?

For participants in the Senate chamber on August 22, understanding depended on a hybrid mixture of written and oral texts.[3] But the mix varied by individuals. Some participants relied principally on the written, and others relied principally on the oral. The president worked from the specific formulations of written text (a draft treaty); the senators worked from listening to him read the draft aloud. What they heard was probably framed by individual prior knowledge. All the senators probably knew about the general problem leading to this treaty, as they had earlier authorized funds for negotiating it (Swanstrom, 1985, p. 117). Some senators may have read the related documents that Washington had sent over a few days before this debate. Additionally, a few may have worked, as Maclay did, from personal knowledge gained as participants in other treaty negotiations.

If they could not hear clearly, the senators might have asked to see the Senate secretary's handwritten minutes as the event progressed. However, it would not have helped much because deliberation was not recorded. Some senators made their own unofficial notes as discussion progressed; Maclay, for example, based his later diary account on the notes he took that day.

So, any participant's understanding of what was happening depended on interdependent oral and written mediations—the carefully formulated written text of a treaty; the partial auditory reception of that text; loose and disrupted oral interactions; cryptic and selective personal notes—factored into personal prior knowledge. Any participant's knowledge could, therefore, have only been a subset, a fragment defined by contingencies, such as whether he was present in the Senate on that day (many sessions were sparsely attended), whether he had background knowledge, whether he could hear the president, whether he had read any of the documents related to this particular treaty, or whether he took his own notes during the discussion. Few, perhaps none, of the senators would have fit in all these categories. Thus, each senator's viewpoint was necessarily partial and different, depending on what he heard, read, or already knew.

---

[3]This discussion of the senators' knowledge construction as it was mediated by the contemporary state of communication technology is indebted to "Collaboration as an Information Processing Activity" (J. B. Smith, 1994, chap. 2).

How about outsiders? How would media of communication have influenced their understanding of this event? Because the Senate conducted all its sessions behind closed doors in 1789, contemporary observers could have known very little by direct observation. (Treaty negotiations remained secret even after other sessions were made public in 1795.) In 1789, no visitors were allowed into the Senate chamber: not from the public, not from the press, not even from the House of Representatives. Moreover, no verbatim record of debate was kept. The Senate secretary kept a constitutionally mandated legislative journal to catalogue legislation and another executive journal requested by the Senate to record executive activities. These journals were for use by the members of Congress, not for public use. The secretary was directed by the Constitution to publish the legislative journal "from time to time;" however, Congress long refused to authorize funding for printing it.

Thus, contemporary observers could learn about this event only if they talked afterward directly with the participants—in boardinghouses where the members of Congress lived, or in taverns where they gathered—or if they corresponded with the members by letter. They might have read summaries of the proceedings in partisan newspapers or occasional "registers" of Congressional debate assembled by printers. Like any other contemporary observer, newspapers and printers compiled their summaries indirectly from conversations and correspondence with Congress members because journalists were not allowed in the Senate chamber. Contemporary observers, like the participants, could therefore only have understood this event selectively, based on an individual subset of information conditioned by the availability of communication media.

Historicity

The conditioning was historical. Mediation intersects *historicity* wherever institution-building as well as contemporary technology, literacy, and culture constrain the availability and use of communication forms and practices.

Constraints flowed immediately from the first senators' intent to define the institution of the Senate, as shown in the protocol they developed for communicating with the president and with the public. The skeptical position the first Senate took on the public's need to know, as shown by meeting in secret and by not publishing records of activity, was historicized in several ways. Precedent was one. The senators looked partly to English precedents. Parliamentary debate in England was not recorded, a practice that evolved to protect the legislature during conflicts with the monarch in the 1688 revolution (Macpherson, 1940, pp. 1-10).

Partisan politics within the Senate may have been a factor. Federalists distrusted democracy and saw no need to encourage popular influence on government by informing the public about it. Both federalists and republicans preferred communicating selectively through their own letters circulated among constituents or through partisan newspapers and printers.

Technological development also mattered. Even if the United States Senators had wanted to record what they said, there was in 1789 no generally accepted system of shorthand for transcribing oral speech accurately. The only available recording method — discursive handwriting — was known to be error-prone (especially in a room where hearing was difficult). As a result, the secretary's minutes of preceding meetings were routinely read aloud to check their accuracy at the beginning of each new meeting. Even if records could have been accurately produced, distributing them was difficult or impossible. The new republic had few roads and little transportation.

Contemporary literacy may have influenced the minimal use of print for communication, as well. Relatively few inhabitants of the United States (unlike the Senators) could read.

Finally, culture was influential, as seen by recalling another interested party to this treaty, the southern Cherokees. Traditionally, their political deliberations were oral. The Cherokee language was only spoken, not written, in 1789. In the U. S. government's choice to negotiate from the basis of written English with the neighboring Cherokee government's representatives, who did not rely on written text and did not use English, retrospective interpreters of this event can recognize the cultural politics of a particular time and place.

Retrospective interpreters (the researcher-writer and readers of this chapter) are the final historical players to consider here. How is our understanding of this event mediated and historicized? It is relevant to compare our process of understanding with the possibilities in 1789. Unlike then, we now have access to official records of the discussion on August 22, 1789 — the Senate legislative and executive journals and Washington's presidential papers regarding treaties. We also have access to a compiled (not verbatim) record of deliberations between 1789 and 1824, the *Annals of Congress*. Additionally, we can search archives for unofficial records in contemporary newspapers, registers of debate, or letters. We can read Maclay's diary, the only surviving diary from the first Senate (published as expurgated by his family in 1880 and verbatim in 1927). And, we can talk about our findings with present-day specialists, as while writing this chapter I discussed it with colleagues in history, computer and information science, literature, composition, and rhetoric.

Because we can read all these records and discuss them widely, it might seem that in the 1990s we can know more than the participants in the 1780s and 1790s did. In fact, comparison suggests that we, as they, know only selectively what happened, based on what we read, to whom we talk, and what we already know.

CONCLUSION

Analysis of the event on August 22, 1789 can be productively cued and constrained by viewing it through an explicit framework for conceptualizing. For that situation, two framing perspectives — performance and mediation — proved most illuminating. When those cues are allowed to intersect and when history is considered, we obtain what is probably a reliable composite view. This view shows that performance is not truly understandable apart from its mediations, nor do mediations make sense outside an embedding institutional history.

Discourse is a texture of constructed meanings. The boundaries of a sample of discourse — where it begins and where it ends — are inherently uncertain. The relations of a sample to its context are multiple, complex, and subject to interpretation at all times. What I have tried to do here is to suggest an approach that is sensitive to these conditions and makes them manageable so that analysis can reliably proceed.

The suggestion is based on my wish that, as specialists in nonacademic writing, we might take up an expanded menu of discourse types to study, enrich our notions of what discourse is, and develop more adaptive instruments of research and scholarship. Conceptual framing is one such instrument. It enables the interpretive observer to (a) keep in mind several patterns of influence beyond simple cause and effect between discourse and its setting, (b) acknowledge variable relationships among components of the discourse that could yield equally true alternative interpretations of the same event, and (c) recognize complex historical groundings of experience.

As an orientation to knowledge, conceptual framing resembles some of the newer philosophical approaches in fields specializing in studies of information processing. One useful analog from information studies is hypertext. I am speaking here of hypertext as metaphor. I am utilizing an idea, wholes-constituted-by-variable-links, made available by late 20th century technology development. The hypertext analog enables me to characterize discourse as the dynamic interaction of parts to wholes, and, most importantly, to recognize the pluralism of wholes that might be derived by linking the same parts differently.

As a characterization of discourse, the technological metaphor of hypertext is more useful than is the organic metaphor of a web. Webs are singular, woven by one spider in one definitive form. Discourse, in contrast, is always plural and interactive, multiple spiders weaving in common a shared web that looks different to each spider. In discourse understood hypertextually, individuals traverse shared information along individual paths. Each traversal is a whole, how the universe looks to that individual.

For the analysis of discourse, conceptual framing is a hypertextual approach. A framework offers specific interpretive pathways through a discourse event; here, they are collectivity, performance, historicity, and mediation. Results of traversing the event along any one of these pathways can be compared with results of journeys along other pathways through the same event, or with those same journeys through a different event.

Why is it useful to think of discourse and its analysis as hypertextual? For the individual contemporary interpreter, the metaphor may provoke fresh insight. For the specialty of nonacademic writing, concepts of hypertext bridge our work and work in other fields, including technology development, attempting to understand and to support communication in human organizations. As analysts of rhetorical practices, we have a contributing role to play in multi-disciplinary research communities now intensively exploring ways that social organization and information technology converge in the settings of human work.[4]

ACKNOWLEDGMENT

For their thoughtful reading of several drafts of this chapter, I am grateful to editors Ann Hill Duin and Craig Hansen; reviewers Marilyn Cooper and Anne Aronson; Syracuse University Writing Program colleagues Duane Roen, James Zebroskie, and especially Kenneth Lindblom. For constructive criticism at all stages of thinking and writing, I am indebted to John Smith. For generous access to sources in Congressional history, I especially thank Richard Baker, the Historian of the United States Senate, and Gregory Harness, Head of Reference, the Senate Library. For sharing their experienced wisdom about present-day Congressional communications, I especially thank Nancy Kingsbury and other staff members of the U.S. General Accounting Office from whom I learn every time I facilitate their training seminars in writing and presenting Congressional testimony.

REFERENCES

Atlas of early American history: The revolutionary era 1760–90. (1976). Princeton, NJ: Princeton University Press.

---

[4]They include special interest groups of the Association for Computing Machinery, for example the Hypertext group, Human-Computer Interaction group, and Computer-Supported Cooperative Work group.

Bowling, K. R., & Veit, H. E. (Eds.). (1988). *The diary of William Maclay and other notes on senate debates.* Baltimore: Johns Hopkins University Press.

Clymer, A. (1993, October 17). Many health plans, one political goal. *New York Times*, p. 22.

DePauw, L. G., Bickford, C. B., & Siegel, L. M. (Eds.). (1972, 1974). *Senate legislative journal and Senate executive journal and related documents* (Vols. 2 and 3 of *Documentary history of the first federal Congress of the United States of America*). Baltimore: Johns Hopkins University Press.

Douglas, M. (1986). *How institutions think.* Syracuse: Syracuse University Press.

Eckert, A. W. (1992). *A sorrow in our heart: The life of Tecumseh* New York: Bantam.

Gadamer, H.G. (1975). *Truth and method.* New York: Seabury.

Gales, J. (Compiler). (1834–56). *Debates and proceedings in the Congress of the United States* (Annals of Congress, 42 vols.). Washington, DC: Gales and Seaton.

Gergen, K. J. (1985). The social constructionist movement in modern psychology. *American Psychologist, 40*(3), 266–275.

Grice, H. P. (1975). Logic and conversation. In P. Cole & J. L. Morgan (Eds.), *Syntax and semantics, vol. 3: Speech acts* (pp. 41–58). New York: Academic Press.

Goffman, E. (1974). *Frame analysis: An essay on the organization of experience.* New York: Harper & Row.

Kintsch, W. (1988). The role of knowledge in discourse comprehension: A construction-integration model. *Psychological Review, 95*(2), 163–182.

MacPherson, E. G. (1940). *The history of reporting the debates and proceedings of Congress.* Unpublished doctoral dissertation, University of North Carolina, Chapel Hill.

Smith, C. F. (1993). 'Is it worth fixing this plane?': The rhetorical life of information in a congressional oversight hearing on the B-1 bomber. In B. R. Sims (Ed.), *Studies in technical communication: Selected papers from the 1992 CCCC and NCTE meetings* (pp. 111–146). Denton: University of North Texas Press.

Smith, J. B. (1994). *Collective intelligence in computer-based collaboration* Hillsdale, NJ: Lawrence Erlbaum Associates.

Swanstrom, R. (1985). *The United States Senate 1781–1801. A dissertation on the first fourteen years of the upper legislative body* (99th Cong., 1st sess, Senate Document 99–19). Washington, DC: U.S. Government Printing Office.

Swift, E. K. (1989). *Reconstitutive change in the United States Congress: The transformation of the Senate 1789–1841.* Ann Arbor, MI: University Microfilms International.

Vygotsky, L. (1978). *Mind in society: The development of higher psychological processes.* Cambridge, MA: Harvard University Press.

10 Participatory Writing: Literacy for Civic Purposes

Sandra Stotsky
Harvard Graduate School of Education

Literacy has been historically associated with the development and maintenance of democratic institutions. Because ancient Athens was a face-to-face
society, literacy may not have been critical for the daily functioning of
democracy, as it was practiced then. Nevertheless, many scholars believe
that it played a crucial role in the development of Athenian democracy and
in the later development of democracy elsewhere. Indeed, the Athenians
also saw literacy as instrumental in its development. As Finley (1983)
commented in a discussion of the nature of self-government in ancient
Athens, "the archaic struggle for a written law code was rightly looked back
upon as critical in breaking the power monopoly of the old aristocracy" (p.
30). It clearly would have been of little use to have laws written down if
none but the aristocracy could read them. Nor would it have been of much
use, in more recent times, to have rights spelled out in writing, as in the
Magna Carta or the charters for the colonies in the New World, if none but
monarchs and their advisors could read them.

The reasons for the positive relationship between literacy and democracy
are not quite clear. As Harris (1989) pointed out in a study of literacy in the
ancient world, literacy has served ostensibly negative purposes throughout
history. He noted that written language "makes empires possible," that it
has been a means of "exercising power," that it has been used by those who
claimed religious authority to "enhance their authority" (such as Moses),
and that it may even have encouraged "a sort of canonization of discourse"
(p. 39). Moreover, 20th-century history teaches us that a high degree of
literacy does not guarantee a democratic society; the populace of Nazi
Germany, for example, was highly literate. Nevertheless, as Harris noted,

writing "gradually came to be associated with the rights of the citizens, their right to exile politicians, their right to know the laws and the proposed laws, and their right to use the law-courts, whether as litigants or as jurors" (p. 115). Even if not a sufficient condition, political scientists and sociologists today still regard literacy as a supporting condition for democratic self-government (e.g., Lipset, 1959). Regardless of cultural differences from country to country, democratic modes of participation seem to require an educated citizenry, as Verba and his associates (1971) found in a cross-cultural analysis.

Curiously, literacy has often seemed to refer only to the ability to read. Even more curiously, it has often been defined in even narrower terms — as the ability to read primarily for occupational purposes. Yet, the ability to convey one's ideas in writing is far more empowering than the ability simply to read or to listen to what others have written. As Levine (1982) commented in an essay on adult literacy efforts, "Writing conveys and records innovation, dissent, and criticism; above all, it can give access to political mechanisms and the political process generally where many of the possibilities for personal and social transformation lie" (p. 262). Further, the ability to write on matters relating to civic or political life is crucial for the proper functioning of the institutions of democratic self-government. For example, in a textbook on how to organize and maintain a democratically run organization, Brewer (1952) devoted an entire chapter to the kinds of writing that its members need to do to preserve its democratic character.

Writing is, in fact, a vital aspect of republican self-government and an inseparable component of almost all the significant activities in which people engage in order to govern themselves in a democratic society. Yet, despite the abundant presence today of participatory writing as well as its historical significance as a phenomenon, political scientists and sociologists have rarely examined the writing people do as citizens for civic or political purposes. A few have looked at letters to editors on political issues to try to understand what kind of people write these letters and why (see, for example, Buell, 1975; Hill, 1981), and one study has explored the quality of the letters that constituents wrote to United States senators on a political issue (Wyant, 1941; Wyant & Herzog, 1941). But other than Sussman's (1963) extensive analysis of the letters sent to President Franklin D. Roosevelt, there seem to be no major studies of citizen writing by political scientists and sociologists despite its extraordinary growth in 20th-century America.

Nor have scholars of rhetoric and composition in general paid much attention to the writing composed by the ordinary citizen for civic or political purposes. They have, of course, paid a great deal of attention to the speeches and other public writings of important elected or appointed public officials and other influential public figures, such as political commentators or business leaders. Although the term frequently used in their work to refer to this writing—*public discourse*—could in theory include the writing of ordinary people in their capacity as citizens (writing which is in the public domain even though it often has no audience beyond the public official to whose office it is sent), in scholarly practice it has not. It seems to designate the writing of only those who hold a major public office or who can easily and regularly command the attention of the media by virtue of their political or professional eminence. And although literary scholars and rhetoricians have also frequently examined the political implications—if not the political influence—of the works of novelists, playwrights, poets, and even other scholars, this writing (as important as it too may be in the political life of a community or society) constitutes nonacademic writing when it is presented publicly by people in their professional capacity.

Even scholars who examine nonacademic writing rarely seem to have gone beyond the workplace to explore the writing that serves other than professional or general occupational needs. Moreover, within the workplace itself, the focus has tended to be somewhat narrow. In a study of the transitions that six college students made as writers in moving from an academic setting to a professional setting in a senior-year professional internship, Anson and Forsberg (1990) pointed out that the bulk of the research on nonacademic writing has focused on the writing of professionals and experts. Together with Ede's (1991) analysis of a series of letters to the editor generated by a controversy over the public school curriculum in her hometown, my own writings on the subject over the past decade (Stotsky, 1987a, 1987b, 1990a, 1991) appear to constitute the only analyses and discussions of participatory writing by scholars in a literacy-related discipline. I have frequently puzzled over why that is the case.

Perhaps an exploration of the nature and significance of participatory writing has been inhibited by the apparent dominance in literacy research of a theoretical perspective that views literacy as a means for oppressing rather than liberating the ordinary citizen (see Stotsky, 1990b, for a discussion of this issue). For example, Graff (1981) claimed that literacy in the west has served as an instrument of "social and cultural control and hegemony" (p. 4). Earlier, Levi-Strauss (1973) articulated an even stronger version of this point of view, stating that writing "seems to have favoured the exploitation of human beings rather than their enlightenment" and that "the primary function of written communication is to facilitate slavery" (p. 299). Perhaps there are other reasons for the lack of attention by writing researchers and scholars to the writing of people in their capacity as citizens. Nevertheless, the contexts and uses for participatory writing remain a fertile area for exploration by those interested in the demands placed on writers as they attempt to transfer ways of thinking about writing and the writing skills they acquired in school to the kind of writing they need to do as adults outside of school in order to participate in the process of representative self-government.

Therefore, the purpose of this essay is twofold. First, based on an examination of a large number of examples of participatory writing at all levels of government, I offer a suggested categorization of the broad purposes for participatory writing in this country. By their very nature, these categories shed light on the nature of the political relationships between citizens and their government—that is, what individual rights they possess that enable them to participate as writers in the process of self-government—thus enriching our understanding of the social context within which literacy education takes place in this country. I then discuss a series of letters written by a group of parents to public officials to obtain their approval and funding of a small-scale community project. These letters illustrate the use of participatory writing in a specific context and reveal the complex interaction of purpose with audience in this writing. They also suggest some of the rhetorical skills that participation in the civic process may require.

A BRIEF HISTORICAL OVERVIEW

In the English-speaking world, participatory writing has a long and significant history with respect to the development of democratic institutions. Throughout history, people have often sought help from their rulers to deal with their grievances against local officials or others who they believed had dealt unfairly with them. In small countries, people often related their complaints directly to their rulers. Where distance prohibited a personal appearance, the grievance was frequently sent in the form of a petition and presented at court by an intermediary. But in medieval England, Maddicott (1981) noted, petitions to the Crown began to be presented at meetings of Parliament as well as at court, a practice that had far-reaching effects on the development of the House of Commons. Although the original and major function of Parliament was to give consent to the Crown's request for taxes, the regular practice of having petitions presented in Parliament gradually led to members of Parliament themselves becoming the vehicle for their constituents' petitions to the Crown. The petition, whether written by a paid scribe or another educated person, or by the citizen himself, soon came to serve the local poor as well as the gentry and townspeople. In this way, Maddicott suggested, members of Parliament ultimately became the "collective voice for the needs of their local communities" (p. 61). Thus did the practice of presenting petitions to the

Crown at meetings of Parliament influence the development of the House of Commons.

Public opinion as a political force in the modern world also made its appearance in written form. During the Civil War period in 17th-century England, thousands of pamphlets about civic concerns were published. In this form, writing became a vehicle of expression for large numbers of people. No longer was it the exclusive province of a handful of the educated.

As pamphleteering was a force in the English Civil War, so also did pamphlets and other forms of civic writing play a key role in prerevolutionary America in its developing quarrel with the British colonial government. Voluminous pamphlets as well as circular letters and protests, such as those drafted by Samuel Adams, argued every shade of opinion and were at the core of the communication of political views that preceded the outbreak of revolutionary violence in 1775. *Common Sense*, written in 1776 by Thomas Paine, was perhaps the single most successful pamphlet of the time, and the Declaration of Independence might be thought of as the culmination of political writing during this period.

The framing of the Constitution in 1787 began an especially fruitful period of political writing. The controversy over ratification of the Constitution occasioned an enormous outpouring of political views in a steady stream of pamphlets and other writing, for and against. The publication of *The Federalist* — as newspaper articles (1787-1788) and then as a volume of its own (1788), written by Alexander Hamilton, James Madison, and John Jay — became the most lasting contribution of this immense literature.

In the next century, civic writing in a vast range of forms became a staple of American democracy. Not limited to an educated elite but practiced by ordinary men and women, this writing delved into such public issues as slavery and the rights of women, as well as innumerable other subjects. It appeared as pamphlets, letters, newspaper and magazine articles, petitions, and in many other forms.

In 20th-century America, civic writing mushroomed at an unprecedented rate in the form of letters from citizens to public officials as well as to editors of newspapers and magazines, according to studies of political letter writing (Sussman, 1959). As the level of literacy of the general population rose, so did the number of communications sent by citizens to public officials and editors. The presidency of Franklin D. Roosevelt (1933-1945) in particular witnessed a dramatic increase in constituent writing to both the president and Congress (Sussman, 1963). By 1976, the Associated Press Managing Editors' (APME) Red Book estimated that letters to the editor column were providing an outlet for nearly 2 million letter writers per year; undoubtedly, many more millions were being sent to editors but never published. And according to a newspaper article (Morse, 1985), in 1984 the

House of Representatives alone received 200 million pieces of constituent mail and the Senate another 41.5 million pieces, figures that represented a fivefold increase in just 12 years.

The phenomenal growth of civic writing in 20th-century America suggests that, despite the revolution in communications technology, Americans believe that participatory writing matters. Moreover, it is also clear that this writing is not the province of only highly educated people. A study reported by Buell (1975), comparing a small group of political letter writers (163 writers) with over 2000 other people in a national sample gathered in 1972, found that income and education were not highly significant factors separating writers from nonwriters. Further, although Verba and his associates (1971) did find a high overall correlation between education and citizen participation in their research on democratic modes of participation in five countries, they also found only a small relationship between "parochial" participation or "particularized contacting" and education. People who contact public officials on personal concerns, whether orally or in writing, seem to come from a wide range of the population, from the highly educated to the barely literate.

PURPOSES FOR PARTICIPATORY WRITING

Although people tend to think of civic or public discourse as persuasive discourse, advocacy is only one of the purposes for the writing that people do as part of the process of democratic self-government. It is possible to identify at least four other broad purposes. Each of these five purposes indicates in a different way the nature of the political relationships that citizens have with other citizens and with their government — their elected or appointed public officials at any level of government and in any political capacity.

Writing to Personalize Civic Relationships and/or to Express Civic Identity

Expressions of joy, gratitude, sympathy, hope, and concern are all a natural part of our personal lives. They are also a part of public life and often constitute purposes for participatory writing to public officials. Citizens may thank a public official for help, send a letter of congratulations to a successful candidate for public office, or write a note of condolence to a defeated candidate they supported.

Citizens also personalize civic relationships in letters to private citizens whom they may not know at all. For example, some citizens wrote welcome-home letters to the former American hostages in Iran when they were released in 1981. In contrast, many people wrote notes of sympathy to the families of the astronauts who lost their lives in the explosion of the Challenger. Many people also wrote letters of sympathy to the widows of President John F. Kennedy and his brother Robert Kennedy after their assassinations. These expressions of welcome or sympathy are an affirmation of the bonds of citizenship, motivated by the perception of a civic identity or a sense of shared membership in a civic community—in the case of the examples here, in a national civic community.

Writing to Obtain Information or Help

Citizens frequently write to other people in their capacity as citizens requesting information or help. For example, members of civic or political organizations may send out questionnaires to gather information for a voter's guide or a survey of public opinion on a particular issue. Citizens, individually or as a group, may also communicate to other citizens to request monetary or nonmonetary donations to cope with a natural disaster that has befallen a community or to locate volunteers for an individual medical need, such as a particular type of blood.

However, public officials are probably the most common audience for citizens' requests for information or help. Citizens may write on behalf of many others or request a service for themselves. Although it may not be apparent to the individual letter writer, a request for a particular service to a legislator or an administrator often has broader significance. A pattern of requests often serves to alert legislators or other public officials and their staffs to the need for new legislation or changes in administrative procedures to improve services to a broad group of citizens.

Writing to Provide Public Information or to Offer a Public Service

Citizens who are members of organized groups—ranging from legally mandated citizen committees such as school or library boards to volunteer organizations, such as parent/teacher, neighborhood, taxpayer, or other civic associations—frequently write to provide information to other citizens or to serve their organizations. For example, the League of Women Voters regularly publishes guides to inform voters of issues in forthcoming elections, whereas parent/teacher organizations often produce handbooks describing a community's schools. Members of civic or political organizations also need to write up calendars of planned activities, minutes of meetings, agendas, memos, newsletters, or announcements of meetings. This writing is vital for maintaining the continuity of these volunteer organizations or public institutions and for providing official records of their policies and activities. The content, organization, and formality of this writing depend on the specific purpose of the board or organization and the needs and skills of its members.

Writing to Evaluate a Public Service, Political Structure, or Public Official

Citizens often write evaluations of public programs, services, or personnel. Sometimes these evaluations are formal. Members of school boards, library boards, health boards, and many other citizen boards are regularly required to assess the performance of the professional person they have appointed to administer the public institution for which they, as citizens, are responsible. Citizens are also often appointed or elected to evaluate a public service (e.g., public safety or crime control) or a political structure (e.g., the organization of state or local government) in order to help legislators or administrators decide what changes if any should be made to improve public services. Evaluations usually contain recommendations for general policies or specific actions as well as information. Those appointed to gather information about the functioning of a service or an individual-or to determine the need for a service that does not yet exist—are expected to proceed impartially and to gather all potentially relevant information before formulating their recommendations. Evaluations of public services, laws, professional persons, or public officials are intended to ensure that the intention of voters is adhered to, that public funds are being spent efficiently, and that the common good is being promoted.

Informal evaluations of a public service, political structure, or public official probably take place much more frequently than formal ones. Citizens informally evaluate public services or officials by writing, as individuals or as groups, to praise or criticize them. Citizens may send their writing directly to officials or public bodies, or they may inform officials and the public of their judgments indirectly through letters to newspapers or other publications. Often writers pleased with or critical of a service will send their letters to the appropriate official and to the editor of a local newspaper to generate wide public awareness of the effectiveness of the responsible official or the seriousness of the perceived problem. Patterns of unorchestrated praise or complaints can call the attention of officials—or the public at large—to excellent performance or deficiencies in public services.

Writing to Advocate Positions on Public Issues, Organizations, or Individuals

Advocacy writing is indispensable for protecting political rights in a democracy and for promoting the common good. There are many specific purposes for advocacy writing, but they can be clustered around five distinct kinds of political activities. The first is soliciting support for a civic or political organization. As de Tocqueville noted in the 1830s, Americans frequently form voluntary associations. These associations, which help constitute civil society, often serve as "mediating structures" between individual citizens and the wider society, and assist in knowledgeable participation in social, economic, and political life. The interests of many citizens are often advanced more effectively by an organized group than by solitary efforts.

A second set of purposes for advocacy writing is embedded in efforts to support or oppose public officials or candidates for office. The bulk of the writing done for this purpose takes place at the local level. Large numbers of citizens annually write letters, postcards, and publicity releases, or design posters and advertisements that urge others to support candidates for the thousands of local public offices for which Americans vote annually. At the national and state levels, most advocacy writing of this sort is now composed by paid professional staff. Citizens may also write to other citizens directly, to the media, or to other public officials to support or criticize a public official in a controversy. And they may also seek removal of a public official by bringing their complaints in writing to higher officials or by bringing their complaints directly to the voters through a recall petition in the 31 states that allow recall in some form.

The ability of citizens to make or influence the making of law, directly or indirectly, lies at the heart of the democratic form of government. Their ability to do so indirectly is most often reflected in personal contacts, telephone calls, and written communications that try to influence others on matters of public policy. These written communications demonstrate a third cluster of purposes for advocacy writing. Citizens may write to other citizens, to the media, or to legislators or other public officials to support, modify, or oppose a proposed or existing law or administrative policy or to support or oppose policy positions of public officials. They may also compose public policy petitions and place them on the ballot in certain elections to register voter opinion.

A fourth set of purposes for advocacy writing is embedded in citizen efforts to create or remove laws directly, in states where it is legal to do so. In this country, citizens may create law directly through the initiative process at the state or local level. Drawing on traditions of democratic literacy, South Dakota in 1898 became the first state to allow private citizens to propose laws to be submitted for popular approval. As of 1984, citizens in 21 states are allowed to place proposed laws on a state ballot by means of an initiative petition. As the counterpart to initiative petitions for creating laws, citizens may also directly remove laws through referendum petitions. As of 1984, citizens in 24 states could directly seek recall of an existing state law through a referendum.

Although many of the laws citizens propose directly have substantive content, they may also propose laws about public issues with purely symbolic value, such as resolutions, but that can strongly influence public opinion. In addition, citizens can propose laws indirectly through their representatives at any level of government.

The writing that citizens do to obtain new political structures or procedural rules constitutes a fifth kind of political activity. Indeed, the most fundamental purpose for which citizens in a republican form of government may write is to devise or modify the very structures and procedures that shape their participation in the governance of their society. The text they propose for their political community, which may be a voluntary organization or a political unit, is often called a constitution or a charter. The opportunity to create a constitution or to revise or amend one arises occasionally not only in civic or political organizations but also at the local or county level. Since the turn of the century, 23 states have amended their state constitutions to permit citizens to propose state constitutional amendments. Although citizens cannot directly propose amendments to the Constitution of the United States, an enormous amount of civic writing underlies any proposal for amendment; consider, for example, the writing for and against the Equal Rights Amendment. This writing can occur in pamphlets, articles, broadsides, petitions, and books, as well as in other forms.

As suggested by these five general purposes for civic writing, it cannot be distinguished by any specific set of language conventions or even literary forms. It can be formal or informal, and it addresses a broad range of audiences, from public officials to other citizens. As writing, it can be distinguished only by its purposes and the context for its use. However, these purposes are often expressed in far more complex and subtle ways than these categories suggest. These different purposes for civic writing frequently overlap in one piece of writing and play themselves out in very subtle ways, depending on how many audiences writers perceive for their writing and the attitudes of all these readers toward the writers' position. To better understand the complex relationship between purpose and audience in civic writing and the rhetorical skills that civic participation may require in a specific context, I looked at a series of letters composed for a particular civic undertaking. They were sent by a group of parents to various public officials in their community as part of an ultimately successful effort to secure an appropriation of money for repairing and upgrading their children's school. These letters also demonstrate concretely the ways in which literacy can empower citizens, that is, how the ability to write facilitates participation in the civic process.

CIVIC WRITING FOR A COMMUNITY PROJECT

This particular community project was selected for several reasons. First, the course of events was not complex, and the span of time involved was relatively brief (less than half a year); thus, a full description of the context for the letters as well as an analysis of all of them could be presented within the pages of an article-length chapter. Second, the letters by themselves tell a complete, self-evident story, one with a beginning and an end, allowing readers to see the evolution of the parents' rhetoric in their written discourse. Third, the chief participant in the project was still available to provide detailed information about the events that occurred, and she was willing to read through my report to assure accuracy. Finally, whereas this particular project might not be of special interest to anyone outside this community, it is precisely the kind of project that is apt to engage the attention and energies of ordinary citizens in their communities, thus suggesting the kind of rhetorical strategies and writing skills that normal civic participation requires. Although this project took place in the 1960s, it is no different from many others that have taken place in many towns and cities over the years. In fact, a new school intended to replace the old school did not get built until 1993; the issues surrounding the repair of the old school had not basically changed in the intervening decades.

Background

This small-scale undertaking took place in a large New England town in the mid-1960s. The school in question was a small 74-year-old brick structure serving about 120 primary grade children. It was situated in a neighborhood containing a mix of middle- and low-income parents. Most of the children who graduated from this school did not do as well in the town's high school as graduates of the other elementary schools, and fewer of its graduates went on to college than did graduates from the other elementary schools in town. In the early 1960s, the town had decided to build a new school plant for the school as part of a long-range capital expenditures program to upgrade all the town's schools. Because the school building was slated for demolition, little money was being invested by the school committee in its maintenance. Moreover, because the playground equipment had been continuously vandalized over the years, the town's Park and Recreation Departments, which were responsible for the care of the school grounds, were making no further repairs. As a result, both the interior and exterior of the school, as well as its play facilities, were in poor condition. However, a new school plant would not be built for at least another 7 to 10 years, and a recent increase in enrollment had meant that the school would have to continue being used until the new building was constructed.

Sizing up the situation, a group of 30 parents, led by the president-elect of their Parent Teacher Council (PTC), decided that the many children who would be attending the school for the foreseeable future deserved a respectable-looking school and decent play facilities. They also felt that, with parental cooperation, vandalism could be reduced if the school and its playground looked like facilities that were valued by the town. After many discussions and meetings, private and public, formal and informal, the Executive Board of the PTC made a decision at a meeting in April 1965 to make a formal request of the superintendent of schools (and, by extension, the school committee) for a program to improve both the inside and outside of the school. The parents felt that many of the town's residents would support their efforts because the school had traditionally served some of the least articulate parents in town, and it was in far worse shape than all of the other schools in town. They also felt they had the support of the superintendent of schools and believed that they had the sympathy of most members of the school committee. On the other hand, they perceived the Board of Selectmen as neutral, the chief of police as not too enthusiastic, and the Park and Recreation Commission as definitely not sympathetic to their efforts.

The Letters

Most of these letters were sent by the parent who served first as the president-elect and then as the president of the PTC. Her formal schooling consisted of a high school education plus a degree from a 2-year community college. Although she composed the first drafts of most of these letters, they also reflect the views and editing efforts of other parents at her school. To protect all identities, I changed the names of all those identified in these letters. Under the cc:s, I listed only the person's position. All the original letters are in the official files of the appropriate town departments.

On May 14, the president-elect of the PTC sent a letter (Fig. 10.1) to the superintendent of schools for consideration at a meeting of the school committee on May 17. The letter, which culminated a number of drafts before its final text was approved, was also read aloud at this meeting. It served two explicit purposes: it formally initiated a process for achieving a civic objective by informing the appropriate authority of a community concern, and it outlined in some detail how the problem might be addressed. After opening with a clear statement of the parents' general objectives, it briefly described the problem and some relevant background to the problem in order to convince the school committee of the rightness of the parents' cause. To address the problem, an outline set forth the parents'

Dear Dr. Sanchez:

On behalf of the Harry Truman Parent Teacher Council, we are writing to formally request a program to improve the inside and outside of the Harry Truman School.

The Parent Teacher Council believes that the appearance and atmosphere of the physical plant is directly involved in the education of the child. Due to vandalism and community neglect, the Harry Truman School is now a dirty, depressing, deteriorating building, with unsafe grounds because of broken glass, and a totally inadequate outdoor area for the children.

We recognize that Town Agencies have attempted to make some improvements over the years, but the whole situation is so complex that the impact has been minimal. We are also aware that a new school plant is planned but we realize that it will be at least 7-10 years before this is accomplished.

We recommend the following immediate improvements and renovations.

I. Outside
    A. Building
        1. complete cleaning and repairing
        2. exterior painting (white paint should be considered)
        3. constant and continuing maintenance
    B. Grounds
        1. immediate removal of all glass
        2. complete redesigning, reseeding and resurfacing of entire exterior grounds with substantial new shrubbery
    C. Play Area
        1. new creative play equipment
        2. outdoor afternoon recreation program with professional, supervised instruction
II. Inside

The Executive Board of our Parent Teacher Council met recently to discuss the Harry Truman School Building. In this meeting, Mr. O'Brien outlined some ideas relating to the present use and future needs of this structure if early relief is not considered for the Harry Truman School with present membership trends. He will, we understand, present these in the Annual Budget. We look forward to the time when it will be possible to discuss his recommendations with you.

III. Maintenance
    A. Refencing of entire area
    B. Floodlighting of school grounds from dusk to dawn
    C. Adequate police protection

We realize that the Park and Recreation Department is involved with these problems and we are already in communication with Mr. Souza of the Park Department and intend to contact Mr. Piatelli in the Recreation Department immediately.

FIG. 10.1. (*Continued*)

Our commitment to the education of our children, and the seriousness with which we take our own responsibility as citizens of the Town of Danford, lead us to believe that concerted action, on the part of the entire community, both official and neighborhood, will eventually result in a new look and a new spirit for the Harry Truman District.

We thank you for your consideration of these matters and hope to have an opportunity to discuss them with you.

cc: School Committee Chairperson
School Principal (Mr. O'Brien)

FIG. 10.1.   Letter of May 14 to the superintendent of schools.

suggestions for improving the outside of the school, its grounds and play area, and for maintaining the grounds around the school. The text also noted the other town officials who had been contacted or were being contacted (the superintendent of the Park Department and the superintendent of the Recreation Department) so that the school committee would know officially about the parents' efforts to involve other relevant town departments. As the *cc*: indicated, the school's principal and the chairperson of the school committee were sent copies; these were some of the key people whose support or cooperation would be necessary for the parents to achieve their objectives.

During the next two weeks, the PTC met first with a subordinate official in the Recreation Department to discuss recreational facilities at the school. It then met twice with a subcommittee on school buildings of the school committee to discuss the PTC's proposal. On June 14, the president of the PTC sent a letter (Fig. 10.2) to the Park and Recreation Commission (the citizen board overseeing the Park and Recreation Departments) to offer the support of the PTC for a program improving the grounds and facilities at the school and to indicate the interest of the PTC in meeting with them to

Gentlemen:

On behalf of the Harry Truman Parent Teachers Council, we are writing to indicate our interest in meeting with you to discuss facilities and programs at the Harry Truman School. We are aware that there are many factors involved.

The Parent Teachers Council stands ready to work with the Park and Recreation Department and the Commissioners to support a program of upgrading and maintaining facilities in this area.

We look forward to meeting with you to discuss these matters.

cc: School Principal
Chairperson of PTC Subcommittee

FIG. 10.2.   Letter of June 14 to Park and Recreation Commission.

discuss these matters. Although this letter might appear to be just a request for a meeting, together with a statement of support and cooperation, it represented advocacy by other means because the Park and Recreation Commission had not agreed to any program for improving the grounds and facilities at the schools and was not in favor of one.

This letter served yet another use: It put the PTC on record as wanting to talk and cooperate with the Park and Recreation Commission, thus allowing any delay in talks between the two groups to be interpreted as foot-dragging or opposition by the commission to the PTC's proposal and recommendations. As the *cc*: indicated, copies of this letter were sent to the school's principal and a parent who chaired a PTC subcommittee on the school building and grounds. The purpose for sending copies of this letter and later correspondence to them was, as is overtly intended, to keep interested parties informed and to let the addressee know who all those being informed were.

In anticipation of another school committee meeting on June 21 that would hear and vote on the recommendations of its own subcommittee on school buildings, the PTC's subcommittee prepared a notice to all residents of the neighborhood urging them to attend the meeting. The notice was also addressed to parents (Fig. 10.3) and distributed to them at the same time, as the PTC was aware that two different although overlapping audiences needed to be reached to encourage attendance by the broadest spectrum of

ATTENTION: ALL PARENTS

As a result of activity by the Harry Truman Parent Teacher Council, a program for the improvement of the interior and exterior of the school is being considered by the Danford School Committee tonight.

The subcommittee on buildings of the School Committee, with Dr. Sanchez, Mr. O'Brien, and representatives of the Parent Teacher Council recently visited the school. The recommendation of the subcommittee will be reported to the School Committee tonight.

It is of the greatest importance that the Harry Truman parents attend the School Committee meeting tonight, June 21.

DATE: Monday evening, June 21, 1965

TIME: 8: 00 P.M.

PLACE: Town Hall, second floor

PLEASE TRY TO ATTEND!

FIG. 10.3.   Notice to the neighborhood and parents.

support possible. At this meeting, the school committee voted to authorize $17,000 to repair and improve the school building even though the town meeting had already approved and passed the school's annual budget 3 months earlier. This favorable vote would not have occurred, the president of the PTC believed, if the parents had not been well organized, knowledgeable, and united in support of a clear and specific set of objectives.

On June 25, the president of the PTC sent a letter to the Park and Recreation Commission that included a proposal listing what the parents believed should be done to improve the grounds around the school (Fig. 10.4). Like the letter in Fig. 10.1, it was a clear request for what they wanted. It also attempted to bring political pressure on the commissioners by mentioning what the school committee had just agreed to do and politely pointing out that quick action by the commission was needed on this proposal, preferably before school began again in the fall. Copies of this letter, as indicated by the cc:, were sent to the school's principal, the superintendent of schools, the superintendents of parks, the superintendent of recreation, and the parent who chaired the PTC's subcommittee.

At a special meeting on June 28, the school committee voted to request bids for sandblasting the exterior of the school — the parents' major priority. On June 30, the president of the PTC received a letter from the superintendent of parks to appear at the next meeting of the Park and Recreation Commission, to be held on July 12, to discuss her letter of June 25.

On July 7, the president of the PTC sent a letter (Fig. 10.5) to the chief of police. Its overt purpose was to request a meeting to discuss cooperation between parents and other citizens and the police department in maintaining security and preventing vandalism at the school and in the playground area. Copies of this letter were sent to the Board of Selectmen, the school's principal, the school committee, the Park and Recreation Commission, and the PTC subcommittee chairperson. A cover letter to the selectmen (Fig. 10.6) accompanied the copy of the letter sent to them.

Although the letter appeared to be chiefly a request for a meeting, its content served additional purposes. By letting the chief of police know about the support the parents had already received from the school committee, it indirectly sought to constrain the chief to cooperate with their request. And by listing the Board of Selectmen as well as others in the cc:s, the parents intentionally or unintentionally strengthened pressure on the chief. If he did not cooperate fully with the parents, he might receive inquiries from his superiors, the Board of Selectmen. On the other hand, the copy of the letter to the Park and Recreation Commissioners let them see that the parents were making connections with two new sources of help — the Board of Selectmen and the chief of police. Whereas they might not be pleased by the letter to the chief of police, the School Committee would.

Dear Sirs:

On behalf of the Harry Truman Parent Teacher Council we are writing to present a proposal for the improvement of the grounds of the Harry Truman School.

The Parent Teacher Council has been concerned about the educational facilities and appearance of the Harry Truman School. An unattractive and deteriorating building and grounds is damaging to both the students and to the surrounding neighborhood. We are fully aware of the many complexities of this situation and of past efforts to improve it. Presently, we see making a concerted effort to upgrade the school and its grounds.

As you may know, the School Committee has approved substantial renovation, both interior and exterior, which will be completed by September. It seems clear to us that the next step is a companion program by the Park and Recreation Department. We would hope that this would be completed, also, by the beginning of school.

We enclose a proposal for your consideration and feel it urgent that we discuss this with you as soon as possible.

cc: School Principal
    Chairperson of the PTC Subcommittee
    Superintendent of Recreation
    Superintendent of Schools
    Superintendent of Parks

PROPOSAL FOR THE IMPROVEMENT OF THE HARRY TRUMAN
SCHOOL GROUNDS

    I. FRONT
        A. attractive and complete grassing
        B. fill in bare foundation with bushes

    II. SIDES
        A. Hanover Street
            1. attractive and complete grassing
            2. complete foundation planting
            3. strip on far side of driveway--groundcover
        B. Town Barn Wall
            1. tear up blacktop from wall to corner of school
            2. plant grass

    III. BACK
        A. Playground at rear, on grass, for Grade 2 and under
            1. complete, creative play equipment
            2. professional personnel and creative program
            3. redwood bench around tree
        B. Resurface blacktop
        C. Complete new chain link fence at back--cedar in play area

    IV. Building--Window Boxes

    V. Maintenance
        A. continuing, scheduled care
        B. Park Police Protection

FIG. 10.4.   Letter of June 25 to the Park and Recreation Commission.

Dear Sir:

On behalf of the Harry Truman Parent Teachers Council, we are writing to inform you of a recently inaugurated program to renovate and upgrade the facilities at the Harry Truman School and to support general improvements for the entire neighborhood. We have received strong support from the Danford School Committee and are meeting with the Park and Recreation Commissioners on Monday July 12th to discuss further improvements.

We feel strongly that in addition to the physical upgrading of the area, there is a need for a conscientious effort on the part of the citizens and the police to work together. Therefore we would appreciate an appointment to speak with you regarding these matters.

cc: Board of Selectmen
     School Principal
     Chairperson of PTC Subcommittee
     Park and Recreation Commission
     School Committee

FIG. 10.5.   Letter of July 7 to the Chief of Police.

Gentlemen:

Enclosed is a letter which we have written to Roman Slezakowski, Chief of Police, on behalf of the Harry Truman Teachers Council.

We intend to keep you informed about our activities and hope that we will have an opportunity to discuss them with you.

cc: School Principal
     Chairperson of the PTC Subcommittee

FIG. 10.6.   Letter of July 7 to the Board of Selectmen.

A copy of the letter was sent to the selectmen for another reason — to inform them officially about the project at this time. Because all budgetary matters normally have to be decided on at the annual town meeting held in the spring, the selectmen would have to be involved if the Park and Recreation Commission approved the appropriation of funds for this project; any appropriation of funds during the summer or fall would have to come from the selectmen's contingency fund. (At this time in Massachusetts, a school committee's budget was autonomous; a school committee could vote at any time to expend funds under its control.) Thus, the letter to the chief of police served as an occasion to alert the Board of Selectmen officially to the parents' activities and to their interest in talking with them in the future.

At the July 12 meeting of the Park and Recreation Commission, the commissioners voted to support improvements at the school. They requested the superintendent of parks to have plans drawn by the town's engineering department and to obtain cost estimates for the work. Their next step would be to ask the selectmen for contingency funds, as the Park and Recreation Commission did not have an appropriation for equipment and materials for this particular school. Immediately following this July 12 meeting, the president of the PTC sent a letter of understanding to the Park and Recreation Commission, thanking them for the opportunity to discuss their problem, confirming what the commissioners had voted on, and urging immediate action because the funds to be requested from the selectmen for this part of the project were contingency funds (see Fig. 10.7). The letter closed with the request that a copy of the plans being prepared by the engineering department be sent to the PTC.

This letter was astute in many respects. Although it was a letter of thanks, together with a request for some information, it served two additional purposes. First, it summarized the results of the meeting (which the minutes of the meeting would confirm) in a form that could be immediately distributed to key people who the parents believed should be informed of the Park and Recreation Commission's vote. Copies of this letter, as indicated by the *cc:*, went to the school principal, the Board of Selectmen, the superintendent of schools, and the PTC's subcommittee chairperson. Second, it placed pressure on the Park and Recreation Commissioners to

Gentlemen:

On behalf of the Harry Truman Parent Teacher Council, we would like to thank you for the opportunity to discuss the school grounds at the meeting of July 12th.

It is our understanding that the Commissioners voted the following: that the Superintendent of Parks, Mr. Manuel Souza, propose plans and obtain cost estimates from the Engineering Department for the improvement of the school grounds; that Mr. Bruno Piatelli confer with the School Committee regarding recreational needs for the school; and that these figures and proposals be sent immediately to the Board of Selectmen with a request by the Park and Recreation Commissioners for funds.

We feel that the emergency nature of the situation and the fact that we are requesting contingency funds highlights the need for immediate action on the part of your agency.

In order to cooperate with you as fully as possible, we would appreciate a copy of the proposal being prepared by the Engineering Department.

cc: School Principal
     Chairperson of the PTC Subcommittee
     Board of Selectmen
     School Superintendent

FIG. 10.7.   Letter of July 12 to the Park and Recreation Commission.

make sure that their departments implemented their vote as soon as possible. Until the parents received a copy of the engineering department's plans, there would be no evidence that the commissioners were following up on their vote.

On July 16, the Executive Council of the PTC met with the chief of police to offer its cooperation. On July 18, the president of the PTC sent a letter (Fig. 10.8) to the selectmen requesting a meeting to discuss the use of contingency funds for their project. This letter was a straightforward statement of concern, as well as a request for help. It expressed the parents' feeling that the Park and Recreation Commission was not moving as fast as

Gentlemen:

You probably are aware that the Harry Truman Parent Teachers Council has been conducting a campaign to rehabilitate the school. The necessity of this activity is painfully obvious to anyone who lives in the area or is concerned with having all areas of Danford conform to minimum standards of appearance.

We have met with the School Committee and were greatly encouraged by their immediate understanding of both the physical and educational problems, and with their prompt guarantee of remedial action. We have met with the Police Department and we feel that their cooperation and understanding will help with the success of our activity. Our meeting with the Parks and Recreation Commission was not as conclusive as we would have liked. We feel that the sense of urgency that this work be done at once was lost.

We do realize that the uncertainty of abandonment has caused a neglect of grounds and creates a problem in quickly changing the appearance of the area surrounding the school. It is precisely for this reason that immediate, effective action should be taken to reverse this condition. The Park and Recreation Commission has informed us that in order to do the proposed work they will need emergency funds from the Board of Selectmen. The commissioners have requested that plans and estimates be obtained from the Engineering Department.

The Parent Teacher Council would appreciate an opportunity to meet with the Board of Selectmen. A great many parents have expressed a desire to participate in this meeting. We would therefore respectfully request that we be able to appear on your agenda in the evening.

Time is a very critical factor in this undertaking. Further delay can negate the progress we have already made and be a dreadful set-back to the entire community.

We hope for an immediate reply.

cc: School Principal
    Chairperson of the Park and Recreation Commission
    Chairperson of the PTC Subcommittee
    Superintendent of Schools

FIG. 10.8.   Letter of July 18 to the Board of Selectmen.

Gentlemen:

On behalf of the Harry Truman Parent Teacher Council, enclosed is a copy of a letter and proposal which was sent to the Park and Recreation Commission on June 25th. We assume that by now the estimates are being obtained so that your board may consider this matter.

We thank you for your cooperation and interest.

FIG. 10.9.   Letter of July 23 to the Board of Selectmen.

it should be; the parents had learned that the commissioners had not yet made a move to request the use of contingency funds. Copies of this letter were sent to the school principal, the chairperson of the Park and Recreation Commission, the superintendent of schools, and the PTC's subcommittee chairperson. The Park and Recreation Commissioners could easily see the letter as a clear attempt to move them to action.

On July 23, the president of the PTC sent a very short letter (Fig. 10.9) to the Board of Selectmen simply mentioning the PTC's assumption that cost estimates for the work to be done by the Park and Recreation Commission were being obtained for their consideration. Enclosed with this letter was a copy of the June 25 letter and proposal to the Park and Recreation Commission. Although informational on the surface, the implicit message of this letter to the selectmen was that if the estimates had not been obtained by now, they should be looking into the matter.

On July 27, the president of the PTC spoke with the superintendent of parks and found no progress. As a result, on July 28, she sent a letter to the Park and Recreation Commission indicating that the parents on the PTC would attend their August 9 meeting to hear what progress had been made since the July 12 meeting (Fig. 10.10). A seemingly informational letter again served as a means to stimulate action without explicitly urging it. As one might expect, copies of this letter were sent to the selectmen, the

Gentlemen:

The parents of the Harry Truman Parent Teacher Council would like you to know that we plan to attend the August 9th meeting of your Board. At that time, we will be interested in hearing the progress of our meeting with you of July 12th, at which time our proposal was discussed.

We thank you for your interest and cooperation.

cc: Chairperson of the PTC Subcommittee
    Board of Selectmen
    Superintendent of Schools

FIG. 10.10.   Letter of July 28 to the Park and Recreation Commission.

superintendent of schools, and the PTC's subcommittee chairperson, letting the Park and Recreation Commission know that the other parties also knew that the parents were going to the meeting to accelerate action by the commissioners.

A successful conclusion to the parents' initiatives was reached within the next month. On August 9, the Park and Recreation Commission voted to request $10,000 in contingency funds from the Board of Selectmen to blacktop grounds and to install a chain-link fence at the school. Because the letter requesting the funds had (inexplicably) not yet arrived at the selectmen's office by the end of August, representatives of the PTC appeared before them on September 1 to support the request for the $10,000. On September 5, they appeared before the Advisory Committee, whose function is to advise the town meeting on all budgetary matters, to seek support for the appropriation there. The official letter of request from the Park and Recreation Commission finally arrived, and the appropriation was authorized. To provide a fitting sense of closure, in October the president of the PTC sent a letter to the local newspaper publicly thanking all town officials for helping the PTC obtain approval and funding for the renovations and repairs the schools needed (Fig. 10.11). This final letter was particularly skillful as it gave all the public officials credit for the parents' achievement and stressed how the whole community had gained from the undertaking.

About a year later, an article appeared in the local newspaper noting that since the "beautification" project had been completed, there had been no acts of vandalism at the school. However, not all of the recommendations in the original proposal were followed up on in the course of time. Over the next 2 years, work to upgrade the playground area of the school continued (as well as work on its companion upper grade elementary school). In October 1967, a letter was sent to the superintendent of parks by new

To the Editor:

The Parent Teacher Council of the Harry Truman School would like to take this opportunity to thank the many town officials--elected, appointed and departmental--who have been instrumental in providing a "new look" for the Truman School. Although the work is not fully completed, it is obvious that the school will be a credit to the Danford Schools and the Park and Recreation Commission, as well as an asset to the physical appearance of the community.

We realize that the Truman School presented a difficult problem in that it had been scheduled for demolition. The patience and understanding of the officials and personnel of the Town, who helped bring about this significant change, is to be commended. Our organization is deeply grateful to them, and eagerly awaiting the completion of the work.

FIG. 10.11.   Letter of October 10 to the local newspaper.

co-presidents of the PTC, one of whom had chaired the PTC's subcommittee 2 years earlier (Fig. 10.12). This letter asked why a request for funds to complete the work laid out in the original proposal for the school had not appeared on a recent agenda for a school committee meeting. This letter, like the letter in Fig. 10.1, was an evaluation of the situation and a proposal for action. Copies of this letter were sent to the superintendent of schools, the new principal of the school, the superintendent of recreation, and the Park and Recreation Commission. As is often the case, the civic process may not always quite end for some projects.

Commentary

What can we learn from the writing in this minicase study? To begin with, we gain some insight into the uses and usefulness of literacy in the process of democratic self-government. Although some of the writing in this civic undertaking might be seen as more facilitative than crucial to the parents' efforts (for example, the notice to parents urging them to show up at a forthcoming school committee meeting—a piece of writing which could be replaced by word of mouth), other pieces clearly led to decisions and actions by others that would not otherwise have taken place. The school committee's discussion and decision would not have occurred without the parents'

Dear Mr. Souza:

We see no mention in the School Committee docket for Monday October 16th of any request for funds to complete the work promised for the Truman playground. I understand that Truman still lacks swings; and that the proposed development of the Lewis School playground which was shown to us in the Spring of 1966 remains to be implemented.

Is it the joint intention of the Park and Recreation and School Committees to abandon these projects without completing them?

We think that it would be highly desirable to show the plan (which I trust is still on file with you) for developing the Lewis School playground to the Truman PTC, so that we may refresh our memories and perhaps have an opportunity to discuss with you the completion of this work.

We would hope that this proposal and the budget request will be approved by the Park and Recreation Commission in time for this year's Town Meeting.

cc: Superintendent of Schools
    Superintendent of Recreation
    School Principal
    Park and Recreation Commission

FIG. 10.12.   Letter 2 years later to the Superintendent of Parks.

request in writing; similarly with respect to the discussion and decision by the Park and Recreation Commission. I do not think that these pieces of writing can be dismissed as mere legal formalities. They seem to have both symbolic and substantive significance. Symbolically, they reflect the parents' knowledge that there are laws governing the use of their local tax money and accepted procedures for addressing these laws. They also reflect the parents' knowledge that their public officials are required to be responsive to them (whether or not they ultimately voted in the parents' favor). Substantively, these pieces of writing were significant because they set forth the parents' claims in detail with a clear and sensible rationale, suggesting how much thinking and work had gone into the request. Without explicit, reasonable, and justifiable objectives available for all to see and understand, it is unlikely that their efforts would have been successful, at least in this community, no matter what else they did.

However, as anyone with political experience knows, the writings would not have been the only mode of discourse in this undertaking nor the only means of influence. It is more than likely that many, many hours of telephone calls and personal contacts took place in addition to these letters. These writings do not and cannot (because some things cannot be said in public writing) reveal all the dynamics underlying their use or their results (and it is unlikely that even ethnographic research at the time could have uncovered all the interpersonal, intergroup, and interinstitutional relationships influencing the course of events), although the cc:s serve as strong clues to these underlying relationships. One might therefore wonder to what extent the writing really mattered in this undertaking. I can only suggest that it must have mattered a great deal because the parents believed it did. Most people do not engage in painstaking, time-consuming tasks that they think are futile or a waste of time. Moreover, a letter to a public official cannot be officially ignored or as easily forgotten as a conversation, for which there is normally no corroborative witness. It must be acknowledged and responded to. And, like physical action, it attests to a seriousness of purpose that oral discourse alone does not.

The letters also served important recordkeeping purposes. Even if the parents' writings had not served to initiate a process for political decision making (which they clearly did), or to accelerate the course of events (which they very likely did, given the length of time it usually takes to accomplish any civic undertaking involving multiple public officials and bodies), their writings did serve to document their problem, their precise demands, and the sequence of significant contacts and activities. Most parents or interested citizens could not be expected to attend all the public meetings that dealt with the parents' proposal. The letters were indispensable as a public record of the parents' problems, their objectives, and the process they followed to reach their goals.

Second, one might hazard the judgment that the tone of the letters served a positive function in this community dialogue. The writers took great pains to establish a tone they judged would be beneficial to their cause. The letters were always courteous and pleasant; they contained no personal attacks, threats, or belittling or sarcastic comments about any individual or event. The theme of cooperation was always stressed even when the parents were concerned, implicitly or explicitly, about the lack of cooperation from their public officials. Much of this stress on cooperation reflected an effort to imply that all parties had a common interest in the school and that this was their common ground, a feature of classical rhetoric, as Ede (1991) pointed out, that is not present as frequently as it might be in public discourse today. Moreover, the parents always acknowledged the complexity of the problem and the previous efforts of others to address the situation constructively, strategies that might mitigate defensiveness in others and prevent dwelling on the past.

Finally, the 12 communications suggest that an understanding of context is required for a full understanding of purposes. All the writers' explicit purposes were intertwined with other, implicit ones that were a function of the many different readers for most letters and their differing attitudes towards the writers' position. Each of the many readers that most letters had could detect several different messages simultaneously, each message dependent on who the other recipients of the letter were. Each reader could also be expected to respond somewhat differently to the same text and then to the other readers. These multiple audiences, multiple responses, and multiples purposes were achieved by means of the cc:.

The cc:s symbolized the formal network of communication that the parents established among all those who were involved in the course of events. But the parents were astute as well as open in informing all relevant parties of their plans, goals, and movements. They were able to use the cc:s as a way to send different implicit messages to both the addressees and those listed under the cc:. The overall purpose of the strategy was to move an indifferent, unenthusiastic, or resisting party—the chief of police or the Park and Recreation Commissioners—toward the parents' goals.

Sometimes the addressee was the intended recipient of an implicit message, and the listing of names under the cc: was used as the way to create the message. One example is the letter of understanding to the Park and Recreation Commission. The Park and Recreation Commission might well be thanked for its vote, but it did not need to be reminded in detail of what it had just voted on the night before. By indicating that copies of the letter were being sent to the selectmen and the superintendent of schools, the cc: in effect, told the commissioners that they were being publicly held to their promises and that action was expected in a reasonable amount of time; this implicit message was the chief purpose of this letter. A second example was the letter sent to the Park and Recreation Commission before the parents' final meeting with them, with copies sent to the selectmen and the superintendent of schools. This cc:, in effect, told the commission that the parents expected a decision that night, and if none were forthcoming, other key people would know that the commission was dragging its feet.

Sometimes one of the names in the list of names in the cc: was the intended recipient of the implicit message. The July 18 letter to the Board of Selectmen is an example of this; the intent was to spur not the selectmen but the Park and Recreation Commission to action. The parents hoped that the commissioners' knowledge of the information contained in the letter to the selectmen would move them to action more swiftly than they otherwise might. Whoever the intended recipient of the implicit message might be in a particular letter, the cc:s served as the signal of the complex relationship between these writers' purposes and their audiences as well as the means for achieving their implicit purposes.

CONCLUSIONS AND IMPLICATIONS FOR THEORY, RESEARCH, AND PEDAGOGY

The minicase study presented in this chapter is only the tip of a vast civic iceberg. There is, literally, a world of participatory writing composed by ordinary citizens awaiting close examination. Clearly, we need to revisit and revise current theories about the uses for literacy. Although, historically, literacy seems to have served many negative purposes and in some respects may continue to do so today, in this country and elsewhere, we need to reassess the validity of theories that have viewed the growth of literacy and literacy instruction as chiefly negative developments in human history and have thus failed to predict its positive, indeed liberatory, role in the lives of ordinary citizens, historically and today. Although educators like Freire and Giroux who write from a Marxist perspective have frequently suggested that literacy may have liberatory effects, never, to my knowledge, have they critiqued these theories or offered a scholarly analysis of any examples, historical or contemporary, to explain what they see as liberatory writing. Indeed, the chief examples one can find in countries with Marxist governments have usually been illegal.

It is ironic that theories centering on notions of power and the ways in which the powerful have used literacy to maintain power have been framed in ways that seem to have excluded an examination of the ways literacy has been used by the average citizen to influence and even restrict the powerful, in some cases simply to ensure that power is shared. As a result, such theories may have served to inhibit the formulation of alternative, more inclusive theories, and, therefore, to inhibit research on the empowering uses of literacy. They may also have served to prevent literacy teachers from discovering that meaningful civic participation can be one result of literacy instruction, even if it may not be its explicit goal (although some might recall that it was the chief rationale for literacy instruction in Thomas Jefferson's thinking and it has always been the chief rationale for public schools in civic republican thinking). This theoretical exclusion or inhibition of other perspectives on the values of literacy may not be the only reason why there has been so little research on the ways in which literacy, especially writing, has served to promote the interests of ordinary citizens and the general welfare of their communities as a whole. Nonetheless, it is undoubtedly a strong reason, and we need to break its hold on our thinking and undertake an examination of other parts of this vast civic iceberg.

A great deal of civic writing is in this country because, despite our limitations and failings, we have been the most participatory of all the democracies in the modern world. But there is much to examine in other countries, especially where people are now striving to establish greater representative democracies for themselves. One has only to think about *samizdat,* or the phenomenon of illegal or underground writing, to recognize the exciting cross-cultural possibilities that await the interested researcher. We know so little about the different ways in which ordinary people use reading and writing today to promote their interests in this and other democratic societies. We know even less about how they do so and have done so in nondemocratic countries. Does a nation's form of government and its political institutions influence both the kind of writing that is taught and the pedagogical practices related to writing instruction?

Reflections by those who participated in the recent 3-year collaboration between American and Polish educators (see Stotsky, in press) to build civic education programs in Poland that will support democracy suggest that this is indeed the case. The development of curriculum guides for civic education, a primary school civics course, a course for preservice teachers, and a network of five centers for civic and economic education to provide inservice training was based on the realization by Polish educational reformers that the ideology and practices of their former government had had an extremely negative influence on their educational institutions and all pedagogical practices, almost totally inhibiting the development of democratic participatory citizenship. Eastern Europe today, among other areas of the world, is a prime area for exploration of the relationship between literacy and the development of democratic self-government. Surely inquiry posed within a social cognitivist framework (e.g., Flower, 1989, 1994) could expand our knowledge of the contexts and motivation for literacy.

We also need to explore whether and how new technologies are altering the uses of literacy for civic purposes. Although one might expect such new modalities as electronic mail and facsimile reproductions to become more commonly used, until most citizens have easy and cheap access to these modalities, the postal service, for letters in particular, is apt to remain as useful as it has been historically. However, as I discovered in an interview with my congressman (Stotsky 1987b), word processors have dramatically increased the capacity of our representatives to respond quickly to their constituents and to individualize their responses, thus no doubt enhancing their constituents' motivation to write and strengthening their belief that they have been heard. The effects of the new technologies on participatory writing might well turn out to be indirect rather than direct, at least at present.

More important, for pedagogical purposes, we need to explore how people acquire the confidence and rhetorical skill they need in order to engage as writers in the civic process, in this country and elsewhere. What role do our many voluntary associations—those mediating structures as they have been called—play in initiating into public life those adults with few literacy skills or without confidence in the skills they have? Do local church-associated groups, unions, fraternal and sororal organizations, and neighborhood groups—the independent institutions that constitute our civil society—provide a more intimate and comfortable setting for public speaking and public writing and build their members' confidence in doing either in larger community settings? Do they give the less literate opportunities to see the value and power of literacy? How do their members learn to anticipate multiple audiences and multiple responses in order to achieve multiple purposes? What role is played by the informal and formal uses of oral language in these settings inasmuch as personal conversations and group discussions are the mainstay or even the *sine qua non* of local civic activity? Do the numerous opportunities for various kinds of talk in these settings increase their confidence to engage in public writing on their own? Does the average citizen acquire in school any of the confidence and skill needed for public writing? A better understanding of how people learn to manage the elements of this complex but intriguing phenomenon could expand our knowledge about the intellectual demands that writing makes on writers, whether in the workplace or in public life. It might also inform pedagogy with regard to the kind of reading and writing assignments teachers give students.

Clearly, the subtleties of purpose and audience in the ministudy as well as the range of genres and audiences suggested by my classification of the purposes for participatory writing suggest that students might benefit from opportunities to write in many genres and for more audiences than their teachers and classroom peers. When appropriate occasions present themselves, students can be asked to engage in participatory writing, although teachers need to observe a number of cautions before inviting students to do any advocacy writing (see Stotsky, 1987a, 1992); a chief caution being that students should always be able to exercise their right not to engage in this kind of writing. Students should not be required to advocate for anything, even for something of their own choosing. However, I do not think it essential that K-12 students write for participatory purposes as part of their school program.

Perhaps the most important implication of the ministudy presented in this chapter is the value it suggests in asking students to read and analyze the participatory writing of the average citizen rather than (or in addition to) the public discourse of eminent public figures. The writing of these letters did not require advanced composition skills so much as it demanded thinking about basic questions of purpose and audience and appropriate ways to communicate in public. These letters demonstrate not only that many different audiences may be relevant for any one piece of writing but also how one piece of writing may differentially affect its many readers — and their relationship to each other — at one and the same time. The phenomenon of multiple purposes, multiple audiences, and multiple responses is not confined to participatory writing. Plural audiences and plural purposes, like plural authorships, are as common in the workplace as they are in civic life. In civic writing, as I have discovered in my research, they come into being by more than the use of a *cc:*. Students might well examine a group of communications on one topic in the letters to the editor column of a local newspaper, or a group of letters sent to a public official on a controversial topic. Inasmuch as these letters are public information, an instructor could obtain copies and, after removing any identification, invite students to think about the kinds of questions that Ede (1991), for example, explored in her study. They could discuss who were the intended readers for each letter with respect to attitudes and values, how might other kinds of readers have reacted, and how they reacted — to their content, tone, and explicit purposes. There might be no better preparation for their own participatory writing as adults than opportunities to critique the strengths and limitations of the communications written by writers in their own community.

REFERENCES

Anson, C., & Forsberg, L. (1990). Moving beyond the academic community: Transitional stages in professional writing. *Written Communication, 7,* 200–231.

Associated Press Managing Editors. (1976). *The APME red book.* New York: Associated Press.

Brewer, J. (1952). *Wellsprings of democracy: Guidance for local societies.* New York: Philosophical Library.

Buell, E. H., Jr. (1975). Eccentrics or gladiators? People who write about politics in letters-to-the-editor. *Social Science Quarterly, 56,* 440–449.

Ede, L. (1991). Language education and civic education: Recovering past traditions, reassessing contemporary challenges. In S. Stotsky (Ed.), *Connecting civic education and language education: The contemporary challenge* (pp. 167–184). New York: Teachers College Press.

Finley, M. I. (1983). *Politics in the ancient world.* Cambridge, UK: Cambridge University Press.

Flower, L. (1989). Cognition, context, and theory building. *College Composition and Communication, 40,* 282–311.

Flower, L. (1994). The construction of negotiated meaning: A social cognitive theory of writing. Carbondale: Southern Illinois University Press.

Graff, H. J. (Ed.). (1981). *Literacy and social development in the West: A reader.* Cambridge, UK: Cambridge University Press.

Harris, W. V. (1989). *Ancient literacy.* Cambridge, MA: Harvard University Press.

Hill, D. B. (1981). Letter opinion on ERA: A test of the newspaper bias hypothesis. *Public Opinion Quarterly, 45,* 384–392.

Levi-Strauss, C. (1973). *Tristes tropiques* (J. Weightman & D. Weightman, Trans.). London: Jonathan Cape.

Levine, K. (1982). Functional literacy: Fond illusions and false economies. *Harvard Educational Review, 52,* 249–266.

Lipset, S. M. (1959). Some social requisites of democracy: Economic development and political legitimacy. *American Political Science Review, 53,* 69–105.

Maddicott, J. R. (1981). Parliament and the constituencies, 1272–1377. In R. G. Davies & J. H. Denton (Eds.), The English parliament in the middle ages (pp. 61–87). Manchester, UK: Manchester University Press.

Morse, S. (1985, May 20). Constituent views keep Capitol Hill letter-writers busy. *Detroit Free Press,* pp. 1F, 3F.

Stotsky, S. (1987a). *Civic writing in the classroom.* Bloomington, IN: Social Studies Development Center, cosponsored by ERIC/RCS and ERIC/ChESS.

Stotsky, S. (1987b). Writing in a political context: The value of letters to legislators. *Written Communication, 9,* 394–409.

Stotsky, S. (1990a). Connecting reading and writing to civic education. *Educational Leadership, 47,* 72–73.

Stotsky, S. (1990b). On literacy anthologies and adult education: A critical perspective. An essay review. *College English, 52,* 916–923.

Stotsky, S. (1991). Participatory writing. In C. F. Bahmueller (Ed.), *CIVITAS: A framework for civic education* (National Council for the Social Studies Bulletin No. 86). Calabasas, CA: Center for Civic Education.

Stotsky, S. (1992). Ethical guidelines for writing assignments. In C. M. Hurlbert & S. Totten (Eds.), *Social issues in the English classroom.* Urbana, IL: National Council of Teachers of English.

Stotsky, S. (in press). Reflections on the Polish project by American participants. In R. C. Remy & J. Strzemieczny (Eds.), *Civic education for democracy: Lessons from Poland.* Bloomington, IN: ERIC Clearinghouse for Social Studies/Social Science Education at Indiana University.

Sussman, L. (1959). Mass political letter writing in America: The growth of an institution. *Public Opinion Quarterly, 13,* 203–212.

Sussman, L. (1963). *Dear FDR: A study of political letter-writing.* Totowa, NJ: Bedminster.

Verba, S., Norman N., & Kim, J. O. (1971). *The modes of democratic participation: A cross-national comparison.* Beverly Hills: Sage.

Wyant, R. (1941). Voting via the senate mailbag. *Public Opinion Quarterly, 5,* 359–382.

Wyant, R,, & Herzog, H. (1941). Voting via the senate mailbag: Part II. *Public Opinion Quarterly, 5,* 590–624.

11 Issues in Hypertext-Supported Collaborative Writing

Stuart A. Selber
Clarkson University

Dan McGavin
Michigan Technological University

William Klein
University of Missouri at St. Louis

Johndan Johnson-Eilola
Purdue University

Collaboration plays a substantial role in the activities of workplace communication, a fact recognized by workplace writers as well as researchers and theorists of nonacademic writing (Couture & Rymer, 1989; Faigley & Miller, 1982; Lunsford & Ede, 1990; Paradis, Dobrin, & Miller, 1985). Recently, for example, it has become evident that communication specialists often collaborate in order to verify technical information (Grice, 1991), to strengthen the quality of documentation through peer and hierarchical editing (Shirk, 1991), and to ensure both the soundness and utility of usability test design for documentation processes and products (Simpson, 1991). It is also apparent that collaboration oftentimes occurs in more subtle ways: as a series of exchanges between writers and readers (Blakeslee, 1993), or as influence exerted from groups and subgroups with which writers regularly identify (Allen, 1993). Moreover, work in composition and rhetoric indicates that writing itself is largely a social act (Bruffee, 1986; Cooper & Holzman, 1989; LeFevre, 1987), and that collaboration is therefore inherent in the day-to-day work of technical communication specialists in workplace settings (Dobrin, 1989; Odell, 1985; Selzer, 1989).

Despite evidence that collaboration is often an integral (if not inevitable) part of nonacademic writing, and that social interactions are generally encouraged by work structures common within organizations (Debs, 1989), writers often find productive collaboration difficult to enact. The reasons for difficulties and failures among and within work groups are numerous and wide-ranging. For example, group leadership may be inappropriate or ineffective (Locker, 1992); labor may be distributed unequally among group members (Forman, 1991; Killingsworth & Jones, 1989); individual agendas may conflict with group agendas (Johnson, Maruyama, Johnson, Nelson, & Skon, 1981); individuals may be unwilling or unable to discuss differences of opinion (Trimbur, 1989); and unequal power relations may exist among group members due to various social forces such as organizational rank (Cross, 1990; Doheny-Farina, 1986), conscious or unconscious political agendas (Myers, 1985), and socioeconomic class, ethnicity, gender, and race (Lunsford & Ede, 1990). As if these complex social concerns were not enough, simple logistical issues of coordinating times and tasks can also make collaboration difficult (Farkas, 1991), thus discouraging useful exchanges that might otherwise occur between writers in workplace settings.

Although the degree to which such circumstances influence productive collaboration varies from group to group, at least three general factors contribute in central ways to the difficulties workers often face in such ventures: authorship, group dynamics, and organizational structures. In this chapter, we investigate the relations between these three challenge areas and hypertext—a relatively new medium for computer-based writing and reading. By examining hypertext's potential to influence notions of authorship, to change and challenge traditional dynamics within heterogeneous work groups, and to help writing specialists communicate in ways not commonly supported by hierarchical corporate structures, we discuss how this emerging technology might affect collaborative writing in the workplace. We begin this project with a brief overview of hypertext, identifying those systems that tend to encourage collaborative activities among users. We then examine the three challenge areas we previously identified—authorship, group dynamics, and organizational structures—and how hypertext might affect working together as well as note potential difficulties of collaborating in this computer-based forum. Finally, through a series of questions, we encourage interdisciplinary research and scholarship directions that explore challenges groups may face when constructing, sharing, and producing information in hypertext-supported collaborative writing environments.

COLLABORATIVE DIMENSIONS OF HYPERTEXT

Hypertext has become a common topic in the literature about nonacademic writing and at professional communication conferences that at least include, if not feature, sessions and workshops on this emerging computer-

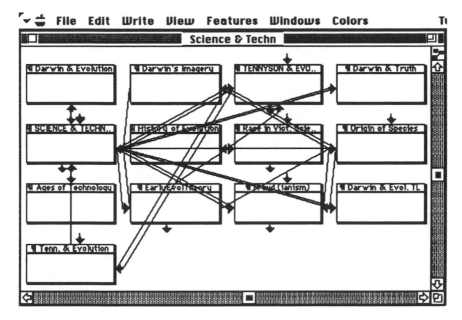

FIG. 11.1.   A screen from Landow and Lanestedt's hypertext version of Tennyson's *In Memoriam*. Readers engage network-structured chunks of information by following paths (or links) through the text. (c) Eastgate Systems. Reprinted with permission.

based technology.[1] Although defining hypertext may therefore seem like a duplication of past efforts, we do so here in order to focus on hypertext's potential to support collaborative exchanges between writers and readers. Briefly, hypertexts are network-structured chunks of information that readers engage by following paths through multiply connected texts (see Fig. 11.1).[2] One chunk of information in these connected texts often fits entirely on one computer screen and potentially contains some combination of text, graphics, sound, and animation. Hypertext is most commonly contrasted with traditional, linear text (Bolter, 1991; Johnson-Eilola, 1994),

---

[1]Both *Technical Communication* (February 1991 and August 1993) and *Technical Communication Quarterly* (1995, Winter) feature articles on hypertext for professional communicators, including various issues relating to pedagogy, practice, and theory. This conversation continues in MIT Press's Technical Communication and Information Systems series in two edited collections: one by Paul Delany and George Landow (1991) and one by Edward Barrett (1992). Discussions relating to hypertext abound at professional conferences as well: the Association for Computing Machinery's Hypertext and SIGDOC solely include sessions about this computer-based technology, while the STC Annual Conference, Computers and Writing conference, and the Conference of College Composition and Communication regularly encourage sessions on various issues relating to hypertext writing and reading.

[2]See Figures 11.1, 11.2, and 11.3 for graphical representations of hypertext systems.

in which readers normally start on the first page of a manuscript and turn successive pages until the end. As we discuss, the type of hypertext in which we are particularly interested allows readers and writers to add information to texts, either by making new connections among elements in the network or by adding entirely new elements to the network.[3]

Although hypertext applications now commonly exist in both academic and nonacademic settings, not all systems ambitiously support collaborative exchanges or textual interactions among writers and readers. For example, one of the most common applications of hypertext in business and industry is automated information retrieval (Charney, 1994; Johnson-Eilola & Selber, in press; Johnson-Lenz & Johnson-Lenz, 1991). This model of hypertext tends to construct users in fairly passive roles that are limited by the application's functionality and/or author's design. In these environments, users primarily search and retrieve information, but do not modify or contribute to the contents of a hypertext document. Typical examples of automating hypertexts include the online help systems that often accompany popular word processing and desktop publishing programs. Although these hypertext environments are important investments for corporations faced with complex information and training needs, they generally hold few opportunities for interactions and collaborations among groups of workers.

A less common but potentially valuable model of hypertext for collaboration provides "interactive" (Landow & Delany, 1990), "constructive" (Joyce, 1988), or "coauthored" (Slatin, 1990) spaces in which users do more than simply retrieve text for viewing. Rather, in varying degrees, users of such malleable spaces can borrow from, add to, or modify texts and their associated links; make personal or communal versions of their modifications; and construct collections of material abstracted from larger documents (see Fig. 11.2). These mutable types of hypertexts move from information-presentation devices to knowledge-working environments. Although systems that support such modifications are less common than automating ones, some R & D and educational projects exist: for example, Xerox PARC's *Notecards* (Irish & Trigg, 1989; Trigg, Suchman, and Halasz, 1986); MCC's *gIBIS* (Conklin & Begeman, 1987) and *rIBIS* (Rein & Ellis, 1991); the University of North Carolina at Chapel Hill's *ABC* (Smith & Smith, 1991), and Brown University's recently abandoned *Intermedia* project (Landow, 1992). Moreover, hypertext systems that support collaborative work in less aggressive ways (offering a simple but powerful facility that allows readers to physically write into the text at some level) are both readily and cheaply available: *Guide* for the Macintosh and IBM PC; *ToolBook* and *PC-Browse* for the IBM PC; and *HyperCard* and *Storyspace*

---

[3]For further discussion about the history and present state of hypertext, see Berk & Devlin, 1991; Conklin, 1987; Nielsen, 1992.

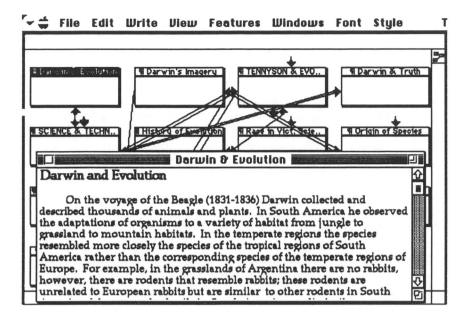

FIG. 11.2.   An open node in Landow and Lanestedt's hypertext version of Tennyson's *In Memoriam*. Readers can modify the text in this node, follow existing connections (or links), and/or create entirely new nodes and links within the network-structure. (c) Eastgate Systems. Reprinted with permission.

for the Macintosh, among many others. It is in these potentially decentralized and nonhierarchical environments — virtual "places" that foster social interactions and networked relations among and between multiple users and their texts — that hypertext holds the potential to help us extend, redefine, and reshape our notions of authorship, traditional group dynamics, and organizational structures conducive to productive collaboration between individuals in work sites.[4]

AGENDAS OF AUTHORSHIP: ENCOURAGING PARTICIPATION AND RESPONSIBILITY

Notions of authorship and their corollary collaborative goals vary widely between academia and industry. In academia, during collaboration both faculty and students are generally encouraged to assume ownership over their texts and the ideas included within them — to claim their work as their own (George, 1989; Trimbur, 1989). In corporations, however, the goals of

---

[4]For a theoretical discussion of virtual reality workspaces, see Pruitt & Barrett (1992).

collaboration are often quite different: people work together to achieve a high level of efficiency and/or quality in their work, often at the expense of exploring differences in perspective and individual identities (Schiller, 1989; Sproull & Kiesler, 1991; see also Slack, Miller, & Doak, 1992). Too often, the collaborative goals of academia and industry are represented as necessary and incompatible opposites, a view that encourages people to accept one goal while rejecting the other. We argue that such a dichotomous view is, in fact, counterproductive at either extreme: Too much emphasis on personal ownership can dislocate the inherent value of working together; whereas too much stress on simple, technically efficient production processes can lead to a consensus that is reached too easily, or to groupthink, the dismissal of valuable, contrasting points of view. In such environments, important ideas and perspectives can be overlooked, especially when individuals are reticent, or when their ideas are dissenting, too complex, or too problematic to be addressed within the time frame allotted for a project.

Unfortunately, in many instances, the inertia of efficiency precludes the productive commentary that might result from strong individual voices. Although an emphasis on reaching consensus is necessary to a functioning corporate culture, or to any culture for that matter, such consensus should be limited in certain ways: "Reaching agreement" or "being a team player" can become an easy habit that overrides critical issues. By not explicitly encouraging individual voices, corporations may implicitly discourage them. The importance of encouraging differing perspectives is exemplified in the downplaying of conflict and individual responsibility in a series of memos immediately preceding the Challenger shuttle disaster (Brown, 1990; Moore, 1992) and the Three Mile Island accident (Mathes, 1986). In less critical but still important ways, encouraging individuals to articulate diverging perspectives may allow them to recognize their personal stake in a collaborative effort; the sense that each individual is both a group member and an author who asserts authority for the overall benefit of the group. Hypertext holds the potential—but only the potential—to become a forum that encourages both group efficiency and individual voices. This balance may result in a more equitable degree of responsibility toward team members and their work, as well encourage environments that both foster and take advantage of the differences inherent in collaborative work groups.

In order to explore the potential of hypertext to support individual voices, we might begin by briefly reexamining what is meant by academic pronouncements for the dispersal of distinctions between authors and readers (Barthes, 1977; Foucault, 1976; see also Belsey, 1980; Eagleton, 1983). In effect, what many poststructuralist theorists claim is that our traditional notions of written texts rely heavily on authorial control: The author decides what text is printed and in what order, and the subsequent textual artifacts are immutable, unchanging, and, importantly, considered separate entities from other related works. For example, this chapter contains numerous parenthetical references to other texts and voices that obviously contribute to and bear great influence on the writing. However, despite these acknowledgments, our text stands explicitly and physically separate. Such distinctions may have implications for how writers and readers operate in collaborative groups. For instance, if a writing project is divided according to task specialization or expertise—a common approach to collaborative work (Bosley, 1991; Killingsworth & Jones, 1989)—individuals may find that they interact very little with other members and other, related texts. Although such segmentation is often necessary due to increasingly specialized work environments and for efficiency (Schrage, 1990), to o sharply defined roles and too rigidly delimited areas of responsibility may discourage interdisciplinary contributions from writers and readers working on other parts of the project. To foster interaction and encourage individual voices, it may be important to collapse the distinctions between writers and readers, to subtly dissolve notions of who owns particular parts of a collaborative text.

Hypertext, with its unique facility for allowing users to store and multiply structure information, may diminish current social conventions that attribute sole authorship to a piece of writing, such as attributing sole authorship of a memo to the name appended after the "From:" field. Although such memos may have been physically written by a single person, they also always refer to a much larger body of text and context—previous memos by the "author" and others, proposals, feasibility studies, progress reports, financial statements, and so on. The existence of that memo in a public hypertext that can be quoted from, rearranged, and associated with different and evolving contexts for various group members can begin to erode a sense of stability and ownership, of a communication being directed "From:" one person and "To:" one or more others. As Moulthrop (1989) explains, hypertext may provide a forum in which reading and writing can be reconceived in such a way that these traditionally separate acts begin to partially collapse (p. 266). Moreover, Bolter (1991) notes that while working in hypertext, "readers cannot avoid writing the text itself, since every choice they make is an act of writing" (p. 144).[5] By diffusing the roles of writers

---

[5]We want to make a clear distinction between the metaphoric and physical senses of writing that is sometimes overlooked in discussions of hypertext. Many existing hypertext systems and texts point *toward* the (metaphorical) idea that each reader "constructs" a new version of the text in their reading of it, both through the divergent cognitive processes of reading and, in hypertext, the navigational decisions they make in following paths through the text. But the robust, collaborative systems we are arguing for here must also combine this psychic sort of "writing" with the physical act of writing new words, paths, and nodes into the collaborative hypertext (see Johnson-Eilola, 1992).

and readers in collaborative work groups, hypertext may help partially shift notions of authority and responsibility from individuals to a larger community of workers. This is a particularly useful activity when messages cross specialty areas or hierarchies in an organization, an issue we return to later in this chapter.

In addition, hypertext may further complicate and challenge traditional notions of authorship by working to involve individuals more fully in collaborative projects. For example, writers working in hypertext systems that allow them to interact with each other and their texts may find incentive to provide honest commentary, even if it is critical, because this medium can show evidence of both group-based work and individual contributions. Although determining authorship in a collaborative hypertext is extremely difficult because of the wide range of input each writer may have made to the text as a whole (Landow, 1992), individual links and nodes may still be tagged in a variety of ways to show the contributions of a specific person, even if that person contributed only a few elements to the full text. As Irish and Trigg (1989) note in their discussion of Xerox's *Notecards*, commenting on successive drafts of a writing project can include worker-specific attributes that make each person's work on the project easily visible. In addition, the *Notecards* program maintains a historical record of the life of a project, including both actual products and meta-discussions about purpose, conventions, design, and other related issues (Trigg & Suchman, 1989), a point we return to more fully in the next section on group dynamics. Other hypertext systems, such as MCC's *gIBIS* (Conklin & Begeman, 1987) and *rIBIS* (Rein & Ellis, 1991), include similar approaches to encouraging workers to gain a sense of responsibility toward group projects. These systems were designed around a stakeholders approach, in which each participant makes comments based on their personal areas of expertise as well as critiques the work of others. By preserving important but perhaps not normally visible contributions in even the late stages of a project, hypertext-supported collaborative work may encourage individuals to attain a greater degree of involvement in the group's activities.

Although little research has been done on the role of ownership of contributions in work groups, systems such as the ones discussed above clearly show how hypertext may work to involve group members more fully in projects. The answers to rethinking traditional notions of authorship, however, are not provided by merely giving workers new hypertext programs. Common strategies and attitudes of workers will need to shift to accommodate such new perspectives. For instance, the individual contributions to a project that can be maintained in systems such as *Notecards* might be viewed by some as a deficit: The speed at which comments can be made and delivered electronically might result in poorly considered comments or, in extreme cases, the "flames" that frequently develop in e-mail communication. Although in many e-mail systems such messages are often quickly deleted, a hypertext system may make these comments a part of the permanent history of the project — either a detriment or an asset, depending on how one views these exchanges. Coping with the existence of a semipermanent record of the often unrehearsed, conversational exchanges inherent in such systems must be an evolutionary process, as group members come to understand and standardize practices and characteristic responses to messages (cf. Hawisher & Moran, 1993).

GROUP DYNAMICS: REFIGURING RELATIONS IN COLLABORATIVE TEAMS

To complete collaborative projects efficiently and effectively, individual group members must be able to speak openly and critically about a wide range of group-related issues, from logistical to political to social (Burnett, 1991; Locker, 1992; Lunsford & Ede, 1990). Despite the need for open dialogue between group members, a number of constraints often exist within collaborative work groups. Some of these stem from the ways in which groups commonly accomplish work: from the often predetermined roles of group members within the larger framework of an organization (and society), and from the unwillingness or inability of group members to explicitly (re)consider their work processes. These limitations may adversely affect group dynamics and, as a result, the subsequent work collaborative teams produce on a day-to-day basis.

As we mentioned previously, work groups often follow methods of task division that encourage each worker to assume the major responsibility for a subtask often assigned to them by a manager or group leader (Lunsford & Ede, 1990, pp. 133–136). In this "divide-and-conquer" strategy, a manager or group leader coordinating a project proposal might have one worker writing the financial section, another the timeline, and a third the resources section; a fourth worker (perhaps the group leader) might combine these three distinct sections with an executive summary and table of contents. In effect, this common organization turns a collaborative project into a related set of individual projects or, even, a project for which the group manager or leader is given primary credit or responsibility. By creating such individual tasks, groups may lose valuable opportunities to rethink entire projects in fundamental ways, missing important input from individuals working in relative isolation.

Similarly, predetermined work roles within organizations (and our larger culture) may hinder or limit productive dialog that might occur within heterogeneous work groups. Although individuals may assume several (and perhaps contradictory) subject positions simultaneously—such as coordinator, leader, silent observer, expert witness, or devil's advocate (McGavin & Sweany, 1993)—group members may feel inclined to assume traditional roles which can influence who may speak and under what conditions (Locker, 1992; Selfe, 1992). For instance, writers, editors, subject-matter experts, and product managers often bring to collaborative tasks individual roles and responsibilities formed apart from a work group. Such external roles and responsibilities may affect behaviors during collaborative projects: It is likely that writers or editors will sit silently and not enter conversations between subject-matter experts and product managers, even if they feel they have much to contribute, because of their relatively low status within the corporation. As a result, groups may lose both synergistic energy as well as important perspectives from individuals who may feel constrained by traditional work roles and responsibilities.

Finally, by not dealing explicitly with the dominant dynamics of a collaborative project, groups may limit productive dialog that might otherwise occur. On some level, groups often engage in the somewhat recursive processes of: (a) forming, gathering ideas and deciding on the purpose, audience, scope and desired effect of a text; (b) storming, dealing with inevitable conflicts that occur between individual expectations and actual performance; (c) norming, agreeing on standards for performance that are consistent with a group's expectations; and (d) performing, making "real" progress on an actual text based on consensual standards (Lunsford & Ede, 1990; McGavin & Sweany, 1993). If conversations are not encouraged about such processes, individuals may not share the same degree of commitment to group goals, and groups may have a difficult time including individual perspectives when faced with difficult deadlines or project inertia.

Although computer-based communication systems such as e-mail provide forums in which individuals can collaborate asynchronously—where each person posts messages and responses and reads those of others at their own convenience—such solutions are only partial to solving problems related to group dynamics. Asynchronous e-mail falls prey to many of the difficulties noted previously: Although coworkers may use computer networks for planning discussions and exchanging drafts of work, these same systems tend to replicate the patterns of paper-based work—memos, reports, and drafts are still sent, received, read, and responded to in relative isolation from project-related writings. In this way, although metadiscussions might still be considered important to the project as a whole, because the history of a project fades quickly (even if preserved by logging mail files to disk), they end up as widely dispersed as paper documents. In this situation, workers may find it important to reach consensus quickly, closing off discussion so that "real work" can begin. And, because of the dynamics of dividing up tasks into isolated subtasks, each task may still be the primary responsibility of only one person. As this primary sense of responsibility for individual sections develops and as the commentary of coworkers disappears at each stage (leaving only the next draft as physical evidence of the actual product), workers may find it difficult to enact the productive type of dissension Trimbur (1989) call "dissensus."

Although dissensus is often seen as inefficient and counterproductive, researchers and theorists have recently claimed that certain types of dissensus are, in fact, extremely valuable counters to groupthink (Burnett, 1991; Morgan, 1991). Hypertext may encourage such productive dissent in two ways. First, by maintaining a public, historical record of a project that is explicitly connected to the current-stage artifact, concerns and comments remain connected. Early brainstorming sessions, drafts, and commentaries related to collaborative work can be stored in a hypertext database, making temporal analyses of group dynamics possible in ways that oral and paper-based commentaries make difficult. Second, by representing in graphical form the individual sections of a project, hypertext may help groups highlight the validity or invalidity of lines of reasoning—a particularly useful function for deciding when dissensus may be justified.

In addition, the open and multiply connected nature of a hypertext document may be used to defuse the tendency toward either/or approaches, with proponents of each idea struggling to position their text as the singularly approved one. In a hypertext system such as *NegotiationLens*, collaborators "are allowed to back off from any initial unilaterally proposed solutions" (Adelson & Jordan, 1992, p. 484). Besides providing the facility for more than one approved position, programs like *Negotiation-Lens* help users categorize and prioritize issues, responses, and goals; assist users in searching the large body of text for important information; and record early brainstorming sessions for later use by storing versions of texts that can be returned to as needed.

Even the earliest, theoretical explorations of hypertext included explicit options for "versioning" or maintaining historical records of revisions to documents (Nelson, 1987). As Halasz (1988) notes, the structure of hypertext systems often implicitly preserve old commentary and drafts even after revisions. In this way, a hypertext-based collaborative project can sustain important—but sometimes overlooked or lost—comments discussing objectives, alternate views, or other concerns. And, although sometimes workers in traditional collaborative projects may find that those who contribute important ideas early in the project lose credit by the time of completion (Trimbur & Braun, 1992), the historical record of the hypertext—centralized and public—might perhaps overcome this tendency. Even in cases where only some contributors are recognized in the final product (a printed report or a working prototype), if management-review takes into account the contributions indicated in the larger hypertext corpus, early stage workers may be more willing to participate in the initial stages of the collaboration.

Even if a public, historical record is maintained, however, in some cases work groups and individuals may want or need to negotiate what constitutes such a record. Although metadiscussion surrounding a project generally contributes in both direct and indirect ways to group work, not all metadiscussion either warrants documentation or may be appropriate reading for all members of a project team. Two examples include the necessary prewriting and brainstorming that inevitably occur in the early (developmental) stages of a project and the "underlife" in which individuals engage as they assert identities different from the ones assigned to them by their organizational roles (Brooke, 1987). Although underlife is useful for helping individuals develop a sense of self — and empower them to practice productive dissent — this conversation may not, on the surface, appear to be "productive" work; in some cases, group members may elect to keep some portions of the metadiscussion from the view of superiors or others.

Hypertext may also help groups reconfigure traditional dynamics by providing a useful tool for reasoning that could encourage group members to critically evaluate the writings of other members as well as their own work (McAleese, 1990; VanLehn, 1986). A common facility for these types of tasks can be found in the graphical maps of hypertext networks that illustrate relationships, dependencies, and conflicts. The structure of hypertext systems such as *gIBIS* and *rIBIS* (see Fig. 11.3) are based on the basic *IBIS* concept — Issue Based Information Systems. *IBIS* systems are designed for solving difficult or "wicked" problems: those types of tasks that do not decompose to easy problem definitions or demonstrably (and singularly) "correct" solutions (VanLehn, 1986). Writing might be considered a general case of wicked problems. For example, there is not one best way to write a progress report, even though some reports are obviously better than others. Clearly, wicked problems are extremely common in the types of tasks on which collaborative groups normally work.

Because systems such as *Notecards*, *gIBIS*, *rIBIS*, *Intermedia*, and *Storyspace* display the network structure of the hypertext in graphical as well as textual format, writers are encouraged to make supporting evidence for assertions explicit. As VanLehn (1986) reports:

> When an attempt was made to browse the [*Notecards*] database, an unexpected property of the argumentation was discovered: the graph created by the browser was disconnected. There were sets of issues that were totally unrelated to other sets. Intuitively, this shouldn't be so. Because the issues were all part of the same theory, they must relate somehow. The browser

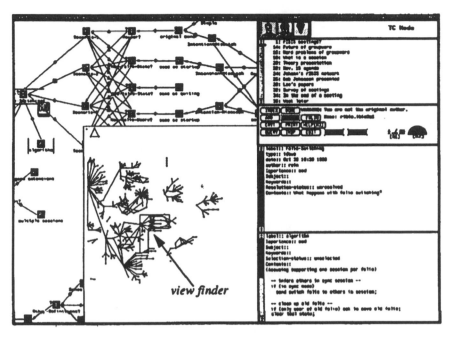

FIG. 11.3.   Graphical map of hypertext networks in rIBIS. These maps, often called browsers, illustrate relationships, dependencies, and conflicts. (c) MCC. Reprinted with permission.

revealed that some essential inter-issue relationships had not been made explicit.

This touched off a [sic] examination of the epistemology of inter-issue relationships. It was discovered that important assumptions had been made without first mentioning them somewhere. (pp. 6–7)

Such characteristics are valuable in both individual and collaborative work. Because the group hypertext can preserve a record of development and discussions (the "metacommentary" discussed previously), group members can return to the assumptions that lay behind the current stage of the project for justification or revision suggestions.

We must caution, however, that this type of productive dissent is not an automatic boon for group members, work groups, or organizations as a whole. At the functional level, including a historical record and examining its underlying assumptions might involve an overwhelming amount of information. Most successful hypertext systems allow users to hide currently unused information from view to avoid cognitive overload, although the current state of hypertext only begins to solve the numerous problems involved in navigating large, interconnected networks (Boyle & Snell, 1991; Lai & Manber, 1991).

However, the issue here becomes more complex for the politically charged arenas of corporate life—who and how is the decision made as to what material is relevant to the current task or subtask? Important information associated with the final draft of a technical report may include a wealth of experimental data, timelines, project goals, individual notes, feedback, and more. Furthermore, the availability of all of this information may foster too much dissent, with group members venting intraoffice problems or pursuing personal agendas by highlighting minor conflicts which do not substantially affect the quality of the project. Group members as well as management must work to define the degree to which they want to encourage productive dissent. This problem is not solved by hypertext software alone, but is related to both software and the social relationships between workers.

TRADING CONTROL FOR QUALITY: COMPLICATIONS IN HIERARCHICAL STRUCTURES OF WORKPLACES

In our discussion thus far, we attempted to avoid giving the impression that hypertext-based collaborative environments necessitate—or automatically lead to—productive reform in work groups. Organizational structures play an important part in the success or failure of hypertext to productively support collaboration. An important issue for us to examine is the degree to which workplace structures will allow (let alone encourage) such reforms: These changes can both support and be supported by certain types of structures and discouraged by others. In terms of collaboration across hierarchical structures, hypertext addresses the problem of the isolated, individual writer by promoting the notion that textual processes are more open than in print or linear electronic files, more likely to include workers from other places in the corporate structure. However, precisely because hypertext can be used to encourage these types of shifts, management may feel threatened and resist using hypertext or only encourage hypertext development and use in certain easily controlled ways such as the auto-mating tasks we discussed earlier.

Advertising hyperbole aside, hypertext is not a very revolutionary tool. As the historical development of hypertext has shown, the technology is frequently used to automate work rather than reform it (Johnson-Eilola & Selber, in press). Whereas such an attribute obviously bears merit in terms of increasing simple, technical efficiency, it is much more difficult to justify the use of hypertext as a way to redistribute control and responsibility in corporations, especially away from the ranks of middle management (who struggle for improved status—often working against each other—between the levels of executive management and workers at the bottom). Management tasks, in this framework, may well depend on controlling subordinates and their communication (Ritchie, 1991; Zuboff, 1988).

Hypertext, then, could become a tool for surveillance and control rather than productive, open collaboration. Computer-based e-mail discussions in the workplace have, in some cases, become a method by which management implies an open forum for private, risk-taking discussion which, in reality, becomes a way in which managers catch petty insubordinate activities (Janangelo, 1991; Zuboff, 1988). Furthermore, although hypertext may, in theory, provide mechanisms by which each person receives credit for their individual work, that capability may constitute something like circumstantial evidence: If the apportionment of real credit—promotions, bonuses, salaries, or other status markers—does not take into account the individual contributions of the hypertext, the hypertext in its entirety may become a background that is ignored by management who might only give credit based on final products.

In these ways, managers working in hierarchical structures may find it difficult not merely to reward, but to promote collaborative activities. These activities encourage a "posthierarchical" or "network" corporate structure, structures that many managers may find threatening (Charan, 1991; Drucker, 1992). As Zuboff (1988) documented in her ethnography of computerized factories and offices, managers frequently find it difficult to give up their authority, as they are often required to do once computer-based communication methods allow individuals at different levels in a corporate or workplace hierarchy to work with and in a body of information. Although apportioning tasks to specialists is a frequent strategy for dealing with large, complex projects, complete compartmentalization can be limiting. As Zuboff indicated, in a posthierarchical corporate structure, "authority is located in the process of creating and articulating meaning, rather than in a particular position or function" (p. 308). If managers encourage the use of hypertext as an open system of discussion and commentary across organizational boundaries, workers in turn may pay less attention to the confines of those boundaries (Thomkins & Cheney, 1985; Weick, 1980). Moreover, although hypertext systems may provide forums in which workers can productively collaborate across job lines, the workplace itself must attempt to accommodate this new sense of responsibility— not merely at the technical level of installing compatible computer and communication platforms, but also at the level of encouraging these new organizational structures and patterns of work. Too frequently, however, bureaucracy provides its own system of logic, resisting change in favor of the conservation of traditional structures and procedures of work (see abundant examples in Drucker, 1992; Hirschhorn, 1984; Zuboff, 1988).

Obviously, then, reforming workplace structures in order to support productive collaboration is no easy task; and hypertext is only one element that might help such reformations. More recently, in addition to considering ways in which corporate hierarchies influence behavior, researchers and reform-minded managers have also considered the impact of managerial philosophy on group work. We believe that collaborative hypertext may offer an important ally for workers and managers attempting to foster these new patterns of work. Interactive or constructive hypertexts may be most useful in organizations that value flexibility and cooperation rather than rigid control, strict divisional chains of command, and individual competition within the workplace. In fact, new "postentrepreneurial" strategies have emerged that aim to accomplish at least three goals: (a) increase the number and variety of communication channels available for workers to take action and exert influence; (b) shift relations from vertical chains of command to horizontal peer networks; and (c) diminish distinctions between managers and subordinates, especially in terms of information control (Drucker, 1992; Kanter, 1989).

As more and more organizations reduce middle management in favor of decision-making and cooperative work groups that communicate across departmental or divisional lines, hypertext might prove useful because it can encourage, create, and reflect an environment that is rich in commentary. In order to benefit from this medium, corporations will have to rethink their approaches to attributing credit and responsibility in group work, their value of dissenting points of view, and their global communication and computerization strategies. Such reconsideration is never easy, but it can be profitable.

In one limited sense, hypertext can provide a back door with which workers and reform-minded managers can decentralize control and knowledge while engaging in work that benefits the company as a whole. In such cases, workers and managers must carefully forefront the ways in which open, collaborative hypertext systems may improve the overall quality of production, provide faster ways of communicating information inside a company, and offer more efficient ways of coordinating workers. At the same time, they must downplay how such hypertext use can potentially decentralize and flatten corporate structures in ways that are useful in the long run but apparently dangerous to those concerned with preserving the status quo for one reason or another (Johnson-Eilola & Selber, 1993). Academic discussions of hypertext frequently center around the perpetual "deconstruction" inherent in this medium, asserting that "a re-analysis of the technologies of writing is in order" (Johnson-Eilola, 1992, p. 100) because "the ideal of stability and cultural cohesion will largely disappear" (Bolter, 1991). In a theoretical sense, these claims are valid; in the conceptual framework of daily experience, however, hypertext does not foster immediate and abrupt changes. These changes are slow and faint, perhaps to be overridden by other social and technological forces. But if we consider the prevalence and importance of another technology—that of print—we can see how a technology that seems to "integrate" well into the current social structure can bring about slow but radical changes in society (Ong, 1982; Poster, 1990). In terms of hypertext, these slow changes must come from both the bottom and the top, with management learning to allow hierarchical structures to flatten and workers taking more responsibility for their own activities.[6]

HYPERTEXT AND COLLABORATION:
RESEARCH QUESTIONS FOR NONACADEMIC WRITING

In this chapter, we briefly examined some ways hypertext may help us rethink traditional approaches to and conceptions of authorship, group dynamics, and organizational structures. While examining these areas, it became clear to us that, as a discipline, technical and professional communication is just beginning to understand the many complicated issues related to hypertext-supported collaborative writing, and that further work is needed to examine the social dimensions of this activity. Although we attempted to outline some productive intersections between social theory and technology, the following questions deserve attention if we hope to articulate the full range of issues surrounding hypertext-supported collaborative writing in workplace settings. Some of the questions we pose draw, in part, on the growing body of theory-based research surrounding hypertext and collaboration. Others challenge us to focus specifically on collaborative efforts in nonacademic settings—to build a foundation of research that rests soundly on observations of groups using hypertext to support writing projects. It is only through such additional work that we can begin to understand the social dimensions of hypertext-supported collaborative writing.

As we recognize the many questions ahead, we might also consider the importance of becoming more fully involved in the development of technologies that support collaboration. If nonacademic writing teachers fail to take active roles in this development, many possibilities may be left unarticulated or problems unsolved: groups may continue to work ineffi-

[6]In addition to the collaboration that occurred between the authors of this essay, we would like to recognize the contributions of others who helped us think productively about the complex relations between technology and people. Cynthia Self, Marilyn Cooper, Ann Hill Duin, and Craig Hansen provided us with generous commentary on various versions and sections of this essay. We thank them for enriching our collaborative experience. A portion of this work was supported by a generous fellowship from the Department of Humanities at Michigan Technological University and the Ford Motor Company.

ciently or unfairly, perhaps failing to take advantage of the various perspectives inherent in group work. Moreover, software developers will continue to build hypertext systems without the important humanistic perspectives offered by what we have learned through our research in both workplace and classroom collaboration—perspectives that offer insights into the social nature of collaboration and how hypertext might affect writers working together in corporate settings. Although research can and should develop in a variety of directions, we feel that the concerns of authorship, group dynamics, and organizational structures represent significant starting places for interdisciplinary study. In addition to the issues we outlined in this chapter, the following questions suggest further starting places.

Authorship

Although we outlined some issues relating to authorship that emerge in group contexts, additional work is needed to further explore the social, political, and logistical dimensions of hypertext-supported collaborative work:

- How might hypertext influence individual voices in collaborative efforts? How might these voices differ from those in non-hypertext-mediated collaborative work?
- If hypertext can encourage individual participation in collaborative efforts, how can we ensure that constructive criticism and dissenting opinions will necessarily follow?
- If hypertext can encourage individual participation in collaborative efforts, will workers feel a greater or lesser sense of personal ownership over texts? How might such changes affect an individual's sense of commitment and responsibility to a larger group?
- If authorial credit is commonly awarded by measuring individual initiative and achievement, how might such measurements be made in hypertext-supported collaborative work? Should such measurements be made at all?
- How might strong individual voices that can emerge from hypertext-supported collaborative work affect the performance of groups, particularly in terms of on-time project completion, the quality of work produced, and efficiency?

Group Dynamics

Although the literature surrounding group dynamics in workplace settings is rapidly emerging, as is literature that focuses on computer-supported collaboration, we need to further explore the ways in which hypertext-supported collaborations may differ from other types of collaboration:

- How might hypertext-supported collaboration differ from face-to-face and other types of computer-supported collaboration?
- Which collaborative activities might best be supported by hypertext and which activities might be hindered or altered in unproductive ways?
- How are work groups commonly configured during hypertext-supported collaborative work? How do these configurations affect group dynamics?
- How do relationships and group dynamics develop in hypertext-supported collaborations? What do these relationships and dynamics look like?
- How do group members define relationships in hypertext-supported collaborative work? Will these new relationships affect the quality and productivity of group work?
- Do relations developed in hypertext-supported collaboration carry over into other kinds of collaboration, virtual or face to face? Can hypertext-supported collaboration influence or change established relationships in other forums?
- If hypertext has the potential to reduce gendered and hierarchical roles within collaborative groups, what might promote and what might impede this process?
- If hypertext has the potential to promote critical inquiry and commentary about interpersonal and social issues related to group work processes, what might promote or impede this process?
- If hypertext has the potential to encourage metadiscussion about group projects, who decides what metadiscussion becomes part of the permanent record of a project and what does not? And how will this metadiscussion be used in corporate/organizational performance evaluations?

Organizational Structures

In terms of organizational structures, we need to further examine the complex relations between hypertext, corporate structures, and managerial techniques and philosophies:

- What organizational structures and communication patterns currently exist within organizations that productively use hypertext to support collaboration?
- How might existing hierarchies and lines of power affect the

structure, use, and development of hypertext-supported writing environments?

- How might hypertext-supported collaboration challenge (or deepen) existing corporate hierarchies and lines of power?
- How is power and hierarchy exercised in hypertext-supported collaboration?
- How might hypertext-supported collaborative work help transform social and political landscapes within organizations?
- What patterns of communication and behavior emerge in hypertext-supported collaboration? Are these patterns useful for helping writers and managers reconfigure and reform organizational structures?
- Will hypertext's potential for surveillance and control suppress and inhibit group members, managers, and organizational stability?
- What management strategies might encourage open, productive collaboration in hypertext environments?
- Will new patterns of reward and recognition emerge as groups begin to think and work in hypertext?
- Who will control or gatekeep hypertext-supported collaborative work within corporations? Writers? Managers? Will writers and managers share this responsibility?

These questions—necessarily and adamantly open-ended and nonexhaustive—mark only the starting point for research in hypertext-supported collaborative work. The technology of hypertext clearly does not provide the utopian workspace some early theorists and researchers suggested. But in continually questioning and testing the patterns of collaborative work in hypertext, we can help map the technology and its use in productive and powerful ways.

REFERENCES

Adelson, B., & Jordan, T. (1992). The need for negotiation in cooperative work. In E. Barrett (Ed.), *Sociomedia: Multimedia, hypermedia, and the social construction of knowledge* (pp. 469–492). Cambridge, MA: MIT Press.

Allen, N. J. (1993) Community, collaboration, and the rhetorical triangle. *Technical Communication Quarterly, 1*, 63–74.

Barrett, E. (Ed.). (1992). *Sociomedia: Multimedia, hypermedia, and the social construction of knowledge.* Cambridge, MA: MIT Press.

Barthes, R. (1977). The death of the author. In S. Heath (Ed.), *Image - music - text* (pp. 142–48). New York: Hill & Wang.

Belsey, C. (1980). *Critical practice.* London: Methuen.

Berk, E., & Devlin, J. (Eds.). (1991). *Hypertext/hypermedia handbook.* New York: McGraw-Hill.

Blakeslee, A. M. (1993). Readers and authors: Fictionalized constructs or dynamic collaborations? *Technical Communication Quarterly*, *1*, 23-35.

Bolter, J. D. (1991). *Writing space: The computer, hypertext, and the history of writing*. Hillsdale, NJ: Lawrence Erlbaum Associates.

Bosley, D. S. (1991). Designing effective technical communication teams. *Technical Communication*, *4*, 504-512.

Boyle, C. D. B., & Snell, J. R. (1991). Intelligent navigation for semistructured hypertext documents. In R. McAleese & C. Green (Eds.), *Hypertext: State of the art* (pp. 28-39). Norwood, NJ: Ablex.

Brooke, R. (1987). Underlife and writing instruction. *College Composition and Communication*, *2*, 141-153.

Brown, M. H. (1990). Past and present images of Challenger in NASA's organizational culture. In B. D. Sypher (Ed.), *Case studies in organizational communication* (pp. 111-124). New York: Guilford.

Bruffee, K. A. (1986). Social construction, language, and the authority of knowledge: A bibliographic essay. *College English*, *8*, 773-790.

Burnett, R. E. (1991). Substantive conflict in a cooperative context: A way to improve the collaborative planning of workplace documents. *Technical Communication*, *4*, 531-539.

Charney, D. (1994). The impact of hypertext on processes of reading and writing. In C. L. Selfe & S. J. Hilligoss (Eds.), *Computers and literacy: The complications of teaching and learning with technology* (pp. 238-263). New York: Modern Language Association.

Conklin, J. (1987). Hypertext: An introduction and survey. *IEEE Computer*, *9*, 17-41.

Conklin, J., & Begeman, M. (1987). gIBIS: A hypertext tool for team design deliberation. In *Hypertext '87 Papers* (pp. 247-51).

Cooper, M. M., & Holzman, M. (1989). *Writing as social action*. Portsmouth, NH: Boynton/Cook, Heinemann.

Couture, B., & Rymer, J. (1989). Interactive writing on the job: Definitions and implications of collaboration. In M. Kogen (Ed.), *Writing in the business professions* (pp. 73-93). Urbana, IL: National Council of Teachers of English.

Cross, G. A. (1990). A Bahktinian exploration of factors affecting the collaborative writing of an executive letter of an annual report. *Research in the Teaching of English*, *24*, 173-203.

Debs, M. B. (1989). Collaborative writing in industry. In B. E. Fearing & W. K. Sparrow (Eds.), *Technical writing: Theory and practice* (pp. 33-42). New York: Modern Language Association.

Delany, P., & Landow, G. P. (Eds.). (1991). *Hypermedia and literary studies*. Cambridge, MA: MIT Press.

Dobrin, D. N. (1989). *Writing and technique*. Urbana, IL: National Council of Teachers of English.

Doheny-Farina, S. (1986). Writing in an emerging organization: An ethnographic study. *Written Communication*, *3*, 158-185.

Drucker, P. (1992, September/October). The new society of organizations. *Harvard Business Review*, pp. 95-104.

Eagleton, T. (1983). *Literary theory: An introduction*. Minneapolis: University of Minnesota Press.

Faigley, L., & Miller, T. P. (1982). What we learn from writing on the job. *College English*, *4*, 557-569.

Farkas, D. K. (1991). Collaborative writing, software development, and the universe of collaborative activity. In M. M. Lay & W. M. Karis (Eds.), *Collaborative writing in industry: Investigations in theory and practice* (pp. 13-30). Amityville, NY: Baywood.

Forman, J. (1991). Computing and collaborative work. In G. E. Hawisher & C. L. Selfe (Eds.), *Evolving perspectives on computers and composition studies: Questions for the 1990s* (pp. 65-83). Urbana, IL: National Council of Teachers of English.

Foucault, M. (1976) *The archeology of knowledge and the discourse of language.* New York: Harper & Row.

George, D. (1989) The politics of social construction and the teaching of writing. *Journal of Teaching Writing, 8,* 1–10.

Guide. [Computer program]. Bellevue, WA: OWL International,

Grice, R. (1991). Verifying technical information: Issues in information-development collaboration. In M. M. Lay & W. M. Karis (Eds.), *Collaborative writing in industry: Investigations in theory and practice* (pp. 224–241). Amityville, NY: Baywood.

Halasz, F. G. (1988). Reflections on Notecards: Seven issues for the next generation of hypermedia systems. *Communications of the ACM, 7,* 836–852.

Hawisher, G. E., & Moran, C. (1993). Electronic mail and the writing instructor. *College English, 6,* 627–643.

Hirschhorn, L. (1984). *Beyond mechanization: Work and technology in a postindustrial age.* Cambridge, MA: MIT Press.

HyperCard [Computer program]. Cupertino, CA: Apple Computer.

Irish, P. M., & Trigg, R. H. (1989). Supporting collaboration in hypermedia: Issues and experiences. In E. Barrett (Ed.), *The society of text: Hypertext, hypermedia, and the social construction of information* (pp. 93–106). Cambridge, MA: MIT Press.

Janangelo, J. (1991). Technopower and technopression: Some abuses of power and control in computer-assisted writing environments. *Computers and Composition, 1,* 47–64.

Johnson, D. W., Maruyama, G., Johnson, R., Nelson, D., & Skon, L. (1981). Effects of cooperative, competitive, and individualistic goal structures on achievement: A meta-analysis. *Psychological Bulletin, 89,* 47–62.

Johnson-Eilola, J. (1992). Structure and text: Writing space and *Storyspace. Computers and Composition, 2,* 95–129.

Johnson-Eilola, J. (1994). An overview of reading and writing in hypertext: Vertigo and euphoria. In C. L. Selfe & S. J. Hilligoss (Eds.), *Computers and literacy: The complications of teaching and learning with technology* (pp. 195–219). New York: Modern Language Association.

Johnson-Eilola, J., & Selber, S. A. (1993, May). *After automation: Hypertext and technical communication.* Paper presented at the Computers and Writing conference, Ann Arbor, MI.

Johnson-Eilola, J., & Selber, S. A. (in press). After automation: Hypertext and corporate structures. In P. Sullivan & J. Dautermann (Eds.), *Electronic literacy in the workplace: Technologies of writing.* Urbana, IL: National Council of Teachers of English.

Johnson-Lenz, P., & Johnson-Lenz, T. (1991). Postmechanistic groupware primitives: Rhythms, boundaries, and containers. In S. Greenburg (Ed.), *Computer-supported Cooperative Work and Groupware* (pp. 271–293). San Diego: Harcourt Brace Jovanovich.

Joyce, M. (1988, November). Siren shapes: Exploratory and constructive hypertexts. *Academic Computing,* pp. 10–14, 37–42.

Kanter, R. M. (1989, November/December). The new managerial work. *Harvard Business Review,* pp. 85–92.

Killingsworth, M. J., & Jones, B. G. (1989). Division of labor or integrated teams: A crux in the management of technical communication? *Technical Communication, 3,* 210–221.

Lai, P., & Manber, U. (1991). Flying through hypertext. In *Hypertext '91 Proceedings* (pp. 123–32). San Antonio: Association for Computing Machinery.

Landow, G. P. (1992). *Hypertext: The convergence of contemporary critical theory and technology.* Baltimore: Johns Hopkins University Press.

Landow, G. P., & Delany, P. (1990). Hypertext, hypermedia, and literary studies: The state of the art. In P. Delany & G. P. Landow (Eds.), *Hypermedia and literary studies* (pp. 3–50). Cambridge, MA: MIT Press.

LeFevre, K. B. (1987). *Invention as social act.* Carbondale: Southern Illinois University Press.

Locker, K. O. (1992). What makes a collaborative writing team successful? A case study of lawyers and social workers in a state agency. In J. Forman (Ed.), *New visions of collaborative writing* (pp. 37–62). Portsmouth, NH: Boynton/Cook, Heinemann.

Lunsford, A., & Ede, E. (1990). *Singular texts/plural authors: Perspectives on collaborative writing*. Carbondale: Southern Illinois University Press.

Mathes, J. C. (1986). Three mile island: The management communication role. *Engineering Management International, 3*, 261–268.

McAleese, R. (1990). Concepts as hypertext nodes: The ability to learn while navigating through hypertext nets. In D. H. Jonassen & H. Mandl (Eds.), *Designing Hypermedia for Learning* (Proceedings of the NATO Advanced Research Workshop on Designing Hypertext/ Hypermedia for Learning, Rottenburg/Neckar, FRG, 3–8 July 1991). Berlin: Spring-Verlag.

McGavin, D., & Sweaney, P. (1993, April). *What students say about collaboration*. Paper presented at the annual conference on College Composition and Communication. San Diego.

Moore, P. (1992). When politeness is fatal: Technical communication and the Challenger accident. *Journal of Business and Technical Communication, 6*, 269–92.

Morgan, M. (1991). Patterns of composing: Connections between classroom and workplace collaboration. *Technical Communication, 4*, 540–545.

Moulthrop, S. (1989). Hypertext and 'the hyperreal'. In *Hypertext '89 Proceedings* (pp. 259–67). New York: Association for Computing Machinery.

Myers, G. (1985). Texts as knowledge claims: The social construction of two biology articles. *Social Studies of Science, 15*, 593–630.

Nelson, T. (1987). *Literary machines*. Palo Alto, CA: Project Xanadu.

Nielsen, J. (1990). *Hypertext and hypermedia*. New York: Academic.

Odell, L. (1985). Beyond the text: Relations between writing and social context. In L. Odell & D. Goswami (Eds.), *Writing in nonacademic settings* (pp. 249–280). New York: Guilford.

Ong, W. J. (1982). *Orality and literacy: The technologizing of the word*. London: Methuen.

Paradis, J., Dobrin, D., & Miller, R. (1985). Writing at Exxon ITD. In L. Odell & D. Goswami (Eds.), *Writing in nonacademic settings* (pp. 281–307). New York: Guilford.

PC-Browse [Computer program]. Seattle: Quicksoft.

Poster, M. (1990). *The mode of information: Poststructuralism and social context*. Chicago: University of Chicago Press.

Pruitt, S., & Barrett, T. (1992). Corporate virtual workspaces. In M. Benedikt (Ed.), *Cyberspace: First steps* (pp. 383–410). Cambridge, MA: MIT Press.

Rein, G. L., & Ellis, C. A. (1991). rIBIS: A real-time group hypertext system. In S. Greenburg (Ed.), *Computer-supported cooperative work and groupware* (pp. 223–241). San Diego: Harcourt Brace Jovanovich.

Ritchie, L. D. (1991). Another turn of the information revolution. *Communication Research, 3*, 412–427.

Schiller, H. I. (1989). *Culture inc.: The corporate takeover of public expression*. New York: Oxford University Press.

Schrage, M. (1990). *Shared minds: The new technologies of collaboration*. New York: Random House.

Selfe, C. L. (1992). Computer-based conversations and the changing nature of collaboration. In J. Forman (Ed.), *New visions of collaboration*. Portsmouth, NH: Boynton/Cook, Heinemann.

Selzer, J. (1989). Composing processes for technical discourse. In B. E. Fearing & W. K. Sparrow (Eds.), *Technical writing theory and practice* (pp. 43–52). New York: Modern Language Association.

Shirk, H. N. (1991). Collaborative editing: A combination of peer and hierarchical editing techniques. In M. M. Lay & W. M. Karis (Eds.), *Collaborative writing in industry:*

Investigations in theory and practice (pp. 242–261). Amityville, NY: Baywood.

Simpson, M. (1991). The practice of collaboration in usability test design. *Technical Communication, 4*, 527–531.

Slack, J. D., Miller, D. J., & Doak, J. (1993). The technical communicator as author: Meaning, power, authority. *Journal of Business and Technical Communication, 7*, 12–36.

Slatin, J. M. (1990). Reading hypertext: Order and coherence in a new medium. *College English, 8*, 870–883.

Smith, J. B., & Smith, F. D. (1991). ABC: A hypermedia system for artifact-based collaboration. In *Hypertext '91 proceedings* (pp. 179–92). San Antonio: Association for Computing Machinery.

Sproull, L., & Kiesler, S. (1991). *Connections: New ways of working in the networked organization.* Cambridge, MA: MIT Press.

Storyspace [Computer program]. Cambridge, MA: Eastgate Systems.

Thomkins, P. K., & Cheney, G. (1985). Communication and unobtrusive control in contemporary organizations. In R. D. McPhee & P. K. Thompkins (Eds.), *Organizational communication: Traditional themes and new directions* (pp. 179–210). Beverly Hills: Sage.

Toolbook [Computer program]. Bellevue, WA: Asymetrix.

Trigg, R. H., Suchman, L. A., & Halasz, F. G. (1986). Supporting collaboration in Notecards. In *Proceedings of the conference on computer supported cooperative work* (pp. 221–228). Austin: Association for Computing Machinery.

Trimbur, J. (1989). Consensus and difference in collaborative learning. *College English, 6*, 602–16.

Trimbur, J., & Braun, L. A. (1992). Laboratory life and the determination of authorship. In J. Forman (Ed.), *New visions of collaborative writing* (pp. 19–36). Portsmouth, NH: Boynton/Cook, Heinemann.

VanLehn, K. (1986). *Theory reform caused by an argumentation tool* (Rep. No. ISL-11). Palo Alto, CA: Xerox PARC.

Weick, Karl. (1980) The management of eloquence. *Executive, 6*, 18–21.

Zuboff, S. (1988). *In the age of the smart machine: The future of work and power.* New York: Basic Books.

12 Technology Enhanced Nonacademic Writing: A Social and Cognitive Transformation

Curtis Jay Bonk
Indiana University

Thomas H. Reynolds
Texas A & M University

Padma V. Medury
West Virginia University

A myriad of reports during the past decade point toward shifts in the economy that demand higher level communication skills and more technologically sophisticated labor markets to function effectively in the workplace (Naisbitt & Aburdene, 1985; Toffler, 1980). As projections become reality, corporate executives are raising concerns about the preparedness of business graduates regarding writing and thinking effectively on the job (May & Arevalo, 1983). From accounting to management to engineering, the everyday workplace has become increasingly writing dependent. Business leaders now realize that writing deficiencies impede financial and economic reporting and seriously impair decision making (Andrews & Sigband, 1984).

Even though the written communication of items such as rebate programs, new product announcements, budget projections, and territorial sales reports has increased in salience in the workplace, the workhorse for this task has been traditionally labeled a *word processor* (Halpern, 1985). Yet traditional visions of writing as *word processing* will no longer suffice. In fact, when hearing references to someone "word" processing, one might conjure up notions of a lonely writer jotting down plans and ideas and then quickly transcribing these thoughts into words and sentences using basic typing, deleting, inserting, saving, retrieving, and scrolling commands. As a result, the "word" processor is deemed a convenient tool for mindless, deskilling activities rather than a technology to enhance the mind (Salomon, Perkins, & Globerson, 1991).

In seeking to supply the necessary writing skills and attitudes, business professors have discovered that more genuine problems can be addressed through writing than when their teaching practices follow a traditional one-right-answer methodology (Smith & Bonk, 1992). Professors realize that the future careers of their students will be filled with a daily array of writing activities (Schrage, 1990; Tebeaux, 1985):

- business forecasts
- sales and budget reports
- press releases
- grant proposals
- letters and speeches
- technical manuals
- feasibility studies
- purchasing justifications
- management briefings.

While business programs incorporate additional writing activities into undergraduate curricula (Kettering, 1989; Smith & Bonk, 1992), nonacademic writing tools and networks are altering the role of nonacademic writing with increases in both group interaction and idea processing tools (Pitturo, 1989). Like the computer revolution of the late 1970s that stimulated the societal transition from "information processing to knowledge processing" (Feigenbaum & McCorduck, 1984, p. 4), revolutionary computer-based writing environments embrace knowledge as well as word processing for nonacademic writing (see Fig. 12.1). According to Dede (1988), these technological advances make possible a shift toward a knowledge-based workplace wherein cognitive partnerships exist between people and machines.

The writing model represented in Fig. 12.1 is designed to encourage questions and answers regarding *who* is involved in this new writing process (i.e., an individual or a team) and *what* is the focus (i.e., word processing or knowledge exploration and idea refinement). The right side of this model focuses on what actions are taking place, whereas the left side centers on who is taking that action. Of course, before considering what is being processed and who is involved in these processing activities, issues of *when* processing might occur should be considered.

In this chapter, we challenge you to think about the different arenas wherein technology alters the writing process, thereby significantly impacting the social and cognitive aspects of nonacademic writing. Using the framework in Fig. 12.1, we:

1. Reconsider workplace writing environments from a reprocessing framework;

2. Discuss how tools employed at different points in the composing process uniquely alter the social and cognitive dimensions of writing;
3. Review how the four levels of software tools—word, self, knowledge, and collaboration—facilitate distinct writing processes;
4. Interconnect these nonacademic writing tools and practices underlying the reprocessing model; and
5. Pose research questions within and between these four levels.

WRITING AS REPROCESSING

Computer tools exist for generating ideas, collaboratively constructing new meanings, and examining surface-level diagnostics of writing. We believe that the cognitive partnerships that formerly occurred between people and machines (once called word processors) now occur between people as a result of advances in the writing tools. As technologies advance, writing models and terminology must expand to reflect the transactions occurring within these altered environments. The model in Fig. 12.1 attempts to refocus nonacademic writing to visions of a reprocessing environment: an environment that includes all aspects of writing from editing mechanical errors to reformulating plans and goals (Scardamalia & Bereiter, 1986). Although planning, translating, and revising acts of the traditional Flower and Hayes (1981) cognitive process model of writing still are evident (although replaced with the terms *preprocessing, in-processing,* and *postprocessing*), our model pushes the text base further away from the written product to focus more on changes in the writer's mind (Witte, 1985), as well as the minds of his or her collaborators, and their joint intermental functioning (Wertsch, 1991). Although it is the social element of collaboration that is perhaps the most distinctive feature of this model, the reprocessing framework also implies constant knowledge construction and meaning negotiation.

Reprocessing expands on the semantically limited term *revision* because it accounts for anything occurring within a writing cycle (e.g., new text, notes, graphs, outlines, diagrams, points, checklists, or ideas that can be used for further reprocessing cycles). When using the term *reprocessing* (Scardamalia & Bereiter, 1986), it is easier to discuss the internal changes or knowledge constructions taking place in the writer's mind before text is actually produced as well as the externally related changes that occur upon discovering errors and inconsistencies in the text produced. Although interactive brainstorming sessions among a group of production control managers might drastically alter a report regarding defective products, these initial planning and pretextual revising processes have been ignored in former notions of revision (Witte, 1985). In conjunction with the social constructivist movement (Nystrand, 1990), the nonacademic writing environment we envision also begins to account for the discoveries of inconsistencies in reports through uncovering the social interactions of a team. In a reprocessing environment, it is assumed, therefore, that the discussion and debate of all team members as well as individual reflection influences the final text product.

REPROCESSING ENVIRONMENT:

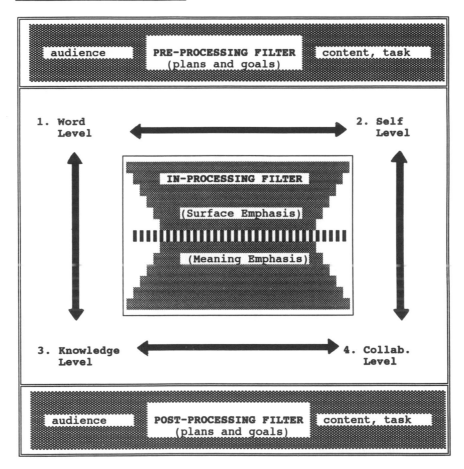

Note: Arrows indicate interdependency among the four levels of computer tools.

FIG. 12.1. Model of social and cognitive processes in writing.

COGNITIVE CONSIDERATIONS OF THE REPROCESSING MODEL

The reprocessing environment also accounts for "when" technology might foster various writing acts, that is, when reprocessing of one's thoughts occurs. As Witte (1985) suggested, planning and revising can occur at any point in the composing process; hence, there are pretextual as well as posttextual revisions. Because linear views of writing have constrained research on revision, we believe that a reprocessing model might better account for these writing activities. Furthermore, as collaborative tools enter the workplace, planning and revision activities prior to drafting texts will increase in importance. New models of writing are needed to better account for writing activities such as:

preprocessing or pretextual filtering, interrelating, and changing of ideas occurring in one's head (i.e., intramental functioning; see Witte, 1985) as well as ideas between coworkers (i.e., intermental functioning; see Wertsch, 1991) before written notation or formal transcription;

in-processing activities such as transcribing and connecting present thoughts and ideas through point-of-inscription shaping (Matsuhashi, 1987); and

postprocessing or the changing of plans and ideas after an initial document is produced through forays back into previously instantiated text (Matsuhashi, 1987).

Because revising occurs both pretextually and on completed text, the main point here is to consider *when* technology might nurture revisionary activities. Instead of assuming that revision occurs on transcribed text, some technologies render greater impact on preprocessing ideas whereas others nurture thoughts during composition (see Kellogg, 1989, for examples).

Preprocessing

Preprocessing of ideas is vital because it establishes writing plans and goals. Witte (1985) established the importance of pretextual filtering and connecting of ideas prior to text instantiation. According to Witte, revision does not just occur on written text; it can occur in one's internal mental representation. In a single-authored document, these pretextual revisions occur in a similar fashion to extant text revision; in a multiauthored document, preprocessing activities divide responsibilities and prepare someone for a later writing task while building consensus about what the final product will look like. As Weber (1991) noted, what feeds this collaborative cognitive process are each writer's memories, prior understandings of professional practice, current goals, and task environment constraints.

Useful idea generation and organization technologies will parallel these preprocessing needs. As Kellogg (1989) pointed out, individual planning aids and idea processing tools are needed for attentional overload, idea bankruptcy, writing anxiety, and other affective interference. Prior to composing the first sentence, for instance, some writers need to overcome writer's block and procrastination, whereas others are distressed over how to organize a wealth of unfocused ideas.

In-Processing

Most word processing packages were developed for translation activities. We refer to software that facilitates such text creation, searching, and movement as *in-processing tools*. Whereas Flower and Hayes (1981) highlighted the transcription function, Matsuhashi (1987) referred to this as *point-of-inscription shaping of ideas* presently in working memory. Pre-textual ideas become instantiated and reconfigured through the drafting of a document on a word processor (including adjoining notes, figures, charts, and other visual representations). In-processing tools such as a thesaurus or word finder assist in sculpting and reshaping one's ideas. In contrast, simple margin and page indicators as well as backup displays are more ubiquitous in-processing tools.

In-processing acts are simultaneously trivial and momentous occasions. Besides textual tinkering, writers internalize both the face-to-face conversation and dialogue about instantiated text (Rogers & Horton, 1992) and the processes displayed by the technologies that led to text instantiation (Salomon, 1993). In a way, in-processing acts are indicators of thoughts on the road to internalization as well as the cognitive residue left behind by the engagement with both tool and human partners (Salomon, 1993). Although we admit that word, phrase, or sentence construction is facilitated by the ideas created during preprocessing and postprocessing activities, the distinction of the three processes should help in the analysis of nonacademic writing. Because in-processing activities include text transcription and shaping, and because it is difficult to determine when one has completed a text sequence and fulfilled a writing plan, it is especially difficult to sever it from the final leg of this writing journey, postprocessing.

Postprocessing

Postprocessing tools include text analysis and editing packages that analyze previously transcribed and solidified ideas. As word processing functions advance, tools for rereading and reevaluating texts multiply. Analyses of word usage and sentence complexity are common in most word processing tool kits. Checklists for certain style and grammar features are available on demand (Friedman & Rand, 1989). It is not surprising that most of this automated editorial feedback is developed using prescriptions or recommendations of psychologists, writing researchers, linguists, and other text design experts (Frase, Kiefer, Smith, & Fox, 1985).

Common postprocessing analysis tools deal with the word level such as pronouns, punctuation, sexist phrases, and transitions (Friedman & Rand, 1989), whereas others encourage collegial review of a document with editing tools for marking, highlighting, annotating, striking out, and rewriting text (Lienert & Cooper, 1992). Frase et al. (1985) pointed out that whereas users of these text analysis programs detect most writing problems, they often fail to heed their advice without additional human guidance.

SOCIAL CONSIDERATIONS OF THE REPROCESSING MODEL

Changes in the social environment, brought about by new technologies, significantly alter reprocessing activities. As cooperative work tools undergo rapid change, there is a greater need to understand human/machine interfaces (Greif, 1988; Robertson, Zachary, & Black, 1990) as well as the resulting human/human interactions. Galegher, Kraut, and Egido (1990) pointed out that these new technologies (e.g., multimedia, hypermedia, and electronic mail) may fail to support the cooperative work they were developed for because they are inconsistent with user goals and needs. In effect, the social interaction and communication patterns of users are often misunderstood by developers, thereby limiting opportunities for intellectual teamwork.

Some instructional designers searching for rationale to account for cognitive and social-cognitive changes in computer-supported collaborative environments have increasingly revived Vygotskian writing for theoretical grounding (e.g., Vygotsky, 1978, 1986). Writing researchers attempting to understand interdependent processes of writing also turn to Vygotsky (1962) for guidance in building a social theory of writing (Faigley, 1985). Of course, one of our premises is that important social dimensions of writing are illuminated by continued advances in technologies that reaffirm the writers' participation in the culture of the organization in which one works (Odell, 1985). Vygotsky's (1978, 1986) arguments about the social interaction mechanisms between learners and more capable peers that assist one in moving to developmental levels previously unattainable are easily extended to nonacademic writing environments. As we described elsewhere (Bonk, Medury, & Reynolds, 1994), technologies change one's relationships with more capable others and increase the avenues to social interaction by providing access to feedback and discussion from peers and supervisors from varying geographical distances. However, the actual form of assistance may depend on the degree of collaboration embedded in the task as well as the assigned roles (Saunders, 1989). As predicted by Vygotsky, expert guidance or scaffolding leads employees into new communication tasks and capabilities, thereby spurring issues important in the design of technologies that support coauthoring and commenting.

We support Pea (1985) and other neo-Vygotskians (Salomon et al., 1991) who claim that technologies designed to encourage teamwork, networking, joint written communication, brainstorming, and problem solving will not only alter interaction patterns and organizational structures, but will also transform definitions of writing and mental functioning. Collaborative writing tools are posited to increase text quality because they reduce the cognitive burden of writing, unlike word processors that mainly reduce the physical labor (Salomon, 1993). According to this view, the forms of support provided by peers can extend the written document to higher levels of communication (Bonk & Reynolds, 1992).

The design of these technologies should include extensive field testing and observational studies by psychologists and anthropologists so that changes based on these observations might be incorporated into the design of systems (Francik, Rudman, Cooper, & Levine, 1991; Olson & Bly, 1991; Tatar, Foster, & Bobrow, 1991). Advances in collaboration tools should encourage continued explorations into the strategies and processes of collaboration (Duin, Jorn, & DeBower, 1991). Writing technologies might even capture and expose writing acts for later replay and analysis (Bonk, Reynolds, & Koury, 1993). For instance, many collaboration tools have saveable chat and dialogue boxes that encourage discussion. Collaboration logs, chat boxes, and transcript replays might provide a window on how managers lend their expertise to a document, how responsibilities are assigned, how questions become raised and revisions accepted, how textual ideas evolve, and how minor modifications in writing environments impact forms of discussion and collaboration patterns. Qualitative text analysis tools and techniques (Ely, 1991; Tesch, 1990) along with videotapes, interviews, and keystroke mapping and replay mechanisms (Reynolds & Bonk, 1990) should foster numerous opportunities to document changes in departmental social interaction patterns and new forms of expert mediation and scaffolding in the workplace.

Such tools might indicate how work groups use common frameworks or socially shared cognition to function effectively. According to Levine and Moreland (1991), knowledge about the group, group members, and the task is critical to the functioning of the group. New workers must understand and be accepted into the existing culture before effective collaborative writing transpires. Witness the new sales order manager who may not be immediately accepted into a monthly shipping and billing reporting scheme or workgroup until there is a sense of trust and shared understanding of roles. Whereas collaborative writing tools typically should increase the quantity of shared knowledge in the workplace, the form of information exchange may harm rather than help the work culture and performance. For example, a sales manager's overstatement of shipments in order to impress top management may be more apparent and embarrassing in a collaborative environment.

As we gain greater knowledge of work group functioning, computer tools are increasingly advocated as a mechanism to enhance the way in which people meet, discuss, communicate, share, and form new meanings in the workplace. As adjunct aids are added to word processors, they play vital roles in the workplace from idea generation to drafting to reanalysis to collegial assistance. These various roles or levels of support transform nonacademic writing environments at four levels.

LEVELS OF WRITING SUPPORT TOOLS

Level One: The Word Level

A main problem in the integration of computers in the meaning-making process of the business world is that reasons for using writing tools often have not kept pace with either rapid technological or theoretical changes; or, as argued by Wertsch (personal communication, April 11, 1994), there is an irreducible tension because the unique uses of many writing aids have not corresponded with the mediational means provided by these cultural tools. Writing tools were originally created for glorified secretaries—the wondrous word processing assistants hired to decipher the scribblings of salespeople, lawyers, engineers, and audit managers. At that time, word processors were just starting to act personal, so struggles with basic commands as well as avoidance and ignorance kept the focus squarely situated at the "word" level for the secretaries to handle. Why leave their dictation machines and secretaries unused? Why expose confidential documents? In any case, notions of processing information at the word level were better left for staff employees, not management.

Although electronic access to thesauruses, encyclopedias, dictionaries, and spell checkers altered most nonacademic writing practices, the focus of business employees and students has often remained at or below the word level (Shirk, 1991). Misspellings and margin problems remain on equal par with whether the right points or recommendations are made. As a result, worker complaints that too much attention is paid to trivial points (see

Locker, 1992, for examples) are often met with reminders that work teams rewriting computer manuals, company policies, or personnel records may need to focus on surface level composing and revision (Van Pelt & Gillam, 1991). Although the next few sections document tools for self-reflection, knowledge acquisition, collaboration, and high-level revision, surface-level revisionary tools clearly can benefit the writer and the text and should not always be trivialized (Beason, 1993).

Level Two: The Self Level

The eventual acceptance of word processors in the nonacademic writing environment has coincided with the advent of more powerful writing tools and resources. Tools at the self level invite reflection on one's perspective as well as building plans and goals for appropriately expressing that perspective. Self-reflection occurs when one is composing according to personal or organizational rules, conventions, goals, and standards. Tools developed at the self level include computer prompting packages, planning aids, text analysis packages, notecard systems, personal note files, and grammar and style checkers (Bonk & Reynolds, 1992; Reynolds & Bonk, 1990).

Tools for individual analysis of written products address both the surface and meaning levels of text. For instance, self-level tools such as the *Writing Partner* (Zellermayer, Salomon, Globerson, & Givon, 1991) provide guidance questions and writing hints (Daiute, 1986), whereas writing aids such as *Wandah* (Friedman & Rand, 1989) and *Writer's Workbench* (Macdonald, Frase, Gingrich, & Keenan, 1982) offer checks for spelling, punctuation, grammar, and style (e.g., readability, sentence length, and passive voice). In comparison, *Writer's Helper* (Wresch, 1984, 1988) segments writing with a number of planning, translating, and revising tools. Although many of these tools were designed for academic writing environments, other software such as *Definitions Plus* (WordScience Corporation, 1989), *Grammatik IV* (Wampler, Haines, Burch, & Moore, 1989), *Microsoft Bookshelf* (Microsoft, Inc., 1991), *Writer's Toolkit* (Systems Compatibility Corporation, 1991), and *Toolworks* (Toolworks, Inc., 1991) provide comparable assistance for corporate writers to appraise their text. While some of these later programs lead to the next level of processing by affording one with knowledge resources such as atlases, world almanacs, thesauruses, quotations, encyclopedias, dictionaries, and various other common knowledge tools, each of these tools provides opportunities for the writer to reflect on the quality of what he or she has written.

Apparently some writing tools offer an investment in writing at the word and self levels that may have immediate benefits in terms of improved writing output, self-confidence, and morale. Although these first two levels of our model operate primarily at the local or surface level of text, they are indispensable to the writing tools and operations in levels three and four. Without the word processing, outlining, spell checking, and note-taking tools of the first two levels, the knowledge and collaboration devices would have limited utility.

Level Three: The Knowledge Level

Technological advances create a frightening amount of information potentially accessible for each writing task. Neuman (1990) cited efforts worldwide that accounted for approximately 14 gigabytes or 7 million pages of humanities text in electronic form at any given time. The wealth of commercially available CD-ROMs and laser discs unequivocally points to the source of the problem—access to information in a timely and efficient manner. Nonacademic writers need to write reports with admission rights to a multitude of data sources. How will they gain access to materials required for knowledge and idea processing?

Development of information access tools may depend on viewpoints of information security and knowledge jurisdiction (i.e., power and control) as well as current notions of what writing is and who is responsible for the text. Although companies vary in knowledge intensity, the wealth of a firm is increasingly determined by how it produces and processes knowledge. As Toffler (1990) pointed out, knowledge embodies value; knowledge production and idea exchanges are no longer equated with worthless paper pushing. As shown in Fig. 12.1, level 3 of our model also values knowledge and idea processing. Knowledge explorations might occur in the workplace when one is collecting, interpreting, creating, combining, deleting, or interrelating information. Tools developed at this level include outline and timeline devices, bibliographic retrieval tools, concept mapping aids, idea generators, database and knowledge-base tools, and hypertext or hypermedia devices (Scardamalia, Bereiter, McLean, Swallow, & Woodruff, 1989).

In library systems, bibliographic retrieval tools offer a number of knowledge, idea, and language processing features. Such devices enable users to perform entire text searchers and manipulate text and visuals. Cognitive processes involved in these searches—goal formation, category selection, and information integration (Guthrie & Dreher, 1990)—will only grow in importance in nonacademic settings since accessibility to more information will not automatically result in enhanced communication (Krauss & Fussell, 1990).

More pristine compositional environments are appearing, in part, due to the design of friendlier retrieval mechanisms. Information can be incorporated into compositions from databanks worldwide. Although these resources are accessed in relatively uncomplicated ways, knowledge- and idea-level tools are not yet seamless. Most access remains at a keyword level as opposed to a propositional or basic idea level. As a result, the search capabilities of full-featured word processors unfortunately are the most primitive examples of full-text searching. Innovations will result from improved processing speeds on computers as well as from additional research and development efforts on search and retrieval mechanisms. All of these factors influence composing in nonacademic environments. From the simple graph or chart to illustrative sound bites or visual sequences, communication in the age of multimedia will involve multiple authors using multiple resources to create multifaceted documents that can be transported as far as one's knowledge- and idea-level tools and resources will allow.

As indicated earlier, new skills are demanded and advanced by this technology. Besides search skills, skills such as planning, translating, evaluating, and revising will become salient (e.g., see Lehrer's [1993] "hypercomposition" environment). Some propose that cutting-edge, knowledge-level tools will soon elevate us to an environment where the typical structure of text itself is no longer two-dimensional (Bolter, 1991), but a network of nonlinear text with unlimited space and viewpoints. As such, knowledge- and idea-level opportunities will increase. It is the opportunity to demonstrate one's linkages among units of information and the nature of these semantic relationships, however, that promotes the collaborative level discussed in the next section. Further fueling the collaborative level is the need not only to widen the social and cognitive resources, but to distribute the intellectual resources of an organization more wisely, thereby reducing technical and cognitive limitations made apparent by the tools themselves (Robertson et al., 1990).

Level Four: The Collaborative Level

Researchers advocate the use of computer tools to increase the efficiency of how people meet, discuss information, and communicate (Adams, Carlson, & Hamm, 1990; Greif, 1988, Newman, 1989). Thus, the final level discussed in this model serves to strengthen collaboration. In another essay exploring the pedagogic value of these tools, Bonk et al. (1994) described coprocessing as activities wherein teams create, reflect on, and exchange viewpoints through interactive dialogue, comments, reasoning, criticism, knowledge pooling, and conflict resolution with potential audiences and coworkers. Each of these activities simultaneously fosters reprocessing at the word, self, and knowledge levels.

There are numerous devices for communicative collaboration:

1. Electronic mail systems are the most successful form of groupware because they use prevailing metaphors of paper-based messages and other

remote interactions (Olson & Olson, 1992). E-mail systems and messaging tools allow users to send entire texts, programs, or files from one computer to the next. In a reprocessing framework, however, even casual comments received via electronic mail are considered significant to understanding the final product.

2. Remote access or delayed collaborative writing programs allow users to access and control files on remote computers and foster collegial editing and idea elaboration. Using packages such as *Carbon Copy* (Microcom, Inc., 1991) and *Timbuktu* (Farallon, Inc., 1992), reviewers can add comments to each other's documents without interfering with existing text. Perhaps, more interestingly, with *MarkUp* (Lienert & Cooper, 1992) editors can customize their palettes by creating frequently used editing symbols and then use them every time they edit a document. The writer, in turn, can view *MarkUp* comments entered by a single individual or the group as a whole. Naturally, the delayed or asynchronous nature of this type of tool has numerous advantages and disadvantages related to accessibility, interactivity, cost, and feedback.

3. Real-time dialoguing and idea generation software consists of those packages that allow for synchronous planning between two or more networked computers. *Conference Writer* (Research Design Associates, 1991) allows individuals working in a particular group to send messages to each other. A transcript window contains the results of the electronic dialogue; users also have access to a composing window for editing the message and a group window that lists the names of group members. One advantage of this package is that users can switch back and forth between discussion groups without exiting the program. According to Harasim (1989), online discussion and debate leads to thousands of interlinked ideas within a relatively short period of time.

4. Cooperative hypermedia tools allow users to share documents that contain multimedia and hypermedia capabilities. Although many tools in this category are available as prototypes, one innovative tool at this level is *Aspects* (Group Technologies, Inc., 1990), which allows up to 16 users to work on the same document from multiple locations at the same time. Text, graphics, and pictures can be jointly or individually created, inserted into documents, and shared in moments. This package has three modes for work groups to use: a free-for-all mode, in which everyone can edit the document at the same time; a medium control mode, in which group members can take turns editing by requesting the pen (i.e., keyboard); and a full mediation mode, in which a moderator decides who can edit at any point by passing the pen to one individual at a time. Obviously, each of these control modes affects the reprocessing cycle in unique but important ways.

Among the concerns for these tools are how many terminals they support and whether communication occurs from one computer to another (i.e., one-to-one communication), one computer to many computers (i.e., one-to-many), or many computers to many computers (Bonk et al., 1994). Potential quandaries over ownership rights may prompt further development of tracking mechanisms regarding who made what changes to the shared document and when. Nevertheless, the issue of real-time or delayed feedback may be most important to consider in collaborative writing because joint viewing, pointing, and modification of text and graphic information is critical to the communication process (Kraut, Egido, & Galegher, 1990) and future reprocessing episodes.

Ishii and Miyake (1991) suggested that the next generation of collaborative tools should assist users in moving easily between individual and collaborative work modes. In this way, there would be a compression between new collaborative patterns and old solo writing efforts. If adoption of these technologies keeps pace with their development, then the study of individual writers will no longer represent writing in nonacademic writing environments.

Groupware systems provide tools for idea generation and online brainstorming, idea synthesis, and ranking of ideas generated. Although the improved productivity and increased solidarity caused by using groupware has been suggested, research studying their impact on quality of decisions is still needed (Kraemer & King, 1988) as is research on tools at each of the other three levels of writing tools in the reprocessing model.

CONNECTING THE MODEL

Given the limited acceptance of word processing for corporate managers in the workplace just a decade ago, it is ironic that so many devices for teamwork and interaction are presently available (e.g., *Cognoter*, Stefik et al., 1988; *GroupSystems*, Valacich, Dennis, & Nunamaker, 1991). Technology has refocused attention on the importance of nonacademic writing. As indicated in Fig. 12.1, advances in technology and research have shifted the focus of writing investigations from the variables operating at the word level and actual texts produced (i.e., writers' in-process struggles at the point of inscription) to global or meaning-related concerns. Clearly, research and practice emphasizing one or more of these four levels currently lacks appropriate unification. In our model, we are not suggesting that effective word processing leads to meaningful knowledge processing or vice versa. Similarly, successful use of tools at the individual or self level does not guarantee more teamwork opportunities. Still, it is plausible that a concentration at the self and word levels would decrease the meaning conveyed. Perhaps an opposite concern is that collaboration and knowledge exploration activities would lead to poorly structured texts. There are many writing concerns that could arise by primarily focusing on any one of the four levels.

The vertical links in the model arise when thinking about:

- Who is involved in the writing process — a solitary writer reflecting on his or her latest budget report (i.e., a self-processor) or a team of auditors mulling over their recommendations for obsolete inventories of a struggling firm (i.e., two or more coprocessors); and
- What is the overriding focus — transcribing one's thoughts and plans into words (i.e., word processing) or elaborating, linking, combining, updating, and exploring one's ideas (i.e., knowledge processing).

The left side of the model concerns what actions are taking place, whereas the right pertains to who is taking that action. This is an interactive model, however, wherein diagonal lines might further illustrate collaborative teams reviewing and reformatting a jointly written brochure or a corporate executive such as a marketing vice president reviewing ideas accessed in a general correspondence database with the intent of writing a critical memo on employee safety. The illustration in Fig. 12.1, basically, was created to remind readers that there is a shift from individual writing environments focused on surface features of composing to a collaborative one rich in knowledge and ideas.

RESEARCH CONCERNS

As the reprocessing framework makes evident, focusing on words alone no longer suffices. As a result, researchers have shifted their focus to the processes underlying word and meaning-making choices (Bridwell, Sirc, & Brooke, 1985; Caccamise, 1987; Matsuhashi & Gordon, 1985). Researchers might embed tracking instruments within writing technologies to assist them in understanding the social interaction patterns these new forms of processing allow (Bonk et al., 1993). Such instruments verify the importance of segmenting the times when writing acts occur, recording how writers switch between word and knowledge processing, between self-analysis and teamwork, or between in-processing and postprocessing. Among the key findings to date is that collaborative writing is linked to a complex web of social relationships in the workplace (Francik et al., 1991; Perin, 1991); adding technology to the process creates new social structures and relationships that result in a reduction of employee visibility (Francik et al., 1991; Perin, 1991; Pitturo, 1989; Schrage, 1991).

Innovative analysis tools also indicate whether there is a balance or optimal configuration at the word, self, knowledge, and collaboration levels. Although our emphasis here is on tools to facilitate higher level thoughts and ideas, the use of writing technologies certainly varies by occupation. For instance, high-ranking managers and corporate executives need more tools for self-processing sensitive documents, whereas clerical staff need continued development within user-friendly "word" processing toys. Entry into and out of collaboration episodes also may be contingent on status, document type, and collaborative role (Saunders, 1989). Hence, the use of writing technologies reflects the level of management and types of tasks wherein these forms of processing increase in salience and importance.

Writing industry prophets acknowledge that these technologies will proliferate in the 1990s. A central theme here is that these advances should allow for nonacademic writers to reflect on the perspectives of potential readers (Bonk, 1990), explore new ideas, solve problems, and make decisions, not just to create neat-looking presentations or persuade people (Schrage, 1990). Unquestionably there is a pressing need for more organizational and real-time participation tools (Sarin & Greif, 1988; Wolfe, 1989). At the same time, however, important decisions remain about the nature, amount, and direction of collaborative composition in the workplace.

Authorship and Other Issues

These forms of processing what one has written lead to many issues; among the most obvious is the notion of authorship and collaboration (Weber, 1991). Because collaborative writing leads to a multitude of drafts and redrafts of one report or announcement, should anyone who provided information or comments have his or her name on the document? What if the comments were not valuable? What if one or more collaborators wish to remain anonymous? Furthermore, how will multimedia and hypermedia documents further muddle the notions of writing, authorship, and intellectual property (Landow, 1990; Selber, McGavin, Klein, & Johnson-Eilola, chap. 11, this volume)? As multimedia electronic mail and collaborative writing tools proliferate in the workplace, primary authorship over a document becomes murky and increasingly controversial (Olson & Atkins, 1990). One individual might be responsible for the text, another for charts and graphs, and still another for sound and animation. Does true "text" creation in a multimedia document determine authorship? What is the primary information source being conveyed in multimedia documents?

Bolter (1991) insightfully noted that while technology vitiates notions of copyright and intellectual property, writers seem more focused than ever on trademarks, copyrights, and securing proper permission before communicating any information. If he is correct, the benefits of the word-, self-, knowledge-, and collaborative-level tools will become blemished by internal struggles for authorship and turf. It is quite ironic, since in knowledge-intensive and collaborative writing environments it should be the content of the message that is more important than who actually produced it.

Other questions surround nonacademic writing environments at each of the four levels discussed earlier:

- Word Level: In what sort of environments will one be able to "word process?" For what sort of corporate writing tasks will simple word processing be sufficient? What features will be added to common word processors during the next decade? Will word processors be designed to toggle between knowledge and coprocessing opportunities? What will the phrase *word processing software* imply in the year 2010?

- Self Level: Will managers reward or value time spent rereading and reflecting on one's writing? How might writing tools better explicate one's composing plans and goals? What sort of tools might assist with self-analysis of written products as well as knowledge exploration and acquisition? What types of self-processing activities might flow from collaborative writing activities and vice versa?

- Knowledge Level: How are knowledge or idea processing tools selected? How do workers utilize the access to more information resources for writing? How does one query knowledge resources? What idea-level tools enliven corporate reporting without losing communicative intent? Does idea processing refocus the writer on meaningful segments of text? Will knowledge processing tools become more prominent than word processors? If yes, how does that change the role of the secretary or office manager?

- Collaboration Level: When are collaborations most important to the writing process? How are collaborations initiated? How are differences of opinion explored and negotiated? What types of tasks are facilitated by group interactions? Will collaborative tools foster new forms of socialization within the organization? How are document drafts and reviews facilitated? How will appraisals of peer talent change as collaborative technology proliferates? How might supervisor-worker relationships be altered in an intensively collaborative environment? Does workplace morale and organizational pride change in an environment that encourages collaborative interactions? How might organizational rewards match collaboration demands?

CONCLUSIONS

As networking and telecommunications tools have elevated writing activities beyond simple word processing, knowledge processing and collaborative writing environments continue to push nonacademic writing in new directions. The status of writing as a work activity and the nonacademic writing environment has irreversibly changed (Landow, 1990). Whether or not writing technologies become so familiar that they are ubiquitous (Weiser, 1991) remains questionable. It is hard to imagine a nonacademic writing environment designed for word, self, knowledge, or collaborative environments that functions invisibly to its users. Whereas word processors might be conveniently melded into most computing systems, new, less amiable knowledge exploration and collaboration software continues to infiltrate nonacademic settings.

We believe that technology will extend writing forms and practices and transform nonacademic writing environments. As technologies add to text-based systems (i.e., graphics, sound, and animation) and nurture connections for creating, viewing, organizing, manipulating, and restructuring ideas, nonacademic writers will be afforded even greater "social and intellectual connectivities" (Harasim, 1989, p. 39). The more mindful participants become of the social and cognitive processing they are engaged in when using these computer tools for writing, the greater the intellectual benefits (Salomon, 1993; Salomon et al., 1991).

Although many writing researchers accept the view that "writing is a way of knowing your own mind" (Bolter, 1991, p. 213), new processing tools offer insights into the minds of others as well as the collective mind of the team or organization (i.e., intermental functioning). "As these technologies converge to create new collaborative environments, people will discover new modes of interaction, new styles of creativity and conversation, and a desire to work with people to solve problems and craft innovations" (Schrage, 1990, p. 185).

Among our hypotheses is that opportunities created by technologies to collaborate on reports and access information provide possibilities for greater "reprocessing" of collective thought as opposed to mere retranscription or "word processing." However, Adams et al. (1990) noted that because collaboration is a complex social and cognitive process, there is no guarantee that collaboration and interaction will trigger critical reflection of one's work. Hence, although we cautiously recommend the development of software that supports higher level processes such as idea generation, text organization, and knowledge linking and integration (Glynn, Oaks, Mattocks, & Britton, 1989), we know that models regarding the social interaction processes involved in nonacademic writing are weak and limit such design.

Conceptualizations of writing as reprocessing or coprocessing highlight these limitations and boundaries; no longer can we envision writing as simply word processing. Instructional designers and researchers must consider the value of coprocessing in nonacademic settings; how people create, reflect on, and exchange ideas and viewpoints through interactive dialoguing and sharing. One need only look at the wealth of collaborative software during the past few years to understand that depersonalized, individual nonacademic writing environments are being reshaped and transformed. Individually focused cognitive models of writing governing attention during the past decade (Flower & Hayes, 1981) will give way to context-sensitive models, and technology once feared to extend our solitary working styles will instead counter workplace disconnectedness.

What emerges as ultimately critical are analyses of how writing tools complement each other at the four levels we outlined as well as specific comparisons of the benefits of different workplace collaboration tools. As tools evolve and their availability increases, the boundaries of writing models change significantly, enabling people to find opportunities to reprocess their ideas whether at the word, self, knowledge, or collaborative level without deliberate reflection on the technology; it will be woven into the basic fabric of one's work culture as well as society (Weiser, 1991). Before that occurs, we need to create, build, and share innovative models for writing for the workplace. If Bolter (1991), Galegher et al. (1990), Greif (1988), and Schrage (1990) are correct in predicting where new technological tools are steering the research, changing structures for computer-supported collaborative work, social interaction, the sharing of minds, and intellectual teamwork are all bound to increase in the workplace.

Although this transformation has not gone unnoticed, those who train future leaders for nonacademic environments need to point out the different levels of writing tools. Nonacademic writing environments will continue to be altered and shaped by ingenious technologies, simultaneously addressing writing problems as well as heightening connections between writers. Hopefully, our model of the social and cognitive processing in writing can shed light on the consequences of who is involved in various writing environments, what level of information is being attended to, and the timing of these acts in terms of the writing efforts.

REFERENCES

Adams, D., Carlson, H., & Hamm, M. (1990). *Cooperative learning & educational media: Collaborating with technology and each other.* Englewood Cliffs, NJ: Educational Technology Publications.

Andrews, J. D., & Sigband, N. B. (1984). How effectively does the "new" accountant communicate? Perceptions by practitioners and academics. *Journal of Business Communication, 21*(2), 15–24.

Beason, L. (1993). Feedback and revision in writing across the curriculum classes. *Research in the Teaching of English, 27*(4), 395–422.

Bolter, J. D. (1991). *Writing space: The computer, hypertext, and the history of writing.*

Hillsdale, NJ: Lawrence Erlbaum Associates.

Bonk, C. J. (1990). A synthesis of social-cognition and writing research. *Written Communication, 7*(1), 136–163.

Bonk, C. J., Medury, P. V., & Reynolds, T. H. (1994). Cooperative hypermedia: The marriage of collaborative writing and mediated environments. In W. M. Reed, J. K. Burton, & M. Lui (Eds.), *Multimedia and megachange* (pp. 79–124). New York: Haworth Press.

Bonk, C. J., & Reynolds, T. H. (1992). Early adolescent composing within a generative-evaluative computerized prompting framework. *Computers in Human Behavior, 8*(1), 39–62.

Bonk, C. J., Reynolds, T. H., & Koury, K. A. (1993, April). *Tracing developmental differences in composing through keystroke mapping.* Paper presented at the American Educational Research Association annual convention, Atlanta, GA.

Bridwell, L., Sirc, G., & Brooke, R. (1985). Revising and computing: Case studies of student writers. In S. W. Freedman (Ed.), *The acquisition of written language: Response and revision* (pp. 172–194). Norwood, NJ: Ablex.

Caccamise, D. J. (1987). Idea generation in writing. In A. Matsuhashi (Ed.), *Writing in real time: Modelling production processes* (pp. 224–253). Norwood, NJ: Ablex.

Daiute, C. A. (1986). Physical and cognitive factors in revising: Insights from studies of computers. *Research in the Teaching of English, 20*(2), 141–159.

Dede, C. J. (1988, April). *Implications of the possible implementation of artificial intelligence based educational devices.* Paper presented at the American Educational Association annual convention, New Orleans, LA.

Duin, A. D., Jorn, L. A., & DeBower, M. S. (1991). Collaborative writing—courseware and technology. In M. M. Lay & W. M. Karis (Eds.), *Collaborative writing in industry: Investigations in theory and practice* (pp. 146–169). Amityville, NY: Baywood.

Ely, M. (1991). *Doing qualitative research: Circles within circles.* London: Falmer.

Faigley, L. (1985). Nonacademic writing: The social perspective. In L. Odell & D. Goswami (Eds.), *Writing in nonacademic settings.* New York: Guilford.

Farallon, Inc. (1992). *Timbuktu.* Oakley, CA: Author.

Feigenbaum, E. A., & McCorduck, P. (1984). *The fifth generation: Artificial intelligence and Japan's computer challenge to the world.* New York: Signet.

Flower, L., & Hayes, J. R. (1981). A cognitive process theory of writing. *College Composition and Communication, 32,* 365–87.

Francik, E., Rudman, S. E., Cooper, D., & Levine, S. (1991). Putting innovation to work: Adoption strategies for multimedia communications systems. *Communications of the ACM, 34*(12), 74–82.

Frase, L. T., Kiefer, K. E., Smith, C. R., & Fox, M. L. (1985). Theory and practice in computer-aided composition. In S. W. Freedman (Ed.), *The acquisition of written language: Response and revision* (pp. 195–210). Norwood, NJ: Ablex.

Friedman, M., & Rand, E. (1989). A computer-based writing aid for students: Present and future. In B. K. Britton & S. M. Glynn (Eds.), *Computer writing environments: Theory, research, and design.* Hillsdale, NJ: Lawrence Erlbaum Associates.

Galegher, J., Kraut, R. E., & Egido C. (1990). *Intellectual teamwork: Social and technological foundations of cooperative work.* Hillsdale, NJ: Lawrence Erlbaum Associates.

Glynn, S. M., Oaks, D. R., Mattocks, L. F., & Britton, B. K. (1989). Computer environments for managing writers' thinking processes. In B. K. Britton & S. M. Glynn (Eds.), *Computer writing environments: Theory, research, and design* (pp. 1–16). Hillsdale, NJ: Lawrence Erlbaum Associates.

Greif, I. (1988). *Computer-supported cooperative work: A book of readings.* San Mateo, CA: Morgan Kaufmann.

Group Technologies, Inc. (1990). *Aspects.* Arlington, VA: Author.

Guthrie, J. T., & Dreher, M. J. (1990). Literacy as search: Explorations via computer. In D.

Nix & R. Spiro (Eds.), *Cognition, education, and multimedia* (pp. 65–113). Hillsdale, NJ: Lawrence Erlbaum Associates.

Halpern, J. W. (1985). An electronic odyssey. In L. Odell & D. Goswami (Eds.), *Writing in nonacademic settings.* New York: Guilford.

Harasim, L. M. (1989). Online education: An environment for collaboration and intellectual collaboration. In L. M. Harasim (Ed.), *Online education: Perspectives on a new environment* (pp. 39–64). New York: Praeger.

Ishii, H., & Miyake, N. (1991). Toward an open shared workspace: Computer and video fusion approach of teamworkstation. *Communications of the ACM, 34*(12), 36–51.

Kellogg, R. T. (1989). Idea processors: Computer aids for planning and composing text. In B. K. Britton & S. M. Glynn (Eds.), *Computer writing environments: Theory, research, and design.* Hillsdale, NJ: Lawrence Erlbaum Associates.

Kettering, R. C. (1989). Meeting the needs of the accounting profession: Requiring more student writing. *Journal of Education for Business, 65,* 64–66.

Kraemer, K., & King, J. (1988). Computer-based systems for group decision support: Status of use and problems in development. *Computing Surveys, 20*(2), 115–146.

Krauss, R. M., & Fussell, S. R. (1990). Mutual knowledge and communicative effectiveness. In J. Galegher, R. E. Kraut, & C. Egido (Eds.), *Intellectual teamwork: Social and technological foundations of cooperative work* (pp. 111–145). Hillsdale, NJ: Lawrence Erlbaum Associates.

Kraut, R. E., Egido, C., & Galegher, J. (1990). Patterns of contact and communication in scientific research collaboration. In J. Galegher, R. E. Kraut, & C. Egido (Eds.), *Intellectual teamwork: Social and technological foundations of cooperative work* (pp. 111–145). Hillsdale, NJ: Lawrence Erlbaum Associates.

Landow, G. P. (1990). Hypertext and collaborative work: The example of Intermedia. In J. Galegher, R. E. Kraut, & C. Egido (Eds.), *Intellectual teamwork: Social and technological foundations of cooperative work* (pp. 407–428). Hillsdale, NJ: Lawrence Erlbaum Associates.

Lehrer, R. (1993). Authors of knowledge. In S. Lajoie & S. Derry (Eds.), *Computers as cognitive tools* (pp. 197–227). Hillsdale, NJ: Lawrence Erlbaum Associates.

Levine, J. M., & Moreland, R. L. (1991). Culture and socialization in work groups. In L. B. Resnick, J. M. Levine, & S. T. D. Teasley (Eds.), *Perspectives on socially shared cognition* (pp. 257–279). Washington, DC: American Psychological Association.

Lienert, D., & Cooper, K. R. (1992). *MarkUp.* Agoura Hills, CA: Mainstay.

Locker, K. O. (1992). What makes a collaborative writing team successful? A case study of lawyers and social workers in a state agency. In J. Forman (Ed.), *New visions of collaborative writing* (pp. 37–62). Portsmouth, NH: Boynton/Cook, Heinemann.

Macdonald, N. H., Frase, L. T., Gingrich, P. S., & Keenan, S. A. (1982). The Writer's Workbench: Computer aids for text analysis. *Educational Psychologist, 17*(3), 172–179.

Matsuhashi, A. (1987). Revising the plan and altering the text. In A. Matsuhashi (Ed.), *Writing in real time: Modeling production processes* (pp. 197–223). Norwood, NJ: Ablex.

Matsuhashi, A., & Gordon, E. (1985). Revision, addition, and the power of the unseen text. In S. W. Freedman (Ed.), *The acquisition of written language: Response and revision* (pp. 226–249). Norwood, NJ: Ablex.

May, G. S., & Arevalo, C. (1983). Integrating effective writing skills in the accounting curriculum. *Journal of Accounting Education, 1*(1), 119–126.

Microcom, Inc. (1991). *Carbon copy.* Danbury, CT: Author.

Naisbitt, J., & Aburdene, P. (1985). *Re-inventing the corporation: Transforming your job and your company for the new information society.* New York: Warner.

Neuman, M. (1990). *States of the art: The development and cataloguing of electronic text.* Paper presented at the joint conference of the Association for Computers and the Humanities and the Association for Literacy and Linguistic Computing, Washington, DC.

Newman, D. (1989). Cognitive and technical issues in the design of educational computer networking. In L. M. Harasim (Ed.), *Online education: Perspectives on a new environment* (pp. 99–116). New York: Praeger.

Nystrand, M. (1990). Sharing words: The effects of readers on developing writers. *Written Communication, 7*(1), 3–24.

Odell, L. (1985). Beyond the text: Relations between writing and social context. In L. Odell & D. Goswami (Eds.), *Writing in nonacademic settings*. New York: Guilford.

Olson, G. M., & Atkins, D. E. (1990). Supporting collaboration with advanced multimedia electronic mail: The NSF EXPRES project. In J. Galegher, R. E., Kraut, & C. Egido (Eds.), *Intellectual teamwork: Social and technological foundations of cooperative work* (pp. 429–451). Hillsdale, NJ: Lawrence Erlbaum Associates.

Olson, G. M., & Olson, J. S. (1992). Defining a metaphor for group work. *IEEE Software, 9*, 93–95.

Olson, M. H., & Bly, S. A. (1991). The Portland Experience: A report on a distributed research group. *International Journal of Man-Machine Studies, 34*, 211–228.

Pea, R. D. (1985). Beyond amplification: Using the computer to reorganize mental functioning. *Educational Psychologist, 20*(4), 167–182.

Perin, C. (1991). Electronic social fields in bureaucracies. *Communications of the ACM, 34*(12), 74–82.

Pitturo, M. C. (1989). Computer conferencing: Brainstorming across time and space. *Management Review, 78*, 43–50.

Research Design Associates. (1991). *Conference writer*. Greenlawn, NY: Author.

Reynolds, T. H., & Bonk, C. J. (1990, May). *Windows on writing: The usefulness of keystroke mapping to monitor writing progress*. Paper presented at the sixth Computers and Writing Conference, Austin, TX.

Robertson, S. P., Zachary, W., & Black, J. B. (Eds.). (1990). *Cognition, computing, and cooperation*. Norwood, NJ: Ablex.

Rogers, P. S., & Horton, M. S. (1992). Exploring the value of face-to-face collaboration. In J. Forman (Ed.), *New visions of collaborative writing* (pp. 120–146). Portsmouth, NH: Boynton/Cook, Heinemann.

Salomon, G. (1993). On the nature of pedagogic computer tools: The case of the *Writing Partner*. In S. Lajoie & S. Derry (Eds.), *Computers as cognitive tools* (pp. 179–196). Hillsdale, NJ: Lawrence Erlbaum Associates.

Salomon, G., Perkins, D. N., & Globerson, T. (1991). Partners in cognition: Extending human intelligence with intelligent technologies. *Educational Researcher, 20*(3), 2–9.

Sarin, S., & Greif, I. (1988). Computer-based real-time conferencing systems. In I. Grief (Ed.), *Computer-supported cooperative work: A book of readings* (pp. 397–420). San Mateo, CA: Morgan Kaufmann.

Saunders, W. M. (1989). Collaborative writing tasks and peer interaction. *International Journal of Educational Research, 13*(1), 101–112.

Scardamalia, M., & Bereiter, C. (1986). Research on written composition. In M. C. Wittrock (Ed.), *Handbook of research on teaching* (3rd ed., pp. 778–803). New York: Macmillan.

Scardamalia, M., Bereiter, C., McLean, R. S., Swallow, J., & Woodruff, E. (1989). Computer supported intentional learning environments. *Journal of Educational Computing Research, 5*(1), 51–68.

Schrage, M. (1990). *Shared minds: The new technologies of collaboration*. New York: Random House.

Schrage, M. (1991). Computer tools for thinking in tandem. *Science, 253*, 505–507.

Shirk, H. N. (1991). Collaborative editing: A combination of peer and hierarchical editing techniques. In M. M. Lay & W. M. Karis (Eds.), *Collaborative writing in industry: Investigations in theory and practice* (pp. 242–261). Amityville, NY: Baywood.

Smith, G. S., & Bonk, C. J. (1992). *Alternative teaching and learning styles in the accounting *curriculum*. Unpublished manuscript, West Virginia University, Morgantown.

Stefik, M., Foster, G., Bobrow, D. G., Kahn, K., Lanning, S., & Suchman, L. (1988). Beyond the chalkboard: Computer support for collaboration and problem solving in meetings. In I. Grief (Ed.), *Computer-supported cooperative work: A book of readings* (pp. 335–366). San Mateo, CA: Morgan Kaufmann.

Systems Compatibility Corporation. (1991). *The WRITER'S TOOLKIT*. Chicago: Author.

Tatar, D. G., Foster, G., & Bobrow, D. (1991). Design for conversation: lessons from Cognoter. *International Journal of Man-Machine Studies, 34*, 185–209.

Tebeaux, E. (1985). Redesigning professional writing courses to meet the communication needs of writers in business and industry. *College Composition and Communication, 36*(4), 419–427.

Tesch, R. (1990). *Qualitative research: Analysis types and software tools*. London: Falmer.

Toffler, A. (1980). *The third wave*. New York: Bantam Books.

Toffler, A. (1990). *Power shift: Knowledge, wealth, and violence at the edge of the 21st century*. New York: Bantam Books.

Toolworks, Inc. (1991). *Toolworks reference library*. Author.

Valacich, J. S., Dennis, A. R., & Nunamaker, J. F. (1991). Electronic meeting support: The GroupSystems concept. *International Journal of Man-Machine Studies, 34*, 261–282.

Van Pelt, W., & Gillam, A. (1991). Peer collaboration and the computer-assisted classroom: Bridging the gap between academia and the workplace. In M. M. Lay & W. M. Karis (Eds.), *Collaborative writing in industry: Investigations in theory and practice* (pp. 170–205). Amityville, NY: Baywood.

Vygotsky, L. S. (1962). *Thought and language* (E. Hanfmann & G. Vakar, Trans.). Cambridge, MA: MIT Press. (Original work published 1934)

Vygotsky, L. S. (1978). *Mind in society: The development of higher psychological processes* (M. Cole, V. John-Steiner, & E. Souberman, Eds. & Trans.). Cambridge, MA: Harvard University Press.

Vygotsky, L. (1986). *Thought and language* (rev. ed.). Cambridge, MA: MIT Press.

Wampler, B. E., Haines, K., Burch, K., & Moore, M. (1989). *Grammatik IV*. San Francisco: Reference Software International.

Weber, J. R. (1991). The construction of multi-authored texts in one laboratory setting. In M. M. Lay & W. M. Karis (Eds.), *Collaborative writing in industry: Investigations in theory and practice* (pp. 49–63). Amityville, NY: Baywood.

Weiser, M. (1991, September). The computer for the 21st century. *Scientific American*, pp. 94–104.

Wertsch, J. V. (1991). *Voices of the mind: A sociocultural approach to mediated action*. Cambridge, MA: Harvard University Press.

Witte, S. P. (1985). Revising, composition theory, and research design. In S. Freedman (Ed.), *The acquisition of written language: Response and revision* (pp. 250–284). Norwood, NJ: Ablex.

Wolfe, R. (1989). Hypertextual linkages on educational computing conferencing. In L. M. Harasim (Ed.), *Hypertextual perspectives on educational computer conferencing* (pp. 215–228). New York: Praeger.

WordScience Corporation. (1989). *Definitions plus*. Concord, CA: Author.

Wresch, W. (1984). Questions, answers, and automated writing. In W. Wresch (Ed.), *The computer in composition instruction: A writer's tool* (pp. 143–153). Urbana, IL: National Council of Teachers of English.

Wresch, W. (1988). *Writer's helper: Stage II*. Iowa City, IA: Conduit.

Zellermayer, M., Salomon, G., Globerson, T., & Givon, H. (1991). Enhancing writing-related metacognitions through a computerized writing-partner. *American Educational Research Journal, 28*(2), 372–392.

13 Contextualizing Technology and Communication in a Corporate Setting

Craig J. Hansen
Metropolitan State University

To understand communication in a corporate setting, one can explore any of several defining characteristics. One characteristic has to do with time: Communicative acts are embedded within a flow of prior and subsequent interaction. Indeed, in a business setting, a document may not have any more intrinsic importance to that community than the process that created it; that is, the real value in the process may come from negotiating a consensus for the final text. Another characteristic relates to form, as the ideas constructed over time may move through many communicative forms: Informal discussion may lead to an agenda item in a meeting, which may result in a request for a document, which may in turn be presented orally in another meeting. An almost endless variety of forms are possible—from formal documents to review comments, from hallway conversations to lengthy presentations, from scrawled notes to multimedia. Not only is the relationship between oral and written texts important (Spilka, 1990; Stygall, 1991), but also the plethora of technology-mediated forms that confound traditional definitions of text [for several examples out of many, see Hansen, 1992 (range of communication technologies); Rice & Danowski, 1993 (voice mail); Selber, McGavin, Klein, & Johnson, chap. 11, this volume (hypertext); Selfe & Selfe, chap. 14 this volume (challenging views of text in networked environments); Sproull & Keisler, 1991 (computer networks); Thralls, 1992 (corporate video)]. Even with so many possibilities, form is a relatively straightforward characteristic in describing communication after the fact. Form, on the other hand, is considerably more complex for the individual doing the communicating. In a business setting, individuals choosing the form of a communicative act must balance a whole range of contextual factors from access to timeliness to appropriateness. In short, the flow of communication over time and the form communicators choose to give it are embedded within a social framework — a set of cultural expectations — that largely define how the individuals within a particular setting interact.

CONTEXT AND NONACADEMIC WRITING

The connection between context and nonacademic writing has been fruitful territory for research (Blyler & Thralls, 1992; Brady, 1993; Spilka, 1993). Nonetheless, it is a difficult concept to generalize. Witte (1992) presents a useful definition of context not tied to a specific research site, which (to paraphrase mightily) focuses on the writer's projected self in light of the writer's understanding of external reality. Context and the social perspective have much to offer in understanding the role of texts in constructing meaning, but they also raise challenging questions when applied to nonacademic research sites. The essential difficulty can be stated briefly: How can we know an unfamiliar context?

Returning to the ideas of flow and form help illustrate this difficulty. As a researcher, I can fairly easily characterize the form of a text; I can also, through various means, explore its flow in terms of precedents and antecedents. Thus, I can describe what a communicative act is and where it fits into the overall conversation. But context, in one simple word, embraces the localized social complexity of communication and all that suggests in terms of what is knowable and what transformations take place in representation. The crux of the difficulty may lie in moving from the familiar to the unfamiliar. In researching writing in the classroom, a familiar setting for many researchers, the barriers to understanding context may not be insurmountable to the extent that we can really understand the context of classroom communication from external points of view. But in many nonacademic settings, writing researchers may find themselves on alien turf (a notion well articulated by Herndl in chap. 2, this volume). Context in a business setting may involve anything from the competitive climate for an entire industry to relations among employees assigned to the same project; from the formal power relationships defined by organizational charts to informal power hierarchies based on information distribution; from managerial attempts to create unified corporate cultures to the unique aspirations of individual employees. Context, in any setting, is layered: The difficulties in its characterization are exacerbated by unfamiliar value systems and distinctly different institutional goals. Yet context can charge texts — even fairly mundane business texts such as memos and meeting minutes — with subtle ironies, implied put-downs, challenges, celebrations, and humor — all difficult to detect for the cultural outsider. For the purposes of this study, however, I chose to impose some boundaries on the idea of context.

Nonacademic writing researchers have most often used qualitative research methods to understand context, generally focusing on individuals (Winsor, 1989) or relatively small groups of employees (Brady, 1993; Cross, 1990; Doheny-Farina, 1991). My own approach is similar but perhaps foregrounds the sources of contextual knowledge to a greater extent in that I asked employees specific questions about context (defined as three layers of corporate culture), supplemented with research into the history of the corporation, where the research took place, and the industry in which it competes. It may be that making explicit the sources of contextual knowledge and relying where possible on the words of cultural insiders to describe their perceptions of context reduces some of the difficulties with representing an unfamiliar culture. This approach, of course, has its limitations: Perceptions of context will differ among any set of cultural informants so that any claim for an overall characterization of context becomes suspect; the selection of which details to present, although in informants' own words, reflect the researcher's institutional biases (Cintron, 1993; Herndl, 1991). Still, as cultures are dynamic, context may be best described as a phenomenon based in individual perception. Construction of meaning ultimately begins in the interaction among and between individuals and small groups (Duin & Hansen, 1994).

TECHNOLOGY AND CONTEXT

The balance of this chapter focuses on the relationship between context and technology (a major influence on both form and flow), providing a sociotechnological perspective on communication at a specific site. I chose this focus for several reasons. First, as noted earlier, connections between text and context are well established, as are links between context and texts over time (Brady, 1993; Witte, 1992). Second, as noted in chap. 1, connections between context and use of technology — from a communications point of view — are not as well understood. Third, choice of technology provides a useful site to illustrate a relationship between context defined as perceptions of corporate culture and decision making about communication. Many decisions about communication are fleeting, recoverable only through means such as protocol analysis. Decisions about choice of technology, on the other hand, are observable and recordable, and other means of gathering information still apply. Finally, like understanding context in unfamiliar settings, understanding the use of technology in a corporate setting presents its own challenges.

In composition and other fields concerned with communication, re-searchers have tended to study technologies as discrete entities, starting with a focus on personal computers and word processing software in the early and mid-1980s, through recent scholarship focusing on new or emerging technologies such as electronic mail over local area networks, hypertext, and multimedia (Elmore, 1991; Horn, 1993; Mabrito, 1991; Slatin, 1990). In many workplaces, and in contrast to the college or university computer lab, employees often choose among many available computer-based tech-nologies (voice mail, fax, and interactive video, in addition to those listed earlier) to communicate a particular message. In terms of technology, then, this research had two goals: first, to explore how people chose among many technological options; and second, to investigate links between employees' perceptions of their context and their use of technology to interact with other employees. And there were links. At the corporate site where I conducted my research, social factors defined the use of communication technologies. Specifically,

1. Communication technology options were determined by contextual factors at the organizational level. That is, technology deployment echoed the organization's goals, values, and conflicts.
2. Choice among the options reflected local culture. For example, widely held perceptions of uncertainty or distrust of management affected which technologies employees used to communicate.
3. Not surprisingly, individual factors, such as an employee's interest in new technology, a need for control, or a dislike of writing further affected choice among communication media.

RESEARCH METHODOLOGY

Research for this study took place at the NetCon Division of Computer Corporation. (All names are fictitious at the request of the corporation.) The research site within NetCon Division was a project team that had just begun working on the development of a new product (Product X), which was based on a technology in which NetCon had little expertise. The purpose of this project team, like other teams at NetCon, was to coordinate the various departments that took part in the product development effort. Team members included representatives from the areas of software, hardware, and performance engineering, product management, marketing, technical publications, technical customer support, and manufacturing. With Product X, coordination was particularly important, as the product combined hardware and software components. Most products at NetCon are one or the other: These two development areas within NetCon have rarely collaborated directly in developing a new product.

Within the project, several individual participants were selected as "cases." They represented a range of job descriptions, departments, and levels in the corporate hierarchy (see Table 13.1). It is important to note that the research results illustrate the relationships of context and technology among these individuals at this particular site; I do not intend them to be generalizable to all corporate settings.

Techniques for Gathering Information

I used a multiphase, qualitative research design, similar to that employed by Spilka (1990) in her study, "Orality and Literacy in the Workplace: Process and Text-Based Strategies for Multiple-Audience Adaptation." Like Spilka, I used several information gathering strategies, allowing for both methodological triangulation and the broadest coverage of group and individual communicative activities within the 6-month period of the study. (Not all results of the research are reported here; see Hansen, 1995.) Specific techniques are described next.

Project Team Meetings. With one exception, I attended all project team meetings over a 6-month period. I particularly noted any discussions that related to the activities of my participants, particularly any "texts" (presentations, memos, formal reports, manuals, etc.) they were involved in preparing, any comments about the work environment, and any discussion concerning technology use.

Questionnaire and Initial Interview. I administered a detailed questionnaire to the four research participants to meet several goals. First, I used it

TABLE 13.1
Research Participants

Participant	Background
Cara, Product Support Engineer	10 years with NetCon; solves product problems for international customers; BA, international relations and MA, library science
Kent, Development Manager	11 years with NetCon; manages software engineers; BS computer science; pursuing MS in same field
Mary, Product Manager	7 years with NetCon; recently moved from software engineering to product management; BS computer science; pursuing MBA
Scott, Technical Writer	13 years with NetCon; senior writer, primarily software documentation; undergraduate work in English, technical school certificate in computer programming

to collect simple demographic information about the participants. Second, I asked them through a series of questions to assess their communicative behavior. I included these questions to establish a baseline of their own perceptions; I later collected information on the same topics through other means. Questions in this series asked them: (a) how much of their time at work they spent writing, what kinds of documents they produced, and how they felt about writing; (b) how much of their time at work they spent reading, and how much they read as a reviewer, how much for their own information; (c) how much of their time at work they spent in meetings, formal and informal; and (d) how they used different communication technologies (including e-mail, voice mail, telephone, and fax).

Another set of questions asked them to describe the corporate culture of their department, of NetCon Division, and of Computer Corporation as a whole. These were general questions and provided a useful springboard for questions in a follow-up, audiotaped interview with each participant.

Logging and Shadowing.   Two weeks after the initial interview, I asked each participant to keep a log of their communicative activities for one week. The goal was to capture a snapshot of their communicative activities that could be compared to their self-assessment and to gain insight into each participant's mix of oral, written, and technology-mediated communicative activity. Detailed log forms were provided to each participant to record and describe acts of reading, writing, and speaking, noting start and end times for each event. However, the logs proved impractical for two of the participants (Kent and Scott). For these participants, I supplemented their log entries with additional interviews and "shadowing," where I followed these participants as they performed their jobs, asking questions and taking notes.

Writing Samples.   I collected writing samples from each participant, which I used for analysis and discourse-based interviews. However, nearly all of the samples I received contained proprietary information. This is a very sensitive issue in the computer industry; thus, I have had to use samples with care as I present them in the discussion that follows.

CORPORATE CULTURE AND TECHNOLOGY USE AT NETCON DIVISION

The sections that follow provide a description and commentary on the use of communications technologies by the four cases. To put this use in its organizational context — and to explore the impact of context on use — I have provided two kinds of information about context at NetCon. In the first section, I provide a brief historical description of NetCon based on articles in the trade press, reviews of company archives (including company newsletters and press releases), and interviews with public relations employees. This description sheds some light on the current work climate and value system at NetCon. The second section presents results from the cases, first presenting summaries of perceptions of corporate culture and then examining each person's use of communication technologies, as reported in interviews and as observed through logging/shadowing.

The Layered Cultures of NetCon Division

NetCon Division, at one time an independent company in the computer industry, had been acquired a number of years previous to the study by Computer Corporation. Shortly after the takeover, like many companies in the computer industry, Computer Corporation laid off significant numbers of employees. These reductions hit NetCon particularly hard. In addition to the impact of takeover, it appears that significant cultural shifts have taken place during the 20 years or so of NetCon's existence. Its initial entrepreneurial culture was, in Morgan's (1986) terms, solidly "organic" (p. 41). The organizational chart was relatively flat (by later standards), and work was accomplished in a project-oriented environment that consisted of teams from many departments. It appears from internal company publications that product innovation and achieving aggressive development schedules were highly valued.

However, the culture of Computer Corporation, as evidenced after the purchase, was quite different. Computer Corporation, although viewing itself as an innovative, adaptable organization, was larger, more bureaucratic—and to use Morgan's terms—more "mechanistic" (p. 25) than NetCon. What followed the acquisition was a difficult mix of Computer Corporation's dominantly mechanistic culture overlaying NetCon's organic one. Although daily work continued to follow established patterns (i.e., project-oriented work teams), a pervasive atmosphere of process control and budgetary accountability began to change interactions within those groups. This conflict is quite apparent in information gathered from research participants.

The Cases: Four Views of Corporate Contexts and Technology Use

Case One: Kent

Corporate Cultures.   Kent did not offer strong opinions about the parent company, Computer Corporation. He described it simply as "conservative": "I guess [they] do things the way that you expect. Pretty hierarchical. People have been here a long time, have done things a certain way. They listen to the same things." Kent had more to say about the culture of NetCon Division. Although he thought current upper management were more "upbeat" than the other participants, he noted that the workforce at NetCon was "mature, dominated by old-timers," and that the division was "struggling to find a new road to travel." Although fairly consistent with the other participants in his views on culture at the corporate and division levels, Kent described a more positive departmental culture, noting the mood of the group that he manages as "fairly loose and upbeat." He said that "it's better than it was. I think people are interested in the [current] project," and in comparing that to recent history at NetCon, noted that, "it's rather bizarre, actually."

Technology Use: Disparate Networks and Voice Mail.   Kent's department uses a sophisticated CASE (computer-aided software engineering) system. This system, beside providing an online environment for writing, compiling, integrating, and testing computer programs, offers an e-mail facility. But this e-mail system has limited usefulness. Kent explained: "There are a lot of e-mail systems here, but they aren't connected. We're on the Internet side of the house. Then there's the Novell side. Basically, I e-mail stuff to my people. I can't, like, e-mail stuff to hardware engineering." Question: "Do you ever converse over e-mail?" Kent: "No. It's one-ended. I don't even get a message every day. [He noted that e-mail is used primarily for departmental announcements.] It's not as important as voice mail for me. We don't have any surveillance anyway." As Kent noted, he makes heavy use of voice mail: "I hate the telephone. I really do. So voice mail frees me a lot. I can pick up messages when I want, and I can leave messages for people when they aren't there. I love voice mail, but I hate the telephone. One I'm in control, the other I'm not in control."

NetCon's voice mail system, unlike the disparate e-mail systems, is company-wide, requires very little effort to learn, and for those who are interested, offers a fairly wide range of features, including broadcasting to a specified user list, forwarding messages with comments, and storage of up to an hour's worth of messages. In many ways, it offers all of the advantages of e-mail without the effort of entering text on a keyboard. Kent's comments about "surveillance" and "control" are interesting in this context. He indirectly associated e-mail with surveillance (and he was not the only participant who made this association). By contrast, the idea that he was in control of the voice mail system makes it appear a more comfortable site for Kent to communicate, and more effective when compared to the ordinary telephone and the limited connectivity of his departmental e-mail system. In composing voice mail messages, Kent was observed to follow generally the same pattern: (a) establish the purpose (e.g., "I have a question about . . ."); (b) provide context and background (e.g., reason for request; allusion to a previous call, conversation, or document); (c) give his own perspective (e.g., a guess about the answer to his question, a possible source for the answer, a possible procedure); and (d) request an action (typically, a return call). This pattern is similar to inductive memo formats where the text builds toward a request for an action. Revision also had a role in Kent's use of voice mail. He noted: "I guess if I'm doing a group delivery, I think about what I'm going to say, and then I record it. I listen to it, and then do it again. About one out of four times I record it again."

Analysis.   The communication technology options facing Kent reflect recent history at NetCon. At the time of the study, Kent could not communicate electronically with Computer Corporation (he later received that capability), highlighting the slow integration of NetCon into Computer Corporation and, perhaps, the latter's conservative approach to conducting business. The lack of e-mail connectivity among departments is more puzzling. Given NetCon's tradition of interdepartmental project teams, one would expect that management would facilitate cooperation among departments with universal e-mail. Yet e-mail system installation occurred after NetCon's acquisition; thus, its insular configuration may not reflect tradition but more recent influences — specifically Computer Corporation's more hierarchical culture. Connecting workers across (not up) the hierarchy — enabling workers to communicate without managerial mediation — may not have seemed desirable to management. That left voice mail, at least for Kent, as the communication technology that best fit his professional and personal needs (i.e., the need to communicate asynchronously and the need to feel in control of his own communicative activities). It is interesting that for someone who indicated that he did not like writing, his composition of voice mail messages almost appeared to be writing in a different medium.

Case Two: Mary

Corporate Cultures.   Mary described the influence of Computer Corporation as "this big wave [that] keeps coming over and washing over us and changing us." Mary described the culture of NetCon Division in less active terms — in fact, as "stagnant" — noting: "It's leveled out. I don't think [morale] has increased greatly. I don't think people are jumping up around saying 'I'm glad to be working here. This is the best company in the world.' 'Cause people are still getting over the layoffs . . . People are looking at their watch. Eight hours, they're out the door."

New to her department, Mary described her department's culture in authoritarian terms: "It's kind of, well, [the overall manager of product management] jokes about it. When you say, 'Well, why are we doing it that way?' he'll laugh and say, 'Because I'm the boss,' and he'll walk away."

Use of Technology: Traditional Text and Voice Mail.   Mary spends about half of a typical work day in meetings, about a quarter of her time reading and writing, and the final quarter on the phone. Her responses to questions about communications technologies were very similar to Kent's— not surprising in that they worked in the same department for many years and have similar professional profiles. While working in software development, Mary used the same e-mail system as Kent. However, the product management department, after years of repeated requests from its workers, had just recently installed a departmental local area network with e-mail capabilities. Like the system in development, the product management system is supposed to communicate with the Computer Corporation system, but otherwise fits NetCon's pattern of incompatible networks. Mary noted: "It [the system] does go to other departments, but I couldn't tell you who right now." Mary expressed the opinion that this defeated the purpose of e-mail: "I think we should have a company system. I should be able to send a memo to anybody in this building, you know. To a janitor if I want to. The phone's a lot easier right now." Mary's use of the phone includes both the traditional, including at least one conference call a week, and voice mail. To Mary, the major benefit of voice mail is its convenience for asynchronous communication. She described composing a voice mail message in the same language she used to describe composing a memo: "For me, it's like a little letter. I think that is the format that people go through mentally."

Analysis.   Overall, Mary spends most of her work time in meetings, in verbal interaction, not with computer-based communications technologies. Even her use of voice mail is somewhat limited. And outside of meetings, most of her communicative activity centers on traditional texts. This reflects her job duties, which focus on the production of planning, marketing, and competitive analysis documents (mostly drawn from other paper documents), and the fact that product management has been slow in adopting e-mail. Yet, Mary's responses highlight the "ease of use" factor for the different technologies. With technical difficulties in installing the local area network, with procedural difficulties in sending e-mail to anyone outside of the department, the default technology for distance communication becomes the familiar telephone and the relatively straightforward enhancement of voice mail. Also, one senses in Mary's responses, as in the other cases, a certain reluctance to pursue electronic communication with Computer Corporation. This, I think, has its roots in the cultural context, in

NetCon Division's sense of separate identity. It is likely that in a more culturally integrated company, the technical obstacles in establishing company-wide e-mail connectivity would seem less significant.

Case Three: Scott

Corporate Cultures.   Like Kent, Scott found the culture of Computer Corporation conservative, but also commented on the power structure. He described Computer Corporation as "a very bureaucratic feudal oligarchy, prone to high level re-orgs that reflect shifts in power." In terms of the culture of NetCon Division, Scott contrasted the current culture with that of NetCon Division in the past: "It's different than it was. There used to be certain movers and shakers who, whether you agreed with them or not, they certainly put their stamp on things. And now that they are gone. . . . People have a strong notion that [business] is declining. Being part of something declining is really a bummer."

Scott described his own department as one that used to be very cohesive, but because he and other technical communicators had been "colocated" with product development groups instead of being located with other technical communicators, Scott thought much of this had changed: "It is easy to see how our own practices have gotten diffuse, when people don't use the same tools, or use them in the same way. They don't necessarily have the same standards applied to everybody, and we don't seem to have anybody who can bring that together."

Technology Use: Reflections on the Use of E-Mail.   Scott has nearly the same technology options as Kent: outside of face-to-face conversation, Scott can communicate with coworkers via e-mail or voice mail. For Scott, a computer network provides a unifying force for a department physically scattered throughout the building, although the network is rarely used as a site for the exchange of important ideas: "I use e-mail to get messages . . . primarily about department business, notices about both personal things — going away lunches — and business stuff — there's a new virus, check your PC. Sometimes [his manager] puts a message out there that he wants you to respond to. . . . It's useful from a business point of view, and also a social point of view, too. It helps to have something unifying." However, Scott noted that there were "no real conversations" over e-mail.

The network, like most others at NetCon, has limited connection to those in other departments. However, according to Scott ,what really prevents electronic communication between departments may be rooted in social factors rather than technical ones:

One of the things that [a previous senior manager] wanted to implement was [a special e-mail system], which is very much a conversational thing, attaching notes and comments to this data base of ideas. It pretty much just sat there. People used it to send mail, but I don't think anybody used it in the way it was intended for a kind of development way of collecting data. Someone would have an idea, and then you could attach everyone's comments to that idea. . . . I'm sure it could work, but not sure it would work here. It would take a certain culture — it would probably work great at Lotus or someplace else that's more open.

Scott attributed the lack of success for this system to several factors. First, it was implemented among a large group of engineers whose project was in jeopardy. With the uncertainty of possible reassignment or even job loss in the air, people did not want to express opinions or complain in so public a forum. Second, Scott said that he and others noticed that management did not use the system. Finally, according to Scott, although presented in a positive light by management, employees felt the system might be used to monitor them. Indeed, Scott, unlike the other participants, did not favor a division-wide e-mail capability.

But like the other participants, Scott thought highly of voice mail. He noted that it can be used to prompt people to attend meetings, by using the broadcast list feature: "It's a good, thorough thing to do." Further, Scott stated: "Voice mail is good for, well, it prevents information from getting lost. You can leave a message and the message will be there. . . . From that standpoint, it's pretty useful. You can call someone and be pretty much assured that they'll pick up the phone at some point. I think it's just primarily more certain." The voice mail system at NetCon really is not that permanent; unless a user takes special actions, the system erases stored messages at regular time intervals. However, as Kent noted, the voice mail system does provide convenient asynchronous communications, one of the major benefits reported for e-mail by researchers such as Sproull and Kiesler (1991).

When asked to comment on composing for voice mail in comparison to composing text, Scott, in contrast to Kent, does not see voice mail as a medium to convey substantive messages: "I would never leave a voice mail message that is too complex to express verbally. . . . I'll say 'Call back.' If I were trying to convince somebody of something, I wouldn't do that on the phone."

Analysis.   Scott, a technical communicator, enjoys writing. He feels more comfortable submitting more complex ideas or requests in written text. Kent finds writing "tedious" and definitely uses voice mail more extensively than Scott. Part of this may be owing to differences in job responsibilities and time constraints, but part, I think, is due to their quite different perceptions of their strengths as communicators. While many other factors may affect technology use, Scott's and Kent's choices among similar media options may be due in part to their differences as individuals.

However, corporate culture enters into Scott's technology use at another level. Scott perceives the various levels of corporate culture in somewhat more negative terms than Kent, particularly upper management. Whereas he sees e-mail as a unifying force for his department and views a sense of cohesiveness within the department as desirable, he is suspicious both of broader e-mail connectivity and of use of e-mail for substantive exchange of ideas. It could be that a certain level of distrust for corporate management has colored his view of technologies that could link employees across departments—that this kind of network, despite its stated purpose, might be a tool for management control.

Case Four: Cara

Corporate Cultures.   Cara, in contrast to the other participants, had daily contact with Computer Corporation's bureaucracy and voiced strong opinions:

> To me they seem—this is just based on impressions—extremely bottom-line oriented. . . . This division used to be real innovation-oriented. And to make employees not think that [it is bottom-line oriented], they pull out some MBA's latest book on management theory and say, "Ahh, we're supposed to have these kind of groups, right? Mission statements, circles of influence." And then there's a flurry of memos. . . . Here's the form you will fill out when you innovate. . . . I don't recall that anything ever got done from any of those.

In contrast to Kent, Cara thought morale was still rather low at NetCon Division: "It still seems pretty downbeat to me. You probably get a sense of community on the small level, but I don't see any division-wide pulling together. I see departments at odds with each other as much as before." Cara described the working environment within her department also as "downbeat" but with complexities:

> There is a huge number of open problems [on products at customer sites] to deal with . . . and there hasn't been money to get more people, so we aren't gaining on the problems. The foreign customers get mad and send angry faxes. . . . People have openly talked to recruiters on the telephone, to their own personal headhunter. Or they set up interviews. They talk amongst each other when they all interview at the same place! But on the other hand, they all have a sense of community, of togetherness. I'm not including me, just them. They are the us-against-them kind of people. . . . So in my department, they have similar backgrounds—age, status, education, things like that. So

depending on how you define culture, it's either very bad or very good. It's complicated.

Use of Technology: Hierarchical Networks and Fax.   Cara's job is very different from those of the other participants. Their jobs, in one way or another, concern the development of new products for NetCon. Cara supports NetCon's existing products; that is, she identifies solutions to errors (program or human) in NetCon's software products. A brief description of this support process is necessary here. When customers experience a problem, they first contact a local support representative. If the local person cannot solve the problem, that support person, or the customer, calls NetCon Division directly for a higher level of technical support. Cara provides this kind of support for international customers. As problems arrive, they are logged into a problem tracking database implemented on a mainframe-based, hierarchical network. It is 15- or 20-year-old technology. Cara's department does have e-mail capability that is accessible even to customers, but it is not heavily used. She noted: "I know we have e-mail. Every time I turn on my PC in the morning it says 'you have no e-mail.' It definitely is not used much internally."

However, although there are no real conversations over e-mail, support engineers have learned to use the problem tracking database as a kind of forum where people can reference each other's work and exchange ideas more actively than on any of the e-mail systems I observed at NetCon. This is not an easy system to use for this purpose: They have adopted a single response area for this, an assigned *field* for providing problem descriptions that permits the entry of free-form text. They refer to this internally as the *status text*. The system does not allow status text entries to be specifically addressed to individuals; however, individual support engineers locate status texts that interest them by referencing problem numbers. They can then enter additional comments to the status text if they wish.

Some exchanges I reviewed in status text fields went on for several days with a variety of support and development engineers involved. In these written conversations, they reference past solutions, documentation, and common experiences. It can become an even larger conversation. Some local support engineers and large customers have access to the problem tracking system but do not have the system security clearance to add to the status text. They read the status text and join the discussion through phone calls, memos, or faxes; often, summaries of their comments are included by engineers who have the required level of clearance.

Fax is another important technology of communication to Cara and the other support engineers — much more important, it appeared, than to the other research participants. In dealing with international customers, Cara must deal with language barriers and significant time differences:

Some people seem to use the phone [to communicate with customers]. It's hard enough just to hear someone long distance on the phone, with the accent on top of that. In talking to places in Africa, you have to be careful taking turns. When I talk, he can't; and when he talks, I have to wait. I have a tendency to interrupt. I had to curb that, and to laugh! I'd lose half a sentence because I laughed. I'm just not polite. So I just send a fax, especially with the time differences. You can fax anytime.

Fax permits virtually instantaneous communication, but minimizes, among other things, the possible pitfalls of different cultural styles of conversation. Voice mail could overcome the time differences, but the need of both engineer and customer in this setting is for highly detailed technical information. Cara noted that fax communication allows the support engineers to specify exactly what kind of information they need from customers.

Analysis.   Cara's case is particularly illuminating for two reasons. First, in a department where she feels marginalized in everyday interaction, Cara contributed regularly to the "status text" conversations, where her technical insight was valued in group problem solving. Cultural norms shifted in this context: instead of gender, common background, or a shared "us against them attitude" that characterized the support department (at least as described by Cara), technical expertise is what counted in the problem tracking system. This is not so much a case of a communications technology masking cues to culture, ethnicity, or gender, as a case of a shift in the value system within the world of the computer system.

Also, the use of the system itself is interesting. It was so dated, had such a complex user interface, and seemed so inflexible that, in my original research plan, I almost ignored it. However, the support engineers felt a strong need to collaborate, an important need to share technical information. The problem tracking system provided a means to accomplish this—between adjacent offices as well as geographically dispersed sites. It provided a site for communication that was all their own as employees in other departments had no interest in using the system, and it was unlikely that management outside of the department, who are viewed with some distrust, would go to the trouble of reviewing status text entries. In contrast to the e-mail system, where electronic communication was possible between NetCon and Computer Corporation but nobody really wanted to communicate, the users here adapted a very difficult computer system to become a vehicle for the vital exchange of ideas. In short, what the problem tracking system illustrates is that (a) a real need must exist to use the technology, (b) the system has to connect the people necessary to carry on the conversation, and (c) a technology can reinforce a sense of community insofar as it is not likely to be monitored. This use of the problem tracking system was not part of overall corporate communication planning, not an anticipated use of technology; yet, it illustrates how important contextual factors become in choice of technology.

Another reason Cara's case is interesting centers on the use of fax technology. Here the contextual factors are not based in perceptions of corporate culture but in the realities of international business. Extensive use of fax with international customers allows Cara and her coworkers to simplify potential language problems, accurately transfer technical information, avoid the time zone difficulties of phone conversation—and still, when required, have virtually instantaneous communication. Fax combines the familiarity of paper with the speed of synchronous phone lines.

DISCUSSION

Table 13.2 summarizes the findings from the case studies. In reviewing theses cases it is important to note, first, that much is missing. I focused on only selected computer-based communications technologies: Others are also relevant. Some of the participants spend a great deal of time at their PCs—

TABLE 13.2
Summary of Cases

Case	Perceptions of Context	Technology Choices	Technology Favored
Kent	Task-oriented departmental culture; awareness of low morale in division	Voice mail; CASE-based e-mail	Voice mail, due to lack of e-mail connectivity, preponderance of short messages, dislike of writing
Mary	Authoritarian departmental culture; awareness of low morale in division	Voice mail; LAN-based e-mail	Voice mail, due to ease of use, lack of departmental use of e-mail; most comfortable with traditional text
Scott	Downsized and "colocated" department; lack of confidence in upper management	Voice mail; LAN-based e-mail	Voice mail for daily interaction; e-mail for routine notices only, due to perceived surveillance
Cara	Cohesive departmental culture to which she felt marginalized; lack of confidence in upper management	Voice mail; problem tracking system; fax; LAN-based e-mail	Problem tracing system for substantive messages; fax for international; less use of voice mail; little use e-mail

particularly Mary and Scott — writing formal documents, creating spreadsheets, graphics, and so on. The communications technologies I examined in this section, those that facilitate the exchange of ideas, relate to their work but are often not the real core of it. Kent, too, spends a good deal of time composing text on his PC; for him, however, the text is more likely to be brief memos. His employees write the formal reports. Cara, whose story I found the most interesting from a sociotechnological perspective, uses those technologies as the main focus of her work at NetCon. Not surprisingly, there is more richness here. And all of the participants spend a good deal of time in verbal interaction, in meetings and other sites of formal and informal communication.

Second, the use of different communications technologies reflects the preferences of different personalities. Scott and Cara prefer to use forms of communication that are text-based. Kent, who prefers to avoid writing, communicates more through verbal media. Job responsibilities also contribute significantly to choice of media. This may seem like a fairly obvious observation, but it underscores a more important and perhaps more subtle point. Most corporate management focus on providing the latest technologies — in the interest of increasing employee productivity — under a deeply seated assumption that each new system improves upon the last. But what may better meet their needs is a focus on the employees, not the technology. A rich variety of communication technologies for all employees (generally, variety comes with a higher position in the hierarchy) may permit employees to accomplish organizational goals by means most appropriate for a given task.

Third, the social context, the culture at NetCon, clearly interrelates to the implementation of communications technologies. I found it interesting that a division that focuses much of its product energy on computer networks, and like the rest of the computer industry, on so-called open systems (i.e., the development of compatible communications across many vendors' products), has such an uncoordinated tangle of computer networks. This, I believe, has resulted from the lack of cohesiveness that grew out of the period of employee layoffs. Indeed, it may reflect an even earlier trend as strong departments supplanted a culture that was weakened by its assimilation within Computer Corporation. These strong departmental identities may have caused internetworking at the divisional level to seem unattractive, perhaps even threatening. (One could turn this argument around and say that the lack of interconnected networks contributes to the feeling of uncertainty.)

In general, voice mail seems to be the most important communications technology among the employees I observed. All the participants used it; all felt positive about its use. Unlike the e-mail systems, voice mail crosses departmental boundaries at NetCon, offers fairly sophisticated features and message storage, is instantaneous, and in light of the context, lacks the apparent permanence that might undercut the attractiveness of technologies such as e-mail. Further, composing a voice mail message seems to draw on generalized composing processes. Based on what I observed, it does not appear all that different from writing, although this clearly needs more research. Fax is similar to voice mail in that it draws on the universal telephone network, similar to e-mail in that it involves written text, but different from both in that it produces an instant physical artifact. It is interesting that Cara uses fax transmissions with customers, but primarily uses the telephone in dealing with Computer Corporation.

CONCLUSION

This research raises several issues. First, a focus purely on written text in a corporate setting would do little to reveal the complexities of composed, planned communication. If we accept writing as a social activity, as part of a constructive process that builds shared concepts of reality, we must consider its place in the overall flow of communication over time, in communication that takes many forms. Even in the very limited setting considered here, one can see that text can be broadly defined to include written documents, various types of electronic texts, and voice mail. Second, defining context so that its impacts can be explored and communicated to others unfamiliar with a particular setting (i.e., through publication) can only be considered satisfactory if it is understood to be limited, perhaps temporary, and in a sense, individualistic. The brief summaries here of participants' perceptions provide some insight into how they experienced their workplace, but the primary interpretive effort, including application of the historical research (which I think proved very useful), comes from the researcher.

Third, it would have been difficult to predict the use of technology at this site or understand the importance of users' choices if one ignored the social context. The sociotechnological perspective that grounded the research questions helps highlight that complex relationship. Use of technology was determined in part by what management made available, which in the case of e-mail networks reflected a lack of coordination between NetCon and Computer Corporation, and by how employees perceived the communication context around them. This sociotechnological analysis resulted in what were to me surprising decisions, such as the support engineers' preference for the problem tracking system over media that were significantly easier to use. Finally, clear links existed between participants' perceptions of context and their choices of communication technology, often relating to participants' sense of privacy in an environment of uncertainty, but also linked to issues such as convenience and a personal sense of control.

None of the technologies considered here are new or emerging. Technologies such as multimedia and virtual reality will strain our definitions of text even more fundamentally and may profoundly affect contexts of communication. To stay relevant as commentators on communication, we must continue our focus on composed communication—but we must be willing to explore it in many forms. We should also, as suggested here, include in our focus how people construct meaning over time and over a variety of media. Finally, as we explore communication in an increasing variety of nonacademic settings, we must give careful thought to how we learn about specific contexts, how we qualify our understanding, and how we convey our interpretations to professional and academic audiences.

REFERENCES

Blyler, N. R., & Thralls, C. (1992). *Professional communication: The social perspective.* Newbury Park, CA: Sage.

Brady, L. (1993). A contextual theory for business writing. *Journal of Business Communication, 7*(4), 452–471

Cross, G. (1990). A Bahktian exploration of factors affecting the collaborative writing of an executive letter of an annual report. *Research in the Teaching of English, 24*(2), 173–202.

Doheny-Farina, S. (1991). Creating a text/creating a company: The role of a text in the rise and decline of a new organization. In C. Bazerman & J. Paradis (Eds.), *Textual dynamics of the professions: Historical and contemporary studies of writing in professional communities* (pp. 306–335). Madison: University of Wisconsin Press.

Duin, A. H., & Hansen, C. J.. (1994). Computer networks as social construction and social interaction: An overview. In C. Selfe & S. Hilligoss (Eds.), *Computers and literacy* (pp. 89–112). New York: Modern Language Association.

Cintron, R. (1993). Wearing a pith helmet at a sly angle: Or, can writing researchers do ethnography in a postmodern era? *Written Communication, 10*(3), 371–412.

Elmore, G. (1991). Planning and developing a multimedia learning environment. *Technological Horizons in Education Journal, 19*(7), 83–90.

Hansen, C. J. (1992). Communication technologies in corporate settings. *Bulletin of the Association of Business Communication, 60*(4), 3–9.

Hansen, C. J. (1995). Writing the project team: Authority and intertextuality in a corporate setting. *Journal of Business Communication, 32*(2), 103–123.

Herndl, C. (1991). Writing ethnography: Representation, rhetoric, and institutional practices. *College English, 53*(3), 320–332.

Horn, W. D. (1993). Network collaboration with UNIX. *Technical Communication Quarterly, 2*(4), 413–429.

Mabrito, M. (1991). Electronic mail as a vehicle for peer response. *Written Communication, 8*(4), 509–532.

Morgan, G. (1986). *Images of organization.* Newbury Park, CA: Sage.

Rice, R., & Danowski, J. (1993). Is it really just like a fancy answering machine? Comparing semantic networks of different types of voice mail users. *Journal of Business Communication, 30*(4), 369–399.

Slatin, J. (1990). Reading hypertext: Order and coherence in a new medium. *College English, 52*(8), 870–883.

Spilka, R. (1990). Orality and literacy in the workplace: Process and text-based strategies for multiple-audience adaptation. *Journal of Business and Technical Communication, 4*(1), 44–67.

Sproull, L., & Kiesler, S. (1991). *Connections: New ways of working in the networked organization.* Cambridge, MA: MIT Press.

Stygall, G. (1991). Texts in oral contexts: The "transmission" of jury instructions in an Indiana trial. In C. Bazerman & J. Paradis (Eds.), *Textual dynamics of the professions: Historical and contemporary studies of writing in professional communities* (pp. 234–255). Madison: University of Wisconsin Press.

Thralls, C. (1992). Rites and ceremonials: Corporate video and construction of social realities in modern organizations. *Journal of Business and Technical Communication, 6*(4), 381–402.

Winsor, D. (1989). An engineer's writing and the corporate construction of knowledge. *Written Communication, 6*(3), 270–285.

Witte, S. (1992). Context, text, intertext: Toward a constructivist semiotic of writing. *Written Communication, 9*(2), 237–308.

14
Writing as Democratic Social Action in a Technological World: Politicizing and Inhabiting Virtual Landscapes

Cynthia L. Selfe
Richard J. Selfe, Jr.
Michigan Technological University

Our intention in this chapter is to identify some of the complex social, cultural, and political forces articulated with the use of computers as wide-area communication devices in workplaces and schools, and to explore both the promise and the terror that come bundled with these electronic communicative networks as they are now designed and used in corporate and public settings. Our goal is to explain why teachers and students of nonacademic writing (our focus here is technical communication) should learn to navigate these discursive territories with purpose and hope.

The analysis we offer is based on three major assumptions that grow out of recent attention to social and political theories of communication and to the ways in which communication practices are enacted in social and political settings. First, we assume there should be some degree of commitment, on the part of most educated individuals, to an increasingly democratic social project—although both the degree and scope of this commitment may vary widely.[1] We maintain that teachers and students of

---

[1] Our personal commitment is best described by the project of "radical democracy," as outlined in the work of Laclau and Mouffe (1985). As we understand it, this project involves the "spread of liberty and equality into increasingly wider domains" (p. 155), but always with the recognition that radical democracy is "a form of politics which is founded not upon a dogmatic postulation of any 'essence of the social,' but, on the contrary, on affirmation of the contingency and ambiguity of every 'essence,' and on the constitutive character of social division and antagonism" (p. 193). As Laclau and Mouffe (1985) point out, carrying out the project of radical democratic politics depends on our ability to identify the "discursive conditions for the emergence of a collective action, directed toward struggling against inequalities and challenging relations of subordination" (p. 153).

nonacademic writing, like other informed and educated citizens, have a civic responsibility to work actively in both local and global arenas to challenge inequities based on oppression, and a civic obligation to enact positive social and political change. We also recognize that such change is enacted only in ways that are partial, momentary, contradictory, and fragmented (cf. de Certeau, 1984; Laclau & Mouffe, 1985).

Second, we recognize that communication, language, is the primary medium for change and reform—as well as stasis—in any culture. Communication, further, is a complex social and political phenomenon itself. This recognition means, at least on some levels, that communication will resist systematic codification, control, and direct instruction (cf. Kent, 1989; Thralls & Blyler, 1993).

Third, our discussion presumes that professionals writing in the workplace, and teachers and students writing in technical communication classrooms, are linked by these issues surrounding language, civic responsibility, and social action. As a result, we believe that technical communicators in the workplace and technical communication scholars in classroom settings should be connected to each other by multiple means of communication. Both groups, although constituted by complex and multiple identities and subject positions, are also part of a larger community that, at some level, shares common purposes, discourses, and responsibilities for social change.

WHY CONNECT COMPUTERS AND COMMUNICATORS? A NARRATIVE AND EXPLORATION

The narrative we want to recount occurred approximately 2 years ago on a *computer listserv*, an online discussion group involving a number of participants—often, although not always, located at different geographical sites. This particular electronic forum, called *TECHWR-L*[2], focuses on the discussion of issues important to technical communicators. We tell this story because it seems to illustrate some of the complexities we wish to frame in this chapter and provides a good point of departure for later analyses.

In the online discussion we want to describe, one participant, called Jackie for the purposes of this chapter, stated that she had been asked to justify why she needed access to Internet as a part of her work as a technical communicator. Jackie sent the following message (TECHWR-L, 1993):

---

[2]*TECHWR-L* (Technical Writers List; for all Technical Communication issues) is a listserv maintained at Oklahoma State University. The e-mail address of this valuable resource is TECHWR-L@VM1.UCC.OKSTATE.EDU).

From: Jackie
Subject: Justifying Internet Access

This message is directed to technical writers and Tech Comm managers who enjoy global network access (which is probably all of us).

The questions: Have you ever been in the position to have to justify having Internet access? If so, how did you do it? If you are a manager, what benefits do you see in letting your workers have the ability to communicate on a global network?

If you care to know why I'm asking these questions, read on:

The story: Less than a month ago, I obtained my address to use my company's Internet connection, which has only existed a few months. Because of the current setup, I did this through a site administrator, but without my supervisor knowing. (Yes, this was a mistake, for I was not trying to be sneaky, just trying to be direct.) Since then, he saw me using my E-mail interface, asked me what it was, and I feebly tried to explain its capabilities. Because I don't want to appear devious, I am preparing a memo to tell my manager what I am using the Internet for and what its benefits are—which leads me to the above questions.

Background info: My manager can be reasonable, but he is admittedly not a high-tech sort of guy. He has also said, "All the information you need can be found within this department," which I think was a hasty statement because it cannot be possible.

For those of you who know my boss, please understand that there are things that I admire about him.

Help me if you can.

The manager's reaction to Jackie's use of Internet, and his remarkable claim about the knowledge Jackie needed to accomplish her work, helps to define, at least in part, a set of commonly held beliefs about the work of technical communicators that is frequently embedded in technical communication textbooks (Ornatowski, 1992; Sullivan, 1990; Zappen, 1987) and that rests at the heart of descriptions about technical communication as an activity. These beliefs are stated simply in the following terms: Technical communicators have enough to accomplish without getting mired down in extraorganizational issues that may distract us from maintaining an edge in an increasingly competitive market environment. As a group of communicators, we are self-contained within our corporate structure; our writing is a small part of a larger process; and we are responsible only to the corporation for the products we produce. The primary characteristics of this argument include a value on corporate loyalty and competitiveness and a rejection of the notion that corporate culture is a necessary and influential element of a larger public sphere. Jackie's response represents, then, a resistance to the notion that technical communication involves a fundamental obligation to serve the interests of the public as well as the employer.

This set of corporate arguments, and the philosophical assumptions they imply, has come under substantial criticism in the last 5 years. A good part of this criticism focuses on the fact that such arguments unnecessarily, and indeed inaccurately, limit the scope of social responsibility of technical communicators in ways that may not be desirable for our culture. Additional criticism stems from the realization that such arguments constitute an identity for technical communicators that is essentialist because it denies the real social and political complexity of their work (Killingsworth, 1992; T. P. Miller, 1991; Mouffe, 1992; Ornatowski, 1992; Sullivan, 1990; Zappen, 1987).

In contrast to this isolationist vision of technical communication as work located within a single department or corporate entity, the online group of communicators to whom Jackie applied for help clearly located its own identity *outside* the boundaries of any single corporation and within a larger public sphere. In its electronic discourse, this group identifies itself as an expanded community of contacts who share common concerns that extend beyond those of their individual employers. Participants on TECHWR-L responded to Jackie's call for help in a way much more apropos of what Sullivan (1990) called for in his essay, "Political-Ethical Implications of Defining Technical Communication as a Practice." Within this piece, which is based on classical rhetorical theory, Sullivan argued for a community of technical communicators that assumes social action as a broad professional responsibility. The participants in TECHWR-L (1993) responded to Jackie as a extracorporate extension of her own local community, and in doing so, defined both her work and their own in terms of an expanded public culture. A quick look at some of the arguments and strategies generated by the group within the next 3 days is illustrative. (We have cited these entries either by the name of the author or by the list name, depending on their request when they granted permission to quote.)

> Keep the memo short. Nothing flowery. No arm-waving. Nothing fuzzy or sociological. Don't even try to be comprehensive. Just a few solid nuts and bolts. ('When the going gets tough, the tough get empirical'—Jon Carroll). . . . If you want to be comprehensive, get a copy of the Whole Internet Guide and plunk it down on your boss' desk. (d'Albenas, 1993)

> The information we've been getting on copyrights [from internet] . . . was more valuable than the info I received when we retained a copyright law specialist last year. (d'Albenas, 1993)

> DO NOT talk about how the Internet helps you do volunteer executive work for your STC chapter. (d'Albenas, 1993)

[After a listing of the names of 59 major corporations excerpted from THE INTERNET LETTER, Vol. 1, No. 1 October 1993]. . . . Given the choice names here, it would seem to me that commercial firms will soon have a hard time justifying *not* being on the Internet. (Showalter, 1993)

[You can receive] information and experience with DTP [desktop publishing] and other products, with indexing, writing formats, etc. (TECHWR-L, 1993)

A simple, non-technical analogy . . . would be a comparison to the telephone. If 'all the information you need can be found within this department,' that's like saying you can do your job without the use of a phone. (TECHWR-L, 1993)

Email is:
- as fast as the phone, but both parties don't have to be available at the same time
- provides immediate access (75% of business calls never get through)
- leaves a written record
- can send messages to multiple recipients at once. (Mitchell, 1993)

[W]e receive material for publication by e-mail (from all over the world) as well as by the postal service, which is worth it if only for what it saves in re-keying. (Rosenzweig, 1993)

This mailing list (and other work-related ones) are resources a lot cheaper than sending people to conferences. (Rosenzweig, 1993)

For us, it interesting to note some of the implications of these suggestions, among them the following:

• Conversations going on within this electronic landscape acknowledge the reality of corporate competitiveness, which in part depends on maintaining information locally and in secret, while identifying the value of collaborative professional exchanges that extend across corporate boundaries.
• This TECHWR-L exchange seems to belie the concept of technical communication as an activity located solely within particular corporate sites.
• This group of technical communicators have assumed subject positions linked to a world beyond the office, indeed beyond national borders.
• These technical communicators recognize a responsibility to contribute *pro bono publico* within larger professional groups that have an extended influence beyond corporate boundaries. The Internet provides them one way of fulfilling this obligation although this work may not be valued on a local basis.

The two conceptions of technical communication illustrated by this narrative—one focused on the private ownership, location, and uses of communication, and one acknowledging a public ownership, location, and uses of communication—identify an important disjunction that complicates the social and political identities of technical communicators. Among the questions that this disjunction raises are the following: To whom are technical communicators responsible? Their corporate employers? The public who uses the corporation's products? The professional societies to which they belong? Who is responsible for the information that technical communicators produce? Who controls the information technical communicators produce? Why is this so? Whose interests are being served in controlling information and in defining the various roles and responsibilities of technical communicators in the way that we now do?

These questions, and others, help define the parameters of a complex debate currently going on among both academics and workplace practitioners about the nature of technical communication as a profession, the multiple roles that technical communicators assume as employees and citizens, and the preparatory education that technical communicators need in order to conduct themselves responsibly within these roles.

THE CHANGING NATURE OF TECHNICAL COMMUNICATION PROGRAMS: THINKING IN BROADER TERMS

In the last half of this decade, the questions that we have identified have begun to influence the ways in which educators prepare students to enter the U.S. workforce. Faced with these unsettling issues, many educators have been forced to reconsider their own responsibilities and identities, as well: to see themselves less as instructors of writing skills in a narrow sense and more as teachers of communication in a field that has broadened considerably in its scope. During this time, teachers of business and technical communication have expressed increasing interest in social theories that help them and the students with whom they work come to a broader understanding of discourse and its roles in shaping cultural formations (e.g., feminism, Marxism, radical democracy, socialism); and address the role of writing and other discursive practices in formulating, examining, and enacting civic responsibilities within broader social arenas (cf., Cooper and Holzman, 1989; Kinneavy, 1982; Stotsky, chap. 10, this volume; Sullivan, 1990). Teachers of business and technical communication have also begun to explore how their own educational responsibilities relate to the expanded program of democratic social action that now informs critical pedagogy, liberatory pedagogy, rhetorical theory, composition studies, and cultural studies (cf. T. P. Miller, 1991; Sullivan, 1990; Waddell, 1990).

As a result of these explorations, the teaching of professional and technical writing, of nonacademic writing, has also begun to expand in dramatic ways. Many programs now include the study of ethics, decision making, social policy formation, rhetorical theory, or risk communication. Increasingly, professional writing courses within these programs are designed to impart to writers not only a sense of responsibility within corporate contexts, but also a sense of responsibility within broader social and civic spheres. Inspired, further, by the direct connections that have been established between the professional practice of technical communication and the social/political decision making in cases such as the Challenger disaster (Moore, 1992; Winsor, 1988) and recombinant DNA research (Waddell, 1990), professional educators are beginning to perceive their responsibility not only as teachers of writing skills, but also as transformative intellectuals who must pass along to communicators both a sense of "public responsibility" (Giroux, 1992, p. 15) and "civic courage" (p. 74).

These perspectives, it is clear, may require communicators to undertake political or civic action that is radically opposed to the official status quo or to a narrow sense of corporate interests. Given this recognition, educators have begun to reason that technical communicators need the ability to think *against* the grain of prevailing thought as well as *with* it. Without this ability, technical communicators, and indeed all students who populate our schools, may prove unable to influence, shape, or change technological and political decision making within the public spheres they inhabit as workers and citizens. As a major part of this expanded course of study, teachers of professional and technical communication are recognizing the need to pass along to students an expanded vision of democratic citizenship and involvement, a sense of the importance of public debate over science policy, and an critical consciousness about the role of language in weaving the cultural fabric of a democratic society (Stotsky, chap. 10, this volume).

Enacting such new pedagogical directions in a meaningful way, however—especially within traditional professional writing or technical writing classrooms—has proven difficult, given the general influence of dominant cultural tendencies (Shor, 1987), the constraints of traditional classrooms (Foucault, 1979), the dynamics of the larger educational system (cf. Foucault, 1979; Hawisher & Selfe, 1993; Shor, 1987), and the expectations of industry. Faced with these tendential social forces, both teachers of written communication and students may find it easier to think and to write *within* the bounds of conventional thinking than outside of them. Educating students to question decisions, to involve themselves in broader social programs, to engage in debates concerning public policy often creates problematic educational feedback. Such feedback comes from parents, who are understandably concerned about the expanded course of study and the effects it will have on their children's future in the workforce; from the public, which may be exposed to students practicing their craft in less that skillful ways within high-stakes arenas; from administrators, who must cope with the institutional costs of an expanded curriculum in technical communication programs.

Similarly, practicing communicators—like Jackie in our earlier example—often find it easier to practice written communication that supports the existing goals of a company, an organization, or an assignment than to resist and interrogate these goals. As Jackie found out, the task of identifying and gaining access to spaces in which writing is recognized and practiced as an activity involving larger social and political dimensions is difficult, albeit possible. At the time of publishing, Jackie had not only kept her access to the technical writing discussion group on Internet, but, by her own admission, made inroads with her supervisor who modified his concept of the corporate good. Equally difficult is the task of coping with the related responsibilities of reflecting on the complexities, subtleties, and challenges of such writing. Often, writers in nonacademic settings perceive themselves as caught in webs of social, economic, and political forces that work against productive social action or involvement—in discursive situations that take place both on and off computers. These individuals may, indeed, avoid talking about writing as a means of participating in expanded social projects because such talk is perceived as dangerous, contentious, or disloyal within existing organizational settings.

TURNING TO THE NETS AS LANDSCAPES FOR AN EXPANDED CURRICULUM: PROMISE AND PROBLEMS

As we have indicated, one area that indicates some potential for supporting an expanded conceptual framework for technical and professional writing is that of computer networks. For the last 8 years, technical communication and composition specialists have devoted increasingly large portions of their scholarly attention to the study of electronic forums—discursive spaces created on local-area networks (LANs) and wide-area networks (WANs)—as alternative communication spaces for professional writers, and for teachers and students of writing. The primary focus of the interest in these forums, to date, has been on the value of the virtual landscapes of networks as alternative communication spaces that have the potential for supporting learning and discursive practices that can be different from, and—some claim — more democratic than, those occurring within traditional corporate or classroom settings.

Claims made for networks in industry, for example, have indicated that they may provide a low-cost, time-efficient forum for communication among expanded communities of individuals and groups; that they may increase the opportunities for democratic participation in problem-solving tasks; that they may encourage individuals to share information across corporate sites in increasingly altruistic ways; that they may encourage expanded opportunities for professional development; and that they may support more responsive, intimate communication environments than do conventional settings for exchange (cf. Hiltz & Turoff, 1993; Kiesler, Siegel, & McGuire, 1984; Mason, 1993; Sproull & Kiesler, 1991). Related claims for computer networks as alternative learning environments in educational settings indicate that they can be structured to provide for student-centered, online discussion groups in which individuals discover their own motivations for using language through actual practice; for online conferences in which writers' race, gender, age, and sexual orientation may not figure in the same ways that they do in more conventional face-to-face settings; for collaborative groups and online editing groups in which students learn to negotiate discursive power for themselves; and for self-sponsored written exchanges among expanded social communities (cf. Barker & Kemp, 1990; Cooper & Selfe, 1990; Eldred, 1989; Handa, 1990; Spitzer, 1989).

Through this work, we have come to recognize some of the potential of computer-supported forums, to see them as intriguing micropolitical spaces within which technical communicators, and teachers and students of technical communication, can seek to address, on a relatively localized level (within a particular classroom or business setting, for example), some of the problems currently plaguing our educational system and corporate culture (Cooper & Selfe, 1990; Forman, 1992; Hawisher & Selfe, 1993; Sproull & Kiesler, 1991). Given this set of circumstances — educational, social, corporate — the widespread exploration of these electronic discursive spaces has become important not only for many technical communication teachers and students, but also for writers and technical communicators in corporate environments.

Importantly, however, we have not yet paid enough attention to the many problems associated with educational and professional discourse within virtual landscapes or to the complicated political issues that permeate and shape communication on networks. Frequently, we have been content to portray these electronic landscapes as one-dimensional, utopian spaces — open to progressive and reformist influences, but not to conservative forces. It is becoming increasingly clear that if these virtual landscapes are conducive to productive discursive involvement in larger social and political arenas, they are also complex, hotly contested public territories shaped by a set of dominant social forces which generally influence and limit this involvement in certain directions and for certain purposes. Given this recognition, teachers of technical communication and professional communicators are beginning to see that electronic landscapes need to be explored with an increasingly critical sense of the ways in which they are constituted and the ways in which they operate.

One important area of concern, for example, is the extent to which these electronic spaces — and the discursive practices that occur within them — are already controlled and shaped by official interests: those of government, business, the military, and educational institutions that conduct research for these entities (sometimes identified collectively as the State or as the military-industrial complex). The combined interests of these groups may serve not to support discursive changes that result in social action and democratic reform, but rather may serve to reproduce forces supporting the status quo. For evidence of this claim, among many other sources, we can point to current work on the National Research and Education Network (NREN), a project being discussed and designed primarily by governmental agencies such as the Defense Advanced Research Projects Agency (DARPA), the Department of Energy, the National Aeronautics and Space Administration (NASA), and the National Science Foundation (NSF), and national research universities which do contract work for these agencies (cf. Bolt, 1979; Cerf, 1991; Gore, 1991; Levidow & Robins, 1989). We can also point to increasing restrictions on agricultural database information by the Office of Management and Budget and the Department of Agriculture (Davis, 1992), and to the work on "weaponized virus" programs by the United States Army ("Attention hackers," 1992).

These examples represent only a fraction of those computer-based projects currently being funded by that collection of corporate, educational, governmental, and military forces. And, although we certainly cannot assume that all such efforts are problematic in terms of their democratic or social goals[3], we can assume that they are shaped by the same

---

[3]The goals of the new National Information Infrastructure (NII), for example, are stated in explicitly democratic terms — not only by official representatives of the current administration, such as Vice President Gore, but also by public collectives interested in the architecture and operation of the NII. The Vice President, for example, listed the following goals for the NII in a speech delivered at the University of California-Los Angeles (11 January 1994): to encourage private investment, to provide and protect competition, to provide open access to the network, to avoid creating a society of information haves and have nots, to encourage flexible and responsive government action. Similarly, the Telecommunications Policy Roundtable, a consortium of more than 70 public interest organizations that have an interest in defining the direction of the government's support of the NII, state the following goals (Renewing the Commitment, 1994): universal access at an affordable price, the freedom for all people to communicate, the maintenance of a vital civic structure that "enables the meaningful participation of all segments of our society" (p. 108), the maintenance of a diverse and

widely dispersed set of complex, shifting beliefs, signification, and material relations that sustains existing social inequities and differentials of power and resources within our government, economic, military-industrial, educational, and welfare systems. What these examples do confirm is the need to understand virtual landscapes as the ground for multiple, ongoing struggles — among them, struggles between official entities that generally have a vested interest in sustaining the current social, educational, political, economic status quo, and the competing interests of citizen groups (some consisting of technical writing teachers and workplace communicators) who are committed to a program of expanded democratic political action that alters the status quo.

The examples we have provided, however, are more complicated than a simple oppositional relationship indicates. They also illustrate the recognition that teachers in state-run, state-sponsored, or state-supported institutions and practitioners in corporate contexts — that is, many instructors of communication and professional communicators — are themselves often representatives of the interests of the military-industrial complex and the State, even as they are simultaneously opposed to many of the goals or practices of these entities. These facts — as scholars such as Laclau and Mouffe (1985), and Virilio (1986) might point out — seriously complicate the ways in which we conceive of communication within electronic spaces, the ways in which we see our roles in shaping and reproducing these spaces, the possibility of undertaking democratic reform within these contexts, and the ways in which we understand our own motivations for civic action.

WHERE WE START: PUBLIC SPHERES AS DISCURSIVE LANDSCAPES AND SITES FOR CIVIC ACTION

To understand how and why the particular discursive spaces of computer networks have come to assume such importance and power as intellectual and political territories for teachers of written communication and for writers in workplace settings, it may be useful to first examine, in a general

---

competitive marketplace, the enhancement of equity in the workplace, the protection and extension of privacy, and access to democratic policymaking. Whereas these terms are explicitly democratic, however, they are also obviously tightly bound up in — articulated closely with — the language and values of our capitalistic culture. The ideological formations underlying — and shaping — these goals illustrate the many contradictions inherent in the public sphere of electronic networks. They sketch not only a complex and overdetermined system of dominant forces (e.g., the interests of the state as a democratic system, the interests of the military-industrial complex, the interests of the class-based system of capitalism, the interests of the science/technology/research community), but also the gaps and antagonisms that characterize this system and that provide some space for agency and resistance.

way, the power of discourse as a force for political action—when it is deployed in public spheres inhabited by members of a body politic. Certainly, scholarship on this subject is abundant in fields as diverse as literary theory, critical theory, radical pedagogy, feminist theory, and cultural studies.

Rhetorical theory, however, may provide the most immediate entry into this conversation for teachers and practitioners of technical writing, given the value it has traditionally placed on civic discourse and its role in political affairs. In the field of rhetoric, a great deal of attention has been paid recently to the role of classical rhetorical studies within the modern academy (cf. Kinneavy, 1982; C. Miller, 1989; S. Miller, 1982; T. P. Miller, 1991; Sullivan, 1990; Waddell, 1990) and the public spheres of civic involvement. Generally, work in this area points to the need for a resurgence of rhetorical study as civic discourse aimed at social action, as a theory-laden practice that reconnects textual invention, arrangement, and analysis to political, legal, religious, educational, and commercial contexts (Kinneavy, 1982, p. 25). Central to these works are two tenets: that the modern study of rhetoric needs to become more "practical" and "politically oriented" (Kinneavy, 1982, p. 22), and that citizens should learn to use rhetoric to increase their effectiveness as "critical thinkers" (S. Miller, 1982, p. 53) capable of social and political action. This work—which Kinneavy, Miller, and other scholars trace back to rhetoric's classical roots—foregrounds the importance of public spheres that are poised, in Eagleton's (1984) words, "between state and civil society" (p. 9), spaces in which individuals employ symbolic and rhetorical systems to discuss, analyze, and transform the complicated forces affecting their lives as workers and citizens.

This notion of rhetorical study departs from the concept of rhetoric—and written communication—as areas of study limited exclusively to the academy. Further, it suggests to teachers in disciplines like professional writing and technical communication—and to writers within nonacademic settings—the importance of entering and working within larger public spheres, taking responsibility for engaging in social and political action, acting as citizens who can be "persuasive in a political environment" (Kinneavy, 1982, p. 21). Such a system, Kinneavy (1982) pointed out, recalls the essential connection among discursive practices, discursive spaces, and political action so fundamental to Athenian culture during the 5th century B.C. where "the implementation of a program by laws and assemblies presuppose[d] individuals speaking freely in a society, the conceptions of freedom, free speech, the city . . . , and an individual's right to make decisions" as "necessary axioms" (p. 21). The essential components of these arguments are the study and practice of rhetoric and its extension into public spheres with a stated commitment to individual or collective civic action and meaningful political involvement on the part of workers and citizens.

Eagleton (1984) and Habermas (1989), in related cases from different perspectives, also argued for a return of open and critical discourse to public spheres. Eagleton, talking about the role of literary critics as it developed in the late 17th and early 18th centuries, describes the discursive spaces of "clubs, journals, coffee houses, periodicals" in which "private individuals" of the European bourgeoisie assembled for "the free, equal exchange of reasonable discourse, thus welding themselves into a relatively cohesive body whose deliberations" assumed "a powerful political force" (p. 9). The critical discourse within this public sphere, as Eagleton noted, also assumed a collective political force that "served the emancipation movement of the middle class as an instrument to gain self esteem and to articulate its human demands against the absolutist state and a hierarchical society" (p. 10). Habermas (1989) provided a related analysis of the public sphere that emerged with the growth of the bourgeois in Europe, "a sphere of public authority, a forum in which the private people, come together to form a public, readied themselves to compel public authority to legitimate itself before public opinion" (pp. 25–26).

The essential argument in both cases—that of the rhetoricians, and of Eagleton and Habermas—is that this public discursive forum, in which people engaged in "debate over the general rules governing relations" allowed for a "public use of . . . reason" (Habermas, 1989, p. 27). As Eagleton (1984) continued, a "ceaseless circulation" of public discourse, of civil and political exchanges within public spheres can serve workers, writers, and citizens who want to form a political collective, a "power bloc at the level of the sign" (p. 14). In short, public spheres as discursive spaces can also serve as powerful political landscapes (de Certeau, 1984), and ones that teachers of written communication and professional communicators may not be able to afford to ignore.

Eagleton also pointed out, however, some of the contradictions and complications connected with the concept of the public sphere, particularly that the exercise of rhetorical power and democratic involvement within these spaces is complicated by the exercise of power and ideology that shapes their nature. The public sphere of the 17th and 18th century, as Eagleton (1984) noted, contained a "concealed problematic" (p. 16) in that it established its own boundaries of rational discourse on the basis of participants' "capacity to articulate" (p. 15) a case through rational conversation, an exercise of power limited to those with property, education, and a certain social status. As Eagleton (1984) quoted Saunders (1964, p. 121), membership within the public sphere of clubs, journals and coffee houses in the 17th and 18th centuries was limited to "politicians, diplomats, lawyers, theologians, scientists, physicians, surgeons, actors, and so on, besides the poets and other writers" (p. 13).

Hence, the legitimacy of the discourse within this particular public sphere in Europe belonged only to propertied classes and was denied those without money and education, people like "farm laborers or domestic servants" (Eagleton, 1984, p. 14). As a result, the legitimating of discourse within this community, Eagleton (1984) commented, was ideologically constrained within "a certain paradigm of reason inscribed in the very event of saying" (p. 15). Given these circumstances, then, free exchanges were possible, but only within a localized "ideal discursive sphere." The ideological apparatus of this sphere allowed what seemed to be the free exchange of civil and political discourse without apparent "domination," "without a breath of exploitation" (p. 17), just as long as participants could ignore those classes outside the political and ideological boundaries of their discursive space. Hence, in Eagleton's (1984) words, irony was inherent in this public sphere during the 17th and 18th centuries: Although it embodied, in one sense, the potential for resistance, democratic change, and a productive "discursive reorganization of social power" (p. 12), it typically proved "conservative and corrective" (p. 12). Given the ideological constraints woven into its fabric, discursive exchanges within this space simply served to redraw "the boundaries between social classes" along different lines, and, hence, to preserve many of the inequities that rested at the heart of social problems characterizing the period.

If we wanted to go back to the roots of classical rhetoric, we could also find, in 5th-century Athens, a similar, localized exercise of free rhetorical exchange, one shaped and constrained within ideological boundaries of another public sphere. Although this period is often heralded as the Golden Age of classical rhetoric and democratic discursive participation, women and slaves — partially because they did not have property rights — were not considered citizens in the fullest sense of the word and were, thus, never allowed to vote on political matters or to sit or deliberate in the *ekklesia* or assembly (Arthur, 1973), the very foundation of Greek citizenship (Glenn, 1994; Kinneavy, 1982).

Hence, the notion of public spheres as forums for democratic discursive exchanges — places for the critical analysis of social issues, for amassing and deploying individual and collective political force — may present an attractive concept to teachers of writing and to writers practicing in non-academic settings who are committed to an expanded democratic project. But if this concept is attractive, it is also problematic and highly complicated. If citizen rhetors, citizen critics, workplace writers, and even teachers of professional or technical writing can find within these public discursive spaces opportunities to exercise power, through discursive strategies to "reconnect the symbolic to the political," and to wield individual and "collective political force" (Eagleton, 1984, p. 123), they also find themselves operating within an existing ideological landscape shaped at fundamental levels by regularly dispersed discursive formations and leveled, at least currently, by our "commodity culture" (p. 122) and its accompanying ideologies. Within such ideological constraints, the potential of fundamental change is clearly limited and controlled influenced by dominant ideologies which generally serve the interests of the status quo.

However, as Laclau and Mouffe (1987) help us see, social contexts are composed of complicated sets of relations among discursively constituted identities, and cannot be either simply or fully articulated by terms like *State*, the *status quo, dominant ideologies*, or *expanded democratic project,* which we have employed thus far. The relations among these social elements, the authors pointed out, are overlapping, "polysemic" (p. 121), dynamic, and continually shifting. Hence, dominant ideologies that broadly support the continued functioning and reproduction of military-industrial or state interests, never exert complete or totalizing control over social identities which oppose these constructs. Nor, at the same time, can opposing, or reform-based, forces hope ever to define themselves in the complete absence of these dominant systems.

Such complicated sets of cultural relations deny "the conception of 'society' as a founding totality" (p. 95), and illustrate the partial, fragmentary, "precarious" (p. 96) nature of all power and its exercise. If the discursive practices of public spheres can contribute to "the maintenance and reproduction" (p. 119) of the status quo—this reasoning suggests—the same practices shift continually in "unstable oscillation" (p. 121) and never crystallize as a "moment" of "unified discourse" (p. 121) that would entirely preclude effective action or change. Rather, as Laclau and Mouffe (1985) pointed out, the contradictions in the "space of hegemony" (p. 93), the "antagonisms" (p. 135) fundamental to discursively constituted identities within cultural and social spaces, the necessary presence of continual subversion and contradiction attest constantly to the possibility of such action. In fact, it is through the exploitation of these discursive antagonisms, through the exploitation of ruptures and gaps in political spaces (and, here, Jackie's efforts come to mind) through the continual transformations of unstable limits and frontiers that "democratic struggles" (Laclau & Mouffe, 1985, p. 133) find life.

WHERE NEXT? VIRTUAL LANDSCAPES AS PUBLIC SPHERES AND SITES FOR POLITICAL ACTION

If a major public sphere of classical Greece was the assembly, and that of 17th- and 18th-century Europe consisted of public houses and periodical publications, certainly a major public sphere of the 21st century is the virtual landscape existing within computer networks linked to Internet — the Matrix in Gibson's (1984) words or the National Information Infrastructure (NII) in Vice President Gore's words — that grids (or will grid) our post-modern world, connecting previously distant parts of our planet in electronic juxtaposition (cf. Bolter, 1991; Dertouzos, 1991; Gibson, 1984, 1986, 1988; Lyotard, 1984; Poster, 1990; Virilio, 1986).

Does this electronic landscape, however, offer any different prospects for enacting individual or collective political action through discursive practices than did the public forums of Athens or 17th- and 18th-century Europe? Can virtual spaces provide the territory, the landscape, for an expanded project of social involvement and action on the part of practicing technical communicators? Can such territories support an expanded curricular framework for communication teachers and students? Or is technology so mystified within our culture that these spaces only *seem* to offer productive landscapes for such projects? Do virtual environments naturalize and mask constraints on civic participation and access within complex cultural contexts? How can teachers of written communication, student writers, and writers in nonacademic settings hope to function as change makers in virtual spaces when they recognize that these territories are shot through with the regularly dispersed social formations that support the status quo and the existence of official systems? Does enough contradiction exist in these spaces, enough multiplicity, enough fracture, enough instability that we can work within them to effect change in cultural systems — in educational systems, workplace settings, political systems, social systems?

The answers to these questions are necessarily partial and contradictory; they lie in multiple and dispersed places, not only in the nature of the electronic landscape but also in the uses that teachers of writing, student writers, and nonacademic writers are able to make of these spaces and the ways in which these groups continually constitute such spaces — and are constituted by them — through discursive practices. Depending on our use of computer networks, the role that we assume as we travel through electronic landscapes, the "tactics" (de Certeau, 1984) that we use to traverse — and create — the discursive spaces contained within computer networks, complex sets of problems and potentials identify and present themselves. To know the territory of electronic landscapes, to perceive the geography, will involve extensive topological surveys — in the spirit of Foucault (1979), Serres (1982), de Certeau (1984), Virilio (1986), Laclau and Mouffe (1985) — explorations that map, in multiple layers and dimensions, the political, intellectual, linguistic, and cultural terrain.

From one perspective, we can see electronic landscapes as spaces controlled, both physically and intellectually, by the complicated interests of official entities (Virilio, 1986) — certainly by those of the military-industrial complex and the State—which depend, to some degree, on the continuation of the ideologically and discursively determined system of relations represented by the status quo. From this vantage point—recognizing, for instance, that the new national computer network in this country is being designed primarily by these official entities—this map of the electronic terrain may appear less than threatening to teachers and students in technical communication programs or to writers in nonacademic settings. After all, most of us understand that the State—partially as an agent of our own interests and values as citizens—delivers much needed social and business services through such networks: jobs, state aid, social security, health care, educational support, for example. Further, we also recognize the economies of scale involved in constructing such networks—and our own technical limitations as individuals or, collectively, as professional educators and writers in nonacademic settings—favor involvement by corporate interests. We have, after all, only begun to learn to use networks; and—although there are individual teachers of writing and writers engaged in large-scale networking projects—we, as a profession, are still very much in the process of developing advanced skills in the design and implementation of network architecture and practice.[4]

However, from another vantage point, another perspective, we might also recognize the State's use—our country's use, our use—of the electronic landscape as involving a more disturbing pattern, one characterized by surveillance, control, violence (de Certeau, 1984; Virilio, 1986), and other activities that may work against the expansion of various democratic projects. In this vision, the State—and the military-industrial complex—employ electronic landscapes to conquer "space-time" (Virilio, 1986, p. 117) through computer-multiplied speed, and to impose control and enact violence over the populations occupying our electronically bounded planet. This particular process, and historical manifestations of the same pattern, are traced by Virilio (1986) in *Speed and Politics: An Essay on Dromology.* If we agree that this perspective of the State as conqueror of electronic landscapes may sound far-fetched, overstated in its dramatic pessimism,

---

[4]For evidence of this statement, we can point to the difficulties and challenges the National Council of Teachers of English is having in designing and implementing a national computer network for English teachers. Council members have been working on this project for at least 5 years. Currently, the effort is being supported by the NCTE Committee on Instructional Technologies, chaired by Tharon Howard (Dept. of English, Clemson University). For teachers educated in the instruction of literacy, composition, and literature, the leap to designing computer networks is seldom an easy or uncomplicated one. There are, of course, instances of success, such as BreadNet that connects teachers of English who attend the Breadloaf School of English. The technical director of this network is Bill Wright (BreadNet Project, 1250 24th St. NW, Suite 600, Washington, DC 20037. E-Mail: BWRIGHT @ TMN.COM).

and unnecessarily totalizing in its description of a monolithic entity whose interests dominate individuals and groups—it can be, nonetheless, informative.

The process, as Virilio (1986) describes it, can be characterized by typical stages. First, an authoritarian State, working to avoid the "direct repression of riots" (p. 26) that have been initiated by oppressed populations, opens new territories to possible settlement by these groups. This action offers discontented populations two unequal choices: liberation and free travel to exciting new frontiers, or the continued "temptation" (p. 26) of bloody rioting against state control. When groups select the obvious choice and move into the new territories—thus participating in their own transformation from discontented to "hopeful populations" (p. 47)—the State exerts increasing control over their free "circulation" (p. 16) and their "power of assault" (p. 27) within these new territories. According to Virilio, the legislation and regulation of official transportation vectors—in various centuries, the open seas, roadways, airwaves, railways, or computer networks—is the first step in this process. State regulation of these vectors, and the speed they allow, is essential because it is partly through these vectors that the State delivers services and enacts strategies of control. In our century, for example, government keeps computerized records of citizen criminals, computerized lists of welfare recipients, computer-supported census records that help determine which citizens in our culture are served by official agencies and in what ways. It is also partly through these official vectors that the State delivers weapons systems—again, in our century, we can point to computerized delivery systems of defensive and offensive missiles, computer-supported Pentagon purchasing, computer-generated data needed to construct Stealth bombers or fire SCUD missiles. The cultural processes that Virilio (1986) sketched, of course, are not instantaneous ones, but complex social movements that vary within particular historical contexts.

Two examples of such cultural processes, enacted over a period of centuries, should suffice to provide a snapshot of Virilio's (1986) thinking. The first involves the State's inexorable extension of control-through legislation and regulation-of the "*open seas*" (p. 41). "The open sea," Virilio (1986) contends, was offered to oppressed populations by sea faring states as a compensation for "every social, religious, and moral constraint, for every political and economic oppression, even for the physical laws due to the earth's gravity" (p. 41). As a significant proportion of the population began to respond to these enticements and to participate in the transportation projects they entailed—for example, the construction of a naval industry, fleets of ships, port facilities, transport infrastructures—the State began to exert increasing levels of control over the nautical territory: levying tariffs on commercial exchanges, enacting licensing procedures for pilots and captains and other nautical workers, charting and formalizing territorial waters, establishing laws to legislate and control activity within these spaces, and finally sanctioning nautical warfare as a way to establish nations' "right to the sea" (p. 45). The State and the military-industrial complex, through this process, thus managed not only to open a huge territory, and to convince populations to settle and civilize that territory in the name of freedom, but also to get these workers to undertake "construction projects headed by the Ministry of War" (p. 114). Among these projects was the task of building transportation infrastructures necessary to the State's own enacting of violence through naval warfare. Hence, as Virilio (1986) said, quoting Lukaĉs, the State transformed an open territory into "an imperial space" (p. 51) within which official agencies could move with enhanced speed and wage war to increase the State's power over population masses.

The construction of the United States' highway system (p. 26), is offered by Virilio (1986) as a companion example. To "survive the economic crises of the 1930s and cure the masses of their 'temptation of the streets'" (p. 26), he contended, the American state initiated a massive program of transportation works involving a system of roads and highways between urban centers. The "social assault" that accompanied this program, Virilio (1986) maintained, modified "the citizen's way of life by transforming all the consumers' needs, and by totally remodeling a territory that . . . at the beginning had no more than 400 kilometers of road" (pp. 26–27). Subsequently, and in some cases simultaneously, he continues, "political control of the highway" (p. 27) was exerted through tolls, licensing procedures, interstate trucking tariffs, and speed limits. Through this procedure, he added, the State created what Bush (quoted in Virilio, 1986) described as a population trained and ready for the war against Germany, "millions of youngsters who could drive cars, or repair them, who could build their own radio sets . . . a whole generation of competent resourceful mechanics and electricians" (p. 27). Finally, the State employed this transportation infrastructure and its "complex implements of war" (p. 28) to enact violence in World War II.

Computer networks for Virilio (1986), then, are "war machines" (p. 61)[5]

---

[5]This key term, *war machine*, indicates how centrally the contributions of colleagues figure in this chapter. Particularly, with regard to this citation of Virilio, we appreciate the generous intellectual contributions of Johndan Johnson-Eilola who helped us see that computers could function as war machines and helped us wrestle with the concepts of nomadism, speed, movement, and cyborgs, among many others. Throughout this chapter, we also appreciate the contributions of Gail Hawisher, our favorite collaborator and alter ego; Bill Klein and Craig Waddell, for help with classical rhetoric; and Jennifer Slack, for bringing the work of Virilio to our attention. We are also in debt to Tim Fountaine for introducing us to the Foreign Agents Series by Semiotext(e). As always, we are also most grateful to good friends-Marilyn Cooper,

that offer a "whole new geometry to speed, to violence" (p. 55) enacted by the State and by its citizens. As he said, "Let us recall that the computers' first task was to solve simultaneously a series of complex equations aimed at causing the trajectory of the anti-aircraft projectile and that of the airplane to meet" (p. 143). In part, these computer networks, Virilio (1987) claimed, serve state violence by deterritorializing existing landscapes, erasing current territorial boundaries separating countries and their peoples, "juxtaposing every locality, all matter" (p. 136), connecting "places and elements that only yesterday were still distinct and separated by a buffer of distances" (p. 136). This disappearance of territorial space (p. 141), the "contraction in time" (p. 140) created within electronic landscapes enables, the State to wage war with increased speed. Speed multiplied by computers and computer networks, Virilio noted, virtually eliminates the time available for a citizenry to reflect, "reducing reaction time, and the time for political decision to nothing" (p. 138).

Once again, if this characterization of the State and its tendency toward violence seems farfetched or exaggerated, we need not look far for evidence that it is—at least partially and at some level—accurate. The Cuban missile crisis became a crisis because the placement of Soviet missiles on the island of Cuba threatened to reduce the Americans' defensive warning time to "thirty *seconds*" (Virilio, 1986, p. 139). Our government has continued to use computer-supported systems both as threats and as powerful weapons. In the December 1991 issue of the *Bulletin of Atomic Scientists*, for example, The United States Army solicited "proposals for the development of a 'weaponized virus' or a piece of 'malicious software' that could destroy an enemy's computers or software ("Attention hackers," 1992). As project engineer Bob Hein explained, "This is the Army. We're in the weapons business" (p. 42).

A final characteristic of war machine technologies, Virilio (1986) added, are their ability to support the State in its occupation of intellectual and spiritual territories as well as geographical territories. Hence, the "animal body of the worker is devalued" (p. 98) not only by the State's continuing coopting, but by technology itself; workers' bodies are transformed by technological "prostheses" (p. 110) into bodies without souls, domesticated robots that serve the State's appetite for additional speed and violence. Those who doubt this merging of humans and machines can refer to any of the current descriptions of projects to develop neural networks, "living brain machines" (Fjermedal, 1986), or biological memory (cf. Fjermedal,

Diane Shoos, Ciro Sandoval, Stuart Selber, Michael Joyce, Jim Sosnowski, and Martin Rosenberg-who introduced us to the works of Michel de Certeau, Claudia Springer, Gilles Deleuze and Felix Guattari, Laclau and Mouffe, among others; and who gently urged us to open our minds to the pleasures of contradiction in this chapter and in life.

1986; Kurzweil, 1990; Pennisi, 1991). A mainstay of funding in such projects is our government, often through its military or industrial agencies.

If, then, the landscape of electronic networks seems to offer promising spaces for local change—either in communication classrooms (cf. Batson, 1988; Cooper & Selfe, 1990; Hawisher & Selfe 1993; Spitzer 1990) or workplace settings (cf. Schrage, 1990; Sproull & Kiesler, 1991)—the chances for making systemic change and progress on a more extensive political level seems less likely within these spaces. If Virilio's vision is accurate, what we are seeing is a kind of double-action containment—an opening up of free spaces, providing a social pressure valve for official state systems; and, at the same time, the increasing regulation and containment of these spaces.

Evidence that regulation and containment is of increasing concern to users of computer networks, for example, can be found in the growing debate over open access and free expression versus the secured access and disciplinary controls on networks—the electronic equivalent of licensing and inspection procedures. Articles such as Welsh's "Developing Policies for Campus Network Communications," in the *EDUCOM Review* (1992, pp. 42–45), for example, point to sites of conflict where First Amendment rights clash with the goals of network administrators charged in official ways with determining whether messages are of questionable "propriety and appropriateness" (p. 43).

A related debate centers on the increasing cost of access to and use of computer networks. As Grimes (1992) noted in a recent *New York Times* article, the subscription costs now associated with commercial networks has become big business. Such costs can be seen, moreover, as the electronic equivalent of highway system tolls, licensing procedures, tariffs, and speed limits. According to Grimes (1992), for example, commercial public networks such as Prodigy and Compuserve now charge approximately $50.00 for starter kits on their systems, between $8.00 and $15.00 for basic use each month, and some additional per-message or per-minute charges as well. The capital stake that commercial groups have in promoting these electronic systems to citizens is not a small one: Approximately 3.4 million people (1.75 on Prodigy and 1.69 million on Compuserve) subscribe to commercial networks at these rates. More than one third of all Internet users are now commercial users.

Within electronic terrains—in the growth of Internet, the development of NREN, the computerization of industry—we could be seeing the ways in which resources (speed and expertise, in particular) are developed and used to support other purposes (education, the delivery of state services, research, commerce) until they are needed to enact violence and war. Indeed, if electronic landscapes are so broadly controlled by the military-industrial complex and the State, and used in the service of these entities—

and, further, if we, as citizens, are partially constituted, and partially constitute, what we recognize as these same entities – can writers and teachers of writing committed to an expanded democratic project and changed sense of community hope to use these discursive spaces effectively for individual and collective political action that may resist such tendencies, however imperfectly and temporarily?

A POSSIBILITY FOR ACTION: TAKING UP RESIDENCE IN ELECTRONIC LANDSCAPES AS NOMADIC, FEMINIST, CYBORG GUERRILLAS

Recognizing the systemic complexity that this last question implies does not provide a justification for individual or collective inaction, especially on the part of educators – as Giroux and Freire (1987) pointed out, teachers who want to enact critical pedagogies of any sort must "steadfastly refuse to engage in a politics of withdrawal or cynicism" (p. xi). Hence, whereas we should remain concerned about the landscape we see from Virilio's perspective, we need to work to identify ways in which technical communicators, professional writers, and writing teachers can most effectively employ their positions and their access to electronic spaces for democratically informed change – even though this change may be partial, temporary, constituted by "singularities" (Deleuze & Guattari, 1987, p. 369), "antagonisms," and "contradictions" (Laclau & Mouffe, 1985, p. 122).

Three ways of addressing the last challenge suggest themselves. First, we may want to educate ourselves to recognize not only the connectedness and extent of the electronic landscapes as shaped by the State and the military-industrial complex, but also its gaps, partiality, complications, contradictions, and schisms. Second, we may want to concentrate not only on the landscape itself, but also on the uses we – as teachers of writing and writers in nonacademic settings-make of that space and of technology itself. Third, we may want to reconceive of our roles within electronic spaces to take better advantage of the terrain within virtual landscapes.

Although there is little reason to doubt the power exercised by the military-industrial complex and State within electronic landscapes, there is also little evidence that such power is seamless or total (de Certeau, 1984; Deleuze & Guattari, 1987; Laclau & Mouffe, 1985). In fact, the very characteristics of virtual landscapes that support the appropriation of these territories as a war machine also offer hope for its use as a habitat supportive of social action and politically based change initiated by citizen writers. The speed permitted the state and the military-industrial complex within the electronic landscape, for example, is currently available to individual writers, or groups of writers, who also dwell within these spaces. And, if official interests have opened up the territories electronic landscapes to a citizen population so that individuals can help construct the infrastructure necessary to the functioning of a war machine, the extent and diversity of the populations now inhabiting these spaces make total control by the State or the military-industrial complex time-consuming, expensive, distracting, indeed impossible.

Currently, millions of technical and professional writers, hackers and bulletin board users, and designers of viruses, and cyberpunks—even teachers of writing—roam the nets, traveling not only official Internet highways constructed by the state and its citizens, and occasionally used as "vectors" (Virilio, 1986, p. 109) for the war machine, but also creating unofficial, unmarked electronic paths into and out of officially sponsored computers.[6] These individuals, carrying forward the tradition of the outlaw hacker, place great value on transversing, cutting across, the official "frontiers dividing time, place, and type of action" (de Certeau, 1984, p. 29), tapping into library collections in search of information and power, hacking from one computer to another via temporarily invisible paths, leaping into the gaps of the power structure they discover.

Although these gaps in the fabric of power and control must be recognized as temporary and partial, the fact that they worry the State and the military-industrial complex as spaces of resistance and political action of an unofficial kind is encouraging. In fact, we can gauge the extent of official concern by looking at the increasingly restrictive regulations and legislation (cf. Branscomb, 1991; Gore, 1991; Kapor, 1991; Valovic, 1991) governmental and corporate agencies—AT&T, the Federal Communications Commission (FCC), and the National Telecommunications and Information Administration (NTIA), National Science Foundation (NSF),

---

[6]A number of these teachers belong to Megabyte University, an online discussion about the teaching of English composition involving more than 100 participants from all parts of this country as well as from Japan, Estonia, Malaysia, Holland, Australia, and England. This electronic list was founded by Fred Kemp (Texas Tech University) in 1989. In recent years, the participants on this list have opposed the Gulf War and the confirmation of Clarence Thomas, challenged the unequal treatment of gay and straight couples, broken the official silence about salaries of academics, and questioned the regulation of bicycle riding on university campuses and public sidewalks. The e-mail address of Megabyte University is MBU@TTUVM1. BITNET.

Evidence that these kinds of online discussions are unsanctioned or unofficial in most academic settings is easy to come by; indeed, the exceptions are rare. How many educational institutions consider participation in online listservs as a viable scholarly activity that counts toward tenure, promotion, salary decisions, teaching awards, or any other official sign of academic success—even when such discussions are immediately and directly relevant to a faculty member's academic work?

among others — feel compelled to impose on individuals in order to control the movement and circulation of "pathfinders" (Virilio, p. 72) who resist official control.

"Power," as de Certeau (1984) pointed out, is after all, "bound by its very visibility" (p. 37) and made vulnerable to individual acts of resistance by that fact. So one useful contradiction for teachers and writers in nonacademic settings, following the lead of Laclau and Mouffe (1985), may be to see virtual landscapes not as totalized by official control, but, rather, open to the necessary partiality of such control. As Deleuze and Guattari (1987) pointed out, every power formation has not only "its zone of power," where it exerts maximum control, but also its "zone of indiscernibility," where it is regularly dispersed throughout a "micropolitical fabric," and its "zone of impotence," where it exerts influence but is unable to "control or define" (p. 226) elements operating at the micropolitical level. Like all discursively constituted spaces, then, virtual landscapes can be understood as a dynamic, gap-ridden fabric, a continually shifting set of "mutually contradictory, discursive surfaces" (p. 93) that we can learn to navigate unofficially as well as officially — even though the ways in which we navigate these spaces as teachers and writers will be informed by our own continually shifting, and mutually contradictory, goals.

A second suggestion — following the lead of de Certeau (1984) — is to think not only about how to *map* the political, intellectual, and ideological terrain of electronic landscapes in order to describe them to ourselves, but rather how to *use* the electronic landscapes within which we exist discursively as both part and not-part of official systems (Laclau & Mouffe, 1985). Maps, after all, are static representations that may do little justice in representing the unstable, continually shifting, contradictory, discursive terrain (Laclau & Mouffe, 1985) within virtual networks. Such a view may help us understand virtual spaces not simply as spaces constituted *within* the complex system of relations represented by the military-industrial complex and the State, but also as places to study and undertake discursive guerrilla actions that are opposed to some aspects of officially supported violence that we cannot condone, even though we might participate in such violence and continually constitute it as citizens. Certainly, teachers and nonacademic writers need look no further than their own institutional or workplace boundaries for evidence of these inequitable practices; among them are included the marginalization of individuals because of their race, age, gender, disability; the intentional or unintentional silencing of certain population groups; and the unequal distribution of power and privilege among economic and social groups represented within the educational systems and workplaces we support with our own labor and constitute through our contradictory discursive practices.

These actions within the discursive spaces of computer networks will not be grand gestures, but rather potent small ones, characterized by quickness (Virilio, 1984) and wit (de Certeau, 1984). de Certeau (1984) calls these actions—those that run against the official channels of thinking within a self-reproducing system—"tactics" (p. 29). Tactics, he noted, are small—and at some levels, partially invisible—ways of "making do" within an oppressive system that reproduces its own power constantly and in extended ways—through discursive practices and social structures. Instructors of technical communication, students, and workplace writers already—and always—have used such tactics to get around the regulations imposed by department chairs, supervisors, and administrators of all kinds.

Currently within the virtual landscapes many of us have set up within technical or professional writing classrooms, we have identified tactics that are already appropriately characterized by speed and the circulation of ideas. We have delighted, for example, in setting up electronic learning spaces that are invisible to departmental or university administrators (Selfe, 1992). In these spaces, we allow—and encourage—students to write to each other without having their words graded. We also use networks, ourselves, to write in ways that are partly unsanctioned and unofficial (e.g., ways that go unrecognized as scholarly activity at tenure and promotion time) when we correspond with colleagues in other countries about their writing programs and their teaching of nonacademic writing; when we use virtual landscapes to compare salaries and promotion criteria among institutions and among writers in various nonacademic settings; when we use networks to put ourselves and our students in touch with individuals from other places and cultures who might be able to see our country's (or our organization's) actions in different religious, economic, social, or mythological lights.

We already participate in informal and unsanctioned electronic discussions about censorship, the electronic complication of intellectual property laws, ethics and social policy, technical journalism and publications management, political involvement and ideology, ecological disasters and union involvement, science fiction and fantasy, speech disorders and Esperanto, health and medicine, workplace relations, and feminist issues. We can learn additional tactics by becoming the students of young network navigators, many of whom—both in academic and nonacademic settings—already *know* the nets as irreverent, "data surfing" (Davis, 1992, p. 46) cyperpunks; many of whom write more and better prose and come to a more effective understanding of those writing concepts and processes we try to teach when they participate on bulletin boards and in e-mail exchanges and silicon love clubs than they do in technical writing classes.

Spaces for such unofficial involvement also exist for many workplace communicators who are connected to the Internet by computer. Although electronic access to the networks is often maintained by corporations to

support *official* communication within or between corporate sites, personnel, and projects, practitioners also frequently subvert these uses by
undertaking *unofficial* communication as well, especially on the Internet.
Listservs, bulletin boards, databases, and newsgroups provide workplace
communicators with extended, and often unofficial, communities of expert
resources, trusted readers and audiences, and professional colleagues. The
growth and vigor of these communities resists at a fundamental level the
concept that the activities of technical communicators are best limited to a
single corporation's boundaries.

Participants on TECHWR-L (1993), for example, listed the following
Internet resources as preferred sites for both *official* and *unofficial*
interaction:

Listservs:

    COPYEDITING-L   editing
            LISTSERV@CORNELL.EDU
    TECHWR-L   technical communication
            LISTSERV@VM1.UCC.OKSTATE.EDU
    CNI-COPYRIGHT   copyright issues
            LISTSERV@CNI.ORG
    DTP-L   desktop publishing
            LISTSERV@YALEVM.YCC.YALE.EDU
    INDEX-L   indexing
            LISTSERV@BINGVMB.CC.BINGHAMTON.EDU
    MBU-L   writing instruction
            LISTSERV@TTUVM1.TTU.EDU
    RHETORIC   rhetoric
            COMSERVE@VM.ITS.VPI.EDU
    WRITERS   writers and writing
            LISTSERV@VM1.NODAK.EDU

Newsgroups:

    desktop publishing: COMP.TEXT
                            COMP.TEXT.DESKTOP
                            COMP.TEXT.FRAME (concerns the Frame-
                            Maker DTP software)
    human factors: COMP.HUMAN-FACTORS
    general: NEWS.ANSWERS (answers frequently asked
                            questions about technical specialties)

These very practical sounding forums—accessed through file transfer protocols (FTP), telnetting, gophers, the World Wide Web, and e-mail—may appear to be primarily transactional, oriented toward official corporate activities. But it takes only a few minutes of reading any list or newsgroup discussion to see how workplace writers use computer networks in complex ways to suit their own personal/professional needs as well as those of corporations.

The most potent unofficial tactics, de Certeau (1984) told us, do not "obey the law" and are unsanctioned within the system governing our own official lives; these gestures cannot be "defined or identified" by that which is official (p. 29). Such tactics come and go so quickly that they lack a "proper locus"; they "trace 'indeterminate trajectories' that are apparently meaningless, since they do not cohere with the constructed, written, and prefabricated space" within which they take place (p. 34). With electronic landscapes, such tactics disappear into "a jungle of procedures" and are thus being "rendered invisible to the conqueror by the very victories he seems to have won" (p. 33).

Because these tactics are essentially invisible in an official terrain, they are also difficult to fix in the sights of the State, the military-industrial complex, or its agents—our official and sometimes professionally bound selves—and, hence, they are difficult to eliminate. The best of these discursive tactics allow both academic and nonacademic writers, for the moment, to "circulate without being seen" (de Certeau, 1984, p, 35) to make temporary use of "the cracks that particular conjunctions open in the surveillance of the proprietary powers" (p. 37) to "poach" on official lands; to enact "guileful ruses" (p. 37) whose value as playful, but purposeful acts of resistance are dependent on their creativity, their speed, and their invisibility. This temporary triumph of absolute speed in the name of an expanded social agenda, of underground teaching and writing in no place and in no time—if we can vary our tactics often enough and creatively enough—may occasionally serve as a counterbalance to the official game of speed and violence.

To get really good at this kind of tactical work, however, we suspect that teachers, students, and practitioners of technical writing are going to have to adopt something of an alter ego. This effort in identity building, which comprises our third suggestion, may be necessary to locate, within the multiplicity of contradictory selves, a persona that will allow individuals—temporarily and in partial ways—to slip into an unofficial role as citizen critic, citizen resistance worker, even while recognizing that the critic, too, exists as part and nonpart of official interests. In many cases, given the more familiar role of intellectual politeness and civility that educators and employees assume as part of their job within a state-sponsored system that serves such a wide variety of people, this new identity might prove both difficult and uncomfortable, even when it proves useful.

The metaphors of electronic landscapes and tactics, however, suggest some aspects of this alter ego: the *nomad*, possessed in Deleuze and Guattari's (1987) terms of multiple identities, absolute speed, and invisibility; and the *guerrilla*, who inhabits the virtual landscape as a home despite an officially imposed grid of power. But the term *nomadic guerrilla* may not entirely suit teachers of writing and nonacademic writers. First of all, if we recognize the multiple contradictions inherent in individuals' relations to official interests, we also recognize that teachers of writing may not be entirely comfortable in building their educational houses entirely on the fractured foundation of conflict and war—especially when the war is, in part, against themselves. The nomad and the guerrilla are never entirely exterior to official interests; in fact, it is only by acknowledging the existence of the State or the military-industrial complex, by tracing the limits of the *official*, that the *unofficial*, the nomad and the guerrilla, are established as social identities—and vice versa (Laclau & Mouffe, 1985).

From another perspective, the term *nomadic guerrilla* does not get at a layer of contradiction that exists in the set of overlapping relations connecting humans and machines—or computer-using writers in academic and nonacademic settings. We do not simply *inhabit* the virtual spaces that exist on computers and computer networks; we do not simply move within these spaces. Rather, we *are*, partially, the architects of these spaces; we *are*, partially, the machines that we have crafted. As Poster (1990) and others (cf. Johnson-Eilola, 1992; Lyotard, 1984; Virilio, 1986) have pointed out—we are already constituted both as technological and cultural subjects, created in part by the machines we ourselves have created and written continually in our discursive practices on these machines. We are, in this sense, part technology ourselves—in the way we write, in the way we see the world, in the ways that we think. We are *cyborgs* in Haraway's (1990) terms—we are makers of the machine, and this activity has made us partially machine ourselves.

Cyborg, then, can serve as a point of entry for this additional layer of contradiction. The term *cyborg*—or *nomadic, cyborg guerrilla*, as it continues to build—may feel uncomfortable to technical communicators and educators. But, as Johndan Johnson-Eilola (1992) pointed out, if it did not niggle, the potency and complexity of the image would be suspect. The word concerns Haraway (1990), too. As she said: "From one perspective, a cyborg world is about the final imposition of a grid of control on the planet, about the final abstraction embodied in a Star Wars apocalypse waged in the name of defense, about the final appropriation of women's bodies in a masculinist orgy of war" (p. 198). However, Haraway also sees a contradictory role for cyborgs, a feminist role; and this aspect helps reveal the intellectual strength and depth of the term.

Cyborgs, as Haraway (1990) notes, carry resistance and contradiction deep within their makeup. First, cyborgs resist definition within the intellectual landscape of the masculinist State; being neither human nor machine, they create a "hybrid of machine and organism" (p. 191) that can recode, rewrite, reconstitute not only the text of their own bodies, but also the larger cultural/economic/ideological narratives and mythologies of the male-dominated war State, the cultural body politic. By altering the meaning of *human* and *machine*, by denying that opposition in a *particular* sense, cyborgs also work against the grain, in a more *general* sense, to show the reductive weakness of the masculinist, oppositional, dualistic thinking that forms the basis of Western tradition, "the logics and practices of domination . . . of all constituted as other" (p. 219). Cyborgs "make problematic the statuses of men or women, human, artifact, member of race, individual identity, or body" (p. 220) break down dualisms such as "self/other, mind/body, culture/nature, male/female, civilized/primitive, reality/appearance, whole/part, agent/resource" (p. 219).

In a practical sense, Haraway (1990) pointed out, these recodings by feminist cyborgs are happening in the challenges to "relatively privileged, mostly white men's unionized jobs" (p. 208) that are now occurring in both the computer and the communications industries, in the erosion of traditional patriarchal concepts of public and private space that is now occurring on computer-based networks in many workplaces, and in the "webs of power and social life" (p. 212) that feminists are already weaving on computer networks around the world.

The notion of a *feminist* cyborg can inform teachers of technical writing and workplace writers committed to a broader agenda of democratic social action and involvement on several counts. First, cyborgs recall the feminist recognition and valuing of plurality and contradiction: of co-existing commitments to life, as well as to death; to resistance in the form of serious play (in language, in scholarship, in politics); and to accommodation, to peace, and to the violence of war[7]. In this sense, the notion of a feminist cyborg can continually remind teachers of writing and writers in nonacademic settings of their own contradictions, their own complicity in the current complex system of cultural relations—as teachers, as workers and writers, as taxpayers. Even feminist cyborgs are part war machine, part humanist; they are partial, faithless, and cynical and—because of these facts—unpredictable.

---

[7]Although we recognize that there is also a tradition of feminist thinking committed to enacting violence and even engaging in war, and that—for some women—this route seems the only possible way of combating the oppression of phallocentric thinking and action, it is not our particular feminist perspective.

But contradiction and plurality can be comforting, too. The concept of a feminist cyborg, for instance, embodies the realization that no discursively constituted political structure—not the State, not the corporation—is totalizing. Thus, cyborgs acknowledge that even though they are part of an official system, they can be involved in "weaving something other than a shroud for the day after the apocalypse" (p. 199). Similarly, if we understand that "cyborgs are the illegitimate offspring of militarism and patriarchal capitalism, not to mention state socialism" (p. 193), we can also recognize that "illegitimate offspring are often exceedingly unfaithful to their origins" (p. 193). In fact, "stripped of identity," in the traditional masculinist sense, cyborgs can teach us "about the power of the margins" (pp. 218–219) and the riches we can harvest by transgressing and transforming traditional educational and institutional boundaries (p. 221).

With this explanation, we begin to see how the contentious identity of *nomadic, feminist, cyborg guerrilla* is suited to the world in which most professional writers, teachers of technical writing, and students must function. The term implies that individuals are already part of regularly dispersed, complexly constituted social formations connected along many lines to the interests of the State and the military-industrial complex and, thus, that teachers, students, workplace writers are already, at some level, implicated in the oppressive or violent agenda sponsored by these official interests. At the same time, the identity also implies that individuals are partly connected with more positive aspects of official action—the government's support of civil rights, as partial and gap ridden as that political fabric is; the State's support of equal employment opportunities for women, as unsystematically and inconsistently applied as that support has proven itself; or the government's commitment to universal education, as problematic and inequitable as that commitment has been.

The term *nomadic, feminist, cyborg guerrilla*, in other words, can serve to remind teachers, students, and practitioners of technical communication that the official institutions in which they work—the government agencies, schools and school systems, corporations for which they communicate—and the computer networks these institutions design and maintain represent potential sites for the "emergence of democratic antagonisms" (p. 180). Within electronic networks, then, there exists what Laclau and Mouffe (1985) call "the possibility" of extending social projects of "radical democracy" (p. 181) through various kinds of discursive action and exploration. Our hope is that teachers, students, and practitioners of technical communication who learn to navigate these new spaces may discover additional territories within which to reestablish the essential connections between a literate citizenry and the important work of communication.

REFERENCES

Attention hackers: Uncle Sam wants you. (1992). *Utne Reader*, p. 42.

Arthur, M. B. (1973). Early Greece: The origins of the Western attitude toward women. *Arethusa, 6*(1), 31–36.

Barker, T. T., & Kemp, F. O. (1990). Network theory: A postmodern pedagogy for the writing classroom. In C. Handa (Ed.), *Computers and community: Teaching composition in the twenty-first century* (pp. 1–27). Portsmouth, NH: Boynton/Cook Heinemann.

Batson, T. (1988, February/March). The ENFI project: A networked classroom approach to writing instruction. Academic Computing, pp. 32–33, 55–56.

Bolt, R. (1979). *Spatial data management* (DARPA Rep. LC# 78–78256). Boston: Architecture Machine Group, Massachusetts Institute of Technology.

Bolter, J. D. (1991). *Writing space: The computer, hypertext, and the history of writing.* Hillsdale, NJ: Lawrence Erlbaum Associates.

Branscomb, A. W. (1991, September). Common law for the electronic frontier. *Scientific American*, pp. 154–158.

Cerf, V. G. (1991, September). Networks. *Scientific American*, pp. 72–81.

Cooper, M. M., & Holzman, M. (1989). *Writing as social action.* Portsmouth, NH: Boynton/Cook, Heinemann.

Cooper, M. M., & Selfe, C. L. (1990). Computer conferences and learning: Authority, resistance, and internally persuasive discourse. *College English, 52*(8), 847–869.

d'Albenas, K. (1993, August 18). E-mail message. TECHWR-L@VM1.ucc.okstate.edu. Stillwater: Oklahoma State University.

de Certeau, M. (1984). *The practice of everyday life* (S. Randall, Trans.). Berkeley: University of California Press.

Davis, E. (1992). Cyberlibraries. *Lingua Franca, 2*(2), 46–51.

Deleuze, G., & Guattari, F. (1987). *A thousand plateaus: Capitalism and schizophrenia* (B. Massumi, Trans.). Minneapolis: University of Minnesota Press.

Dertouzos, M. L. (1991, September). Communications, computers and networks. *Scientific American*, pp. 62–69.

Eagleton, T. (1984). *The function of criticism: From the spectator to post-structuralism.* New York: Verso/New Left Books.

Eldred, J. (1989). Computers, composition, and the social view. In G. E. Hawisher & C. L. Selfe (Eds.), *Critical perspectives on computers and composition studies* (pp. 201–218). New York: Teachers College Press.

Fjermedal, G. (1986). *The tomorrow makers: A brave new world of living-brain machines.* New York: Random House.

Forman, J. (1992). *New visions of collaborative writing.* Portsmouth, NH: Boynton/Cook, Heinemann.

Forman, J. (1994). Literacy, collaboration, and technology: New connections and challenges. In C. L. Selfe & S. Hilligoss (Eds.), *Literacy and computers: Complicating our vision of teaching and learning with technology* (pp. 130–143). New York: Modern Language Association.

Foucault, M. (1979). *Discipline and punish: The birth of the prison* (A. Sheridan, Trans.). New York: Random House.

Gibson, W. (1984). *Neuromancer.* New York: Ace Books.

Gibson, W. (1986). *Count zero.* New York: Ace Books.

Gibson, W. (1988). *Mona lisa overdrive.* New York: Bantam Books.

Giroux, H. (1992). *Border crossings: Cultural workers and the politics of education.* New York: Routledge, Chapman & Hall.

Giroux, H. A., & Freire, P. (1987). Series introduction. In D. Livingstone (Ed.), *Critical pedagogy and cultural power* (pp. xi-xvi). South Hadley, MA: Bergin & Garvey.

Glenn, C. (1994). Sex, lies, and manuscript: Refiguring Aspasia in the history of rhetoric. *College Composition and Communication, 2*(45), 180-199.

Gore, A. (1994, January 11). Speech presented at the University of California, Los Angeles.

Gore, A. (1991, September). Infrastructure for the global village. *Scientific American*, pp. 150-153.

Grimes, W. (1992, December). Computer as a cultural tool: Chatter mounts on every topic. *The New York Times*, pp. C13-15.

Habermas, J. (1989). *The structural transformation of the public sphere: An inquiry into a category of bourgeois society* (T. Burger & F. Lawrence, Trans.). Boston: MIT Press.

Handa, C. (Ed.). (1990). *Computers and community: Teaching composition in the twenty-first century*. Portsmouth, NH: Boynton/Cook.

Haraway, D. (1990). A manifesto for cyborgs: Science, technology, and socialist feminism. In L. J. Nicholson (Ed.), *Feminism/postmodernism* (pp. 190-233). London: Routledge, Chapman & Hall.

Hawisher, G. E., & Selfe, C. L. (1993). Tradition and change in computer-supported writing environments: A call for action. In P. Kahaney, J. Janangelo, & L. A. M. Perry (Eds.), *Theoretical and critical perspectives on teacher change* (pp. 155-186). Norwood, NJ: Ablex.

Hiltz, S. R., & Turoff, M. (1993). *The network nation: Human communication via computer*. Cambridge, MA: MIT Press.

Johnson-Eilola, J. (1992, May). *Process, control, and the cyborg: Writing and being written in hypertexts*. Paper presented at the Eighth Conference on Computers and Writing, Indianapolis, IN.

Kapor, M. (1991, September). Civil liberties in cyberspace. *Scientific American*, pp. 158-164.

Kent, T. (1989). Paralogic hermeneutics and the possibilities of rhetoric. *Rhetoric Review, 8*(1), 24-42.

Kiesler, S., Siegel, J., & McGuire, T. W. (1984). Social-psychological aspects of computer-mediated communication. *American Psychologist, 39*(10), 1123-1134.

Killingsworth, M. J. (1992). Realism, human action, and instrumental discourse. *Journal of Advanced Composition, 12*(1), 171-200.

Kinneavy, J. (1982). Restoring the humanities: The return of rhetoric from exile. In J. J. Murphey (Ed.), *The rhetorical tradition and modern writing* (pp. 19-28). New York: Modern Language Association.

Kurzweil, R. (1990). *The age of intelligent machines*. Cambridge, MA: MIT Press.

Laclau, E., & Mouffe, C. (1985). *Hegemony and socialist srtategy: Towards a radical democratic politics*. London: Verso.

Levidow, L., & Robins, K. (Eds.). (1989). *Cyborg worlds: The military information society*. London: Free Association Books.

Lyotard, J. F. (1984). *The postmodern condition: A report on knowledge* (G. Bennington & B. Massumi, Trans.). Minneapolis: University of Minnesota Press.

Mason, R. (1993). *Computer conferencing: The last word*. Victoria, British Columbia: Beach Holme.

Miller, C. (1989). What's practical about technical writing? In B. E. Rearing & W. K. Sparrow (Eds.), *Technical writing: Theory and practice* (pp. 14-26). New York: Modern Language Association.

Miller, S. (1982). Classical practice and contemporary basics. In J. J. Murphy (Ed.), *The rhetorical tradition and modern writing* (pp. 46-57). New York: Modern Language Association.

Miller, T. P. (1991). Treating professional writing as social praxis. *Journal of Advanced Composition, 11*(1), 57-72.

Mitchell, S. (1993, August 17–18). E-mail message. TECHWR-L@VM1.ucc.okstate.edu. Stillwater: Oklahoma State University.

Mouffe, C. (1992). Feminism, citizenship and radical democratic politics. In J. Butler & J. W. Scott (Eds.), *Feminists theorize the political* (pp. 369–384). New York: Routledge & Kegan Paul.

Moore, P. (1992). When politeness is fatal: Technical communication and the Challenger disaster. *Journal of Business and Technical Communication, 6*(3), 269–292.

Ornatowski, C. M. (1992). Between efficiency and politics: Rhetoric and ethics in technical writing. *Technical Communication Quarterly, 1*(1), 91–103.

Pennisi, E. (1991, December 21 & 28). New analog chip acts just like a nerve cell. *Science News, 140*, 407.

Poster, M. (1990). *The mode of information: Poststructuralism and social context.* Chicago: The University of Chicago Press.

Renewing the commitment to a public interest telecommunications policy. (1994). *Communications of the ACM, 37*(1), 106–108.

Rosenzweig, V. (1993, August 18). E-mail message. TECHWR-L@VM1.ucc.okstate.edu. Stillwater: Oklahoma State University.

Saunders, J. W. (1964). *The profession of English letters.* London: Routledge.

Schrage, M. (1990). *Shared minds: The new technologies of collaboration.* New York: Random House.

Selfe, C. L. (1992). Preparing English teachers for the virtual age. In G. E. Hawisher & P. LeBlanc (Eds.), *Re-imagining composition in the virtual age: Research and teaching* (pp. 24–42). Portsmouth, NH: Boynton/Cook, Heinemann.

Selfe, C. L., & Hilligoss, S. (1994). *Literacy and computers: Complicating our vision of teaching and learning with technology.* New York: Modern Language Association.

Serres, M. (1982). *Hermes: Literature, science, philosophy.* Baltimore: John Hopkins University Press.

Shor, I. (1987). *Critical teaching and everyday life.* Chicago: The University of Chicago Press.

Showalter, M. (1993, August 18). E-mail message. TECHWR-L@VM1.ucc.okstate.edu. Stillwater: Oklahoma State University.

Spitzer, M. (1989). Computer conferencing: An emerging technology. In G. E. Hawisher & C. L. Selfe (Eds.), *Critical perspectives in computers and composition instruction* (pp. 187–200). New York: Teachers College Press.

Spitzer, M. (1990). Local and global networking: Implications for the future. In C. Selfe & D. Holdstein (Eds.), *Computers and writing: Theory, research, and practice* (pp. 187–199). New York: Modern Language Association.

Springer, C. (1991). The pleasure of the interface. *Screen, 32*(2), 303–323.

Sproull, L., & Kiesler, S. (1991, September). Computers, networks and work. *Scientific American*, pp. 116–123.

Sullivan, D. L. (1990). Political-ethical implications of defining technical communication as a practice. *Journal of Advanced Composition, 10*(2), 375–386.

TECHWR-L. (1993). E-mail messages sent to TECHWR-L@VM1.ucc.okstate.edu. Stillwater: Oklahoma State University.

Thralls, C., & Blyler, N. R. (1993). The social perspective and pedagogy in technical communication. *Technical Communication Quarterly, 2*(3), 249–270.

Valovic, T. S. (1991). Conflict or cooperation? NREN and US Telecom policy. *Whole Earth Review*, pp. 12–14.

Virilio, P. (1986). *Speed and politics: An essay on domology* (M. Polizzotti, Trans.). New York: Semiotext(e).

Waddell, C. (1990). The role of pathos in the decision-making process: A study in the rhetoric of science policy. *Quarterly Journal of Speech, 76*, 381–400.

Welsh, G. (1992). Developing policies for campus network communications. *EDUCOM Review, 27*(3), 42–45.

Winsor, D. A. (1988). Communication failures contributing to the Challenger accident. *IEEE Transactions on Professional Communication, 31*(1), 101–07.

Zappen, J. P. (1987). Rhetoric and technical communication: An argument for historical and political pluralism. *Iowa St. Journal of Business and Technical Communication (JBTC), 1*(2), 29–44.

Author Index

Subject Index

M

Maclay, Senator William, 211, 213, 216, 219, 220, 223
  diary of, 211–213
Macromedia Director, 9, *15*
Management philosophy, 272
Maps, 9
MarkUp (software), 293
Marxism, 189, 252
Marxist/critical theory, 188–191, 193, 197, 199
Masculinism, 352–353
Mathematics, 60, 64
McClintock, Barbara, 60
Mediation (and discourse development), 209, 219–222
Megabyte University, 347
Men, 191, 192, 198, 199, *see also* Gender, Women
Metadiscourse, 43
Metaphors, 8, 9, 73, 224, 263
Mexico, 188
Military-industrial complex, 179, 191, 334, 335, 339, 341, 346–349
Microsoft Bookshelf (software), 290
Microsoft Kids, 9, *15*
Models
  research, 6–7
  use of 163, 169
Modes of discourse, 23
Multimedia, 323

N

NAFTA, 188
National Aeronautics and Space Administration (NASA), 334
National Council of Teachers of English (NCTE), 341
National Educational Goals Report, 38
National health care reform, 206–207
National Information Infrastructure (NII), 334, 340, *see also* Gore, Vice President Al
National Research and Education Network (NREN), 334, 345
National Science Foundation (NSF), 334
Negotiation, 195, 197
Newsgroups, 350
Nomadic guerrilla, 352
Nonacademic writers, 174, *see also* Nonacademic writing, civic writing, technical

writers, technical writing, workplace writers
  and community, 12
  as researchers, 13
Nonacademic writing, 1–13, 30, *see also* Civic writing, participatory writing, workplace writing, research
  architectonics of, 114–119
  and computer tools, 281–299
  and context, 224
  definitions of, 1–2, 11, 81
  and distance, 9–10
  issues surrounding, 3–4
  and organizational communication, 5
  and professors, 174,
    areas, 10–13, 31–32, 48–52, 75, 167, 170, 295–297, 323
    methodologies, 4, 18, 23–26, 35, 45
  and social context, 5
  and social theory, 176
  teaching of, 7–8, 10, 12, 13, 30–31, 47–48, 167–170, 254, 331
  and technology, 4, 7–12
Nonverbal cues, 174
Notecards (software), 260, 264
Novice writers, 164, 168, 187

O

Office of the Future, 40
On-the-job training, 144
Oral discourse vs. written, 250, 254, 321, 322
Organization rhetorical patterns of, 187
Organizational chart, 117
Overnominalization, 166

P

Page design, 41, 42
Pamphlets, 231
Parliament (England), 222, 230–231
Participant observer, 21
Participatory writing, 227–255
Pedagogy, 30, 35, 36, 37, 39, 42, 152, 168
  nonacademic, 13, 23, 36, 254–255
    and ethnography, 18, 19, 25–32
    and theory, 22, 25–32
Performance (and discourse development), 209, 214–219
Persuasive writing, 186
Petitions, 230, 235